Crippled Justice

Crippled Justice

THE HISTORY OF

MODERN DISABILITY POLICY

IN THE WORKPLACE

Ruth O'Brien

The University of Chicago Press

Chicago and London

Ruth O'Brien is associate professor of government at the John
Jay College of Criminal Justice and deputy chair of the political science
program at the Graduate Center of the City University of New York.
She is the author of *Workers' Paradox: The Republican Origins of
New Deal Labor Policy, 1886–1935.*

The University of Chicago Press, Chicago 60637
The University of Chicago Press, Ltd., London
© 2001 by The University of Chicago
All rights reserved. Published 2001
Printed in the United States of America
10 09 08 07 06 05 04 03 02 01   5 4 3 2 1

ISBN (cloth): 0-226-61659-2
ISBN (paper): 0-226-61660-6

Library of Congress Cataloging-in-Publication Data

O'Brien, Ruth Ann, 1960–
    Crippled justice : the history of modern disability policy in the
workplace / Ruth O'Brien.
        p.   cm.
    Includes bibliographical references and index.
    ISBN 0-226-61659-2
    1. Handicapped—Employment—United States—History.
    2. Vocational rehabilitation—United States—History.   I. Title.
    HD7256.U5 O27   2001
    331.5'9'0973—dc21   2001001896

♾ The paper used in this publication meets the minimum requirements of
the American National Standard for Information Sciences—Permanence of
Paper for Printed Library Materials, ANSI Z39.48-1992.

For Rudi

CONTENTS

PREFACE

As is true of most big projects, writing this book has been a long journey. What distinguished this journey from my last, however, is the personal circumstances leading to it. Had I not sustained what is now a ubiquitous workplace injury, a debilitating case of bilateral tendinitis in my hands and forearms, I might never have explored the development and implementation of such a significant social policy as disability policy. Because of this injury, which turned out to be temporary, I got a glimpse of the frustrations that disabled people face when they ask for help at the workplace.

Photocopying all my archival documents rather than taking notes as I completed research for my first book, I found myself getting into arguments with archivists. A conflict would result if I asked for permission not to put down the machine's lid. After having one discussion too many about what a bad precedent I would set with this or other requests, my interest as a student of American social policy was piqued. I was fascinated, however, not by the similarities the Americans with Disabilities Act (ADA) shares with the Civil Rights Act, of which there are many, but by the differences between these two public policies.

First, I discovered that I could not guess how someone would respond to a request for an accommodation. I could never anticipate if someone would help, oftentimes generously offering more assistance than was necessary, or if someone would stand in my way. Self-proclaimed progressive people could react with as little understanding as those identifying with conservative causes, or vice versa. This is not to say that the disability rights movement did not struggle over the same issues that women and minorities battle—bias, prejudice, stigma, and fear. Although political demands for disability rights and civil rights were essentially the same, I realized that many people responded without regard to their partisan affiliation.

Still looking for some sort of pattern to explain people's behavior, I noticed that the response I received about accommodations were influenced by cultural values. My own experience helped me understand how I, too, had been shaped by a cultural understanding of disability. No one brought this home to me better than Judith Heumann, the assistant secretary for education, in charge of the Office of Special Education and Rehabilitative Services.

Elated that this former activist and now the person in charge of all rehabilitative services agreed to an interview, I was mortified when she scolded me for distinguishing what I perceived as my minor impairment from her more debilitating one. Out of misplaced respect that she used a chair, I saw the difference between our impairments, whereas she focused on our similarities. What difference would the difference between our impairments make, she asked, if we were both out of work?

Heumann and other activists taught me that the disability rights movement is an inherently political movement—based on a consciousness about how a "normal" environment creates obstructions for those who do things differently. Focusing on the nature of different physical and mental impairments, they argue, only confuses the issue that disability rights are civil rights *and* human rights. I have also profited from the British school of disability studies because of its emphasis on the universal nature of disability rights. The pathbreaking work of Henri-Jacques Stiker and James Charlton gave me further insight about the universal roots of animus toward disabled people.

Nonetheless, in limiting my inquiry to the workplace, I discovered that the universal roots of bias and prejudice manifested themselves in a distinctly American way when employers reacted to their employees' requests for accommodations. Not the cost of an accommodation, but its precedent-setting capacity insinuated an element of need that was foreign in the American workplace. It was this need that employers balked at providing. While civil rights policy has some employers concerned about opening doors to minorities and women, American disability rights policy worries some employers that disabled people will keep adjusting the width of the doorway. Since the term "disability" encompasses so many different types of physical and mental impairments, people with disabilities present a perpetual precedent-setting threat to the workplace.

Armed with these insights, I began digging in different libraries and archives. I found that a book about the origins of disability rights in the workplace, and the resistance to these rights, ought not to start with Section 504 of the Rehabilitation Act of 1973. Rather, the story begins when physicians and policymakers advanced the idea that people with disabilities should be let out of the "warehouses" and that they could become productive members of the work force, albeit without rights to nondiscriminatory treatment. Hence, I start this story just after World War II when physicians, who had helped during the war effort, and public officials in the Federal Security Agency began lobbying for vocational rehabilitation. They tried to establish a vocational rehabilitation program, not just for veterans or those injured in industrial accidents, as the program had in the 1920s, but for any person with a physical or mental impairment worthy of the benefits of their program.

Given great discretion by the Vocational Rehabilitation Act of 1954, the rehabilitation counselors decided who could compensate for their disabilities, not just in mind or body but, more important, by strengthening their so-called maladjusted personalities. Following what was called the Whole Man Theory, the counselors thought these candidates would be able to make the accommodations necessary to fit into the workplace. This is not to say that people with disabilities were given a voice. Like the physicians who treated disabled people in the warehouses, vocational rehabilitation experts had complete control over candidates for rehabilitation. Since the 1950s, these experts have decided that only very few people with disabilities are eligible for rehabilitation.

Next, the book addresses the formation of disability rights with the passage of the Rehabilitation Act of 1973, the development of the regulations implementing the rights-oriented Section 504, and the federal judiciary's interpretation of this disability legislation. It also reviews how the disability rights movement influenced the passage of the ADA of 1990. Yet, while the book explores the role the disability rights movement played in the public policymaking process, it should not be confused with a book about the movement. Many articles about the disability rights movement have been published, but a comprehensive history of the movement has yet to be written.

The story ends nine years later when the Supreme Court construed the employment provisions within the ADA so narrowly that disabled people were placed in an awkward position. People with disabilities are either not disabled enough to be covered by the ADA or they are too disabled to work. The Supreme Court also upheld the notion that people could mitigate their impairments with medication or equipment and, consequently, should not be covered by the law. And, indeed, this idea about mitigation has become very significant. In less than one year after the Supreme Court rulings, the lower federal court judges have transformed mitigation into their own version of the whole man theory. Still dismissing most cases on summary judgment, many judges have decided that people who compensate for their disability are "whole" and, consequently, not deserving of antidiscrimination protection in the workplace.

I have many people to thank for help in writing this book. Not only was it exhilarating to meet Judith Heumann, a former disability rights activist who filled Mary Switzer's seat in the federal government, but she introduced me to Fredric Schroeder, commissioner of the Rehabilitation Services Administration (RSA), and to Beverlee Stafford, director of the planning, policy, and evaluation staff at the RSA. Interviews with Fredric Schroeder and Beverlee Stafford, which came at the final stage of my research, gave me more confidence about my work on the vocational rehabilitation ethos. Mark Shoob, the deputy commissioner of the RSA, and Judy Tynes, who recently retired from the program, gave me a good depiction of the vocational rehabilitation program in the 1960s.

Interviews with Mary Lou Breslin, Arlene Mayerson, Patricia Wright, Kenneth Stein, and Kitty Cone from the Disability Rights Education and Defense Fund, along with meetings with Gerald Baptiste and Terry Herkheimer from the Center for Independent Living in Berkeley, and the disability rights activist Hale Zucker provided me with insight about the disability rights movement that could not be gained from articles and books. Kitty Cone gave me a particularly vivid account of the movement, drawing a colorful picture of the sit-in demonstrations for the Section 504 regulations. My time spent with Mary Lou Breslin provoked a great deal of thought about some disability rights issues in general. What is more, she graciously opened more doors to members of the disability rights community. Meanwhile, Arlene Mayerson and Patricia Wright gave me a legal insiders understanding about all the unanticipated problems inherent in Title I.

The research trips that enabled me to talk with the above-mentioned people were funded by two Professional Staff Congress Fellowships that the City University of New York generously provided. These funds also gave me the resources to hire Jocelyn Boryczka, a graduate student, to sort through many of the Title I cases. I also appreciate staff members and undergraduate students at John Jay College of Criminal Justice for the time they spent photocopying many of the cases when I could not do so myself.

Further, the library staff at Alexander Library and the Library of Science and Medicine at Rutgers University must be cited as examples of how supportive people can be when they are fulfilling their obligations under the ADA. Also learned and cooperative archivists and staff members from the National Archives II, the Jimmy Carter Presidential Library, and the Schlesinger Library at Radcliffe college aided my research. I am particularly indebted to Connie Mast, a volunteer, who spent many hours duplicating documents at the National Archives when she could have been doing more exciting tasks.

Given the interdisciplinary nature of the book, I asked colleagues from different disciplines for assistance. Gerald Grob shared some of his abundant knowledge about the history of American psychiatry, which helped me gain more of a grasp of all the material about the medical community in the 1940s and 1950s. Incisive criticism that Simi Linton rendered made me rethink some issues about disability studies. Karen Orren, Chloe Atkins, Andrew Polsky, and Howard Gillman provided apt comments about particularly problematic chapters or research proposals. I also benefited immensely from an opportunity that Martha Fineman created when she brought me up to Cornell Law School on a Clarke minifellowship. In addition to the fact that the universalizing nature of Martha's own work has been a source of inspiration for this project, the fellowship that she organized also gave me a chance to gain a legal perspective on employment discrimination, civil rights, and administrative law, since meetings were set up with Diane Avery, Cynthia Farina, Winnie Taylor, and Kathryn Abrams, some of her colleagues at Cornell. Finally, I have thoroughly enjoyed working with John Tryneski, who could not have been a more astute and attentive editor. John may not realize it, but were it not for a long stimulating conversation we had I might not have turned a vague idea about disability rights into a book.

While this project was underway, I also leaned on close friends for intellectual and personal support. Martha Campbell fueled my interest in employment-at-will with her thoughts about economics and American capitalism. Molly Greene often let me ramble on long after she must have been interested in disability cases. Teaching me something about their own crafts, Cate DuPron, Robyn Laisure, and Lila Weinberg helped me smooth out some of the writing problems. I also appreciated the friendship of Dubravka Knezic and Jaap Spaans, particularly during the very final stage of this project's completion.

To my family I owe the biggest debt. Not only have they always sustained an atmosphere of encouragement and love, but they accepted what can only be dubiously described as invitations to research trips. Forgoing some museum trips in Washington, D.C., my mother spent quite a few days behind a photocopy machine, never once asking why it was necessary to copy such a large bulk of material. Most important, it was my mother who endowed me with the tenacity it took to finish this project. Kathleen, my sister, flew out from San Francisco, generously spending her vacation time on a research trip in Massachusetts. Although not always appreciated at the time, my children, Max and Theo, were the source of many distractions, which undoubtedly gave me more distance and perspective about the project.

Finally, it is to Rudi Matthee, my husband, and the most generous person I know, that I dedicate this book. While still reading and rereading drafts of this project, Rudi shouldered the entire weight of our household for five years. And as I slowly recovered from my injury, he somehow always understood that it was vital for me to put what physical stamina I had gained into my research rather than into running the household. Despite all of his hard work, he had enough love and energy left over to encourage me to keep writing.

INTRODUCTION

Disabled people have physical and mental impairments as a result of birth, an injury, or an illness. Impairments include such conditions as orthopedic, visual, speech, and hearing problems, epilepsy, multiple sclerosis, cancer, diabetes, mental retardation, and mental illness, among others.[1] The Americans with Disabilities Act of 1990 (ADA) was passed to free people with disabilities from discrimination for their impairments. Not only did Congress address the discriminatory treatment disabled people face, but it also safeguarded those who either have a history of an impairment or are regarded as having one.[2]

Given this broad definition of a disability, few people die without experiencing the debilitating effects of an illness or an injury. According to the National Council on Disabilities, 49 million Americans currently have physical or mental impairments, most of them resulting from injuries or illnesses that occurred in adolescence or adulthood.[3] As Justin Dart, a disability rights activist, explains, "Disability used to signal the end of active life. Now it is a common characteristic of a normal life-span."[4] Robert Murphy, an anthropologist who had a severe physical impairment himself, suggested that disability is an apt metaphor for the human condition: it represents humanity.[5]

Nonetheless, few people identify with those who have impairments or are regarded as having a disability. When viewed as the "other," people with disabilities become reified and dehumanized because of their distinctiveness.[6] As Murphy expressed it, people with disabilities are "the living symbol of failure, frailty, and emasculation, a counterpoint to normality." The distance between the self and the other creates a wall that blocks understanding, denying any type of equality to whoever is categorized as the other. The "very humanity" of the person with a disability, as Murphy elaborates, "is questionable."[7]

Well aware of this distinction, the disability rights movement has long fought to put an ordinary face—not that of a victim, a hero, or a martyr—on people with disabilities. Only by ridding society of its belief in their "otherness" could disabled people become full-fledged citizens. Most important, this otherness shields mainstream society from facing how it has designed a social and political environment that "cripples" people with disabilities. Hence, the disability rights movement centers on the idea that it is sociopolitical obstructions, not physical or mental impairments, that restrict disabled people.

Although the disability rights movement formulated this idea in the 1960s, and would succeed in incorporating its spirit into the ADA, it still faces great resistance. In an effort to universalize the notion of disability, some members of the movement came up with the rather infelicitous term "temporarily able-bodied," which gathered everyone together, suggesting that each of us is either living with a disability or will be in the future. This rankled many Americans. According to Irving Zola, a disability studies expert, most people do not appreciate being considered only a "banana-peel slip away from disability."[8] They resist being categorized as temporarily able-bodied because it is tantamount to saying that they are temporarily alive.[9]

Resistance to the idea that disability is part of the human condition, however, arises not just from the political weakness and vulnerability of disabled people. It is also paradoxically a product of their strength. I argue in this book that disabled people derive power from alternative means of performing the ordinary and the extraordinary tasks of everyday life, because what circumscribes disabled people from completing these tasks the "normal" way gives them special insight.[10] The forethought and creativity required to develop the alternative means to accomplish the tasks provides disabled people with the capacity to help themselves and, sometimes, others.[11]

What is more, this search for alternative means is perpetual, permeating all aspects of life, because there are all kinds of different disabilities and all kinds of different means to deal with them. The means that a person in a wheelchair uses are different from those used by someone with impaired vision. What gives one person more independence, in other words, could well restrict another. At the same time, the alternative means used by someone in a wheelchair can also help someone pushing a baby stroller. Alternative means are just that, *alternative,* and as such they open new doors and create new possibilities of how to live.

Society, however, is not always open to change. Using alternative means can cast doubt on existing opportunities and modes of operation and, therefore, can be considered disruptive or a threat. Hence, as each person with a disability creates his or her own alternative vision of life, he or she has the capability to upend the civic order. People with disabilities, in other words, have the potential to disturb every stage of life and upset the natural order and hierarchy of a society.[12]

This book describes how the unique vision of people with disabilities undermines one particular society—American society. Tracing the legislative development of the history of employment provisions in disability policy from World War II to the present—namely, those in the Vocational Rehabilitation Act of 1954, the Rehabilitation Act of 1973, and the Americans with Disabilities Act of 1990—it shows how the employment rights within disability policy give people the capacity to subvert the workplace, one of this society's most confining everyday structures. When employers realized that disability rights could turn this subversive potential into a reality, they turned to the federal courts, which concurred, rendering a very narrow construction of these rights.

Workplace Hierarchies

Nowhere in the United States are hierarchal relations more visible, and ultimately restrictive, than at work. In the American workplace, the hierarchal relationship between employers and workers is best denoted by the employment-at-will doctrine.[13] This legal doctrine, which no other industrialized nation uses, stipulates that employers have the right to fire employees for "a good reason, a bad reason, or no reason at all."[14] It exemplifies the hierarchal nature of the American workplace because, as one legal scholar said, "[E]mployment-at-will is the ultimate guarantor of the capitalist's authority over the worker. . . . If employees could be dismissed on a moment's notice, obviously they could not claim a voice in the determination of work or the use of the product of their labor."[15]

To be sure, civil rights laws have had a mitigating effect on the employment-at-will doctrine. Employers cannot fire workers on account of race or gender. Unlike statutes prohibiting discrimination of people with disabilities, these civil rights laws, however, do not change the nature of the hierarchal relationship between employers and workers. Rather, they eliminate two specific reasons that an employer can use as cause for termination: race and gender. Assuming that employees were not chosen on the basis of gender or racial criteria, an employer still retains the prerogative to fire them.

Although some states have modified the employment-at-will doctrine by requiring employers to list the cause for termination, few people question the workplace hierarchy that this doctrine helped to cultivate. It is accepted as an integral part of American capitalism in which an employer purchases labor for a set amount of time. When employees sell their labor in the hiring process, as economists see it, they relinquish control over their time. What is not factored into this equation are employee needs. As long as needs do not interfere with the ability to maximize profits, an employer remains indifferent to them.[16]

From the employers' standpoint, a request for an accommodation does not sit well with business rationality. This is true even for accommodations that have no monetary cost, because they have the capacity to challenge the logic underlying work rules and regulations instituted by employers to maximize profits. Indeed, some workers without disabilities recognize requests for accommodation for what they are: leverage that gives employees the opportunity to negotiate work conditions.

The only other means of providing employees with bargaining leverage is unionization. Yet, unlike a disabled person's request for an accommodation, labor leaders seek collective bargaining agreements that try to minimize disruptions at the workplace. Whereas employees can make requests for accommodation at any time, employers negotiate with labor leaders at specifically scheduled times. And, while an employee's request for an accommodation is spontaneous, a collective bargaining agreement contains its own set of carefully considered rules and regulations. Collective bargaining agreements increase the amount of power and leverage that workers have with their employers, but they do so by trying to substitute the workers' version of workplace normalcy. By contrast, no matter how cooperative or well-intentioned an employee with a disability might be, his or her request for an accommodation cannot be governed by a similar set of rules and regulations. Accommodation requests, therefore, can be perceived as disruptive to employers and threaten or potentially threaten workplace normalcy.

Disabled people have been seen not only as a threat to the workplace hierarchy but also to the principle of business rationality underlying American capitalism. This helps to explain the opposition they face from employers and the federal courts. My purpose in this book is threefold. First, I intend to show how the postwar disability policy that pertained to work—vocational rehabilitation—initially tried to "normalize" people with disabilities. Inspired by physicians who pioneered the very notion of rehabilitation during World War II, this policy provided that disabled people accommodate society rather than have society accommodate them. Disabled people must compensate for their physical or mental impairments with their whole minds and bodies to gain entrance into the work force. Showing how these physicians and policymakers made disabled people pursue normalcy, particularly in the workplace, not only recounts the history of disability policy. It also uncovers the conformism underlying the conception of democracy during the Cold War.

Second, I will relate how remnants of the cultural values embedded in postwar policy influenced the rights-oriented disability policy created in the 1970s. In 1973, Congress passed an amended version of the Vocational Rehabilitation Act, which renamed the Rehabilitation Act, gave people a statutory right to be free of discrimination for physical or mental impairments. The rights provision, Section 504, however, was an unanticipated consequence of the policymaking process. Staffers from congressional offices included this one-sentence section in the legislation without realizing that it would become the cornerstone for disability rights. As such an accident of history, Section 504 was not given the forethought that might have effectively eradicated the compensatory values associated with the earlier vocational rehabilitation program. Both the Department of Health, Education and Welfare (HEW), which came under pressure from members of the disability rights movement to draft regulatory guidelines to implement this section, and the federal courts, which enforced it, maintained enough leeway in their respective interpretations to soften the blow that disability rights had on employers.

Finally, I will suggest that public support for the cultural values behind vocational rehabilitation and the commensurate lack of support for the rights orientation help explain why the employment provisions within the ADA have been so ineffectual. While Congress passed the ADA with overwhelming majorities and the full support of the disability rights movement, employers have turned to the federal judiciary, which has enfeebled the employment provisions. Rather than viewing the alternative means that disabled people use as potential for power as a benefit for people with and without disabilities, employers and members of the federal bench have portrayed it as a zero-sum threat that must be thwarted.[17] They challenge the antidiscrimination employment provisions because they believe that few people with disabilities should have a *right* to accommodation. They subscribe to the postwar values of compensation and normalcy, which propagated the idea that people with disabilities should take responsibility for making their own accommodations. An accommodation, moreover, involves not just equipment but also the attitude that a person with a disability adopts at the workplace. Containing language that is reminiscent of that of the pioneers of vocational rehabilitation, the federal courts have suggested that, if people can mitigate their impairments, whether or not they have cerebral palsy, a back injury, or multiple sclerosis, the courts need not protect them from employment discrimination, knowing that this would undermine the employers' right to manage a workplace.[18]

Striving toward Normalcy

When Drs. Howard Rusk and Henry Kessler, two of the founders of rehabilitation medicine, and Mary Switzer, the leading federal bureaucrat who instigated and ran the vocational rehabilitation program from World War II until 1970, conceived, drafted, and lobbied for the Vocational Rehabilitation Act of 1954, they were influenced by a prominent political value associated with the 1950s—democratization. Like other advocates of democratization, they thought people should join nongovernmental institutions and associations, such as places of work, schools, churches, and local communities, as a means of developing their full potential. Participating in such nongovernmental institutions would give each individual an outlet for personal and political expression. It was believed that the aggregate of these individuals' actions would make the United States more democratic. Underlying this belief that the nongovernmental organizations could bring about social reform was an abiding faith that American political institutions would respond to such reform efforts.

To Rusk, Kessler, and Switzer, people with disabilities had to be included in the democratization process. Although most disabled people were not warehoused, all three used the discourse about institutionalization and democratization to portray themselves as reformers. They distanced themselves from the public spaces that had characterized treatment for people with disabilities in an earlier era—the hospital and the mental asylum. Rusk, Kessler, and Switzer envisioned a new public space—the rehabilitation center—that would treat disabled people, preparing them for reentry into private life, particularly employment.

Modeled after the Manhattan Project, the rehabilitation center was staffed by an interdisciplinary team of experts, which ideally included a psychiatrist, a physician, social workers, occupational and physical therapists, vocational rehabilitation experts, *and* even an anthropologist. After each expert examined a candidate for rehabilitation, the whole team would put together a diagnosis. This diagnosis, however, was grounded in one assumption—that most people with physical and mental impairments were "maladjusted." It was the job of this new team of rehabilitation experts to make such people fit in with society.

For Rusk, Kessler, and their colleagues, a large part of the attitudinal adjustment necessary for disabled people revolved around diminishing what made them different from the rest of society. Rehabilitation was to help disabled people maximize their potential by compensating for their problems. Although none of them would ever become the "employee of the month," Rusk and Kessler thought disabled people could, by striving, achieve normalcy.

Rusk and Kessler derived these ideas about normalcy and compensation from two interrelated sources. First, rehabilitation medicine was based on the principle that the anatomical model of the mind and body should be replaced by a functional one. That is, rehabilitation medicine no longer concentrated on what disabled people could not do but what they could do. This "can do" perspective became known as the "whole man theory" of rehabilitation.

Second, rehabilitation medicine took the belief structure behind the whole man theory from the American version of psychoanalysis, psychosomatic medicine, and cultural anthropology. Rehabilitation doctors found the intellectual means in these disciplines to focus not on physical loss but rather on modeling the personality that could compensate for this loss. Building strong and healthy egos was crucial, these rehabilitation doctors proclaimed, because people suffered more from the so-called emotional maladjustments or personality defects that accompanied their physical impairments than from the impairments themselves.

Borrowing loosely from an American version of Sigmund Freud's ideas about the personality problems of people with disabilities, rehabilitation experts believed that their problems came from a conviction that they should be exempt from the normal customs and laws that govern society. It was this attitude that gave disabled people license to "wreak havoc" upon the rest of society. The supposed hostility that they manifested, as well as other similar personality disorders, could be attributed to their frustration with their physical or mental impairments.[19] Disabled people were unemployable, the argument went, because of their "twisted and maladjusted personalities," which was what the rehabilitation experts sought to change.

According to Rusk, Kessler, and other advocates of vocational rehabilitation, people with disabilities, unlike "normal" healthy people, particularly needed to develop their potential, because a "sick" individual led to a "sick society." The federal government's commitment to vocational rehabilitation was, therefore, justified on the basis that it strengthened the whole of American society.

Put differently, the rehabilitation experts from the 1950s were engaging in what Michel Foucault called "normalizing judgments" or a "metric" mode of thinking.[20] Within the context of democratization, rehabilitation was dependent on normalizing judgments, which assessed each person in relation not to a fixed standard like law but to each other.[21] People with disabilities were compared to those without. Rehabilitation experts, however, hoped that most disabled people could fit in what statisticians described as the arch of a bell-shaped curve. Although a minority hung to one side or the other of average, the democratization process featured the majority in the middle. It was this majority that those in rehabilitation centers were measured against.

The revolutionary idea that people with disabilities could be compared to people without them dated back to World War II when Rusk and Kessler abandoned the anatomical notion that there was an ideal body type. Relinquishing the concept of an ideal was revolutionary in that it was democratic. Unlike the preceding generation of physicians and biologists who believed in eugenics, Rusk and Kessler developed rehabilitation as a means of offering hope to disabled people: hope not to be themselves, but hope to be freed from the so-called abnormalities that rehabilitation experts assumed plagued people with disabilities. Disabled people were no longer measured against an ideal, and as a result some of them could compensate for their "deficiencies" and could be welcomed into mainstream society.

Rusk's and Kessler's democratic perspective about the body was not the only value they drew from the 1950s. Their emphasis on normalcy also exemplified this era. Many professionals extolled the virtues of societal conformity, and Rusk and Kessler were no exception. To them, disabled people had to counterbalance what distinguished them from the rest of society, carefully conforming to its notion of normalcy. Experts did not think that disabled people should have the autonomy to decide what would be in their best interest. So as not to be seen as "abnormal," they were encouraged to mask their physical or mental impairments, thereby exhibiting or expressing as little of their individuality as possible. Societal acceptance or rejection, according to Rusk and Kessler, depended on how well disabled people conformed to society. They would not be accepted by virtue of how their physical or mental impairments contributed to, or detracted from, a community on their own terms.

Hence, Rusk and Kessler and other physicians in rehabilitation medicine, who came into prominence after World War II, and the disability policy they advanced, paid virtually no heed to the voice of the disabled people they served. They supported a policy that, while being justified on the individualistic grounds of aggregate behavior, gave little weight to the individuality of disabled people.[22] As these rehabilitation doctors advised, disabled people should accommodate society rather than expecting society to build accommodations that would include them.

By providing an understanding of the postwar period, it will be shown here that disability activists could not just refashion the old vocational rehabilitation program by interjecting a new rights orientation. To ground disability policy in rights, activists would have to displace what Foucault would have described as a discursive practice. The history of vocational rehabilitation, it will be illustrated, followed the three axes of such a practice. First, Rusk and Kessler created a whole new medical speciality—rehabilitation medicine—that established its own "domain of recognitions." As the fathers of this speciality, they became the experts of this "specific knowledge."[23]

Second, the passage of the Vocational Rehabilitation Act, as well as amending and adding complementary legislation, like the Hospital Survey and Construction Act of 1946, allowed these physicians, along with Switzer, to build a rehabilitation empire. This field supporting rehabilitation medicine funded and trained several generations of experts like vocational rehabilitation counselors, and occupational and physical therapists and social workers who also supported the field. Like the punitive rationality Foucault described in *Discipline and Punish,* the vocational rehabilitation ethos was "endowed with its own rules for which external determinations could not account." In other words, vocational rehabilitation had its "own structure as a discursive practice."[24]

Finally, not only did the discursive practice underlying vocational rehabilitation affect ordinary people with disabilities, it also helps explain why leaders of the disability rights movement had problems undermining the authority and expertise of the vocational rehabilitation experts. Being antithetical to the rights orientation, the vocational rehabilitation ethos has strongly influenced those with disabilities as well as society's perception of them. Vocational rehabilitation helped, and still helps, to sustain the idea that disability is not part of the natural course of life, and that those with physical and mental impairments must be normalized. The federal courts still make normalizing judgments, comparing a person with a disability to the "average person in the general population."[25] By perpetuating such an us versus them binary, the vocational rehabilitation ethos continues to give employers tight control over their workplaces.

Parking Lots and Workplaces

The disability rights movement came into being in the mid-1960s. A small group, headed by Paul Strachan, fought for disability rights in the 1940s, but it was almost completely overshadowed by the advocates of vocational rehabilitation. Influenced by the poor people's movement, feminism, the student movement, and the civil rights movement, the disability rights movement, not surprisingly, was founded in two university towns—Champagne-Urbana, Illinois, and Berkeley, California. Seeking an alternative space to the rehabilitation center, with its emphasis on striving for normalcy and "creaming," which referred to the vocational rehabilitation experts' practice of placing those people who had the least debilitating impairments, people at both universities started what were called Centers for Independent Living (CIL). Most notably, Edward Roberts, who is often seen as the father of the movement for independent living, and other disability rights activists at Berkeley in the 1960s developed the principles behind independent living, free from the gaze of rehabilitation experts, to help foster the dignity and self-determination of people with disabilities.[26]

Questioning the power and prestige of the rehabilitation professionals, the first disability rights activists challenged the fundamental principles behind the vocational rehabilitation ethos or the psychoanalytical approach to disability.[27] Roberts in particular rejected the authority and expertise of rehabilitation professionals in favor of inventive self-help groups. To Roberts, disabled people had a better understanding of what they needed than did the rehabilitation experts.

Initially concentrating on wresting control over the minds and bodies of disabled people from the rehabilitation experts, the disability rights movement could devote little time to fight for employment rights of disabled people.[28] Then, in the mid-1970s, employment became a much bigger concern to the movement when, albeit unanticipated, Section 504 of the Rehabilitation Act was passed.[29] After discovering this section's importance, the disability rights movement began wielding it to make public places accessible, including public schools, colleges, and universities, *and* sought relief from employment discrimination. At the same time, the general spirit of rights that had been inculcated by the different rights movements in the 1960s inspired disability rights activists who began to make their movement more coherent and cohesive. Using the 1980s to strengthen its ranks, the disability rights movement reached a peak in 1990 when, as a cross-coalescing movement uniting disabled people with all types of physical and mental impairments, it helped pass the Americans with Disabilities Act.

Despite its eventual success, the movement for disability rights did evolve at a much slower pace than other civil rights movements for three interrelated reasons. First, the movement was plagued by its particular history. The disability rights movement could not fight for a policy based on rights without first freeing disabled people from policies that had been enacted, supposedly, to help them. While the movement was critical of these existent policies, like the vocational rehabilitation program, many people with disabilities still had to rely on them.

Second, this movement had special difficulties mobilizing members. Richard Scotch, a disability policy expert, observed, "Disabled individuals in noninstitutional settings are geographically and socially dispersed, and this fact constitutes a barrier to collective political action."[30] Unlike other movements, such as the women's movement, which rallied people on the basis of their identity, many disabled people either try not to be identified as disabled, or they identify with those who share their particular disability by joining an organization that caters to their specific needs. Harlan Hahn also observed that disabled people "are understandably reluctant to focus on that aspect of their identity that is most negatively stigmatized by the rest of society and to mobilize politically around it."[31]

Third, despite its efforts, the disability rights movement had trouble becoming a coherent, national movement because some activists, particularly those from the deaf and hearing impaired, developed their own distinct culture and saw little reason to reach out to people who had different physical and mental impairments.[32] The different disability cultures, in turn, have spawned disparate tactics and strategies.[33] Some of the pivotal provisions within the 1992 Rehabilitation Act amendments, for instance, were included because of a particularly effective demonstration that the National Federation of the Blind (NFB) staged during committee hearings.[34] Meanwhile, disability rights activists from other organizations had not participated in this demonstration, preferring to rely on less militant lobbying tactics.[35]

Despite these organizational problems, a national disability rights movement did come into its own in the 1970s. Unlike many other movements which emphasize identity politics, this one is held together by a sociopolitical vision that most people with disabilities share.[36] Simi Linton, a disability rights expert, observes that "we are all bound together, not by the list of our collective symptoms but by the social political circumstances that have forged us as a group."[37]

Indeed, the disability rights movement's belief in self-help has remained constant from the 1960s to the present. It has wavered little from its original belief that what hobbles people with disabilities are the personal attitudes or prejudices of people without them, not the disabilities themselves. Disability rights activists know that the state has less difficulty passing policies for people with disabilities that appeal to someone's sense of charity or pity than it has enacting policies that promote their equal rights. What is perceived as "the 'normal,' 'natural' response to a person with disabilities," according to Lennard Davis, a disability studies expert, "is in reality a socially conditioned, politically generated response."[38]

To be sure, everyone is bound by the norms and conventions of society. The disability rights movement does not question the need for societal conventions; it promotes the idea that people with disabilities should help shape them. It rejects the notion that people with disabilities are distinguished from those without. In fact, a whole field of study—disability studies—has emerged in colleges and universities to revisit what Linton depicts as "the critical divisions our society makes in creating the normal versus the pathological, the insider versus the outsider, or the competent citizen versus the ward of the state."[39]

Most important, the disability rights movement has questioned the pity that underlies modern disability policy. "To be identified with the young poster people in wheelchairs dressing the set on the Jerry Lewis muscular dystrophy telethon each year," Hockenberry explains, "was the lowest of the low."[40] Or as James Williams Jr., the Easter Seals president, described the Lewis telethon, "One of the biggest problems facing disabled people is stereotypes. If you portray people as objects of pity, in a mass medium like a telethon which has sixty million viewers, then it only reinforces those stereotypes."[41] Both Hockenberry and Williams realize that people with disabilities who insist on equal social, economic, and political rights make the rest of society uncomfortable. "No one would think of having a telethon," Hockenberry adds, "to raise money to build accessible housing for wheelchair consumers or to find jobs for them."[42]

Policies and programs based on pity are acceptable because they make disabled people nonthreatening. When people with disabilities challenge the monopoly of power and control held by the able-bodied, their efforts have been met with loud protest. The blue-lined parking spots are emblematic in this regard. For some people without disabilities, a specially reserved set of parking spaces represents a privilege and a convenience they would like to enjoy themselves. The inconvenience of finding a regular space becomes tantamount to the inaccessibility that drivers with disabilities face. The situation gets worse if one believes, as Andy Rooney exclaimed on *Sixty Minutes,* that people exaggerate their claims about disabilities to gain this privilege. When Rooney and other drivers equate their parking problems with accessibility issues, they are essentially saying, "How dare these people with disabilities inconvenience me?"

Parking lots are one thing; work is another. In the workplace, no presumption of accessibility exists. The privileges associated with ownership and job qualifications make equal access unattainable. A concrete hierarchy between employers and workers, extended by the aforementioned employment-at-will doctrine, governs the workplace. When workers with disabilities successfully use alternative means of performing their jobs, these means can be perceived as special work conditions which upset the hierarchy of the workplace.

Sometimes workers with disabilities present such a threat to the workplace that they become the target of disaffection from coworkers as well as employers. Casey Martin, the professional golfer who has grave difficulties walking, encountered this type of resentment when he asked to use a golf cart during a tournament. Brad Faxon, a fellow golfer, said Martin "is a great player, and he deserves all the accolades, but I don't see guys in the NFL, who have knee injuries getting mopeds. Where do you draw the line?"[43] Workers with disabilities like Martin's are imperiled because some able-bodied workers might consider these means better than what the able-bodied rely on to fulfill their job requirements.

The disability rights movement did penetrate American culture in the 1960s and 1970s, while Centers for Independent Living have not displaced but do coexist with rehabilitation centers, and the rights perspective became the basis of Section 504 of the Rehabilitation Act and later the ADA's employment provisions. Nonetheless, this perspective has not fully succeeded in supplanting the values about normalcy and compensation that underlie the policy from the 1950s. These values have been expressed by employers, federal court judges, and Supreme Court justices, who characterize workplace requests for accommodation as either an excuse for not wanting to conform to work rules, or as the means to overturn the supposedly rightful hierarchal relationship between employers and their employees. After all, people with disabilities may expose the rules and regulations that shackle other employees, and it is this fear, not the actual accommodations made, that convinces employers and federal court judges and justices not to accommodate them.

ADA Creates a Catch-22

Two-thirds of disabled people want to work, yet only two-thirds of those have found a job.[44] Almost half of the people, moreover, have moderate disabilities that do not hinder their capacity to work. Their disabilities limit only their job choice or the length of their workday or workweek. One report indicated that "this enormous employment gap cannot be fully accounted for by limitations imposed on the work-disability population because of their disabilities."[45] According to many members of legislative and executive branches, along with disability rights activists, these figures indicate that disabled people still face discrimination.

Beginning in the 1980s, politicians and policymakers started questioning the idea entrenched within American disability policy, particularly the income maintenance programs run by the Social Security Administration, that the very definition of disability rests on someone's inability to work. In other words, they began exploring the notion of the disability rights movement that it was discrimination, not the physical or mental impairments of people with disabilities that in large part accounted for their high rate of joblessness and poverty.[46] Culminating in the passage of the Americans with Disabilities Act in 1990, the disability rights movement convinced Congress and the president that people with disabilities constituted one of the last minority groups that needed relief from discrimination.

Yet, despite the ADA's passage, few people with disabilities have found relief from employment discrimination. Before the Supreme Court ruled on disability rights under Title I, the lower federal courts decided on 94 percent of all litigation in the employers' favor.[47] Then, in 1999, the Supreme Court issued a trio of rulings that upheld and extended the lower federal court decisions.[48] To be sure, the disproportionate number of courtroom battles that employers have won includes what critics of Title I call "frivolous" lawsuits. This figure, however, does not account for all 700 federal court cases rendered before the Supreme Court issued its rulings.[49] What helps explain these figures is that people filing lawsuits have been caught up in a battle over the functional definition of who has a disability.

Unlike other civil rights categories, like race, people with disabilities must prove that they have one. African Americans seeking protection under the Civil Rights Act, for instance, do not have to provide evidence of their racial lineage. While the disability rights movement was well aware of this difference, neither it nor any groups representing employers fore-saw the problems associated with defining a disability. Instead, disability rights activists thought the primary point of contention would involve what constitutes a reasonable accommodation, not a disability. After all, they had no courtroom experience that pointed to the contrary.

Moreover, since the definition of a disability had not been a significant issue in litigation about Section 504 of the Rehabilitation Act, disability rights advocates, who lobbied for the ADA, suggested that the broad def-inition of a disability in the Rehabilitation Act of 1973 be retained. It in-cludes people with a physical or mental condition, those who have a history of one, like cancer, and those perceived as having a disability, like a facial scar. Catching the disability rights activists off guard, it was when this broad definition of a disability was applied to the private work force that some federal court judges and Supreme Court justices issued an in-terpretation of it that excluded most disabled people from the ADA's cov-erage.

First, the federal courts have cultivated a broad and free-wheeling func-tional definition of a disability. Few people within the federal government, nor lobbying from the outside, have opposed functionalism. It was the Equal Employment Opportunity Commission (EEOC) that first issued a functional definition articulating that a disability is determined by what a worker or an employee can and cannot do: it must substantially limit a major life activity like walking.

The disability rights movement, moreover, has never taken issue with functionalism. To the contrary, it has always fought against any percep-tion of a person with a disability that could be described as essentialist. Activists, for instance, insisted that the ADA's title must clearly articulate that it benefits a person *with* a disability rather than a *disabled* person. Furthermore, the functional definition is often juxtaposed with the med-ical definition and, having long battled with the medical community about their autonomy, disability rights activists abhor the idea that physicians should decide what constitutes a disability. The federal courts' definition of a disability, therefore, has not limited coverage because it is functional but rather because of how they have interpreted functionalism.

To the federal court judges, a functional definition of a disability must take into account not just medical and scientific evidence of what the per-son can do but also personal and societal considerations. A person with a debilitating impairment with more education than the "average person" can do more than a person without this education. The courts, in other words, look at how a person functions *generally,* essentially making normalizing judgments about people with disabilities in comparison with "normal" people. Evaluating each person with a disability on a case-by-case basis, the federal courts have ignored the EEOC's expansive guidelines about what constitutes a substantial impairment, for example, a missing extremity, epilepsy, or diabetes. They have used this case-by-case basis, not to avoid stereotyping people as the disability rights activists had hoped but as a means of scrutinizing the personal, societal, medical, and technological ways that someone has to mitigate their condition.

Second, the federal courts' interpretation of a disability has had punitive results. Judges and justices have not simply failed to protect people from employment discrimination by wielding this definition. Filing a suit against an employer for discrimination has given some employers cause to fire people with disabilities. The federal courts have ruled that if a person does not have a severe enough disability to warrant protection under Title I, this disability can be considered limiting enough to provide grounds against hiring or, further, for dismissal if he or she already has the job.

Writing for a seven-to-two majority in *Sutton and Hinton v. United Air Lines,* the Supreme Court's leading case, Justice Sandra Day O'Connor, held that "an employer is free to decide that physical characteristics or medical conditions that do not rise to the level of an impairment—such as one's height, build or singing voice—are preferable to others, just as it is free to decide that some limiting, but not *substantially* limiting, impairments make individuals less than ideally suited for a job."[50] An employer, in other words, can refuse to hire someone *because* of his or her disability. Rather than providing antidiscrimination protection, many federal court judges and justices have turned Title I on its head, giving employers cause for letting someone go.

Overall, the federal courts' functional definition of disability has been, as Justice John Paul Stevens, one of the two dissenters in the *Sutton* decision, called it, "especially ironic." The Supreme Court's interpretation denies "protection for persons with substantially limiting impairments that, when corrected, render them fully able and employable."[51] Hockenberry said that "by this definition the fact that I use a wheelchair to mitigate my paraplegia suggests that I am not disabled."[52] Or as Chai Feldblum, a law professor, explained, this definition creates "the absurd result of a person being disabled enough to be fired from a job, but not disabled enough to challenge the firing."[53]

Given the irony of the Court's opinion, some critics have questioned the majority's motives. In particular, Stevens argued in his own dissenting opinion that the majority has tried to reduce the number of people seeking relief under Title I. As he saw it, this goal of limiting legal access represents a significant departure from the Supreme Court's own history of interpreting other civil rights statutes. Barring one exception, Stevens elaborated, the Court has been more inclusive in defining who should be protected under civil rights statutes. For example, while the House and Senate Committee reports about the Civil Rights Act of 1964 refer to African Americans, the Court also made Hispanics and Asians part of the protected class.[54]

Stevens takes this position, in part, because providing an expansive definition of who qualifies for statutory protection, be it under the Civil Rights Act or the Americans with Disabilities Act, does not give minorities, women, and/or people with disabilities a courtroom advantage. Extending coverage, as he explains, would mean that fewer cases could be dismissed on summary judgment. Juries, not judges, would decide if employers had discriminated against them on the merits of the case. Once inside the courtroom, in other words, people with disabilities still must prove, first, that they are qualified for the position; second, that their requests for an accommodation are reasonable; and third, that these requests would not cause the employer undue hardship. As a reader of the *New York Times* wrote, "The law never gave anybody with a disability the right to a job for which they weren't qualified or which they couldn't perform without a reasonable accommodation that he or she would not pose an undue burden for the employer."[55]

While disabled people primarily have been caught up in the struggle over this definition, another part of the explanation stems from the similarities that disability rights and other civil rights legislation, including labor legislation, share. Neither Section 504 nor Title I of the ADA gives disabled people employment. Disability law for employment has, therefore, bestowed people with distinctly American rights. Title I gives disabled people the right to work. This is not a positive right, however, like the right granted by the British quota system, for instance, which makes employers hire disabled people. Rather, employment rights for disabled people are civil rights, and they are based on what Isaiah Berlin described as a negative conception of liberty or freedom. Embodying this type of negative liberty in disability policy means that the government juxtaposes the rights of disabled people with the employers' right to contract.

What explains this attitude toward negative liberty and rights, moreover, is the deep strain of individualism in American liberalism. According to the American creed, every citizen has the prerogative to determine what is in his or her best interest. Individualism rejects any explanations of social phenomena other than those couched in terms of the abstract individual. All rules and regulations to the contrary are artificial. People with disabilities have a right to work *and* employers have a right to manage, which means that disability rights policy intervenes at the workplace only when an employer violates a disabled person's right to work. It is the juxtaposition of these rights that explains how the United States can have both strong statutory rights and an ineffectual policy that provides little protection in the workplace for people with disabilities.[56]

Further tipping the balance toward employers in this contest over rights is the fact that disabled people need accommodations to exercise their right to work. These accommodations make the federal courts more reluctant to recognize their rights because they require positive state action, instead of negative or prohibitive action. Yet, throughout the Supreme Court's history, a negative type of statutory protection, in which the state prohibits an action or activity, is more likely to be accepted by the Court than a positive one that compels state action. For instance, legislation that provides a positive type of protection, like wage-and-hour legislation that gives only women a higher wage and a shorter workweek, would undoubtedly be overturned by the Court. Even if the federal courts gave a more expansive reading of what constituted a disability, the disability rights movement would face this legal hurdle, which is a hurdle that few social movements have cleared.

The Theory of Ideas and Epistemic Communities

While the federal judiciary has treated disabled people as one of the last minorities, including presenting this group with the same problems that other minorities have faced, it did not develop this response fully as a reaction to civil rights. The judiciary has been influenced by the attitude that the vocational rehabilitation program had fostered since the 1950s, which made people with disabilities ready to accommodate their employers. The federal court judges and a majority on the Supreme Court have subscribed to the values that lay behind the whole man theory of rehabilitation.

Yet, why did policymakers incorporate this theory into disability policy in the first place? This book maintains that policymakers relied on the whole man theory at the exclusion of other models of rehabilitation because they were receptive to the beliefs and values of what has been called an "epistemic community," a group of "experts" who share a set of ideas and beliefs. Experts—the doctors who lobbied for vocational rehabilitation in the 1940s and 1950s—convinced the policymakers to rely on the whole man theory of rehabilitation.

Political scientists like Judith Goldstein and Peter Hall have introduced the notion of an epistemic community to show how ideas affect the policymaking process.[57] "A supply of ideas," according to Goldstein, "can satisfy the demands for policy change."[58] An example is American trade policy, which she argues switched from protectionism to liberalism because of the influence of an epistemic community. This occurred once members of the community convinced policymakers that protectionism was no longer a viable political idea. The policymakers, Goldstein suggests, knowing that they themselves lacked the expertise to solve the economic crisis in the 1920s, solicited advice from experts.[59] They deferred to an epistemic community that already had a network of professionals with expertise engaged in analyzing trade policy.

Goldstein and Hall essentially have superimposed the theory of ideas on the neo-institutionalist approach. That is, first, they assume that political institutions structure state and societal relations. Governed by a set of rules and regulations, institutions create a context that then determines different types of political opportunities. They mobilize organized interests, shape the strategies that the leaders of these interests pursue, and assert political legitimacy.

Second, Goldstein and Hall speculate that while these institutions and the policies the institutions implement are important, they also are bogged down by inertia. As a result, institutional changes of any consequence rarely can happen without a crisis that exposes the limits of an institution. It is the crises, then, that provide policymakers with opportunities by making their institutions amenable to change.

Third, neo-institutionalism, as Theda Skocpol suggests, "holds that politicians and administrators must be taken seriously. Not merely agents of other social interests, they are actors in their own right, enabled and constrained by the political organization within which they operate." This is not to say, however, that there cannot be what she describes as "dual lines of determination." Policymakers institute social policies, which in turn affect the social identities and group capacities of those who become involved in the politics of social policymaking.[60]

This study also relies on both neo-institutionalism and the theory of ideas to explain the development of disability policy. First, it recognizes institutions, as Thorstein Veblen did, as "habits of thought."[61] The bureaucratic apparatus that developed implemented the first vocational rehabilitation program but did not simply constrain or channel actions of self-interested individuals. Acting with purpose and forethought, it created a whole new discipline, producing a context that helped shape the strategies of organized interests emerging within this new field of vocational rehabilitation. This program prescribed the actions of the state actors and advanced a new notion of legitimacy about how to rehabilitate the whole man. Finally, the history of vocational rehabilitation exposes how political institutions structure policies, which in turn define political opportunities that influence the construction of future policies. Having vocational rehabilitation molded, fashioned, and refashioned by physicians and bureaucrats, from the 1940s until the late 1960s, created a discourse that those pursuing rights, beginning in the 1970s, would be compelled to follow.

Second, this study applies the theory of ideas to new institutionalism. It underscores that, as Karen Orren and Stephen Skowronek point out, political institutions are "steeped in ideas."[62] Institutions give expression to ideas, Orren explains, both "by the way that they enforce norms, and by the manner in which they shape opposition."[63] What is more, this book highlights the role the epistemic community of physicians plays to show how it brought the ideas into the initial policymaking process. It suggests that this community based vocational rehabilitation upon the political value of democratization, which included a notion of normalcy and compensation, which still bog down those seeking disability rights today. Finally, this book suggests that a field of rehabilitation is mobilized and organized around a set of beliefs and values that arose during a specific moment in history.[64] It uses history as a theory, however, not as a method, as historians do. It does so by highlighting the irregularities rather than the regularities of time.[65]

While this study utilizes Goldstein's notion of the theory of ideas, it does modify her model in one crucial respect. It avoids her assumption that "good ideas, like science, will be recognized for their objective merits."[66] The persuasiveness of ideas arises not because of their "objective merit" but because they are articulated in a context that combines knowledge *and* power. The book adopts Foucault's supposition that knowledge is imbued with power. The belief system underlying rehabilitation created what Foucault would have designated as a new discourse of power.

Before the nineteenth century, Foucault argued, power was visible. To illustrate this point, Foucault opened *Discipline and Punish* with a graphic description of a prisoner being drawn and quartered. The prisoner had committed a crime against the king. The public, which was expecting a spectacle worthy of a king, was not disappointed. The prisoner's gruesome punishment served as a spectacular display of royal power, reinforcing the idea that the king was valued because of what distinguished him from his subjects.[67]

For Foucault, the modern age began with the end of these public spectacles, not just with corporal punishment but in terms of all aspects of state-societal relations. Although power is no longer vividly displayed, everyday rituals and procedures impose rights and obligations on society in the modern era that Foucault considered to be more invasive and oppressive than before. Essentially, the modern notion of power reversed relations between the sovereign and his subjects. This is because crimes are no longer committed against sovereigns or any other symbol of the state but against the whole of society.[68] A crime against the state is equivalent to a violation of the social contract that governs society. "We punish," wrote Foucault, "but this is a way of saying that we wish to obtain a cure."[69]

As explained earlier, rehabilitation medicine engaged in a similar discourse of power. Physicians sought cures for people with disabilities, not by healing their bodies but by curing them of their so-called personality abnormalities and disorders. An interdisciplinary team of rehabilitation experts, Rusk and Kessler maintained, could restore disabled people to normalcy. Disabled people themselves could not be involved in the healing process that rehabilitation experts should control because, as Rusk and Kessler saw it, they were not to express their individuality. After all, this was what prevented them from being accepted as "normal" members of society in the first place. Thus, candidates for rehabilitation had to compensate for their disabilities by building stronger personalities instead of working with what distinguished them from the rest of society. Once their personalities were healed, disabled people could be returned to mainstream society.

Before World War II, few physicians or physical therapists thought disabled people could be rehabilitated. Instead, many were warehoused in hospitals and institutions, where state authorities stripped them of any shred of visible power. Even the president of the country was affected by this. Aware of the stigma attached to physical disability, Franklin D. Roosevelt went to great lengths to hide his own so as not to shake the public's faith in his ability to lead the nation.[70] In the 1950s, power relations changed with the creation of a new vocational rehabilitation program. At this time, experts suggested that rehabilitation offered disabled people more humane treatment than hospitalization. Yet, by making the assumption that disabled people all suffered from emotional maladjustments, the rehabilitation experts created a system of power relations that still gave them great control over disabled people.

This book concludes that an attempt to alter a person's attitude was oppressive because the rehabilitation experts' notion of normalcy had been internalized. Moreover, the power of the rehabilitation expert was hardly discernible. The all-encompassing nature of incarcerating the minds of disabled people only came to light when one of them refused to cooperate. The expert then condemned this person, not for rejecting rehabilitation but for the chance to gain societal acceptance. After all, rehabilitation was justified as a state expense because, again, according to the experts, a sick individual could lead to a sick society.

This model of rehabilitation medicine, and the discourse of power underlying it, was at odds with the demands of the disability rights movement for individual autonomy. When the movement began pushing for the implementation of the rights perspective included in Section 504 and Title I, it encountered a type of resistance from some employers and federal court judges and justices that revealed the success of the vocational rehabilitation program. This program has helped shape cultural attitudes about disabled people for almost fifty years.

Constructing Disability Policy

Chapter 1 explores the origins of the set of values and ideas that the rehabilitation movement cultivated, beginning in World War II. It shows how the behavioral revolution, particularly cultural anthropology's contribution to it, and the American version of psychoanalysis or psychodynamic therapy influenced the emerging field of rehabilitation medicine. Rehabilitation doctors thought that building patients' egos would help them compensate for their physical and mental impairments. A healthy personality, free from the emotional maladjustments that accompany physical and mental disability, would ensure a patient's rehabilitation and help that patient find a job. Physicians like Rusk and Kessler did not cultivate what disability studies experts like Hahn call a "medical model of disability."[71] Rather, they developed a medical model of the whole of society. To them, a so-called weak individual weakened society. Hence, rehabilitation was vital, not just to help the individual with an impairment but to help all of society.

Chapter 2 demonstrates that the epistemic community that made up the rehabilitation movement influenced the formation of modern disability policy in the 1940s and 1950s. Key officials in the federal government, most notably Switzer, incorporated the psychoanalytical principles propagated by the rehabilitation experts. Switzer also gave the rehabilitation movement an important role in vocational rehabilitation. Finally, she subscribed to the Cold War philosophy that the federal government should fund research and development in medicine and science without questioning the expertise of the doctors and scientists completing it. Like Rusk and Kessler, Switzer believed that rehabilitation was essential, not just to help the individual but to build a stronger society. Indeed, she made a link between rehabilitation and anticommunism with the argument that unrehabilitated, disabled people fostered a diseased society that, if left untreated, would make the United States vulnerable to Communist infiltration.

Chapter 3 shows how the rehabilitation movement and critical federal officials shaped the whole field of rehabilitation, primarily with federal funding. It argues that the psychoanalytic model of rehabilitation was dominant throughout the 1940s, 1950s, and 1960s. Governmental officials and doctors were so impressed with their success at rehabilitation that they wanted it to be expanded to the poor. Poverty could be solved by rehabilitating the poor, Switzer and Rusk proclaimed, by helping them compensate for their cultural and social impairments. This chapter accentuates how adamantly opposed the rehabilitation movement and critical members of the federal government were to employment rights for disabled people.

Chapter 4 traces the formation of the rights orientation that was included in the Rehabilitation Act of 1973. This chapter shows that Section 504 had an unintended consequence: it gave the disability rights movement the opportunity to begin to fight for disability rights. Since Section 504 had been included as an afterthought and was loosely crafted, its implementation was fraught with problems. HEW, which had been the champion of the psychoanalytic approach to vocational rehabilitation, obstructed the implementation of Section 504 by not issuing the necessary federal regulations. It was only after a federal court ordered the secretary of HEW to comply and the disability rights movement staged the longest sit-in demonstration in U.S. history that the regulations became operational.

Chapter 5 argues that the Supreme Court used the legislative ambiguity of Section 504 to render its own weak interpretation of disability rights. The Court held that disabled people had no constitutionally guaranteed rights. Yet, it also decided that disabled people were not always afforded equality of opportunity. Finally, the Court made a narrow rendering of Section 504 by determining the order of the thresholds that a person with a disability must clear. By examining qualifications of a person with a disability before reasonable accommodations, the Court created a precedent for the federal courts that ensured that few school officials or employers would be found guilty of discrimination. What is more, the Court did not take into account in its findings the disaffection that the able-bodied felt toward disabled people.

Chapter 6 explores the passage of the Americans with Disabilities Act and the federal courts' interpretation of its employment provisions. In their interpretation of these provisions in Title I, many federal courts have placed workers with disabilities in a double bind in that, by exposing the full extent of their limitations, disabled people become vulnerable to termination. The federal courts also have extended the Supreme Court's construction of a long series of thresholds that workers with disabilities must cross before they can be said to suffer discrimination. Most disabled people do not cross the first threshold, and their suits are dismissed on summary judgment, which means they do not proceed to trial. This chapter reviews how the Supreme Court entrenched the idea that most workers do not have disabilities severe enough to warrant protection under the ADA. In three cases, the Court ruled that people with disabilities can mitigate their impairments with medication or equipment. While some people may have a debilitating illness, like epilepsy, if they can treat it effectively with medication they do not have a disability in the eyes of the Court that should be safeguarded under Title I.

Finally, the Afterword describes how the lower federal courts have advanced the precedents established by the Supreme Court. Yet, rather than clarifying the issue about who can receive statutory protection, as the business community and other critics of Title I had hoped, this chapter reveals that the Supreme Court's declaration about mitigation has muddled the issue more than before. In the first year following the Court's decisions, the lower federal courts handed down more than 150 cases which not only maintained the high threshold limiting who Title I covered, but they broadened the Court's notion of mitigation. It demonstrates that some federal courts are asking whether plaintiffs could employ mitigating measures even if they have chosen not to. Others have begun evaluating mitigating measures themselves, while deciding if their usage is debilitating.

The irony imparted by this Afterword is that while the legal reasoning behind these ideas about mitigation discloses just how resistant the federal court judges remain to the ADA's rights orientation, they have allowed more cases to be heard by a jury. Thus, the federal court judges have become the modern-day version of the vocational rehabilitation experts. Instead of using the term "compensation," they rely on the idea of mitigation to exercise their power and authority over people with disabilities. By probing and investigating every minute detail about how a person can mitigate his or her disability, the federal court judges have essentially adopted the whole man theory of rehabilitation. Instead of asking who is whole and can be brought back into the work force because they compensate for their respective impairments, the federal court judges allow into the courtroom only those they regard as "unwhole" to protest employment discrimination.

" 'Deform'd, Unfinish'd,' and Maladjusted": The Psychoanalytical Model of Disability

In 1941, many American scientists, physicians, and social scientists offered their services to defeat Hitler. Most notably, an interdisciplinary team of scientists and engineers worked on the Manhattan Project which built the atom bomb. Meanwhile, physicians examined and treated servicemen and women. Social scientists also conducted research during World War II. Anthropologists, for instance, studied the "national character" of the enemy. As scientists, physicians, and social scientists relied on their professional expertise to build tools and weapons in the fight for democracy, what they abandoned was the assumption that academic research was "value-free."

The war effort illustrated that science, medicine, and social science could be used to effect large-scale change. Some professionals expressed grave reservations about this capacity for change. To other professionals, who would later participate in the Cold War, the Manhattan Project provided evidence that a long-term research project could be successfully completed with reference to a specific set of values.[1] Rehabilitation medicine was one of these disciplines. As Dr. Howard Rusk said, "[U]nder the stress of danger and urgent necessity, we make spectacular advances."[2]

The very idea of rehabilitation medicine, according to Drs. Rusk and Henry Kessler, was derived from the notion that science, medicine, and social science should promote democratization.[3] This is not to say they furthered what disability studies experts like Harlan Hahn have called a "medical model of disability."[4] Rusk and Kessler advanced a much more sweeping and ambitious plan that medicalized not just disability but the whole of society. Rehabilitation was promoted to ensure the health of the individual *and* that of society. According to them, an unrehabilitated person could weaken and erode society's health.

Starting from the perspective that advances in medicine and the behavioral social sciences, like psychology and anthropology, could help disabled people develop themselves as human beings, Rusk and Kessler promoted what they called a "rehabilitation center." In such a center, an interdisciplinary group of experts—including a physician, a psychiatrist, a psychologist, several social workers, a vocational training specialist, and an anthropologist—worked as a team to prepare people with disabilities for their eventual return to mainstream society. Rusk and Kessler then associated the rehabilitation center with democratization by extrapolating the health of society from that of the individual.

Developed in the late 1940s and in the 1950s, democratization was a loosely defined political movement which purported that nongovernmental institutions and associations gave people collective choice, and was thereby an instrument for social reform. Borrowing from the logic underlying the capitalist market system where every choice made by sellers and buyers determines the fate of a commodity, the advocates of democratization maintained that the aggregate of individual choices within a nongovernmental institution represented a collective choice. While democratization involved a scheme for participation in that each individual had a choice, there were two formal means of channeling this choice. First, the nongovernmental institution relied on a set of rules that each individual could explicitly *or* implicitly agree to follow. Second, it deferred to the existing political institutions and their underlying values and beliefs, seeking only gradual reform.

Democratization was, therefore, an inherently conservative reform movement. It created a formal system of political participation, which often gave elites the authority to speak for the members of the nongovernmental institutions and associations pursuing reform. Indeed, proponents of democratization opposed the very idea of a mass movement, arguing that this type of movement was by nature associated with fascism and communism.

Equating experts with political elites, Rusk and Kessler thought the rehabilitation center could be one of the nongovernmental institutions that help to gradually reform society. To them, the rehabilitation center could compile an aggregate of individual choices, not so much from disabled people but rather from the team of experts serving them. The person with a disability contributed to a "collective" choice simply by seeking treatment in a rehabilitation center. It was the rehabilitation experts who, in writing the rules and regulations that guided the individual choices disabled people made, restored them to "normalcy" and thereby furthered democratization.

Put differently, democratization was the political expression of the tension between individualism and normalcy found in Rusk's and Kessler's notion of rehabilitation. On one hand, Rusk and Kessler insisted that rehabilitation helped disabled people fulfill their individual potential. On the other hand, they insisted that it was the experts who helped them develop this potential. Portraying disabled people as "malformed and maladjusted," only the rehabilitation experts could show them how to strive toward normalcy. To Rusk and Kessler, the rehabilitation center represented a vital means of fostering democracy, because a "sick" individual led to a "sick society."

Rusk and Kessler were so committed to this conception of rehabilitation that they waged a public campaign to propagate it. Without a trace of irony, Rusk and Kessler identified themselves as members of a movement —"the rehabilitation movement." To do so, however, they had to misconstrue the definition of a social movement. Although disabled people were supposedly at the center of the rehabilitation movement, there was no indication of any grassroots participation generally associated with a social movement.[5] This said, Rusk and Kessler were not out to promote their own self-interests. The rehabilitation movement may not have been a social movement, but it did advance an ideological position—one that purposefully gave people with disabilities no voice in it. Hence, Rusk and Kessler formed what some political scientists have described as an epistemic community, one united by a coherent set of ideas, values, and beliefs that influenced public policymakers.

What united this epistemic community was the belief structure that they cultivated—"the whole man theory of rehabilitation." This belief structure had rehabilitation experts cast aside the anatomical model of the mind and body in favor of a functional one. That is, physicians in the rehabilitation movement no longer focused on what disabled people could not do but on what they could do. Rusk and Kessler distinguished the ailment from the cure by studying how healthy limbs could compensate for missing ones.

Rusk and Kessler also believed that the focus on a person with a disability must be switched from the problem—the loss as a result of the physical or mental disability—to the solution—building a healthy personality that could cope with such a loss. No longer rendering a diagnosis on the basis of a set of symptoms, doctors in the rehabilitation movement abandoned the notion that they could cure or prevent disabilities. They still relied on a medical diagnostic unit of analysis, however, though they replaced symptoms with the "personality," a term studied in the 1950s by physicians, psychiatrists, psychologists, anthropologists, and even political scientists. Rehabilitation medicine rested on the idea that the mind, and more specifically the personality, provided the key to rehabilitation because it helped disabled people regain their equilibrium as whole people.

This "can do" perspective gave physicians an opportunity to determine if a person with a disability had what they described as a "malformed" or "maladjusted" personality that could be nursed back to health. Neither Rusk nor Kessler, however, generated the means to make this assessment. They borrowed a set of ideas, values, and beliefs from a distinctly American version of psychoanalysis called "psychodynamic therapy," which was practiced by prominent psychiatrists like William Menninger, one of the founders of the Menninger Clinic, and Franz Alexander, who held the first chair of psychoanalysis in an American medical school.[6]

With Menninger and Alexander in the lead, psychodynamic therapy took the country by storm after World War II.[7] This type of therapy had wide appeal because, while being loosely drawn from Sigmund Freud's notion of psychoanalysis and psychosomatic medicine, it did not share his pessimistic worldview. Menninger and Alexander "Americanized" Freudian thought, turning it into a practical course of therapy that, with strong teleological overtones, embodied the postwar spirit of optimism and hope for the future.

Rusk and Kessler took the idea of intertwining the fate of the individual with that of society from psychoanalysts who thought psychodynamic therapy had the capacity to heal not just the patient but also society at large. Heavily influenced by the Franz Boas school of cultural anthropology, psychodynamic therapists claimed that norms and social customs, not biological determinants, molded a specific culture and shaped society. These norms and social customs and, most important, how people reacted to them, they maintained, were both fluid and malleable and, therefore, could be changed for what they perceived as "the better."

The optimistic outlook inherent in psychodynamic therapy's emphasis on culture meant that doctors and psychiatrists in the rehabilitation movement thought not only that disabled people *could* be rehabilitated but that they *were worthy* of rehabilitation.[8] They distinguished rehabilitation from eugenics, a science that spawned some of the horrors of the holocaust which led to the death of untold thousands of disabled people.[9] Yet, this is not to say that Rusk and Kessler accepted diversity. Instead of exterminating or sterilizing disabled people, Rusk and Kessler insisted that, with the new behavioral perspectives in medicine and social science, they could be healed of their abnormalities.

In making normalcy the goal or aspiration that the whole person would try to achieve, rehabilitation experts practiced what Michel Foucault called "normalizing judgments."[10] That is, they ordered the capacities of people with disabilities, not in relation to an abstraction or nothing at all but in relation to one another. The rehabilitation movement was, therefore, united as an epistemic community around the belief that disabled people should be valued not for their differences but for their ability to surmount them. How they surmounted them, however, was not determined by the disabled people themselves, since rehabilitation medicine made little room for them to exercise their autonomy. Rusk and the rehabilitation movement harbored a belief system that promoted not the freedom and individuality of disabled people but their normalcy.

Part I: Treating People with Disabilities before World War II
No Cure—No Hope

The fundamental idea that rehabilitation must concentrate on how patients could compensate for missing legs, not so much with their prostheses but with the rest of their minds and bodies, was not practiced until World War II, when medical treatment for people with disabilities merged with vocational education and training.[11] The prevailing medical perspective before the 1940s had doctors examining what caused, and how they could prevent or cure, a disability. According to a team of medical historians, a chronic illness or injury was not regarded as a medical or social problem in the United States before World War II. "Prior to World War II," Rusk himself described, "the great majority of the medical profession looked upon rehabilitation as an extracurricular activity of medicine, something dealing with social work and vocational training, but which had little concern or which held few implications for medicine."[12]

The care people received after being injured during industrial accidents was illustrative of the type of medical treatment from the late nineteenth century until World War I. While physicians gave victims of industrial accidents medical attention when they were first injured, the permanent injuries they sustained were generally overlooked by the medical community. If a miner lost both legs, for example, it was assumed that he could no longer provide for his family. The accident transformed the miner from a breadwinner into what the community perceived as a burden on his family. To ease a family's burden, it was reported that some miners even left home, spending their final days in isolation.

World War I changed this situation, giving physicians the medical resources necessary to help soldiers who incurred permanent physical or mental disabilities. These resources did not produce rehabilitation medicine. Instead, the two medical specialities that cared for soldiers with permanent physical disabilities during World War I—physical therapy medicine, and orthopedic surgery—focused on curing or restoring the soldiers back to health instead of helping them cope with their losses. Treating over 123,000 soldiers who returned home with permanent physical disabilities, physicians in these two medical specialities concentrated on the curative and restorative, not the rehabilitative, aspects of disability.[13] The hospitalization of almost an equal number of soldiers for psychiatric help—122,000 soldiers—also provided evidence of the need for the treatment of neuroses. Before World War I, psychiatrists gave more attention to discovering the means of treating psychoses or severe mental illnesses like schizophrenia.[14]

Emphasizing either the cure or the prevention of physical and mental disabilities brought physical therapy medicine and orthopedic surgery closer to the mainstream medical community. Since the nineteenth century, physical therapy physicians had worked with patients who suffered from acute diseases, for example, tuberculosis or cancer.[15] These physicians insisted that they could either cure or restore their patients back to health with one of three types of physical therapies: electrotherapy, hydrotherapy, or massage and exercise. Physical therapy medicine made little attempt to help people who had chronic problems like back pain. When a chronic condition like arthritis received attention from physical therapy physicians, these physicians stressed curative rather than rehabilitative treatment.[16]

Yet, physical therapy medicine did not have a very high standing in the medical profession. While no speciality effectively treated acute diseases before World War II, it was thought that internal medicine and surgery, for example, were more successful in taking care of patients than physical therapy medicine. Electrotherapy and the other types of physical therapy paled in comparison with the surgical procedures and techniques being discovered by physicians in other medical specialities. Moreover, physical therapy physicians often competed with orthopedists in hospitals over who could best serve people with physical disabilities.

During World War I, orthopedists gained the upper hand over physical therapy physicians. Approximately 75 to 80 percent of soldiers with wounded extremities were treated in orthopedics. Orthopedists had had as long a history of trying to either cure people with disabilities or restore them back to full health as physical therapy medicine had. In the late nineteenth century, orthopedists had been described pejoratively by other physicians as "the society of buckle and strap men," a term that reflected how little prestige this speciality commanded.[17] Orthopedists had a chance to elevate the professional standing of their speciality during the Great War because of two medical advances.

First, some physicians discovered that their patients could fully recover from serious wounds as long as they prevented infection. Second, the invention of the X-ray machine meant that orthopedists could better set fractures, thereby leaving fewer people with permanent disabilities. One orthopedist estimated that "the total amount of 'crippling' disabilities could be reduced by 10 percent because of the X-ray machine alone."[18]

While physical therapy physicians and orthopedists both accentuated the curative aspects of their specialities, some orthopedists, like Dr. Joel Goldthwait, the chief of orthopedics at Massachusetts General Hospital, took advantage of the emergency wartime situation to enlarge their conception of how best to care for people with physical disabilities. Goldthwait believed that soldiers with permanent disabilities should be gainfully employed once they returned to civilian life. Only if veterans become "happy, productive, wage-earning citizens, instead of boastful, consuming, idle derelicts," said one orthopedic surgeon, "would the work of an orthopedist be done."[19] Medical treatment of people with disabilities, claimed some physicians within the medical department of the army, must include a plan for their vocational training and education.

The orthopedists' attempts to broaden their medical outlook, however, went largely unfulfilled during World War I. They were defeated both by political constraints the army imposed and by the opposition raised by the vocational training experts. When the United States entered the war in 1917, the surgeon general created a Division of Orthopedic Surgery in the medical department of the army.[20] Assuming the orthopedic surgeons had more experience working with injuries than other medical practitioners, the surgeon general put them in charge of the war wounded. Physicians from other medical specialities objected, insisting they, too, could care efficiently for the wounded.

A group of physicians began lobbying to change this arrangement. With so few orthopedists trained in the new speciality who could respond to the protest, doctors from other specialities wrested control over the wounded from the Division of Orthopedic Surgery. The surgeon general reconsidered his initial position and put the Division of Special Hospitals and Physical Reconstruction in charge of handling wounded soldiers. Instead of having any one speciality oversee the wounded within the Division of Special Hospitals and Physical Reconstruction, the surgeon general appointed medical officers to represent a myriad of specialities, including general surgery, head surgery, neurological psychiatry, *and* orthopedic surgery.[21]

The idea for widening the conception of how to treat disability, however, was not lost. Other physicians thought that vocational training and placement should be part of the medical regimen. Most notably, the head of the Division of Special Hospitals and Physical Reconstruction proposed that doctors in his division prescribe vocational training along with medical treatment. This official, however, had no more success than the orthopedic surgeons had because the Federal Board for Vocational Education, and a number of private agencies who dealt with people with disabilities, for example, the Red Cross and the Institute for the Crippled and Disabled, balked at the idea. These experts, who were either involved in vocational education or worked with disabled people, convinced the secretary of war that there should always be a sharp distinction between medical and vocational programs.[22]

One last attempt was made to merge medical treatment of disabilities with vocational education. Just before the war ended, federal legislation was introduced that would have created a civilian board to control vocational rehabilitation, in part to advise vocational officers on the surgeon general's staff about soldiers who had been discharged.[23] Again, the idea that vocational education remain distinct from medicine prevailed. While the military nursed soldiers back to health, it was the Federal Board for Vocational Education that oversaw their vocational education and training. The medical treatment of people with physical and mental disabilities remained separate from vocational training and education until the idea of rehabilitation was promoted again by doctors during World War II.

Eugenics, another Form of Prevention

During the intrabellum period, vocational programs maintained their focus on education and training, while physical therapy physicians kept concentrating on how to cure, restore, or prevent physical disabilities. Orthopedic surgeons, moreover, gave up broadening their ideas about caring for people with disabilities. Physical therapy medicine and orthopedics were not the only fields to underscore how disabilities could be prevented. The eugenics movement, which reached its apex in the 1920s, also addressed the prevention of physical and mental disabilities.

Most eugenicists conducting research in the United States, unlike orthopedic surgeons or physical therapy physicians, had been trained in biology. From a research laboratory, not a clinic or a hospital, eugenicists examined the so-called victims of nature who suffered from birth "defects." Accordingly, most of their research was devoted to the prevention of congenital physical and mental disabilities.

Furthermore, eugenics was not confined to the scientific community. From the late nineteenth century until the mid-1920s, eugenics constituted a social movement—the eugenics movement—that constructed a public policy that spurned those who had imperfect minds and bodies. Most important, eugenicists constructed a movement that campaigned for the systematic prevention of bringing people with disabilities into the world. This movement tried to stop people with disabilities from endangering society by lobbying for laws that prohibited them from having their own children. Eugenicists applied Charles Darwin's theory of natural selection to American society as a means of demonstrating that people with mental and physical disabilities had adapted poorly to environmental obstacles. Many eugenicists, moreover, subscribed to Aristotle's notion of "the great chain of being." That is, they believed that all animals, including people, should be graded in accordance with their level of anatomical perfection.[24]

The American eugenics movement presented anatomical imperfections or physical and mental birth defects as evidence that society must defend itself from them.[25] By 1914, thirty states had laws prohibiting the mentally "deficient" from marrying.[26] Three years later, fifteen states passed sterilization laws to prevent the "biologically inadequate" from procreating.[27] After the Supreme Court upheld Virginia's sterilization law in 1927 in *Buck v. Bell*, many more states put these statutes on the books. By 1938, thirty-three states had sterilization laws.[28] "Better for all the world if instead of waiting to execute degenerate offspring for crime, or to let them starve for their imbecility," Oliver Wendell Holmes Jr. said in *Buck v. Bell*, "society can prevent those who are manifestly unfit from continuing their kind."[29]

The eugenicists' emphasis on innate character and genetic determinism meant that they were deeply pessimistic about making any social improvements for people with disabilities. Indeed, the eugenics movement's distrust in democracy showed how little faith they had in people generally, not just those with disabilities. As Donald Pickens, a historian, described, the eugenicists' misgivings about democracy stemmed from their having rejected the eighteenth-century notion of rationalism, which had long served as the source of American democratic ideals.[30] In other words, the eugenics movement, like other movements during the Progressive era, expressed little confidence in the power of scientific inquiry and education.[31]

The eugenicists did not believe that the United States should support positive social reform programs that helped people alter their standing within society. These programs, they claimed, offered little hope of change. Prohibition, for example, could not stop people from imbibing liquor. The Progressives supported the ban on the sale of liquor, but they put little stock in suppressing a person's desire for alcohol. To them, society should be a replication of nature. Members of the eugenics movement thought it was futile to try to change the natural hierarchy of American society.

Eugenicists went to great lengths to ensure that other members of society understood that this hierarchy was natural. Their explanations of how society could better itself by excluding people with disabilities were generally couched in scientific terms. Aristotle's great chain of being, according to the eugenics movement, was not based on subjective criteria. Supposedly, biology, not a political perspective, gave eugenicists the proof they needed to show that people with disabilities must be segregated from the rest of society. In fact, a large part of the eugenics movement's appeal stemmed from its "scientific" basis.[32]

Part II: A Social Scientific Perspective
The Fight for Democracy: A Purpose for Study

By the mid- to late-1920s, scientists began questioning some of the basic assumptions about heredity.[33] An overly enthusiastic eugenics movement in the United States and Great Britain undermined the science of eugenics. With editors of the leading eugenics journals allowing their enthusiasm for policy to overshadow their interest in scientific integrity, the study of eugenics as a science, and not a social science, was compromised. This practice became self-reinforcing and undermined the legitimacy of eugenics.

Meanwhile, racists increasingly relied on eugenics to justify Jim Crow laws, among other things. The questions raised about hereditary and the role of biology led to more than a repudiation of eugenics in science. Once the scientific facade began crumbling, eugenics started to lose its appeal to social scientists. It was difficult for reformers to defend the harsh pronouncements about disabled people, for instance, without scientific data to support them.

What is more, a new perspective in social science emerged in the late-1920s and 1930s—behaviorism—that called into question the eugenics movement's most basic values and beliefs. This methodology changed the focus of study from an environmental to a biological explanation of individual behavior. By the late-1930s, this methodology posed a formidable challenge to the significance of heredity in science, medicine, and social science.[34] Overturning the emphasis on genetic determinants, behaviorism was adopted by so many disciplines and schools of thought that by the 1940s it constituted a revolution in thought. In particular, the behavioral revolution had a tremendous effect on shaping the course of rehabilitation medicine.

Although no one field or discipline can be credited with initiating the behavioral revolution, it was anthropology in the form of the Franz Boas school of cultural anthropology that reinitiated the study of humans as individuals. Beginning in the early 1900s, Boas began formulating the basic principles underlying cultural anthropology. He did so by disputing some of the rudimentary elements in the type of genetics that anthropology had borrowed from Charles Darwin and J. B. Lamarck. Boas constructed the argument that specific cultures, not universal laws of behavior, affected people and, therefore, determined the nature of a society.

Although Boas's argument about the significance of cultural determinants founded a subfield in anthropology, that of cultural anthropology, and influenced social and psychological anthropology, his greatest contribution was that he trained a whole generation of graduate students, such as Ruth Benedict, Margaret Mead, Melville Herskovits, and Ralph Linton, who themselves became prominent anthropologists.[35] Boas's students helped extend his perspective about studying individual cultures before positing general laws of human behavior in the 1930s and 1940s. They not only shaped the field of cultural anthropology but had some influence on behaviorism within social science as a whole.[36]

What became known as the Boasian school of cultural anthropology had an effect on other behaviorists because of its dynamic definition of culture. Recording how social norms and customs dictated cultural habits and rituals provided Benedict, Mead, and other members of the Boasian school of anthropology with evidence that culture was a dynamic concept. The whole culture, they contended, was greater than the sum of its parts. "Culture . . . is that complex whole," explained Edward Tylor, "which in-

cludes knowledge, beliefs, art, morals, law, custom, and any other capabilities and habits acquired by man as a member of society." In her pathbreaking book *Patterns for Change,* published in 1934, Benedict also
described a culture as an organic whole, bringing her definition to life with
a reference to gunpowder. Gunpowder only explodes, she observed, as a
composite.[37]

Benedict, Mead, and their colleagues did not develop their ideas about
culture as an organic whole in a theoretical vacuum. In addition to Boas,
they were influenced by the work of cultural *and* social anthropologists,
including A. R. Radcliffe-Brown and Bronislaw Malinowski, who relied
on the interdisciplinary notion of functionalism, and Edward Sapir, who
practiced Gestalt psychology.[38] Holism, as it was defined in both functionalism and Gestalt psychology, meant that one could study the parts in
relation to the whole and, in turn, the whole in relation to the parts, by
concentrating on how these parts worked. As Linton explained, a member
of society can use an axe to cut wood for fuel or decapitate prisoners in a
tribal ritual. Hence, no one particular function could be ascribed to an
axe: its meaning changed depending on the context or environment in
which it was used. To fully comprehend how an axe functions, an anthropologist must know not just what it can do but what purpose a society,
which is constrained by specific social norms and customs, has bestowed
upon it.[39]

As Benedict, Mead, and other cultural anthropologists conducted field
research in Japan and Samoa, they discovered not only the significance of
social norms and customs but also how these norms and customs affected
people differently. Every culture, they argued, contains a wide range of
personalities, and for anthropologists to appreciate a culture they must
also have an understanding about the different types of personalities
within it.[40] The dynamic between a culture and a personality was so fluid,
Mead, Linton, and Benedict suggested, that the definitions they advanced
for each could be described as almost interchangeable. As Benedict revealed, "[C]ulture is personality writ large."[41]

The argument that the two were interchangeable was not to say that
cultural anthropologists advanced their own theories of the personality.
Most anthropologists relied on members of what became known as their
sister disciplines—psychology and psychiatry—for theories of the personality. Not only were Benedict, Mead, Herskovitz, and their colleagues influenced by the sum is greater than the parts notion underlying Gestalt
psychology, they also liberally borrowed ideas about personality types
from the branch of American psychoanalysis that practiced psychody-

namic therapy and psychosomatic medicine.[42] "Psychology, which is concerned with the study of the individual, joins anthropology," explained the psychoanalyst Solomon Ginsburg who would run the Committee for Social Issues for the Group for the Advancement of Psychiatry after World War II, "because of its understanding about culture."[43]

Together, some anthropologists, psychoanalytic psychiatrists, and psychologists went so far with their interdisciplinary ideas as to start what became known as the personality-and-culture school. As the anthropologist A. L. Kroeber later noted, the personality-and-culture school "started out self-consciously as a revolutionizing new dimension of anthropology."[44] Some anthropologists, who initially identified themselves as cultural anthropologists, started calling themselves psychological anthropologists.[45] Although this was an interdisciplinary endeavor, members of these different disciplines did not agree on how much the psychic variables were dependent on the cultural ones or vice versa.[46] Nonetheless, what they all shared was the focus on the correlation between a culture and different personalities.

The personality-and-culture school, moreover, also acquired strong teleological overtones from Gestalt psychology and functionalism, which gave it the normative dimension shared by all the anthropologists, psychologists, and psychiatrists who belonged to this school.[47] That is, by studying the personality as a means of studying the individual as an organic whole and, in turn, arguing that the culture was also greater than its parts, this school ultimately maintained that the purpose of a society was its preservation. All societies had a goal, an end-state, or what was described as an equilibrium, that they would try to achieve and sustain.[48] This was not to say that all cultures and societies had equal standing. Some anthropologists maintained that cultures that actively promoted democratization had better goals than those that did not.

The values underlying cultural anthropology of holism, change, and teleology would greatly influence psychiatry and psychology. But these were not the only disciplines that profited from them during the 1930s. Disciplines ranging from sociology, history, economics, and specialities within the fields of social work and medicine were indebted to cultural anthropology's notions about holism and its deep and abiding belief that individuals and whole cultures could be reformed. Cultural anthropology created a theoretical framework for social scientists who sought an alternative to objective or value-free social science.

In the 1930s and 1940s there were two types of social scientists who found this framework appealing. First, there were what historian Mark

Smith calls "social service intellectuals," who demonstrated their commitment to cultural anthropology and dedicated their work to the community. Second, there were "purposive" social scientists, who insisted that social science must have a preconceived set of goals and, ultimately, a vision for society, and who embraced the values underlying cultural anthropology. Unlike social service intellectuals, who placed little emphasis on the scientific method, the key source for purposive scholars was a quest for scientifically determined values.[49]

Initially, neither the social service intellectuals nor the purposive social scientists dominated the profession. According to the standard historiography of behaviorism, social scientists claiming that the different social sciences must be practiced with scientific objectivity largely controlled the profession during the 1920s and 1930s, not the social scientists who were influenced by cultural anthropology.[50] Nonetheless, the latter social scientists, who were also called "purposive social scientists" and "social service intellectuals," with their anthropological values that called into question the neutrality of social science, increasingly gained influence.

By the late-1930s, many social scientists concluded that the Great Depression in the United States, the rise of the Third Reich in Germany, and fascism in Italy and Japan made it difficult for them to conduct research they could call either "abstract" or "objective." Social science demanded a normative theory, they argued. Indeed, when the United States entered the war in 1941, the purposive school had gained such prominence and constituted a formidable challenge to the objectivist approach to social science.[51] What is more, the value-laden theoretical framework advanced by cultural anthropology began to influence medicine, particularly psychiatry and rehabilitation medicine, as physicians lent their professional expertise to the war effort and, in the words of one anthropologist, practiced "action research."[52]

Out of Bed and into Action

While many social scientists lent their expertise to the war effort, almost all the physicians who qualified for military duty offered their medical services. The medical discoveries made in the twenty-three years since the American involvement in World War I gave these physicians an advantage over their counterparts. New medical treatments and procedures significantly reduced mortality rates during World War II.

First, new diagnostic tests, developed in the 1930s, helped physicians save soldiers' lives. While the wounded benefited from the X-ray during World War I, blood transfusions became a basic hospital procedure and saved many lives during World War II. Other diagnostic instruments, like the electrocardiograph, also helped doctors make better diagnoses and consequently lowered mortality rates.

Second, disease, which had been the number one noncombat killer, no longer demanded as much attention from physicians as it had in other wars.[53] The ratio of disease to noncombat injury was reversed during World War II. At this time, one of every twentieth person died because of disease.[54] By contrast, sixteen people died from disease for every person killed by a noncombat injury during the Spanish-American war.

Third, new techniques in neuro- and urogenital surgery made it possible for people with paraplegia to survive. When soldiers became paralyzed on the battlefields of World War I, doctors put them to bed. The combination of bed rest, which caused severe bedsores, and kidney infections gave few veterans much hope of living out the year.[55] Physicians discovered that bed rest had no recuperative powers and actually exacerbated a paraplegic's condition.

Given such medical advances, after the Second World War people with physical and mental disabilities were more likely to live a longer time. Like most physicians, Rusk and Kessler championed these new advances. Discussing medical breakthroughs on a more abstract level, both Rusk and Kessler echoed ideas that Arnold Toynbee, the British historian and social thinker, had expressed. Like Toynbee, they maintained that technological developments were responsible for the great advances in Western society.[56]

Nonetheless, Rusk and Kessler believed that the medical advances made between the world wars only provided the tools rehabilitation medicine needed, not the outlook or perspective that accounted for its status as a new medical speciality. Most telling about what distinguished Rusk and his conception of rehabilitation from the mainstream medical community that dealt with disabled people, namely physical therapy medicine and orthopedics, was that many members of these specialities viewed both the rehabilitation movement and Rusk with suspicion. Rusk, whom other physicians credited with being the single most influential founder of rehabilitation medicine and the rehabilitation movement, had been trained as neither a physical therapy physician nor an orthopedist.

Speaking as an outsider, Rusk first introduced the idea behind rehabilitation when he designed and directed the convalescent program for the Army Air Forces. Before enlisting, Rusk had practiced internal medicine in St. Louis. It was at the Army Air Force's Jefferson Barracks that Rusk devised what he initially called "reconditioning." This meant that doctors helped seriously wounded veterans reformulate their career goals in accordance with their physical condition, encouraging them to learn new skills. Rusk had some bedridden veterans, for example, practice identifying enemy planes from a mobile he put over their beds.[57]

If the traditional emphasis doctors placed on sickness was downplayed, according to Rusk, rehabilitation medicine could take the man from the bed to the job. He developed what Edward Berkowitz describes as a "new type of medicine, one which went beyond the highly specialized processes of diagnosis and treatment of well-defined pathologies. It took more than an organ-by-organ view. It looked at the effect of a disability on the whole man."[58]

Yet orthopedic surgeons had grave reservations about Rusk's notion of the functional conception of the body. They wondered what the idea of rehabilitating the whole man, and not just the damaged part, had to do with medicine. Making a critical reference to the influence that social science had on his perspective of rehabilitation medicine, some orthopedists called Rusk a "social service boondoggle."[59]

Rusk had no problem with what orthopedic surgeons said about his commitment to social service. To him, it only showed how resistant they were to his ideas. Rusk had not looked to orthopedics for help or inspiration when he developed rehabilitation medicine. Instead, he had turned to social science and other medical specialities that identified with social science for assistance, namely, the branch of psychoanalytic and psychosomatic medicine that practiced psychodynamic therapy. To Rusk, the social science underpinning the functional conception of the body or the whole man theory was what accounted for the transformation from physical therapy medicine to rehabilitation medicine.[60]

Along with Rusk, Kessler also established one of the first rehabilitation centers in the United States. Like Rusk, Kessler had generated his views about rehabilitation during World War II. Kessler's background was similar to Rusk's in that he too had not been trained to practice physical therapy medicine. Just before he went into practice as an obstetrician, Kessler met Dr. Fred Albee and Colonel Lewis T. Bryant, who were credited with introducing physical therapy medicine to the United States after the Great War. As a result of their influence, Kessler abandoned obstetrics and started practicing rehabilitation medicine in Newark. Kessler left New Jersey during the war, joining Dr. Albee at an amputation center on Mare Island near San Francisco. In compensation for the grim task of amputating wounded arms and legs, he and Albee concentrated on how they could help their patients cope with physical impediments.[61]

Like Rusk, Kessler had ideas about rehabilitation that featured coping skills and vocational adjustment, which he called the "creative process." Echoing Rusk's belief in the team approach, Kessler described rehabilitation as a "composite science bringing into focus various professional services required by a disabled child or adult to achieve normal living."[62] Finally, Kessler also subscribed to the whole man theory. As he saw it, rehabilitation "is a broad term, enveloping the whole gamut of surgical and medical treatment and aftercare that will make an individual employable. It is not confined to one phase of medical care but is regarded as the total approach to human welfare and medical service."[63]

The Roots of the "Can Do" Perspective

Although the whole man theory can be traced back to the branch of behaviorism in social science initially cultivated by anthropology, Rusk and Kessler, among others in the rehabilitation movement, were not discriminating about the origins of their ideas. The conceptual framework for the whole man theory of rehabilitation came from a myriad of disciplines: cultural anthropology, Gestalt psychology, psychoanalytic medicine, psychosomatic medicine, and history. What these different disciplines did share, however, was a theory of functionalism.

First, functionalism within anthropology, Gestalt psychology, and psychoanalysis necessitated that rehabilitation physicians discard the anatomical concept of the body. "When physical standards were drawn up during the first and second decades of this century," Mary Switzer, the longtime director of the Office of Vocational Rehabilitation, recounted that "they were influenced by the 'anatomical' concept of medicine. . . . Competence was measured in terms of anatomical perfection."[64] A patient could either perform a task or not. Rather than concentrating on what disabled people could not do, rehabilitation medicine focused on what they could do. The rehabilitation movement spurned this notion of anatomical perfection, opting for a functional conception of the body.

Second, rehabilitation physicians highlighted the fundamental principle within functionalism itself, the notion that the whole—be it a body or a society—was greater than the sum of its parts. Moreover, this notion of an organic whole was dynamic. That is, one could study the parts in relation to the whole and, in turn, the whole in relation to the parts that constitute it by examining what these parts could accomplish. While an orthopedist might help his patient walk after operating on a leg, the orthopedist would still be concerned with the patient's glaucoma, as one anthropologist explained it, because vision problems would also hinder his patient's ability to walk. The whole patient as a biological organism might be affected by trying to reinstate this equilibrium. Taking this example to heart, Rusk and Kessler made this idea about the organic whole the cornerstone of rehabilitation medicine. One part of the body could compensate for another part, restoring the whole body. In other words, the compensating part of the body provided the equilibrium of health.

Third, Rusk incorporated Toynbee's functionalist interpretation of the history of Western civilization. Rusk argued that disabled people could be regarded as whole because of technological developments. To substantiate this argument, he referred to Toynbee's idea that technological developments led to the rise of specialization and the division of labor in the modern world.[65] The very concept of a division of labor emerged, according to Toynbee, because the economy could no longer be dependent on labor that embodied the "all around man."[66] What is more, Toynbee contended that people in primitive societies with physical impairments inspired the very idea of the division of labor and the feasibility of specialization.

Taking this idea further, Rusk and Kessler argued that disabled people could be regarded as full participants in society and, therefore, should be considered "whole" people. "To be a whole man one must be more than an individual functioning as an individual," wrote the rehabilitation expert C. Obermann. "One of the most important tokens of being a member of his group is awarded when he can participate and interact, through work."[67] This notion of rehabilitation, according to Rusk, "epitomizes the prime democratic concept of equal opportunity for all."[68]

Fourth, Rusk applied the functionalist perspective or systems theory within international relations to his own international outlook about the hope for disabled people. We live in "an age in which human society dare to think of the welfare of the whole human race as a practical objective," wrote Rusk.[69] He was not literally addressing the whole of the human race with this statement. Rather, he was acknowledging his debt to Toynbee, who had been influenced by the value of holism within cultural anthropology and functionalism within international relations.

Finally, the place of treatment—the rehabilitation center—for disabled people also reflected the emphasis that functionalism placed on interdisciplinary work. Rusk modeled his rehabilitation centers after those he created for the army. He believed firmly these should not be housed in a hospital.[70] After all, he said, the people with a disability who received treatment were not actually sick. Nor should they receive treatment administered solely by doctors. In a rehabilitation center, a doctor, psychiatrist, psychologist, social worker, vocational rehabilitation counselor, and an anthropologist worked in concert to assess the potential of a person with a disability. Once these assessments were complete, he believed, the rehabilitation experts, as a team, would determine the best course of treatment.[71]

Rusk was not the first physician to apply what was called the "team approach" to rehabilitation. Switzer described it as "the team approach, a by-word today in rehabilitation medicine—[which] first came into my consciousness as I was learning about the whole area of mental illness from the Menningers and those leaders in postwar psychiatry to whom we owe so much." The Menningers, Switzer, and Rusk placed this notion of teams at the forefront of the atomic age, characterizing the Manhattan Project as part of the team approach. As Switzer explained, "Teamwork is neither in medicine or public health. Actually this concept of cooperative effort is taking hold in all types of scientific and professional circles." The team revealed the interdisciplinary nature of postwar psychiatry and rehabilitation medicine. "The psychiatrist, social worker, the aide in the mental hospital—yes, and the anthropologists—all became part of the treatment team in those places," she added, "where history was being made in mental health."[72]

Part III: The Medical Roots of Rehabilitation
Whole People, Not Damaged Parts

The functionalism underlying both Rusk's idea about reconditioning and Kessler's notion of the creative process not only indicated their support for holism. It also changed the entire concept of a medical diagnosis. To apply functionalism to rehabilitation, Rusk and Kessler had to surmise the motivation for a person's actions *without* treating the symptoms of the disability.[73] The key, they found, was the personality. Just as the personality became the unit of analysis for cultural anthropology, the study of the personality replaced the physical symptom as the primary unit of analysis in rehabilitation medicine.[74]

Studying someone's personality, as opposed to examining the symptoms of the person's illness or the effects of his or her injury, was also significant in that it gave the doctor room to maneuver. A symptom or an effect pertained only to an illness or an injury, whereas a personality described every aspect of the whole person—sick and well. Doctors could nurse the maladjusted personality—developed as a result of a disability—back to health with rehabilitation.

Rehabilitation physicians derived their perspective on the personality from psychoanalysis. It was Freud who first suggested that the study of the whole person was united by the personality.[75] Freud's work helped change the focus in psychiatry from addressing a specific problem to examining how the composition of the whole person could help solve this problem. Freud was one of the first psychiatrists to turn against the localistic approach to disease that had led doctors to practice narrow specializations that concentrated on curing a diseased part of the body.[76] The psychoanalyst must treat the total individual, declared Freud, not merely one malfunctioning organ.

Rehabilitation physicians, however, did not draw the idea of the whole person directly from Freud. It was the psychiatrist, William Menninger, responsible for popularizing psychoanalysis after World War II, who first applied the concept to rehabilitation. As a leading member of the group of American psychiatrists who practiced psychodynamic therapy and was influenced by the Boasian school of cultural anthropology, Menninger derived this notion of the whole man theory from his own experience during World War II.

The Menninger Clinic that he founded with his brother Karl and their father Charles was a product of the slow transformation that the discipline of psychiatry itself had undergone. Between the 1880s and the 1940s, psychiatrists altered the foundation of their specialty. As Gerald Grob, a medical historian, describes that psychiatry, they "expanded the jurisdiction and boundaries . . . to include psychologically troubled individual as well as allegedly dysfunctional social structures and relationships." These changes were made, in part, because of psychiatrists who lobbied for new laws that gave them patients who were abnormal or maladjusted, not clinically insane.[77]

What was called the "new psychiatry" became a discipline that looked at life's normal activities, including marital problems and alcoholism, and took a hand in resolving them. Psychiatrists in places like the Menninger Clinic dealt with everyday problems of mental health as much as mental illness. Psychodynamic therapy had no classifications, charting instead the behavior of all people along a continuum from normal to abnormal behavior.[78] This medical speciality was fundamentally transformed from a discipline concerned with insanity to one interested in normality.[79]

Psychodynamic therapy had practical applications which imbued it with a spirit of optimism that was uncharacteristic of Freud. From the moment they were introduced to Freud's thought, many prominent American psychiatrists, including William White, Adolf Meyer, Franz Alexander, and the Menninger brothers, had been less interested in his theory than in how they could turn it into a practical course for therapy. Freud put less faith in the healing potential of psychoanalysis than the new psychiatry did. This new type of psychiatry developed psychodynamic therapy, which was a broad catch-all phrase for therapy that stripped psychoanalysis of many of Freud's thoughts about sexuality, culture, and religion.[80]

Indeed, a fundamental rift that divided two schools of psychoanalysis in the United States in the 1920s and 1930s involved the debate over whether psychoanalytical theory, which strayed little from Freud's own thought, or therapy should be emphasized. The New York Society for Psychoanalysis believed that laymen, with no medical schooling, could still be trained as analysts, that with broad educational backgrounds they could help advance Freudian thought. The American Psychoanalytical Association (APA), by contrast, maintained that only physicians who, as Alexander expressed it, made therapy their primary interest should practice psychoanalysis.

The APA's position prevailed in 1929, and the medical perspective toward psychoanalysis became increasingly prevalent throughout the 1930s. The dominance of the medical outlook of psychoanalysis became evident when the United States entered World War II, and William Menninger was appointed director of psychiatric services in the Office of Surgeon General.[81] Menninger, who was active in the APA and had become its president in 1948, was a prominent member of the second generation who practiced the new psychiatry.[82]

Menninger championed psychoanalysis for its "study [of] the individual as whole" and suggested that doctors should "treat the person and not the disease." To Menninger, psychiatrists were the only doctors who "practice[d] comprehensive medicine." As Menninger portrayed it, "[W]e have been trapped, because of medical evolution, into a concept of disease as affecting *an* organ or *a* system."[83] William's brother Karl Menninger described it similarly, pointing out that "medicine's frantic search for a single diagnosis of every case . . . turns bacteria into demons and medicine into a demonic science." Disease must be thought of "in terms of the total economics of the personality."[84] Or as John Stone, from the Menninger Clinic, described, "In this business of seeing the patient as a whole, psychiatry has an illuminating contribution to make in terms of ideas."[85]

It was William Menninger's experience and training as a psychoanalyst that led him to apply the whole man theory to rehabilitation. First, he dealt with the rehabilitation of people with mental disabilities during World War II.[86] Aware that almost the same number of soldiers had been hospitalized for mental problems that were physically injured, psychiatrists were prepared for rehabilitation. This resulted despite the fact that physicians had screened out more people from the military during World War II than in World War I.[87]

Second, William Menninger thought that psychiatry, with its insight about the personality, provided the key to the rehabilitation of people with physical disabilities. According to William Menninger, candidates for rehabilitation were generally located toward the abnormal end of the psychiatrists' dynamic continuum. Disabled people were placed on this end, he argued, not on account of their physical impediments but because of their maladjustment to them. William Menninger, along with most prominent psychoanalysts, presumed that most people with physical disabilities were emotionally disturbed. Psychodynamic therapy, he insisted, could help strengthen their personalities, giving them the capacity to cope with their disabilities and, therefore, become healthy members of society. William Menninger thought that psychodynamic therapy offered hope that disabled people could become "normal." Rusk concurred with William Menninger, adopting not just his methodology but also the phrase "the whole man theory of rehabilitation."

Determined to Prove a Villain

Rusk and Kessler did not just rely on William Menninger for ideas about rehabilitation. Physicians practicing rehabilitation medicine had ample evidence that disabled people were maladjusted. They gathered this evidence from medical journals, which beginning in the late-1930s and 1940s began publishing studies on the personality problems of disabled people. Whether the authors of these studies cited Freud or not, none of them contested his conclusion that disabled people were "malformed and maladjusted." The reason that disabled people had personality problems, Freud thought, came from their denial about "the reality principle."

Freud applied the notion of the reality principle to disabled people in *Character and Culture*. In a short essay, he used the text of Shakespeare's play on Richard III to illustrate his argument. As the story goes, Richard III was "cheated of feature by disembling nature, deform'd, unfinish'd, sent before my time into this breathing world, scarce half made up, and that so lamely and unfashionable, that dogs bark at me as I halt by them." For this reason, Richard wreaked havoc on the world. As Shakespeare said, "[S]ince I cannot prove a lover, to entertain these fair well-spoken days, I am determined to prove a villain."[88]

According to Freud, Richard III felt that he was exempt from the laws that governed his society. Because of his congenital deformities, life owed him reparations. Richard, therefore, denied his own conscience and indulged in self-destructive behavior. Having a disability, in other words, entitled Richard to be ruthless.[89]

Freud used Shakespeare's play as a means of explaining how the king's behavior represented a victory of the unconscious desires all people harbor.[90] Richard III was a magnified representation of something Freud thought we could all discover in ourselves given similar circumstances.[91] To Freud, Richard's behavior constituted a desperate cry for love he had never received. Richard III felt that he was inherently inferior and unworthy of being loved by his mother, the one person who should love him the most.[92]

The fact that Richard III was not to blame for his deformities, which Freud conceded was "unjust," simply made him more neurotic than the able-bodied. The legitimacy of the grievances of disabled people, in other words, only increased their righteousness and, concomitantly, their anger. "The privileges that they claimed as a result of this injustice, and the rebelliousness it engendered, had contributed not a little to intensifying the conflicts leading to the outbreak of neurosis."[93] Freud stipulated that all those suffering from congenital defects or debilitating injuries were, almost by definition, neurotic.

Freud went on to argue that disabled people manifested their hostility toward society by trying to claim unfair privileges over others. They saw themselves as "exceptions," and thought they should be exempt from the normal rules of society.[94]

Citing this essay from *Character and Culture*, one psychologist applied Freud's findings to patients who had a congenital injury or a physical affliction, like polio, in early childhood. This study demonstrated that these patients exhibited resistance to the reality principle. They rebelled against the frustrations imposed on them. Because they suffered enough, disabled people behaved as if they were exceptions who were above societal rules and regulations.[95] According to this study, the greatest problem for disabled people was that they could not subscribe to the reality principle.

This study was an exception; most research did not make direct references to Freud's work. Nonetheless, the conclusion that people with disabilities were hostile, rigid, or had immature personalities appears in many studies conducted in the late 1940s and in the 1950s. "[N]eurodermatitis patients," one study claimed, "tend to show marked signs of repressed hostility."[96] A tentative interpretation of ulcer patients revealed that "as a group [they] tend to deal with their environment at an impulsive, emotionally immature level leading to conflict in the area of social interpersonal relationships."[97] In a study of the deaf, another analyst concluded that they showed either a complete reaction or no reaction at all, which proved that they had "less differentiated and more rigid personalities."[98]

Studies maintained that people with coronary occlusion, for instance, supposedly showed a distinctive pattern of aggressiveness and compulsive striving for power and prestige.[99] Two-thirds of patients with urticaria or gallstones, according to another study, missed parental and especially maternal affection. The remaining third of the patients had so great a need for love that "they demanded what they regarded as their due, complained if they did not get it, became embittered, hard, and harsh, or adopted a manifestly vindictive attitude."[100]

In study after study, rehabilitation doctors were shown that disabled people had severe psychological or emotional problems. Psychoanalysis and the psychosomatic movement, therefore, taught doctors caring for people with physical and mental disabilities that their patients probably suffered from immature personalities. It was concluded, however, that the emotional problems of disabled people came not just from their personal reaction to this physical or mental limitation. Disabled people were also crippled by a society that held them in low esteem. But rather than placing the burden on society, psychiatrists thought the person with a disability should shoulder it.

Evidence of the influence of these studies and the predeliction of their belief was that one of the first things a rehabilitation center did was give a patient a projective test that assessed what type of personality problems he or she suffered from.[101] Then, another test would be conducted to project whether this candidate had the potential for growth. Could rehabilitation medicine transform the maladjusted personality into a healthy one?

The Power of the Mind

The idea that disabled people had emotional disturbances provided the team of healthcare providers in the rehabilitation center with a great opportunity. Psychiatrists, psychologists, physicians, rehabilitation counselors, and social workers cared for patients whose chronic problems had heretofore been neglected by the medical community.[102] The psychosomatic movement influenced rehabilitation medicine after World War II by proving that psychoanalysis could be applied to people suffering from all types of illnesses and injuries.[103]

Adolf Meyer, an exponent of psychobiology, was one of the first proponents of psychosomatic medicine to render this expansive definition of it. But it was Helen Flanders Dunbar, a psychoanalyst interested in psychobiology, who wrote the book *Emotions and Bodily Changes* that "many consider to have launched the movement" in the United States.[104] Dunbar presented evidence that personality types caused physical ailments and disabilities.

Examining the life histories of 1,600 patients, Dunbar categorized people into specific "personality profiles." In the first large-scale psychosomatic research program in the United States, she investigated how certain diseases and injuries affected patients with particular personalities, patterns of behavior, and modes of feeling and thinking.[105] For example, patients with rheumatoid arthritis were identified as "quiet, sensitive individuals who combined posing as a good sport with ingratiating appeal for sympathy beneath which much hostility was present." These patients suffered from many neurotic traits that Dunbar and other psychoanalysts perceived as defenses against guilt, depression, and sexual conflicts.[106]

Dunbar locked horns in an academic battle with Franz Alexander who repudiated her personality-specificity concept, replacing it with his own conflict-specificity theory.[107] He suggested that disease and injury could not be correlated with a specific personality as Dunbar had found.[108] Instead, Alexander argued that a basic conflict sparked a psychosomatic illness. As he explained it, a person's repressed drives and emotions were discharged through the automatic nervous system. This caused a functional disturbance that led to irreversible changes in the person's tissue. Alexander held that an ulcer, for example, resulted from an unconscious conflict between the wish to be loved and cared for and the adult patient's aspirations for independence. The wish to be loved, Alexander asserted, was converted into the wish to be fed. In turn, overeating would stimulate the stomach to secrete acid, which ultimately produced the peptic ulcer.[109]

Alexander discredited Dunbar's work and became the most influential leader of the psychosomatic movement throughout the 1940s and 1950s.[110] Nonetheless, the primary contribution that Dunbar and Alexander made to psychosomatic medicine was their departure from Freud's previously accepted concept that psychosomatic illness occurred because of "conversion hysteria."[111] Both Dunbar and Alexander carried conversion hysteria far beyond Freud's findings by showing that organ neurosis should automatically be associated with emotional conflict. For Alexander, the symptoms of this disease did not have a specific psychic meaning. They were the final result of a prominent physiological change that accompanied repressed, unconscious psychological needs.[112]

Alexander extended the view of the specificity of unconscious psycho-

logical conflict as the determinant of various psychosomatic disorders. He
was not alone in believing that psychosomatic medicine could be applied
to more than hysterical women. Most psychiatrists practicing psychodynamic therapy agreed with Alexander. Karl Menninger, for instance, was
fascinated with Freud's general theories about the unconscious and the
subconscious. Yet, ever since he was introduced to psychoanalysis, Karl
Menninger thought that Freud's emphasis on sexuality was "fishy."[113]
Repressed sexuality could not account for everything. Menninger constructed his own theory about what influenced a person's life and death instincts. He maintained that these influences happened during the oral,
rather than the genital, stage in childhood.[114]

Although doctors practicing rehabilitation medicine were not particularly interested in judging who was responsible for patients' debilitating
injuries or diseases, and hence made little mention of the causative role of
emotional factors, they were impressed with how psychosomatic medicine
demonstrated that the mind could control the body. "The interrelationship
between emotional factors and physical well-being, which has been explored in psychosomatic medicine," a report for the Office of Vocational
Rehabilitation stated, "needs to be applied particularly to the area of individuals confined to the home because of physical disability."[115]

Psychosomatic medicine could help disabled people adjust to their limitations on an emotional level. Rusk echoed this sentiment in his explanation about the emotional adjustment of disabled people. Emotional
adjustment, not physical adjustments, represented the greatest hurdle for
disabled people. In a study of adults with ambulatory cerebral palsy, a
physician practicing rehabilitation medicine wrote that "to all intents and
purposes, these emotional problems, rather than the physical disability,
precluded employment."[116]

The pioneer doctors and psychiatrists in rehabilitation medicine also
believed that "emotional factors play a large part in the extent to which
the disabled individuals will cooperate in the treatment process." Karl
Menninger highlighted this point at a conference on medical and psychological teamwork in the care of the chronically ill. Rusk explained that
"the prognosis of rehabilitation does not depend as much on the severity
of the handicap as it depends on the patient's psychological adjustment to
his disability."[117]

Compensation as Cure

Psychosomatic medicine provided rehabilitation medicine with evidence
for hope that people with physical disabilities could become productive

members of society. The optimism expressed by psychodynamic therapy, in combination with the American ethic of self-help, helps explain why psychiatry provided the medical foundation for rehabilitation medicine. It also accounts for how Alfred Adler's pathbreaking book, *A Study of Organ Inferiority,* directly influenced Rusk and other doctors in rehabilitation medicine.[118]

Rusk incorporated some of Adler's central ideas about compensation into his own work on rehabilitation.[119] Adler's work not only convinced Rusk that somatic disease and one's constitution affected an individual's psychic functioning, but it had wide appeal in the medical community, particularly with psychoanalysts and psychobiologists.[120]

Adler's argument in *A Study of Organ Inferiority* was that an actual or imagined physical defect represented a common source of a feeling of inferiority, and that in neurotics organ defects gave rise to heightened feelings of inferiority. Adler's pathbreaking idea, however, was that a primary organ weakness did not necessarily lead to an actual deficiency. He argued that the organ could make an adjustment. For instance, Adler explained that a heightened sense of touch could compensate for a weak eye, or the normal foot of a child might grow longer to compensate for a club foot.[121]

Adler's argument about compensation went so far that he claimed that "an imperfect organ can turn out to be the source of great advantages." Stronger feelings of inferiority produced greater attempts at compensation, or what he called "overcompensation." Disability when compensated for could be better than normal activity. A disability could become a stimulus that impelled someone toward a higher level of achievement than an able-bodied person would attempt.[122]

Adler referred to this relationship among inferiority, compensation, and overcompensation as a dialectic. Like any dialectic, Adler's was teleological. People naturally strove to overcome their inadequacies. Overcompensation could help someone if the mind had found the technique for overcoming difficulties.[123] Adler maintained that "[t]he personality is not determined by the inferiority, but by the reaction of the individual to the inferiority."[124] The personality represented a goal-directed unit aimed at maintaining the individual's wholeness.

The foundation for psychosomatic medicine that Adler constructed embraced an optimistic, not a pessimistic, view of disabled people. Instead of underscoring the damaged part and its implications, he examined how the whole body could compensate for the damaged part. Thus, Adler developed his individual psychology, or the psychology of the "in-dividual [*sic*], the unit which is indivisible."[125]

Adler, moreover, combined his optimism with a strong belief in socialization. According to Adler, communal ties helped people transcend their biological limitations. Initially, it was the mother who instilled social interest or *Gemeinschaftsgefühl* in her child.[126] Perceived organ weakness of all kinds could make a child feel inadequate and might become a permanent form of weakness. But a child could learn to compensate for these weaknesses and for his or her helplessness by developing social ties. In other words, feelings of inferiority were assuaged when the child felt the support of the community.

The community was the source of all useful compensation and overcompensation. When an individual's social interest remained undeveloped, biological and social handicaps evoked unsuitable responses, such as character anomalies, neuroses, psychoses, criminality, and psychosomatic disturbances. Neurosis was an accentuation of human helplessness and existential problems that could be cured by improving one's self-esteem.[127]

For Adler, culture and civilization were all about man's efforts to control his imperfection; a person was determined neither by his biological constitution nor by his environment. Adler spurned the Freudian idea that the drive mechanism was responsible for the human personality. Instead, he viewed the community as the origin and the matrix of the truly creative personality.[128]

Rusk and Kessler incorporated Adler's findings into rehabilitation medicine with their ideas about the whole man, compensation, and the value of the community. As Rudolf Dreikurs, a rehabilitation expert, explained, "No condition lent itself as readily to such [Adler's] investigation as physical disability."[129] Kessler echoed the same sentiment with the announcement that the very idea of rehabilitation was derived from the Latin term "for return of ability." Rehabilitation, therefore, involved "any process which overcomes disturbance of ability."[130] Meanwhile, Rusk accepted Adler's conception of social interest or *Gemeinschaftsgefühl*, going so far as to argue that rehabilitation would further democratization in the United States.[131]

A Sick Society?

Psychoanalysts like William Menninger, Alexander, and Solomon Ginsburg, and rehabilitation physicians like Rusk and Kessler did not restrict their ideas about rehabilitation to their patients.[132] In 1946, William Menninger and a number of prominent psychiatrists formed the Group for the Advancement of Psychiatry (GAP), which was to advance psychiatry, not as an interest group or lobby but through education and social activism.[133] What was unique about the GAP's notion of activism, moreover, was that its members joined this organization not just to make patients whole again but to help society at large.[134]

Like the cultural anthropologists, the psychiatrists in the GAP thought they should use their professional expertise for social reform. This was not to say that they wanted to provide "expert" opinions based solely on data gathered in the course of treating hospital patients. Rather, William Menninger and Ginsburg, among others in this group, advanced a set of values and beliefs about social reform. Most notably, they believed in the idea that the sum is greater than the parts, and that both the individual and a society, which made up the organic whole, had the capacity for change.[135]

Psychiatry's idea of holism rested first on the assumption that environmental conditions were a significant determinant of mental health, and that these conditions were deteriorating. As William Menninger described it, "If psychiatrists are to be concerned with the conditions which give rise to psychogenic illness at its present rapidly increasing rate, they must begin to turn their attention to the 'sick' society as well as to the sickness of the individual personality." After making this assumption, psychiatrists in the GAP could render what the cultural anthropologists described as an organic or a dynamic view. In other words, these psychiatrists could show how the individual and society were inextricably linked by mental illness. A sick individual led to a sick society; and, conversely, a sick society could make an individual ill.[136] Psychiatrists in the GAP underscored the process of "give and take," or the interconnection that characterized the individual's relatedness to his or her group.[137]

Concentrating on members of a sick society, the psychiatrists in the GAP described them as "lacking in productive purpose and capacity, and failing to develop as a fully mature personality."[138] James Halliday, a prominent physician from Scotland, who was invited to address the Menninger Clinic, described it best with his British examples.[139] He said that "bricklayers in Britain today lay fewer bricks in a given period of time than did their forefathers, because they were members of a sick society." Halliday viewed "[a]bsenteeism, strikes, and a feverish enthusiasm for dog races" as "manifestations of the worker's lack of purpose," which stemmed from the fact that they had been part of a "sick society." Members of this society were far more susceptible to psychiatric and psychosomatic illnesses than people whose group relations had always been "healthy." According to the GAP's credo, "A poor environment or social reality, or what the psychoanalysts called a sick environment, therefore, could weaken an individual."[140] Psychoanalysts extrapolated the health of the individual to the environment in what some called "biopolitics."[141]

Rusk incorporated this same dynamic notion of the interplay between the health of parts and the whole, also referring to it as biopolitics. To him, a political system could best be characterized as a biological organism as Toynbee had done. "Every living species and every specimen is affecting and modifying the biosphere," Toynbee declared, "with its efforts to keep itself alive during its brief lifetime." Applying this idea of biopolitics to disabled people, Rusk explained, in an article coauthored with Switzer and E. Taylor ("International Programs in Rehabilitation," 527–48), "One, and perhaps the most significant, feature of social development which gives hope for Mr. Toynbee's objective becoming a reality is the increasing recognition throughout the world that the security and welfare of the human race are interdependent within each geographic area of the world, and that the security and welfare of each geographic area is dependent upon the security and welfare of the world as a whole."[142]

Rusk had high hopes about the possibility that the world could become an organic whole. Before this could happen, however, disabled people would have to be healed. On the basis of their work with disabled people in psychosomatic medicine as well as with neuroses attached to mental disabilities, the psychoanalysts thought that people with physical and mental disabilities, by nature, could not be considered part of a healthy society.[143] They must be restored or rehabilitated before reentering society. William Menninger as well as other members of the GAP echoed Freud's belief that people with either mental or physical disabilities were maladjusted. In fact, the Menninger Clinic sponsored research that applied psychosomatic medicine to disabled people in hopes of discovering precisely how they manifested their hostility toward society.[144]

Hostility could be so debilitating, wrote the Committee for Social Issues in the GAP, that it could trigger another world war. The GAP predicted, "Psychodynamic considerations such as these are of immediate relevance to the critical problem which presses upon us all; namely, the defective control of aggression in individuals and between groups, which imminently threatens a new World War." To be sure, the hostility of disabled people was different from that of those whose aggressions might lead to World War III. Nonetheless, psychiatrists within the GAP understood that hostility stemmed not from the disabled people themselves but from their relation to society. "A harsh, restrictive environment in the formative stages of personality tends to weaken those powers," the founding pamphlet of the GAP noted, "and thus indirectly undermines the individual's capacity for coping with conflict." Disabled people had to cope with the scars that this type of harsh environment caused.[145]

Disabled people, however, could be freed from a restrictive environment. The key was not to change the environment but to change a person's reaction to this environment. Making an indirect reference to Adler, the GAP pamphlet explained, "In special circumstances, a harsh environment may mobilize in an adult, a higher potential of integrative powers, provided such capacities have been earlier induced by a favorable emotional environment."[146]

From the Ideal to the Norm

With their sweeping proclamations about the sickness or well-being of a society, psychiatrists in the GAP realized that they needed a standard of normality. "Whether we admit it or not," the GAP newsletter proclaimed, "in our everyday psychotherapeutic work with patients, we are continuously applying both an ideal of 'normal' for the individual and 'normal' for the social environment."[147] Unlike psychoanalysts who rarely strayed from what they described as "pure" Freudian thought, members of the GAP had little trepidation about defining normalcy. Indeed, sharing a definition of culture was one of the characteristics that separated the American version of psychodynamic therapy from what its critics call "pure" Freudian thought. "The difference between Freud's theoretical orientation and that of the present-day 'cultural school,' . . ." said Clara Thompson, a psychoanalyst, is "Freud not only emphasized the biological more than the cultural, but he also developed a cultural theory of his own based on his biological theory with his notion of instincts."[148]

Members of the GAP ignored the biological determinants in Freud's work and developed a cultural explanation of normalcy which they derived largely from cultural anthropology. Whereas Freud was pessimistic about the future of humankind, cultural anthropology gave psychiatrists and psychologists practicing psychodynamic therapy reason for hope. As Thompson explained, the psychoanalysts thought personality is largely determined by cultural conditioning and were very optimistic about "building a more constructive society."[149]

From cultural anthropology, members of the GAP also learned that no universal conception of normalcy could be advanced. "All psychology, and especially psychoanalysis, is concerned with the genetic process, the way in which the individual develops from his beginnings and then it thus emphasizes his earliest life experiences," said Ginsburg. "Anthropology demonstrates how these experiences are culturally determined," he elaborated. "From one culture to another, the content of what is repressed in the developing personality varies and, parallel with this, the content of neuroses and psychoses varies."[150] Normalcy, in other words, is culturally determined.

Finally, members of the GAP also regarded normalcy as a state that people should aspire toward. For this reason, the GAP called upon psychiatrists to discover the "emotionally-weighted and elusive problem of what constitutes a 'normal' environment."[151] Psychiatrists and psychologists in the GAP rendered a teleological explanation of normalcy since, after all, they were members of the helping professions.

Rusk and Kessler, with their emphasis on healing the emotional maladjustments of people with disabilities also relied on a concrete notion of normalcy with teleological overtones. While they believed that disabled people had the capacity for change, the extent to which they could change was offset by the idea that they could not be measured against an ideal. Rusk and Kessler gave up the notion of anatomical perfection, having their patients strive instead for success as a culturally driven norm.

According to Lennard Davis, a disability studies expert, the terms "norm," "normal," "normalcy," "normality," "average," and "abnormal" entered European languages relatively late. It was not until the 1850s that the word "normal," defined as "constituting, conforming to, not deviating or differing from the common type or standard, regular, usual," was used in most European languages. Earlier, normal meant that something was perpendicular or in what was called a carpenter's square. The norm did not exist as a point of comparison or as a means for conformity. As Michel Foucault explained, this "metric" mode of thinking came about only in the late nineteenth century.[152]

Before that time, people were measured against the ideal and the grotesque. Unlike the term "norm," the term "ideal" characterized an elite. The ideal was held over people as something they could strive toward but that few people could achieve. At the opposite end of the spectrum was the image of the grotesque, which was simply the inverse of the ideal. By the late nineteenth century, the twin notions of the ideal and the grotesque were abandoned and the norm was accepted.[153] The norm, or what Foucault called "normalizing judgments," consisted of classifications that recognized people in hierarchical terms. Unlike the ideal, the norm ordered the capacities of people not in relation to an abstraction but in relation to one another.[154]

Unlike the ideal of Aristotle's great chain of being, these normative judgments were inherently democratic. A society with a norm expected that the majority of the population could comply to its standards. By definition, this majority fell under what early statisticians described as the arch of a bell-shaped curve. A minority would be charted as above average on this curve and a minority as below average.

In the United States, the rehabilitation movement embraced the norm. This meant not only that it rejected anatomical perfection as part of an unobtainable ideal but that it abandoned the accompanying notion of the grotesque. The functional conception of disabled people cast aside both the ideal and the grotesque and rested upon a definition of normality. Rehabilitation doctors treated disabled people with the hope that they, too, could fit into the middle of the bell-shaped curve.

This acceptance of normalcy had profound consequences for the rehabilitation movement because it redefined what an impairment was. Originally, a physical or mental impediment was referred to as a handicap. This term "handicap" was taken from a game played by the ancient Greeks. The handicap was the money that one of the players paid because he or she was more adept at the game. It leveled the playing field so that players were evenly matched. A handicap, as in golf today, was used in games that had competitors who were not equal. The fact that they had unequal standing did not stop them from competing.

The functional conception of disability, by contrast, accepted that a handicap meant that a person was less competitive.[155] It made no attempt to restore what made the player less competitive since physicians sought the means to compensate for this person's deficiency. The key was to strengthen what was already healthy. In particular, rehabilitation doctors strengthened the personality, because it, unlike diseased or injured parts, governed the whole body. Rehabilitation medicine emphasized that patients must be perpetually striving toward normalcy. This new medical speciality was, therefore, indebted to the American culture of equality of opportunity and democratization. As the story goes, with enough hard work people could achieve their dreams. For those with physical or mental disabilities, the dream was to be accepted by American society.

Rejecting the concept of the ideal, rehabilitation medicine also lowered the competitive threshold for all of society, as physicians encouraged their patients with disabilities to aspire toward normalcy. For both Rusk and Kessler, the descriptive and normative dimensions of normalcy depended upon one another. What is most common, they claimed, defines what ought to be. Rehabilitation medicine measured what disabled people could do by virtue of what normal people did. It downplayed what distinguished people with physical and mental disabilities from those without them.

On one hand, Rusk and Kessler argued that rehabilitation showed not only that people with a physical disability could be restored to health but also that they were worthy of restoration. "The basis of strength of our Western democratic system lies in the worth of each individual as a matter of paramount concern. The state exists for the individual and not the reverse."[156] "Society," Arthur Bierman, a director of vocational services in New York, argued, "is in one sense only an aggregate of individuals."[157]

On the other hand, normalcy constrained the notion of individualism outlining the whole man theory of rehabilitation. Individuals within the aggregate that Rusk described were measured in relation to one another. Abnormal behavior was defined by virtue of how it was a departure from normal behavior. It was, literally, the aggregate in society that constituted the norm. Rehabilitation experts used a norm, not a fixed standard or no standard, as a means of assessing if a person with a disability was "maladjusted."

Anthropology and psychodynamic psychiatry helped members of the rehabilitation movement formulate their idea of the whole body theory of rehabilitation. The dynamic aspect of their definition of holism also helped them preserve and foster a specific culture. Just as holism helped people compensate for the whole body, making these disabled people whole would also restore the whole society. For Rusk and Kessler, the society in question was in the United States. Needing the federal government to fund rehabilitation, Rusk and Kessler primarily concentrated on the political aspect of American culture, trying to show how vocational rehabilitation could foster the democratization process.

Rusk and Kessler agreed with the Menningers that people with physical disabilities suffered from emotional adjustments more "crippling" than their physical handicaps. While these so-called maladjustments stemmed from the disabled people themselves, they were exacerbated by the community at large. The injustice of society's inability to recognize disabled people for who they were made them all the more hostile. Yet, Rusk, Kessler, and the Menninger brothers believed that disabled people must depend on themselves, not society, if they wanted to be free from emotional maladjustments. They must, in other words, be normalized.

This process of normalization represented a great departure from how the medical community had treated disabled people before World War II. First, it meant that the rehabilitation movement opposed the practice of warehousing disabled people. Before rehabilitation, disabled people were often warehoused with the understanding that they could not be cured; there was nothing society could do with disabled people but put them out of sight. By contrast, the rehabilitation doctors made no claims about curing their patients' particular disabilities.

Second, rehabilitation medicine progressed beyond physical therapy medicine and orthopedic surgery in that it no longer concentrated treatment on the symptoms of a disability. A prosthesis, for instance, was not enough to help someone stand on his own two feet. This was not to say that, when rehabilitation medicine gained acceptance in the medical community, it was welcomed in the mainstream community. Rehabilitation medicine, with what doctors learned from psychiatry and social science about the personality, tried to heal the whole person. Because of this emphasis it remained on the fringe of the medical community.

In all, the rehabilitation movement's belief in the functional conception of disability was based on two competing values—individualism and normalcy—that were also part of the political culture cultivated during the postwar and Cold War periods. On one level, Rusk and Kessler placed great value on the individual's worth, arguing not only that people with a physical disability could be restored to health but also that they were worthy of restoration. On another level, normalcy constrained the notion of individualism behind the whole man theory of rehabilitation because disabled people were measured in relation to one another. Abnormal behavior was defined by virtue of how it constituted a departure from normal behavior.

The rehabilitation movement's reliance on what Michel Foucault would describe as normalizing judgments undermined its emphasis on individualism. The worth of the individual was not judged alone but by virtue of his or her relation to the rest of society. In other words, disabled people were maladjusted not in comparison to some ideal of adjustment but in relation to the able-bodied. This relative type of thinking was in conflict with Rusk's conception of developing the potential of each individual.

Henri-Jacques Stiker's analysis of a nineteenth-century conception of French equality that leaned toward innate similarity also captures the friction between these competing values.[158] He demonstrates that this notion of equality made both the state and society intolerant of innate difference. To him, equality undergirded by individualism denied the social nature of a community with its citizens striving toward similarity and, therefore, trying to repress diversity. "The defective," he describes in *A History of Disability*, "takes the ordinary as model."[159]

The history of rehabilitation followed a similar trajectory. Encouraging the American state and society to rely on both individualism and normalcy meant that members of the rehabilitation movement thought everyone should be free to become normal or, conversely, that no one should be permitted to be abnormal. Not only did these physicians show little tolerance for difference, but promoting the idea that disabled people exercised their freedom to be normal gave them little insight into the repressive nature of their actions.

2

From Warehouses to Rehabilitation Centers: Restoring the Whole Man

From the moment they became involved in the war effort, Rusk, Kessler, and the Menninger brothers advanced the functional perspective about rehabilitation with an eye toward influencing postwar disability policy.[1] Physicians who cared for the wounded used the federal government's commitment to veterans as an opportunity to entrench the new discipline of rehabilitation medicine, which they proposed should treat veterans and civilians alike. World War II presented these physicians with a great opportunity to show that rehabilitation was a viable policy option.

This war afforded more possibilities than the preceding one, in part because more people could live now with serious physical and mental disabilities than ever before. Nevertheless, the symbiotic relationship that Rusk, Kessler, and the Menningers held with key public officials, most notably Mary Switzer, accounts for the type of vocational rehabilitation program constructed. These physicians belonged to a part of the medical community that had flourished during World War II. Overlooking death and destruction, Rusk, Kessler, and the Menningers had been impressed by what scientists, physicians, and federal officials had achieved during the "good war."

Few officials were more aware than Switzer of the potential for power that this type of relationship would yield. It was during World War II, when Switzer worked for the Assignment and Procurement Board, that she established a good rapport with experts in the medical and scientific communities and realized what they could accomplish together. When President Harry Truman's universal healthcare plan failed, other federal officials, like Switzer, saw this as an opportunity to further their own plan—one based on creating a partnership among the federal government and the scientific and medical communities to ensure better healthcare. As Switzer envisioned it, research would be controlled by scientists and doctors, yet paid for by the public.

Championing this new role for the state, Switzer was particularly interested in the ideas of Rusk, Kessler, and the Menninger brothers. These physicians, forming what political scientists have described as an epistemic community, had great influence over the federal bureaucrats who ran the rehabilitation program, in part because their ideas were so cohesive. Without Switzer, however, these physicians would not have wielded as much influence as they did.

Switzer was deeply committed to the values and beliefs of rehabilitation medicine, the Menninger's conception of psychoanalysis, and psychosomatic medicine.[2] She also told Menninger that she was "deeply interested in" his "application of psychiatry to problems of human welfare."[3] Being a pivotal player in the development of the postwar disability policy program, it was Switzer, therefore, who interjected vocational rehabilitation with the rehabilitation movement's values and beliefs.

Switzer's success, however, was not immediate. While the 1940s and early 1950s helped the rehabilitation movement cultivate its ideas, it was only at the end of another crisis, the Korean War, that Switzer and other public policymakers put these ideas into practice. When Dwight D. Eisenhower came into office these policymakers convinced members of his administration that the vocational rehabilitation program should be enlarged and expanded. Since Eisenhower was casting about for a domestic policy that was not part of the New Deal heritage, and the conservative self-help ethic underlying the vocational rehabilitation program played well with the Republican party, the president sponsored the Vocational Rehabilitation Act of 1954, which finally created the vocational rehabilitation program that Switzer and the rehabilitation movement had been working toward since World War II.

First Legislative Initiatives

Like most governments, the United States government made it a priority to help wounded soldiers return to civilian life. Given the tremendous medical advances in the early part of the century and increased life expectancies of injured soldiers, it was not until World War I, however, that the first vocational rehabilitation program took shape.[4] Inspired by what a rehabilitation program had done for soldiers with disabilities, President Woodrow Wilson signed the Smith-Fess Act on June 2, 1920, to help civilians. This law gave a person with a physical disability the chance to meet with a counselor who would help him find educational opportunities and provide medical services that might make him employable.[5]

As explained in Chapter 1, the initial idea of vocational rehabilitation differed from the World War II and postwar notion of rehabilitation medicine, because the physicians who treated people with disabilities focused on curative and restorative rather than rehabilitative practices. Similarly, the first vocational rehabilitation program accepted only people with disabilities that could be "cured."[6] Unlike the physical therapy physicians and orthopedic surgeons, the vocational rehabilitation officials emphasized curability out of programmatic necessity. As the historian Edward Berkowitz writes, "[A]ccording to the ideology that developed to justify the new program, it generated economic returns like a profit-making loan company. Like any loan company, the government had to take the best risks."[7]

The first vocational rehabilitation program accepted "risks" that included workers who stood the greatest chance of being cured, and thus had a greater likelihood of securing a job. This was called "creaming." It also risked including those workers who were socially acceptable. Vocational rehabilitation, therefore, mirrored the existing societal prejudices against minorities, women, and the aged—all people who had less chance of being gainfully employed. In the 1920s and 1930s, the average person rehabilitated was white, male, and thirty-one years old.[8]

The first vocational rehabilitation program also reached relatively few people with physical disabilities. From 1920 to 1943, the vocational rehabilitation program served only 12,000 people, while approximately 250,000 were disabled every year. At the same time, the vocational rehabilitation program was designed to serve people who were hurt in industrial accidents, not those injured in nonindustrial settings or debilitated by congenital defects.[9] Workers who had been hurt in industry needed retribution, Berkowitz said, whereas those slighted by nature needed nothing. An official in the vocational rehabilitation program explained that "the justification of vocational rehabilitation is based on its economic returns to society."[10]

Little changed in the vocational rehabilitation program during the New Deal. Although the Great Depression softened the public attitude about people with disabilities, the program still served the so-called deserving people who had been injured at work.[11] One notable administrative change, however, was that the vocational rehabilitation program became a permanent part of the executive branch. Funding for the program was included in the Social Security Act of 1935, which meant that by 1938 it was placed under the jurisdiction of the Federal Security Agency (FSA).[12]

Housed in the FSA, the vocational rehabilitation program gained a supportive bureaucratic family. Paul McNutt, the FSA administrator, and Switzer, who was his assistant at the time, became enthusiastic supporters of the vocational rehabilitation program. While Switzer acted as McNutt's "watchdog," promoting and guarding the integrity of the programs in the Public Health Service, the Office of Education, and the National Youth Administration, she became particularly interested in rehabilitation.

Switzer had first become engaged in rehabilitation in 1935 after a friend, Tracy Copp, who worked as a regional field officer for the vocational rehabilitation program, called her attention to it. At that time, the vocational rehabilitation program was part of the Public Health Service in the Treasury Department. After learning about rehabilitation, Switzer immediately asked for a transfer so that she would have the opportunity to work with Josephine Roche, the dynamic director of the Public Health Service who oversaw the vocational rehabilitation program. From 1935 until Roche's retirement in 1937, Switzer was her assistant and had an experience she would later describe as "thrilling and educational."[13]

Roche's departure did not dampen Switzer's enthusiasm about public health issues. In the late-1930s and the 1940s, Switzer and others in the FSA developed strategies that would give their programs more independence from the executive branch. They hoped to be more effective in creating and controlling specific programs, for the most part because they had been disillusioned with the Roosevelt administration's work on public health. As these federal officials perceived it, President Roosevelt kept backing away from supporting their plan for national health insurance. Congress also refused to pass universal healthcare or disability insurance. Drawing one lesson from their disappointment, agency officials learned to be more "sophisticated" in presenting their legislative ideas to the executive and legislative branches. In particular, they developed new, yet less sweeping, programs that could create constituencies for the FSA, which, in turn, could help them lobby for specific programs.[14]

Switzer, who had started working in Washington before the New Deal and had invested less in molding its ideas into a public policy platform, appreciated working in the innovative atmosphere brought on by the disillusionment others had with Roosevelt. It created a climate that gave her an opportunity to develop new programs. She was also very adept at cultivating relationships with many of the groups, for example, the Group for the Advancement of Psychiatry that would become part of the FSA's clientele.

World War II and Whole Men

The involvement of the United States in World War II presented the FSA with the chance for great expansion, and McNutt, the agency's administrator and also head of the War Manpower Commission, seized the opportunity. Most notably, McNutt dramatically increased the power and scope of the vocational rehabilitation program during the war with the passage of the Barden-LaFollette Act of 1943. This legislation transformed the vocational rehabilitation program most significantly by shifting the program's focus from job training to what Rusk and Kessler called mental and physical "reconditioning."[15] It also established the Office of Vocational Rehabilitation (OVR).[16]

Armed with this new emphasis on reconditioning, officials in the FSA upstaged the officials in both the Labor Department and the Interior Department who had been fighting since the Great War about whether the program should stress education or vocational training.[17] Switzer and other agency officials in the FSA, however, had not conceived of this new vision of vocational rehabilitation alone. Rusk and Kessler convinced them that it was best not to limit vocational rehabilitation to either education or vocational training.[18] Rehabilitation must deal with the health of the whole man, they claimed, which was exemplified by the personality of people with disabilities and not merely by their education or job history.

The Barden-LaFollette Act, however, did not go as far as Rusk and other members of the rehabilitation movement had hoped. First, Rusk thought that rehabilitation centers should be constructed with public funds. Second, although the Barden-LaFollette Act no longer limited its services to those who were injured at the work force, it still emphasized curability. If a person could not return to work, he or she was supposedly not worthy of treatment.[19] This policy promoted "creaming" (mentioned earlier), the practice of rehabilitating people who had a greater likelihood of securing a job.[20] Third, Rusk was disturbed that the federal office never pushed the state offices into sending people with disabilities to any one of the seven existent rehabilitation centers, which already practiced this specialty from the rehabilitation movement's perspective.[21]

Rusk held Michael Shortley, the first OVR director, responsible for these three problems. To be sure, Shortley had had grave difficulties directing the vocational rehabilitation program. He never gained the confidence of the "old timers" in rehabilitation in the federal government, nor the bureaucrats in the regional offices, who responded to few of Shortley's directives and made no secret about how they resented him. Initially, Shortley scrutinized the activities of the state directors, but he eventually gave this up as a losing proposition. By so doing, Shortley traded this conflict for one with Rusk, who thought he should have continued fighting with the state directors.[22]

Rusk's frustrations with Shortley were primarily bureaucratic, since this director championed both the rehabilitation and the psychosomatic movements.[23] Evidence of Shortley's support surfaced in 1949, when he advanced Rusk's whole man theory of rehabilitation by advising all the state directors they should read an address by Wilma Donahue, which reviewed this theory and traced its psychoanalytic and psychosomatic origins.[24] This approach, Shortley said, was "vital to the development of the rehabilitation program."[25]

Donahue's conference paper defined the whole man theory, citing Alfred Adler's influence on it.[26] She also underscored the significance of the team approach and other trends in the psychosocial aspect of rehabilitation.[27] Most notably, Donahue's work discussed how recent developments by Gestalt, the American interpretation of psychoanalysis or psychodynamic therapy and psychosomatic medicine, influenced rehabilitation medicine.

According to Donahue, it was Gestalt psychology that had inspired Rusk and other doctors in the rehabilitation movement to conclude that the whole man was more than the sum of his parts. "Personality was assumed to be the sum total of distinct traits which were measurable by psychological tests similar to those used in the measurement of intelligence." Uniting the parts of the person into a whole, the personality was seen as the outcome of interaction between the individual and his environment. "On the basis of this concept," she added, "a new notion of personality was developed which has become known as the holistic organismic theory of personality."[28]

Finally, Donahue noted how important projective tests were in vocational rehabilitation: "For the first time there is recognition of the psychologists's clinical concern about the individual and of his responsibility in the clinical diagnosis and treatment of maladjustments." These projective tests utilized "new techniques designed to tap the deeper strata of personality in terms of unconscious motivation," maintained Donahue.[29] Projective tests, like the Rorschach test, she concluded, could measure a person's potential.[30]

Although Shortley subscribed to the whole man theory of rehabilitation as Donahue described, using its vision to sustain the OVR before Congress and the public, Rusk had become increasingly dissatisfied with his efforts.[31] Indeed, by the fall of 1948 Rusk had had enough of Shortley's rhetorical support. As he saw it, Shortley's support translated into little actual support for the rehabilitation centers relying on the whole man theory. Rusk was annoyed that Shortley acted as if the federal government sponsored these centers, while in fact the government did little to disturb the old practice of having local doctors refer patients to hospitals. Rusk's own rehabilitation center had not received one patient from such a referral in 1948. To rectify this problem, Rusk told Shortley, he must end this practice; otherwise Rusk would call attention to the discrepancy in his weekly column in the *New York Times*.[32]

With the exception of Virginia, neither the federal government nor any other state had put public money behind the rehabilitation centers promoted by Rusk and other members of the rehabilitation movement.[33] Also, rehabilitation medicine had missed out on the research and development bonanza after World War II. The newly formed National Institutes of Health (NIH) gave money primarily to the old, established medical specialties.[34] Further, within these specialties, the doctors who were rewarded were those who explored etiology. Recognizing this bias, some of the NIH's critics called etiology the "disease of the month club."[35]

Given these frustrations, Rusk shifted his attention from working with the OVR to changing the structure of the program.[36] Already in 1947, he had directly appealed to President Truman to build more rehabilitation centers and cautioned that "an adequate program of medical rehabilitation soundly conceived and now well through its formative stage is now operating in the Veterans Administration hospitals. . . . [the] real need in the U.S.," wrote Rusk, is "for the establishment of community rehabilitation centers."[37] After 1948, Rusk pushed even harder for legislative reform.

Meanwhile, Kessler was also lobbying for reform. He took advantage of writing a report for the Postwar Retraining and Resettlement Administration, sponsored by the Truman administration, to recommend creating more rehabilitation centers. Like Rusk, Kessler declared that physical medicine and rehabilitation should be included in civilian hospitals and that the federal government should help build rehabilitation centers.[38]

In 1950, Rusk and Kessler had the chance to address the Senate Committee on Labor and Public Welfare on just these issues. Rusk impressed upon the subcommittee that 98 percent of disabled people were "warehoused" and thus remained out of work. In dramatic testimony, Rusk told the subcommittee that epileptics were sharing rooms with the feeble-minded when the only thing they had in common was their destitution. Rehabilitation centers, by contrast, would "help the[se] clients attain maximum adjustment." Since the average person, he reasoned, used only 25 percent of his potential, the highly trained team of healthcare providers at the rehabilitation centers could work with the remaining 75 percent, helping them to reenter mainstream society.[39] With these calculations, Rusk outlined the whole man theory of rehabilitation to the Senate Committee on Labor and Public Welfare, professing that most people with disabilities could compensate for their impediments. Rusk explained that his rehabilitation center was studying the "emotional problems connected with physical disability." Further, underscoring the importance of the psychosocial elements, Rusk said that "medicine is allowed to aid psychiatry, and psychiatry to aid medicine" when a hospial makes a diagnosis.[40]

Rusk was not the only person to lobby for the whole man theory of rehabilitation. The OVR also endorsed it. Speaking for this office, Donald Dabelstein, who was the assistant director, testified that rehabilitation should strive for "the total evaluation of the individual—physical, psychological, and social."[41] Finally, the testimony of Rusk, Kessler, and Dabelstein came on top of the Baruch Committee Report, which also had given evidence about how important rehabilitation centers were given their capacity to provide medical, educational, and psychosocial services.[42]

Influenced by the lobbying efforts of Rusk, Kessler, and other members of the Baruch Committee, the Senate Labor and Public Works Committee issued a report that called for the construction of eighteen rehabilitation centers.[43] They failed to convince the Committee as a Whole in either the Senate or the House, however, and the legislation that was passed—the National Services for Disabled Persons Act—provided little money for rehabilitation centers. Rusk and Kessler were also disappointed that the federal government maintained its commitment to the traditional sources of vocational rehabilitation: sheltered workshops and licenses to the blind to operate vending stands in federal buildings.[44]

Although the National Services for Disabled Persons Act was not the legislative victory the rehabilitation movement hoped for, its passage did provide Oscar Ewing, the federal security administrator, with the impetus to appoint a new director to the OVR who stood firmly behind the movement's ideals.[45] Shortley was "kicked upstairs" to become the regional director of the FSA, and Switzer, who had been his assistant since 1943, took over the OVR.[46] Switzer's appointment showed that the climate for reform was beginning to change in the rehabilitation movement's favor.

Mr. and Miss Rehabilitation: Switzer's Work with an Epistemic Community

During World War II, Switzer had forged a symbiotic relationship with many members of the medical community. She knew many prominent doctors who had served on the wartime Procurement and Assignment Service, which designated where doctors could best serve the armed forces. Switzer's service made her privy to the internal politics of the medical community.[47] This service, which the American Medical Association (AMA) and the FSA ran together, had been organized in 1941.[48]

Following her prewar experience with rehabilitation, Switzer showed great interest in the work of physicians, like Rusk and William Menninger, who devised systematic means of helping the wounded resume normal lives. She got along well with these members of the medical community, having been accustomed to working with them, and also because she shared the values and beliefs underlying the whole man theory of rehabilitation.

Switzer's wartime experience also taught her that it was vital to have a respected authority in the form of rehabilitation advocate Rusk on her side.[49] Switzer had great respect for Rusk, whom she referred to in correspondence as "Mr. Rehabilitation."[50] First meeting him when he appeared before the Procurement and Assignment Board to explain his rehabilitation program in the Army Air Force, Switzer was so struck by Rusk's idea that the "hospital environment" could be "normalized" that she adopted his saying "out of bed and into action" as her own.[51]

Given her commitment to Rusk's notion of rehabilitation and her enthusiasm about cultivating informal relationships with experts like him in the private sector, it came as little surprise to those who knew Switzer that she and Rusk, as her biographer, Mary Walker, describes, "entered what was almost a partnership to run the vocational rehabilitation program." Rusk not only advised Switzer in private; she brought him along to many high-level meetings at the FSA.[52] The greatest testament of their close relationship became apparent when Rusk advanced Switzer's candidacy for the head of the OVR.

Rusk's faith in Switzer was well-founded since she internalized his beliefs about rehabilitation and the whole man theory, giving speeches that referred to it as "an emerging concept."[53] Moreover, the depth of her commitment to the whole man theory was not born solely from her experience with Rusk. Switzer underscored how she and Rusk had been influenced by William Menninger's conception of psychoanalysis or psychodynamic therapy and psychosomatic medicine.[54]

As Walker writes, Switzer, working with both Menninger brothers during World War II, was "devoted to psychiatry as Karl Menninger described it."[55] Switzer herself said that Karl Menninger's "personality made me feel that anything he asked for I would try to get for him with all my might and main."[56] Realizing just that, Switzer had solicited Karl Menninger's advice on what became of the National Mental Health Act of 1946, which she then based on his vision of psychiatry. This legislation also promoted research and education, another one of Karl Menninger's suggestions, with psychiatrists running the two advisory bodies—the National Institute of Mental Health and the National Advisory Mental Health Council—which determined what institutions would receive public funding.[57] Finally, the National Mental Health Act fulfilled William Menninger's dream that the United States have a community mental health program.[58]

Switzer again in 1948 pledged her commitment to this eclectic type of psychoanalysis and psychosomatic medicine practiced by the Menningers.[59] Years later, reminiscing about the postwar years with great fondness, Switzer relayed how William Menninger "broke new ground in alluding how the insights of psychiatry allied with the other related professions could change the attitudes not only of individuals with mental illness, but of societies." She also applauded the Menningers' commitment to social activism. Indeed, Switzer offered her support for the Group for the Advancement of Psychiatry (GAP), which William Menninger helped found, stating that "there has always been for me a sense of responsibility for helping psychiatry play its full role in human affairs."[60] Switzer wrote to William Menninger that "it is a tremendous satisfaction to be connected with one group [GAP] devoted to the development of ideas."[61] Switzer backed the psychodynamic branch of psychiatry so fully that the Menningers made her the only layman trustee of their clinic.[62]

For Switzer, the social activism practiced by people like William Menninger made the period after the war memorable and "exciting."[63] She also knew that psychoanalysis and psychosomatic medicine had been essential to rehabilitation medicine during its formative years and thought it was imperative to maintain this connection.[64] In the earlier 1950s, for instance, Switzer repeatedly wrote to R. H. Felix, the director of the National Institute for Mental Health (NIMH), encouraging him to fund a project that would explore "what psychiatry can do to illuminate the need for understanding the emotional aspects of work with the disabled."[65]

Finally, Switzer was committed to something that rehabilitation medicine, psychoanalysis, and psychosomatic medicine all shared: an emphasis on interdisciplinary work and thought. In a speech called "New Horizons in Rehab," she gave a ringing endorsement to rehabilitation because it included "a tested and comprehensive science of human behavior" from an interdisciplinary perspective. "The disciplines represented," Switzer told the audience, "are sociology, social anthropology, clinical and social psychology."[66]

Switzer was so enamored of interdisciplinary teams and projects that she placed them at the forefront of the postwar atomic age. To her, the Manhattan Project had been one of the first interdisciplinary projects, composed of a team of scientists, that illustrated how well business and the government could work together. In 1945, the editors of *Fortune* magazine captured the spirit by writing that "a stream of new scientific knowledge [could work] to turn the wheels of private and public enterprise."[67] Switzer said that "teamwork is neither in medicine or public health. Actually this concept of cooperative effort is taking hold in all types of scientific and professional circles. The mental hygiene clinic, TB, surgery team, social agencies, industry, Manhattan [P]roject and development of atom bomb."[68] She thought the government should provide funds for similar projects.[69]

Switzer's Atomic Age Pattern Prevails

Switzer's ideas about the new role for the federal government prevailed as the National Mental Health Act of 1946 established a pattern for postwar health legislation.[70] Bolstered by this success, Switzer thought that many other health measures should be implemented with the help of other advisory board members, which could lend the government their expertise without compromising the integrity of medical professionals. Grants-in-aid would be used as a nonthreatening means of increasing governmental involvement in healthcare. In the words of Walker, "[S]cience would be governed by scientists and paid for by the public."[71]

Characterizing the Hospital Survey and Construction Act of 1946 in the same light, Switzer advertised the benefits of financial aid for the purpose of the construction of hospitals for the public, which would help build hospitals for the next twenty-five years.[72] Switzer's biographer wrote, "The federal government took the initiative and the medical establishment took the control. Mary Switzer had helped to assemble the pieces."[73]

Switzer had no problem securing the AMA's support for this type of partnership between the federal government and voluntary agencies. The Hospital Survey and Construction Act promised to expand medical, dental, and nursing schools; construct more medical facilities; and facilitate more medical research.[74] To be sure, Rusk also endorsed this new relationship, hoping that rehabilitation medicine would benefit from it.

Rusk's hopes were not in vain, since he worked with Switzer on creating a plan for the vocational rehabilitation legislation that followed the same pattern as the National Mental Health Act and the Hospital Survey and Construction Act. Not only did Switzer make the rehabilitation center the primary focus of this legislation, but she proposed that a board of rehabilitation experts modeled after the NIMH convene to fund research and development in rehabilitation medicine.

Switzer understood how the rehabilitation center departed from traditional treatment because of an opportunity she had earlier. Josephine Roche had first shown Switzer how effective rehabilitation centers could be when she took over the United Mine Workers' (UMW) Welfare and Retirement Fund in 1938. After discovering that miners received only immediate care for debilitating injuries that often left them paralyzed, Warren Draper, a former deputy surgeon general, set up ten regional medical offices for the fund—the first rehabilitation centers—to help them.[75] Switzer became involved with this experiment when Roche convinced her to become a trustee of the UMW's Welfare and Retirement Fund. Even before Rusk had become interested in rehabilitation, Switzer had been involved in one of the first experiments with rehabilitation centers. According to Berkowitz, Switzer was particularly proud to have "gotten in on the ground floor of America's experience with disability programs."[76]

Not only had the UMW's experiment with rehabilitation taught Switzer that rehabilitation centers were the key to returning disabled people back to work, but her work with the fund helped keep Rusk's and Kessler's rehabilitation centers afloat.[77] The UMW Welfare and Retirement Fund referred a steady supply of patients to their centers in New York City and Newark, respectively, during the late 1940s before the federal government changed its position.[78]

Further, Draper and Rusk found themselves involved in what Switzer called a "demonstration project," or a project that would educate the public and other members of the government about the need for rehabilitation, because she hoped to bring them closer together. Switzer used this demonstration project in the same way that she had always used them: to provide her with concrete evidence of the deficiencies in the delivery of medical care. She often used demonstration projects as a platform to launch a new program.[79]

An Early Resistance to Rights

The rehabilitation approach promoted by Rusk, Kessler, the Menningers, and Switzer represented only one of the many approaches available in the 1940s. Another approach was the quota system, which was founded in Great Britain, for instance, in 1944. This system required employers with over twenty employees to make 3 percent of their work force people with disabilities.[80] Although the proponents of the rehabilitation approach may have been aware of the debate about quotas, no one in Congress introduced legislation based on this ideal. Switzer and other bureaucrats in the FSA, moreover, opposed any policy that in any way compelled employers, let alone one that would require them to hire a specific number of people with disabilities.

The idea that people with disabilities should have a right to employment was foreign to American policymakers both in Congress and the federal bureaucracy. Disability policy pertaining to employment was no different than so many other social policies passed in the United States, in that it was a product of an "exceptional" liberal state.[81] With many pivotal social policies resting on a classical interpretation of liberalism, the American state differed from its European counterparts by promoting liberty and equality of opportunity rather than equality per se. Freedom to contract, which extended to an employer's right to manage a workplace, was one of the primary manifestations of this conception of American liberalism.[82]

Indeed, when several members of Congress attempted to pass legislation in 1940 that gave disabled people not a right to a job but a right to work free from discrimination, federal bureaucrats opposed it, describing this prohibition as too invasive of an employer's freedom to contract.[83] In particular, the bureaucrats expressed their resistance to this approach when Senator Elbert Thomas, who chaired the Senate Committee on Education and Labor, asked Leonard Cohen, general counsel for the FSA, to present a comprehensive critique of the rights-oriented legislation. In his critique, Cohen concluded that it "does not appear to present the proper approach to this problem." This legislation, he explained, "would inject the element of penal compulsion in a situation of delicate personnel relationships calling for human sympathy and a willingness to cooperate." In addition to being wrongheaded and "costly," Cohen thought the bill "would give rise to extensive litigation . . . and in most instances it would be difficult to determine reliably whether refusal to employ a particular individual arose from disability or from other consideration." In conclusion, Cohen added, "It would be next to impossible to prove conclusively that the rejection was due to his [the job applicant's] former physical disability. Serious administrative difficulties would result from attempts to settle disputed cases, and these difficulties might be expected to have [an] adverse effect far beyond the value of the potential objectives."[84]

Cohen opposed any measures that pitted the rights of employees against the rights of management. "I believe that greater success can be achieved in the placement of physically handicapped persons through voluntary action," he said. "It may be expected that there would frequently be a difference of opinion between the physically handicapped applicant and the employer concerning the former's competence. Apparently, then, whenever the applicant felt that he was competent to do the job, he could insist upon the summoning of a rehabilitation agent to preside over a demonstration or test. Frequent recourse to such a procedure might well increase the resistance of management to the employment of handicapped persons."[85]

Despite the FSA's opposition, the rights-oriented approach to vocational rehabilitation was introduced in the Senate again in 1941. At that time, the FSA rendered the same critique. Arthur Altmeyer, chairman of the Social Security Board, purported that this bill suffered from the same problems as the last.[86]

Members of the FSA held onto their opposition to a rights perspective for over a decade, when Switzer and the OVR began lobbying for legislation. In 1952, Public Health Service officials suggested that there should be "entitlement to rehab" in the same way that there is "entitlement for cash benefits." Undermining their own suggestion, however, these officials conceded that it would be difficult, if not impossible, to give everyone this entitlement. "If there were such entitlement, however, it is recognized that the total public and private facilities and personnel would not be sufficient for all who would be entitled. The suggestion is made, therefore, that a limited rehabilitation right could be provided."[87]

When Switzer's OVR raised the issue of providing employment rights to people with disabilities, it again rejected the proposal that "within the mechanics of the state vocational rehabilitation service the disabled person who fails to obtain rehabilitation services should have an appeal beyond the local counselor to a state board for similar authority." One official argued, "There should be no provision of this sort in the act." At best, rehabilitation as a right could only be a sharply limited right, which Switzer and other officials thought should be more appropriately labeled a "privilege." Switzer never supported the idea that people with disabilities should have rights in the workplace.[88]

On a practical level, Switzer worried that providing the disabled with rights would open the floodgates. "Furthermore, the automatic payment for certain rehabilitation services for *all* individuals would give rise to pressures on rehabilitation agencies to make them available to people who could not be employed."[89] At the time, Switzer did not want any new program to call into question that vocational rehabilitation experts worked with only the "cream" or the people who had the greatest chance of successfully finding employment. The so-called practice of creaming dramatically increased the vocational rehabilitation program's rate of success that the bureaucrats involved with the program did not want to compromise.

While these legislative attempts failed, Paul Strachan tried to carry on a fight for civil rights for people with disabilities. Strachan, who founded the American Federation of the Physically Handicapped, and had succeeded in establishing the National Employ the Handicapped Week in 1945, opposed Rusk's and Switzer's approach to rehabilitation.[90] An earlier proponent of what would become the rights model of disability, Strachan lobbied for civil rights legislation that would protect people with disabilities from discrimination and would provide for an affirmative action plan for hiring them. Moreover, he suggested that a federal commission for the physically handicapped be established along with other benefits programs, like subsidized loans to disabled people. Rejecting the paternalist and patronizing attitude underlying the "rehabilitation philosophy" touted by Rusk, Kessler, and Switzer, Strachan insisted that the federal government should invest more money into benefits programs, programs that would give people with disabilities the opportunity to care for themselves. Given his emphasis on civil rights for people with disabilities, Strachan, as Berkowitz describes, was "out of step" with "the era of rehabilitation centers and professionalization."[91] What is more, he failed to convince members of the rehabilitation movement and federal bureaucrats involved in vocational rehabilitation that the whole man theory of rehabilitation was patronizing and that a rights model of disability should be utilized, let alone a quota system.

Switzer's position to both the disability rights legislation and Strachan's lobbying attempts again made it clear that she and the doctors in the rehabilitation movement shared the belief that vocational rehabilitation would profit from the whole man theory, not from the institution of civil rights for people with disabilities. Under the whole man theory, disabled people could develop their potential by compensating for their injuries. This theory focused on barriers in the minds of disabled people. It was the people with disabilities who made accommodations so that they could be accepted by society. The rights approach to rehabilitation, by contrast, emphasized that society must accommodate disabled people by removing the obstacles society had erected.

Pledge Allegiance to the Handicapped

With the passage of the National Mental Health Act, Switzer had become "health care's guide to federal dollars," and the rehabilitation movement certainly hoped to profit from her guidance. Rusk envisioned vocational rehabilitation legislation that would establish a framework similar to the one provided by this legislation. He hoped it would create a long-lasting relationship between the private and public sectors which would not endanger the autonomy of the rehabilitation professionals.[92]

While Rusk, Kessler, and others campaigned for these changes, it was Switzer who rallied the support from the oldest organization of rehabilitation experts—the National Rehabilitation Association (NRA). Switzer challenged NRA members to "think beyond the present law, to remove themselves from 'silent isolationism' and 'don the cloak of dynamic leadership.'" She wanted the group to "pledge allegiance to the handicapped, using a multidisciplinary approach to correctly analyze individual limitations and potentialities and develop the maximum of services authorized under the Vocational Rehabilitation Act."[93] To stir up the audience, Switzer dangled money and power in front of them all the while reminding them that such action resulted only when "the state leadership demonstrated the urgency of the need."[94]

Despite Switzer's efforts to drum up more constituent support for the construction of rehabilitation centers, it was the Korean War that gave her the greatest opportunity to make real changes in the vocational rehabilitation program.[95] As Walker describes, American involvement in the Korean War meant "the time was ripe" for reforming the vocational rehabilitation program. Not only did wartime inspire private-public sector cooperation, but Switzer, Rusk, and other members of the rehabilitation movement could argue that coping with the wounded and the manpower shortage caused by the Korean War demanded that they build more rehabilitation centers.[96]

Moreover, Rusk, as chair of the Health Resources Advisory Committee of the National Security Resources Board during the Korean War, was in a good position to make these arguments.[97] Acting in that capacity, Rusk wrote Senator W. Stuart Symington, chair of the National Security Resources Board, about the critical need for placing disabled people in the work force, which had been depleted by defense mobilization. Symington responded by encouraging the director of Defense Mobilization, Arthur Flemming, to create a task force. In turn, Flemming asked Rusk for suggestions of persons to sit on the task force. Taking advantage of this opportunity to set the task force's agenda, Rusk selected doctors who supported the rehabilitation movement. Not surprisingly, the task force report combined the "needs assessment" with the "rehabilitation philosophy," or the whole man theory of rehabilitation.[98]

Then, in 1951, to illustrate how successful the rehabilitation center could be, Switzer and Rusk developed a demonstration project called "Operation Knoxville."[99] Switzer and Rusk pointed to Knoxville as proof that the rehabilitation process was already at work in Tennessee. In Knoxville, rehabilitation teams were utilized in which a doctor dictated the physical needs, a social worker interpreted the social problems, and a psychologist "pointed out neurotic symptoms" of people with disabilities. Finally, rehabilitation counselors in Operation Knoxville "explor[ed] the individual's perception of the disability, as well as the cause and course of the problem."[100]

It was no coincidence that Switzer had located her demonstration project in Knoxville, which housed the Oak Ridge atomic energy plant.[101] She hoped to use the association with atomic energy to show that rehabilitation could help fight not only the Korean War but also the Cold War. Supposedly, Operation Knoxville promoted democratization by having "public officials keeping citizens productive and self-reliant by working together with traditional American institutions such as Kiwanis clubs and local chambers of commerce."[102] These nongovernmental organizations fostered democratization by helping American citizens develop their full potential. On a practical level, she added, rehabilitation teams could treat Americans wounded in a Communist attack.[103]

"Beating the bushes in the states to understand the problem, Switzer [was] build[ing] support and spurr[ing] action." As Walker describes, Switzer's "brainstorming paved the way for legislative change." This change finally occurred in 1954 when the Korean War ended, and Dwight D. Eisenhower was swept into office. Switzer refashioned the whole man of theory so that it promoted a conservative notion of individualism and anticommunism and also saved taxpayers money.[104]

The Crowning Glory: Eisenhower and the Vocational Rehabilitation Act of 1954

When Eisenhower became president, one of Vice President Richard Nixon's political allies was slated to replace Switzer as the director of the OVR. Upon hearing this news, Rusk dropped everything in New York and immediately flew to Washington, D.C. The rehabilitation movement could not afford to lose Switzer, its strongest advocate within the government. To convince Eisenhower not to let Switzer go, Rusk used the connections he made during his service in World War II and the Korean War. He persuaded Sherman Adams, Eisenhower's chief of staff, and General Snyder, the president's personal physician, among others, that Switzer must retain her position.[105]

Despite this awkward beginning, Switzer had little difficulty convincing the Eisenhower administration that the rehabilitation movement's vision of vocational rehabilitation should be adopted.[106] In fact, vocational rehabilitation became a central part of the Eisenhower administration's domestic agenda. Not only did the vocational rehabilitation program reflect this vision, but it followed the postwar cooperative model of government, initiated with the passage of the National Mental Health Act, with a panel of rehabilitation experts awarding grants for research and training.

Eisenhower, however, was not the first executive to promote the idea that the federal government should sponsor research and development in the private sector. During World War II, the Roosevelt administration had been working on such a program for peacetime. After Roosevelt's death, President Truman extended this notion during the reconversion to peace.[107] Truman signed both the National Mental Health Act and the National Science Foundation Act (NSF) into law in 1946, though he voiced grave objections about the extent of professional autonomy that protected scientists and doctors, arguing that the federal government should retain more control over what type of research they conducted.[108] Hence, Switzer's plan that the federal government sponsor research and development in the field of rehabilitation may not have been the first one suggested, but it was more compatible with Eisenhower's theory of conservatism than with either Roosevelt's New Deal or Truman's Fair Deal.

Eisenhower was comfortable with cultivating this new relationship because it safeguarded professional autonomy, which undergirded his notion of welfare capitalism. To him, the federal government was the "financier, and expeditor of the efforts of the states, localities, and private groups."[109] As a result, governmental involvement, Eisenhower thought, should be manifested as the research and development of new products, like federal aid to education, roads, health, safety and relief, and social welfare techniques. Unlike Roosevelt or Truman, he maintained a reserved, nonpartisan approach to politics and administration, which produced rational solutions to policy problems that were often based on an efficient system of decentralization.[110] Eisenhower preferred, moreover, to promote policies that could be administered by existing programs.[111]

Reforming the vocational rehabilitation program fulfilled all of these criteria and had the added advantage of having been around long before the New Deal.[112] Members of the Eisenhower administration, however, did not immediately see the appeal of this program. To convince them that vocational rehabilitation would fulfill their objectives, Switzer first persuaded them that such a program could appeal to both conservatives and liberals. She knew the existing vocational rehabilitation program had a special allure for Republicans because it fulfilled fundamental principles of the conservative agenda.

Switzer's efforts paid off as Nelson Rockefeller, an undersecretary of the Department of Health, Education and Welfare (HEW), who was part of the new crowd of welfare capitalists in the Eisenhower administration, came to support the program for precisely that reason.[113] In 1953, Rockefeller, Oveta C. Hobby, the new secretary of HEW, and Roswell Perkins, an assistant secretary, decided that the vocational rehabilitation program constituted the type of comprehensive and "nonsocialistic" social program that the administration wanted to advance. The vocational rehabilitation program reduced dependency, saved taxpayers' money, and operated under state, rather than federal, control. It also furthered the Eisenhower administration's position on fostering technology by being associated with advances in medical technology.[114] As an added bonus, the program complemented Eisenhower's proposal to elevate the status of the FSA into a department.[115]

Eisenhower unveiled his proposal for vocational rehabilitation on January 18, 1954.[116] Addressing Congress, he proposed, first, that vocational rehabilitation be expanded by the allocation of more funds for state vocational rehabilitation programs. Second, he suggested that basic support funds be provided for these programs as well as new ones in the public and private sector.[117] Third, grants would be awarded for special projects, research, and training, particularly to those who developed creative new services and programs.[118] Eisenhower's proposal also included a demonstration project or a showcase rehabilitation center that was to be built in the Washington, D.C., area. Finally, the vocational rehabilitation proposal established a twelve-person National Advisory Council on Vocational Rehabilitation, modeled after the National Institutes of Health, that would be staffed by experts who determined which projects would be funded.[119]

Switzer, Dabelstein, Rockefeller, and Perkins, who had drafted Eisenhower's proposal, oversaw the passage of the Vocational Rehabilitation Act of 1954.[120] To do so, they all testified before the House and Senate and attended the markup session for the legislation.[121] They did not have too much trouble convincing Congress about the merits of the program. The support was so strong that the House and Senate conference bill passed by voice votes with no amendments.[122]

Part of the explanation for the vocational rehabilitation program's support stemmed from the fact that no outside interests opposed it. Although the AMA opposed disability insurance, it had no problem with the rehabilitation legislation because it promoted professional autonomy.[123] The AMA was pleased to have another health advisory council, which was staffed by professionals who provided funds for vocational rehabilitation.[124]

Ultimately, Switzer was so satisfied with her role that she wrote to a friend: "The excitement of a change-over such as we are having is very great. Being a top staff member and in addition having responsibility for the administration of an important program of service like rehabilitation puts me in just about the most interesting, if exposed, position I could have."[125] Five months later she wrote to Secretary Hobby, "This is a 'new day' in rehabilitation. . . . To have this program recognized by the President is the 'crowning glory' of years of effort."[126]

On August 3, 1954, Eisenhower signed the Vocational Rehabilitation Act, with Switzer, Rockefeller, Rusk, and E. B. Whitten, the head of the NRA, in attendance. During the signing ceremony, Eisenhower praised the program, emphasizing that it was "a humanitarian investment of great importance, yet it saves substantial sums of money."[127] While it furthered the Eisenhower administration's notion about welfare capitalism, the real victors were the doctors in the rehabilitation movement who were not interested in saving money but rather in advancing what Switzer described as a "bold and advanced social experiment."[128]

While this may have constituted the crowning glory for Switzer, the Eisenhower administration's support for vocational rehabilitation did not end with the signing ceremony. The president also sponsored the Medical Facilities Survey and Construction Act of 1954, amending the Hill-Burton

Hospital Survey and Construction Act by providing funds for rehabilitation centers as well as for hospitals and other medical facilities.

Switzer and the rehabilitation movement relished their legislative victories in 1954. Indeed, they had been so successful in influencing the Eisenhower administration regarding the vocational rehabilitation program that the president extended the notion of rehabilitation to the whole society. Rehabilitation, he purported, could help people regain control of their lives. Just how seriously Eisenhower took this became apparent when he began peppering his speeches about social programs with the metaphor of "government action as rehabilitation."[129]

Tooling Up: Implementation of the Rehabilitation Act of 1954

With guidance from Rusk, Kessler, and the newly established National Advisory Council on Vocational Rehabilitation, Switzer immediately began to reshape vocational rehabilitation and rehabilitation medicine.[130] She particularly relied on Rusk, whom she still saw as "an outstanding medical authority from outside [g]overnment . . . to whom she [Switzer] can turn for professional advice as often as necessary."[131] Switzer dedicated her efforts to what her biographer called "tooling up" by facilitating training and research in the rehabilitation profession. Walker describes her as "in the birth of rehabilitation research, Switzer was often the midwife, encouraging mavericks as well as the established to initiate research proposals."[132]

The OVR's newly expanded budget and its commitment to rehabilitate 200,000 people gave Switzer a good deal of room for maneuvering. Since the AMA endorsed the program, Switzer anticipated that the only opposition would come from members of the old rehabilitation establishment, who were associated with running the state vocational rehabilitation programs.[133] As a means of ensuring their cooperation, Switzer and Rusk had been careful that Eisenhower's proposal for vocational rehabilitation gave them more funding than they had requested.[134] Switzer's plan worked. Satisfied with their budgets, the state directors put up no opposition when she took vocational rehabilitation in a new direction.

First, Switzer expanded vocational rehabilitation services by awarding grants to special projects. Under her direction, more money was allocated for these special projects than for the improvement and extension of the old vocational rehabilitation program. For example, these projects developed psychiatric techniques with deaf persons to help epileptics find work. She also wielded her power with discretionary grant funds by strengthening the basic grant program, giving some of these grants to private, voluntary agencies involved in research and demonstration projects. She found people who widened the reach of rehabilitation—like Hank Viscardi, who had founded Abilities, Inc., which encouraged employers to give the disabled "just one break"—and she built a sense of unity among the emergent groups.[135]

Second, Switzer ensured that the Vocational Rehabilitation Act provided training for a whole cadre of vocational rehabilitation professionals.[136] Switzer had long insisted that the shortage of trained people was "the greatest single obstacle to the more rapid expansion of all rights of day by day activity" that would strengthen the vocational rehabilitation program.[137] The OVR, therefore, gave grants that founded professional training programs in universities, subsidized research on rehabilitation methods, and awarded students in this field scholarships and fellowships so they could attend the new programs at public expense.[138]

Still showing the influence of Rusk and the Menningers, Switzer left her mark on the training programs by insisting that the rehabilitation professions remain interdisciplinary.[139] Most important, these ideas underlying the rehabilitation movement and psychoanalysis influenced the creation of the "infant and emerging discipline" of rehabilitation counselors.[140] When training rehabilitation counselors was first proposed in the OVR, there was some question about whether they should be trained in psychology or in a separate program for vocational rehabilitation. Dabelstein, who had initially developed the rehabilitation counseling process along with Terry Foster, suggested that this program be housed in psychology departments.[141] Cecile Hillyer, one of Switzer's staff members, disagreed. Trained as a social worker, Hillyer argued that rehabilitation counselors should understand social forces and develop leadership in public affairs.[142]

Switzer settled the stalemate about psychology and social work by making rehabilitation counseling a new profession that would be neither "profession-centered" nor "agency-centered," but would reflect the "fast-changing scene in the community" by remaining a hybrid or interdisciplinary field.[143] The counselor would be influenced by psychology and social work, since Switzer wanted the training to stress philosophy, not techniques, and a sense of history and purpose, not a commitment to a particular profession or agency. Nonetheless, Switzer thought the rehabilitation counselor must concentrate on helping people with disabilities resolve their emotional problems.

As Switzer and the OVR intended, rehabilitation counselors wielded enormous power and control over their patients. They singlehandedly decided whether the patient would receive vocational rehabilitation services. As a director in Maryland said, rehabilitation was "not an entitlement."[144] Clients could be turned away by the counselors whose professional training gave them the expertise to judge if a disabled person could profit from rehabilitation. Because the candidate for rehabilitation might challenge the authority of the counselor, the counselor was instructed to try to gain influence when the person was at a most vulnerable point in the process.[145] During "the early chronic phase," one expert described it as "the patient went through a period of depression" and would be "exquisitely sensitive to the attitudes of the attending physician's ancillary personnel."[146]

Whether candidates for rehabilitation would be rejected by counselors depended largely on the candidates' motivations.[147] If candidates had the "wrong" attitude, they would be turned away. Similarly, candidates needed to exhibit a "certain type of temperament"; otherwise they would be labeled "infeasible" or a "low promise case." Rehabilitation counselors sought out people with disabilities who were "responsive from the first" and rejected the rest.[148]

This emphasis on attitude and motivation in the vocational rehabilitation program was different from that of most other social programs which gave their officials little discretion and latitude. For this reason, officials in workers' compensation disparaged "the links between psychology and a worker's performance."[149] They challenged the idea that the counselor should evaluate both the occupational problems and the nonoccupational problems. Workers' compensation separated the job from the person, whereas vocational rehabilitation did not.

Construction of Rehabilitation Centers

Switzer's strategy of promoting research and training in vocational rehabilitation was a great success. The OVR sponsored four training programs the first year with five students graduating in 1955. By 1970, there were forty programs, which trained over 800 students every year.[150] Research in the field of vocational rehabilitation also proliferated with over 2,000 references to rehabilitation between 1958 and 1968, as compared to only five articles referring to the subject from 1942 to 1950.[151] Finally, many local communities had begun building rehabilitation facilities and workshops at a rate five times faster than had been the case between 1920 and 1954. From 1954 to 1960, almost 200 rehabilitation facilities and workshops were established.[152]

What is more, the rehabilitation centers, which had been the brainchild of Rusk, Kessler, and others in the rehabilitation movement, continued to be bolstered by Switzer's grants. Rehabilitation experts at George Washington University Hospital were awarded a large research grant "to develop effective methods of dealing with the psychological and vocational adjustment problems of individuals with multiple sclerosis." Meanwhile, the Los Angeles Orthopedic Foundation received funding "to explore techniques for assessing the vocational rehabilitation potential of disabled persons based on analyses of personality factors." Rusk's own Institute of Physical Medicine, Rehabilitation at Bellevue Hospital in New York was given funds "to study the effectiveness of various medical, psychiatric, social and counseling services in the vocational rehabilitation of facially disfigured persons."[153]

The rehabilitation center remained distinct from hospitals because it relied almost solely on the team approach. A team of rehabilitation experts diagnosed, analyzed, and treated every patient with, in particular, a psychologist who "pointed out neurotic symptoms" that supposedly plagued this patient.[154] While rehabilitation counseling became its own field, experts in rehabilitation thought psychology was the most important aspect of the rehabilitation counselor's job.[155] The psychiatrist often headed the team because of the belief that the biggest obstacle confronting people with disabilities was not their physical impediments but their inability to adjust. While rehabilitation centers had a team of physicians, psychiatrists, nurses, and social scientists, it was known that those who played with the mind had the most important role on the team. As Switzer explained, "Psychiatry can . . . illuminate the need for understanding the emotional aspects of working with the disabled."[156]

Nine years after World War II ended, the rehabilitation movement's campaign to reshape the vocational rehabilitation program finally succeeded. Overall, the movement's success can be attributed to four interrelated factors:

First, Rusk's and Kessler's commitment to the whole man theory of rehabilitation never wavered.

Second, not only did the rehabilitation movement make Switzer into a governmental spokesperson for its ideals, but it could not have chosen a more effective one. Switzer played the crucial policymaking role during almost every stage of the reform effort. She worked with both the congressional policymakers and the policymakers in Eisenhower's administration, persuading them that rehabilitation centers, staffed by an inter-disciplinary team of experts, were necessary for restoring disabled people to normal lives.

Third, Switzer made the vocational rehabilitation program appealing to both Democrats and Republicans by characterizing it as neither liberal nor conservative, but rather as part of the bipartisan effort to win the Cold War. To do so, she associated vocational rehabilitation with democratization and anticommunism. Helping people develop their potential in rehabilitation centers, she maintained, brought them back into the work force where they could be productive citizens. According to Switzer, the vocational rehabilitation program gave disabled people the will and the strength to exercise their democratic rights and duties, which, in turn, strengthened the nation and made it less vulnerable to communism.

Fourth, physicians from the rehabilitation movement continued to influence the course of vocational rehabilitation by being involved with its implementation. These physicians, after all, were the ones providing care for disabled people. The vocational rehabilitation program was changed in accordance with the feedback that they provided to the bureaucrats funding the program. Meanwhile, when the Vocational Rehabilitation Act came up for periodic renewal, the physicians in the rehabilitation movement would present testimony at the congressional hearings and, more important, work with Switzer and other members on her staff drafting the legislative changes.

With Switzer describing herself as Miss Rehabilitation and referring to Rusk as Mr. Rehabilitation, or the father of rehabilitation, the ideas underlying the vocational rehabilitation program changed little until her retirement in 1970. These ideals were found in the type of research that the federal government funded and the kind of programs that received money for the education and training of rehabilitation personnel. What was most important was how it shaped cultural attitudes about the first employees who reentered the work force. Employers came to expect disabled workers to bend over backward to fit into their workplaces. One rehabilitation counselor went so far as to liken himself to a temporary employment agent who works in the interest of employers. Not quite realizing how inappropriate his behavior was, this counselor confessed to Fredric Schroeder, the commissioner of the Rehabilitation Services Administration during the William Clinton administration, that he paid such close attention to employer preferences that when an employer said no African Americans need apply, he sent only white disabled people for interviews.[157]

3

From the Whole Man to the Whole Family: Rehabilitating the Poor

Switzer and the rehabilitation movement transformed American disability policy with the passage of the Vocational Rehabilitation Act of 1954, just before the Supreme Court handed down *Brown v. Board of Education*.[1] The rehabilitation movement, however, was not part of the civil rights revolution. While the rehabilitation movement and the civil rights movement both fought against segregation, they employed vastly different strategies to achieve that end, with the former hoping to usher disabled people into mainstream society, particularly into the work force. The civil rights movement, by contrast, battled for the political and economic equality of African Americans and women by demanding their rights. It also fought for rights that the American state and society had long withheld, whereas the rehabilitation movement had never supported extending antidiscrimination employment rights to disabled people.

The rehabilitation movement did not think rights represented the primary, or even the secondary, issue for people with disabilities who worked or sought employment. Although Switzer and Rusk knew how unkind American society had been to disabled people, they thought it was vital to change the people themselves, not the society they lived in. To Switzer and Rusk, the subjective self, not the objective world, was the subject of rehabilitation. Rather than emphasizing why society was hostile to disabled people, they focused on how "these" people could stop expressing their presumed hostility against society, especially at the workplace.[2]

The rehabilitation movement and the officials implementing this policy were so satisfied with their approach that when Presidents John F. Kennedy and Lyndon B. Johnson initiated a "war on poverty," they had "the solution." Why not rehabilitate the poor? To both Switzer and Rusk, poverty was a cultural, social, and personal finance problem, not an economic and political problem. Offering their own interpretation of the so-called culture of poverty, they believed that, like people with physical or mental disabilities, the poor lacked a healthy personality with which to compensate for their cultural and social disabilities. To strengthen their "ego defenses," people in poverty needed what Switzer called "social rehabilitation."

Switzer and Rusk were not the only ones engaged in the war on poverty. The poor people's movement had been mobilized by this war also. Taking its cue from the civil rights movement, the poor people's movement made relief from poverty a right. The poor were entitled to welfare, the activists within this movement argued, because poverty was a societal, not an individual, problem, and, therefore, society owed its members relief. Meanwhile, the rehabilitation experts resisted the very concept of relief. While Switzer and Rusk led the initiative to rehabilitate the poor, which did not include making welfare an entitlement, the poverty movement fought for the rights of the poor.

By 1967, the rehabilitation movement and the poor people's movement, along with the Office of Economic Opportunity (OEO), were locked in a struggle over what direction the war on poverty should take. Neither approach—making poverty a right or socially rehabilitating the poor—succeeded: the poor people's movement realized only part of its goal of making poverty relief into a right, and Switzer and the rehabilitation movement failed to achieve their objective.

Although the campaign for social rehabilitation was a categorical failure, it demonstrated the depth of the rehabilitation experts' commitment to making disabled people accommodate society rather than having society accommodate them. This campaign revealed how little the rehabilitation movement's position against employment rights had changed from the 1940s until 1970. Rights were not spurned because the rehabilitation movement was unaccustomed to this type of orientation in the 1940s and 1950s, but because Switzer and other policymakers made a conscious decision not to pursue disability rights.

Given their perspective on rights, neither the officials overseeing the vocational rehabilitation program nor the physicians running it helped launch the disability rights movement during the heyday of the rights revolution. This movement had few allies in the federal government when it started calling for reform. What, therefore, accounts for the rights orientation of the Rehabilitation Act of 1973 cannot be attributed to the rehabilitation movement, to federal or state officials in vocational rehabilitation, or to the fledgling disability movement. The impact of Section 504—the provision establishing rights for disabled people—was unanticipated. This chapter will examine the groundwork that helped push the movement toward maturity and action.

Fighting Infantile Urges: Treating the Culturally Disadvantaged

From the 1940s through the 1960s, the doctors' commitment to rehabilitating people with disabilities, not rehabilitating the society they lived in, stayed constant.[3] The inattention that the rehabilitation experts exhibited was amply demonstrated by the activities of Switzer, while she was director of the Office of Vocational Rehabilitation (OVR). During the mid- to late-1960s, Switzer tried to extend the rehabilitation model to poor people, who were often viewed as victims of their objective circumstances.

Just as Switzer had made an association between the postwar vocational rehabilitation program and the public debate about democratization in the 1950s, in the 1960s she linked her ideas about rehabilitation to the debate about the culture of poverty.[4] This debate, which most historians credit the anthropologist Oscar Lewis with initiating, referred to a culture in an attempt to distinguish poverty from economics.[5] A culture of poverty was universal, Lewis argued, transcending regional and even national differences.[6] It was "a design for living" that children inherited from their parents.[7]

Although Switzer's ideas were still steeped in psychological and psychiatric references, she quickly picked up on this notion of the culture of poverty. But Switzer did not adopt the notion of a culture of poverty advanced by Lewis as much as the one promoted by Daniel Moynihan. For Moynihan, the culture of poverty was bred by deviancy or social pathology, which he claimed was especially virulent among African Americans.[8] Although Switzer avoided making any overt associations between poverty and African Americans, she relied on Moynihan's characterization of the culture of poverty as a mental health problem.

Switzer's position stemmed, in part, from the fact that she started her career in the federal government during President Herbert Hoover's administration. Switzer had only supported President Franklin D. Roosevelt's poverty relief programs in the 1930s with the understanding that such programs would last just as long as the Great Depression. By the 1960s, she was clearly discouraged that "welfare remained essentially a 'relief' program, despite all we have learned of the psychology of the underprivileged, despite all the social science research and demonstration projects." Switzer claimed that "welfare failed to provide real relief, it failed because . . . it told people what they could have and what they could do with it; . . . it did not involve assistance recipients in the solution of their problems; . . . it did not provide incentives toward self-development and self-help." For this reason, Switzer had shown a greater commitment to rehabilitation than to relief. "What is social rehab[ilitation]?" she asked. "Put simply: the substitution of 'rehabilitation' for 'relief.'"[9]

Always a team player, Switzer saw the Great Society as an opportunity to expand rehabilitation from serving people with physical and mental disabilities to those who had social, economic, and cultural ones. "In essence, there was a growing consensus that problems of the perennially poor and fundamentally disadvantaged," as she put it, "should be at-tacked on the same general basis as had been used for the physically and mentally handicapped."[10] Rehabilitation could offer poor people what they needed most: "special counseling to give them the motivation to up-grade their basic education, to enter work-training programs, and to help them make the adjustments necessary in the difficult transition from un-employment to regular work."[11] Like those hindered by physical and mental impairments, motivation was the biggest obstacle those in poverty faced.

Switzer's emphasis on rehabilitation indicated that she thought the poor, like disabled people, suffered more from a maladjusted perspective on life than from concrete material problems. As she saw it, rehabilitation could "treat maladjustment, underdevelopment, lethargy, antisocial be-havior, outright hostility; rebelliousness based on fear, sense of inferiority and rejection and on lack of protective framework for support through ethical, moral, religious standards and disciplines." Switzer argued that rehabilitation provided hope in that it could "restore to satisfactory living those whose hearts and minds have not yet been destroyed by poverty, by broken homes, by unequal opportunity to compete with peers." A pro-gram in vocational rehabilitation, she promised, would allow the poor "to return or redirect to the mainstream of productive citizenship." In her mind, the poor were defeated by "hopelessness, through the inability to find or accept a suitable challenge."[12]

While Switzer picked up on the literature about the culture of poverty, she never let go of the debt that rehabilitation owed to the new psychiatry "as it emerged to meet the need of World War II," which she "character-ized by its recognition that it often takes more than the physician psychia-trist to restore a patient with mental illness to his full capacity for community living."[13] Switzer thought that, similarly, people in poverty would profit from psychiatry. The primary problem of the poor, she argued, was that they lacked the personality to change their objective circumstances. Just as the physically disabled needed to be adjusted, so did the socially, culturally, and economically disadvantaged.

Another rehabilitation expert, David Malikin, put Switzer's sentiment a different way. Disabled people, this expert noted, lacked motivation and the psychological resources necessary to establish successful coping mechanisms. The internal force was generated by the socially disabled themselves, and it could be rehabilitated.[14] Using the vocabulary of a psychoanalyst, Switzer herself said that the poor were plagued by an "infantile urge to return to the anonymity and security of the womb."[15] Rehabilitation centers, Switzer contended, could rebuild the egos of the poor so they could cope with society, which in turn would give them the opportunity to rebuild their lives. "Rehabilitation principles eliminate polarization," she said, "by restoring the handicapped person to the mainstream of society."[16]

For Switzer, disabled people and people who are poor must break from the cycle of dependency that restricted their lives. "Our heightened efforts toward elimination of dependency that arises from disability serve to point the way of our emphasis for the immediate future. But the work of rehabilitation has far wider horizons. . . . Our projects," she decried, "have added to our knowledge and we are setting out on an all-out attack upon the disability dependency front."[17] Switzer went so far as to show how the team approach could help those in poverty.

Rehabilitating the socially, culturally, and economically disadvantaged or people with behavioral disabilities was first included in the Social Security Amendments of 1962. Secretary Abraham Ribicoff and Wilbur Cohen, the assistant secretary for legislation, drafted the Social Security Amendments with Switzer's notion of rehabilitation in mind. These amendments provided for the "individual identification of problems, counseling, [and] referral to other community agencies."[18] They stopped short of championing the broad social objectives, like self-support, and strengthened family life which Switzer promoted. Switzer's perspective was also manifest in the Public Welfare Amendment of 1962 and the Manpower Development and Training Act of 1962. These two pieces of legislation "stressed services in addition to support, rehabilitation instead of relief, and training for useful work instead of prolonged dependency."[19]

After she gained more institutional power in 1962 when Kennedy reorganized the Department of Health, Education and Welfare (HEW),

Switzer convinced HEW officials that a program to rehabilitate the poor should be implemented as soon as possible. She became the commissioner of the Vocational Rehabilitation Administration and, taking advantage of her new position, campaigned to include people with behavioral disabilities in vocational rehabilitation. "I have wondered many times," said Switzer, "if some of the concepts and methods of operation of the vocational rehabilitation program might not be profitably put to use in attacking some of the unemployment problems of the nondisabled as well as the disabled."[20]

Social Rehabilitation versus Rights

After Kennedy's assassination, President Johnson also made rehabilitation, rather than relief, one of the many themes of the Great Society. When the Vocational Rehabilitation Act came up for renewal in 1965, the Johnson administration sponsored amendments that provided a broader base of services than before. The vocational rehabilitation program now included those who suffered from socially handicapping conditions. Enthusiastic about how these amendments would change the face of vocational rehabilitation, Switzer characterized them as "the first major legislative change in eleven years," or since the groundbreaking passage of the 1954 legislation under the Eisenhower administration.[21]

In addition to including the socially handicapped, the Vocational Rehabilitation Act Amendments sponsored the construction of more rehabilitation facilities, doubled the vocational rehabilitation program budget, and instituted two advisory boards—the National Commission on Architectural Barriers and the National Citizens' Advisory Committee on Vocational Rehabilitation. The OVR cashed in on what one official called the federal "gold rush of 1965 and 1966."[22]

While the new emphasis in vocational rehabilitation on social disabilities was couched in terms of the Johnson administration's attempt to eradicate the culture of poverty, it provided only one means of eroding this so-called culture, whereas the Office of Economic Opportunity (OEO) presented another. To officials in the OEO, the community action provisions provided the best hope of breaking the cycle of dependency.[23] Mobilizing the community, they argued, offered the poor a sense of autonomy and entitlement that they needed.

Switzer, however, did not see eye-to-eye with the OEO on this issue. Testifying before the House Committee on Education and Labor, she insisted that there was an inherent tension among community action plans, rights, and rehabilitation.[24] Switzer applauded the vocational rehabilitation program for its contribution to poverty relief, arguing that, unlike some of the OEO's new programs, it constituted the best antipoverty program. In private, Switzer was even more critical of the men working in the OEO, referring to them disrespectfully as the "poverty boys."[25]

Switzer disapproved of the poverty boys' outlook, not just for substantive reasons but also for political reasons. She resisted the idea that community action programs should bypass the old sources of control and establish a direct relationship between the federal government and leaders in the urban ghettoes. The new Democratic administration did so because President Johnson wanted to bring in the new population to support his Great Society programs. He sought the support of a whole new set of constituents whose assistance would not disturb the Republican city and state governments in the North and the anti–civil rights groups in the South. Meanwhile, Switzer was comfortable working with the existing rehabilitation experts and social workers.[26]

Switzer had little faith in the war on poverty's emphasis on community mobilization because she distrusted the urban leaders. With their emphasis on rights, these leaders shared none of her views about the poor. Indeed, just as Switzer was developing social rehabilitation, welfare rights had become a national issue. Social workers, churchmen, lawyers, civil organizations, public welfare employees, private foundations, activist students, antipoverty employees, civil rights organizations, family agencies, settlement houses, and the poor themselves mobilized and took advantage of the war on poverty policies causing an explosion in people eligible for relief. These programs mobilized the poor by establishing new services, both public and private, that offered them information about welfare entitlements.[27] The war-on-poverty programs provided the poor with the assistance of experts to obtain the services, lawyers to initiate litigation to challenge a number of local laws and policies that kept the poor off the welfare rolls, and new organizations to advertise what entitlements existed.[28]

Although Switzer opposed community action programs and poverty rights, she was careful to distinguish these programs from the community development plans she did support. Community development provisions differed because, instead of recognizing the autonomy of their beneficiaries, they provided experts with the means to fight the "pathology of the ghetto," which professionals like Switzer and Rusk insisted provided the rationale for their paternalistic attitudes. They thought that neutral "scientific cures," like the rehabilitation of the poor, would best eradicate poverty. Experts like Rusk lent their scientific authority to what at a different time might have been perceived as political rhetoric.[29] According to Frances Fox Piven and Richard Cloward, scientific references had been included in the war on poverty to reassure white liberals that the crisis in urban areas revolved not around the issue of rights but around welfare dependency.

Institutional Changes in Rehabilitation

Throughout the mid- to late-1960s, the rights approach versus the rehabilitation approach to the war on poverty came into conflict. By 1967, however, social rehabilitation began to gain ground since it could not be blamed for the eruption of inner-city violence and urban strife that was plaguing the nation.[30] Switzer herself thought that some programs within the war on poverty had contributed to this strife. Just as she never associated rehabilitation with rights, so Switzer never thought welfare should be considered a right or an entitlement. In fact, one of the mainstays of the poor people's movement—that the poor should have legal representation —Switzer considered absurd. For people on welfare to demand "the right to have a lawyer," she proclaimed, "was ridiculous."[31]

Switzer was so dedicated to making her vision happen that from 1965 until her retirement in 1970 she grabbed every chance to expand and enlarge the definition of disability, including rehabilitating people with behavioral problems and also the poor. One of her greatest opportunities for change came when John Gardner became the secretary of HEW shortly after the Vocational Rehabilitation Act Amendments and the OEO passed Congress in 1965.[32] While Gardner initially devoted his energy to educational reforms, by 1966 and 1967 he began reexamining welfare and concluded that Switzer was on to something about rehabilitating the poor.[33]

Gardner began tackling the issue of welfare when he sensed that by early 1967 the war on poverty was in trouble. From 1966 to 1967, the number of welfare recipients increased from 7.8 million to 8.4 million, and both Republicans and Democrats charged that the OEO was responsible for this dramatic increase.[34] As a reporter for *Time* magazine described, "The welfare colossus has lately received its most telling blows from liberals, who accuse it of subverting the people it is supposed to sustain."[35] Part of the frustration, these liberals charged, stemmed from the fact that the Office of Legal Services in the OEO had been so effective in counseling the poor about their rights it had made them militant. Conservatives and liberals alike thought that inner-city riots, "from Harlem to Hough, Chicago to Cincinnati, Boston to Buffalo," had been ignited by the failed promises of the war on poverty.[36] As Theodore Lowi, a political scientist, explained, "Unprecedented generosity—as measured by transfers, cash grants, and assistance-in-kind—had not made much of a dent in the poverty, dependence, delinquency, or despair against which the 1964 war had been declared."[37]

For Gardner, a reexamination of welfare represented the best means of helping the war on poverty change direction. Like Moynihan and Switzer, Gardner dismissed the idea of welfare rights and wanted to feature programs that could diminish the mental health aspects of the culture of poverty.[38] Gardner underscored that "the Negro family in the urban ghettoes [was] crumbling."

Gardner also gave the expert a significant part to play in the restorative process. Gardner joined Switzer and her colleagues in expressing a renewed faith in the role of the expert that had been accentuated during the first years of the war on poverty. They argued that rehabilitation experts could rehabilitate the poor.[39] Gardner and Switzer were not the first to express this faith in experts in the 1960s. On one of its covers in 1967, *Time* magazine featured what it called "the new poverty expert"—the "urbanologist." In the lead article, a reporter proclaimed that a "new scientific diagnostician has been born" who could help end urban strife and poverty.[40]

Whether it was to be achieved by the rehabilitation expert or the urbanologist, Gardner, Switzer, and other white liberals favored reducing dependency, not by providing the poor with rights but by changing their attitudes. In Gardner's mind, the poverty rights movement had contributed to the dramatic swelling of people on the welfare rolls, yet increasing the number of people on welfare would not help get rid of poverty. It would only make poor people dependent on a governmental program.

Knowing how Gardner's position regarding poverty resembled Switzer's, one of Switzer's aides, James Garrett, urged her to take advantage of this opportunity by placing Social Security payments, welfare, and aging programs under the jurisdiction of the rehabilitation program. "It was well and good to think of the Vocational Rehabilitation Administration—David using his meager sling shot of pressures to slay the Health or Education—Goliath," he said, " . . . but our total program could compete more equitably in an Individual and Family Services army than it could in Health or Education."[41]

Switzer followed Garrett's advice and made a pitch for the program, telling Gardner that they should "attack the problem of public assistance, or dependency, with the rehabilitation approach." As Switzer explained, her office could "embark on large-scale programs to serve the socially and educationally and economically disadvantaged, because vocational re-habilitation had demonstrated its effectiveness in serving disabled citizens."[42]

Gardner reacted enthusiastically to Switzer's suggestions, asking her to draft a report about the new opportunities that the Vocational Rehabilitation Act Amendment of 1965 could provide the poor.[43] Pleased by the secretary's response, Switzer said, "I look upon our new legislation as both a door to a new horizon and a revolutionary thread running through all that we do."[44]

One of the contributions that Switzer brought to social rehabilitation was the rehabilitation counselor. Just as this counselor had been important for rehabilitating disabled people, so Switzer thought the rehabilitation counselor was "the instrument for focusing the talents of many different specialties upon the unique problems of one [socially] disabled person to gain a full understanding of the obstacles to be overcome and to make the disabled person an active partner in the process of building his own future."[45]

Switzer was so eager to implement her plans for social rehabilitation that, even before the Vocational Rehabilitation Act Amendments of 1965 were enacted, she suggested that the state vocational rehabilitation programs start rehabilitating the poor. "I don't think there is a more urgent job facing state vocational rehabilitation programs today," Switzer wrote to all the state directors, "than attempting to help people out of poverty.... For many welfare clients, vocational rehabilitation is the last hope they have for a better life.... We can't ignore them and feel that vocational rehabilitation is achieving its full potential."[46]

Switzer also rallied support from her usual backers, including Rusk. In fact, Rusk had gone on record in favor of social rehabilitation, even lobbying for it until Switzer's retirement in 1970.[47] Upon Switzer's urging, the National Rehabilitation Association (NRA) also voiced its support for the idea of social rehabilitation.

Like Switzer, Gardner, and Rusk, many rehabilitation experts professed that poverty had more to do with a maladjusted personality than with objective conditions. Lee Rainwater, for instance, contended that the main component of poverty is a "maiming of personality."[48] Another expert, Walter Neff, constructed the argument that the poor suffered from a weak work personality, distinguishable from the individual personality. A weak work personality, he concluded, meant that a person lacked the right attitude as well as the aptitude for work.[49]

To be sure, not all rehabilitation experts agreed with Rainwater, Harrington, and Neff. Joseph Kunce and Corrine Cope had a more moderate argument: although there did not "appear to be a personality of poverty, some psychological attributes associated with the role of disadvantage-ment stand out . . . [including] . . . pervasive negative and self-defeating attitudes toward achievement; and higher incidences of maladaptive be-haviors such as passivity, crime, and emotional disturbance."[50]

Other rehabilitation experts were wary of treating people in poverty; these experts focused more on the practical problems associated with so-cial rehabilitation. The rehabilitation experts were concerned that the poor, who they characterized as ungrateful and antagonistic, would be un-receptive to their help. As one rehabilitation expert said, the socially, culturally, and economically disadvantaged would reject the verbal, prob-lem-solving counseling approach, whereas those with physical and mental disabilities did not. "Overwhelmed by the struggles of survival, they shrug aside 'empty' words and seek actions," this expert related, "that might produce favorable and alleviating changes in their everyday lives." This type of client, the expert maintained, had a pessimistic outlook on life compared to those with physical and mental disabilities, who the coun-selor could presumably fill with optimism.[51]

The attitude of the rehabilitation experts about the difference between disabled people and those in poverty left out one important detail. Over the years, rehabilitation experts had had a good deal of control over their environment by being highly selective about who they served. Vocational rehabilitation counselors accepted just 1 percent of all disabled people into their programs. Most applicants were rejected for two reasons.[52] First, counselors took part in the practice called "creaming," that is, they chose people with the most moderate impairments, thinking they stood the greatest likelihood of success. Second, candidates for rehabilitation were rejected if they did not exhibit the "proper attitude"—meaning that they were not highly motivated, cooperative, or appreciative.

Building a Rehabilitation Empire

Undaunted by these potential problems, Gardner, Switzer, and Rusk viewed rehabilitating the poor as a rewarding challenge. Gardner agreed with Switzer's and Rusk's assessment that vocational rehabilitation was a great program, calling it the best of all the "so-called helping professions." He added, "The idea of expanding our operation to assist with the culturally, educationally, or socially deprived appears to have real merit." To him, this merit stemmed from the fact that "social rehabilitation proposes to use these same tools to help people to improve the quality of their lives and to do their own part, along with professional assistance, to begin the climb up out of poverty." Gardner "chose REHABILITATION as the most desirable method to influence change in public welfare."[53]

Gardner was still exploring the idea of social rehabilitation in May of 1967, when he instructed Dr. Worth Bateman to tell Switzer that she should begin thinking about how the poor could participate in sheltered workshops originally designed to employ disabled people. Shortly thereafter, Switzer sat down with William Gorham, Dr. Alice Rivlin, and Bateman, senior HEW officials, to discuss more comprehensive legislative proposals.[54] "There should be available a residual public employment program for those severely disadvantaged persons among the poor," she said, "who are not able to perform as a member of the regular labor force."[55]

Switzer convinced these officials from Gardner's office that her office should oversee this program. The "Vocational Rehabilitation Administration has an excellent image with respect to our experience in and support of workshops. We have a good program in our workshops and should not proceed too fast in expanding so as to degrade what we have." Bateman agreed with Switzer, both about the concept of rehabilitation and about the idea that social rehabilitation should be housed within the Vocational Rehabilitation Administration. "He considers that these individuals could be regarded as having a type of disability," said Switzer, "and come within the scope of the vocational rehabilitation program."[56]

Sigmund Schor, head of the Division of Statistics and Studies in the OVR, and Bateman concurred with Switzer that the psychological problems of the poor, not the environmental or material ones that plagued them, were the most serious. They compared the potential of social rehabilitation with the job-training programs provided by the Economic Development Act. To them, the Economic Development Act had not succeeded because it provided "little more than [what] WPA provided in the 1930s." What the poor needed, they reasoned, was not just a program that accepted the environmental conditions of poverty but one that addressed the psychological reasons. The "Happy Pappy" program in eastern Kentucky, created under the Vocational Rehabilitation Act (VRA), was ideally suited because it had "income maintenance, counselors, vocational education, and other facilities which some of these major community programs require."[57]

After these preliminary discussions, Switzer launched a campaign to transform the OVR. Gardner responded by not only "plac[ing] the concept of rehabilitation at the very heart of the new agency" but also by modifying the entire HEW as an organization.[58]

Originally, HEW had been designed so that there would be little room for empire building. Unlike personnel in most other executive departments, assistant secretaries in HEW had difficulty creating constituencies for themselves. Aside from the secretary for health and medicine, HEW had only a secretary for legislation and federal-state relations. While assistant secretaries in other departments worked with specific constituencies, HEW assistant secretaries did not.

This arrangement had been set up by the Eisenhower administration at the behest of the American Medical Association (AMA). Members of the AMA worried that if officials in HEW cultivated their own constituencies, it might jeopardize their position of influence. The AMA, therefore, championed Eisenhower's reorganization plan with the proviso that governmental involvement in health issues would not imperil the autonomy of its organization. The creation of the Social Rehabilitation Service (SRS) in 1967 changed all this. Gardner reorganized the department so that each division—health, education, and welfare—had a separate secretary.[59]

For the OVR, the first part of the transformation was reflected not only in its new name, but also in the fact that it wrapped into a single agency all the major federal programs geared to improve the comprehensiveness of social and rehabilitation services.[60] Vocational rehabilitation services for those on welfare, as well as for the aged, were combined under one roof. As explained earlier, this new service provided "a unified approach to the problems of needy Americans, with special emphasis on the family, and at the same time to assure continued special emphasis upon servicing the aged, the handicapped, and children." This unified approach was created, as a reporter for *Time* described, to "better coordinate the programs" in HEW, since the war on poverty had "spawned a vast, ever-growing nexus of federal programs and agencies designed to help the poor."[61]

The structural transformation of HEW occurred because the whole notion of "welfare is undergoing reassessment," the *Time* reporter noted. According to him, Switzer was "first to admit the shortcomings of the present system."[62] For this reason, the Social and Rehabilitation Service "placed a rehabilitation philosophy in all the programs that serve those who cannot achieve their rightful place in our society without some assistance." Or, as Secretary Gardner elaborated, the purpose of social rehabilitation "is to foster the strengths and capabilities that enable individuals to function as free and responsible citizens."[63]

Along with Secretary Gardner, Switzer had played the most critical role in the creation of the SRS. She had masterminded the idea behind social rehabilitation and also mobilized support for it in Congress. In Switzer's mind, the head of the SRS would oversee an empire, particularly since this person would also have "the budget of an empire." The most telling sign of its expansion was that the budget increased more than eighteen-fold, from 300 million to 6 billion.[64] Although there was no guarantee that Switzer would lead this empire, Gardner, being so pleased with her work, gave her the position.[65]

From the Whole Man to the Whole Family

On August 15, 1967, Switzer became the head of the SRS, undertaking her new position with great enthusiasm and the "deep conviction" that rehabilitation could help the poor solve "the welfare problem."[66] Gardner predicted that Switzer would "make history for all of us." Switzer also had great expectations, which she communicated by proclaiming that "we stand or fall together."[67]

Switzer applied the rehabilitation idea in its entirety to poverty relief, albeit with some modifications. Instead of emphasizing the whole man theory, she now developed what could be called the "whole family theory." That is, the SRS oversaw programs with the intent of rehabilitating the entire family.[68] As Switzer explicated, "[I]ndividuals suggesting such a concept believe that we can't solve the plight of the average family working in poverty by helping only the wage earner. It was suggested that a family rehabilitation center or workshop be considered." By undergoing rehabilitation, "a wage earner might learn a trade; women might learn to cook, care for children, and perform properly other family work. . . . Recreation, education, medical service, or other family needs might be supplied during the training period for the entire family."[69] A second effort was to eradicate illegitimacy and improve family planning.[70]

In 1967, the SRS also helped the Labor Department formulate the Work Incentive Program (WIN), which sought to make the poor employable.[71] This program, which was administered by the Labor Department, compelled the states to establish community work and training programs in hopes of decreasing the number of people on welfare. The Work Incentive Program was initially called WIP; the acronym was changed to WIN to prevent possible detractors from making light of it. WIN required fathers, mothers, and some older children to register for work with a state employment service and be active in job searches or training programs.[72] In particular, the program was designed to make it profitable for mothers to work.[73]

With a 1-billion-dollar budget, WIN could not be described as a small program. Switzer herself thought it would become a great success, proclaiming that it "should have 100,000 of these clients placed in full employment, increasing to 500,000 by 1974." Switzer also thought the program might provide her with another venue for practicing social rehabilitation. It was "more important for our immediate consideration," she said, "that public discussion and knowledge of what rehabilitation had accomplished might be extended to reach other millions, people who were not victims of precise physical or mental disability, but who were handicapped at least as seriously by social, educational, cultural, economic, and other limitations."[74]

Trying to Mobilize the Community

Despite all of Switzer's hopes and expectations, her plans for social rehabilitation were not well received. According to her biographer, the press quoted Switzer as saying that "welfare head calls program a disgrace."[75] In an article for *Time* magazine, a reporter characterized Switzer's answer to welfare programs as more work. Switzer's notion of social rehabilitation was vilified by the press.

The following year, 1968, proved even more trying for Switzer and thwarted her plans to rehabilitate the poor. By early spring, when Lyndon Johnson announced that he would not seek a second term, it became apparent to Switzer how little time she had to make social rehabilitation a viable policy program.[76] Despite the initial lack of public enthusiasm for social rehabilitation, Switzer continued publicizing the ideals behind it, increasing her number of speaking engagements to a frantic pace.[77]

Just as she had done with the rehabilitation story in the 1950s, Switzer brought the welfare dependency story to the public. "[I]t seems to me," Switzer claimed, that "we have an even greater inspiration to apply what we have so successfully done in the conventional rehabilitation program." Trying to mobilize support, she said that "it would be an impressive demonstration that there is within our possibility the will and the skill to break this cycle of dependency for vast numbers, particularly for our black migrants from the south who have come out of their communities because of a loss of opportunity, or a lack of education, or a desire to find a better way of life for themselves and their children."[78]

Switzer's efforts were frustrated, however, by the riots that erupted again in the summer of 1968, which produced more violence and chaos in many inner cities and put the war on poverty on the defensive. Switzer also met her match when she faced the demonstration staged by the poor people's movement. On June 19, 1968, Reverend Ralph Abernathy, a civil rights leader, led what was considered Reverend Martin Luther King Jr.'s last, posthumous enterprise—a march in Washington, D.C., for poor people's rights.[79] Over 55,000 people turned out for the march, including groups that referred to themselves as the "Sisters of Watts" and the "Concerned Citizens from the Slippery Slope." After the march, a small group of people decided not to leave the capitol until the federal government changed its policy, setting up camp next to the Lincoln Memorial in what they called "Resurrection City."

Switzer herself came face-to-face with the leaders of Resurrection City when they stormed into HEW with a long list of demands. Although she took their demands seriously and wrote a thirty-four-page response, Switzer never changed her position about rights for people in poverty or with disabilities. She vehemently opposed the rights orientation to these issues.

Switzer faulted the government for the mobilization of the poor people's movement because, as she explained it, programs within the war on poverty had helped promote the new emphasis on rights. Switzer was not alone in her assessment that the OEO had facilitated the growth of the poor people's movement by creating welfare rights services. By 1968, more than 100,000 professionals and community residents had been hired. Welfare rights litigation also increased the number of applicants for welfare, the OEO spent 85 million dollars providing these legal services.[80] Those receiving welfare were now awarded all the rights and privileges that other citizens enjoyed, no longer having to waive privacy rights, the right to travel, or family autonomy to be eligible for welfare.[81]

Switzer and the SRS realized that the poverty movement's victory to change welfare residency laws "will have a tremendous impact on practically all social and rehabilitative programs throughout the nation."[82] Most important, the poor people's movement argued that poverty was caused by social forces outside the realm of the individual's control. Indeed, legal activists relied on the Fourteenth Amendment to fight to make welfare a right or entitlement.[83] Society, therefore, had an obligation to support these rights.[84]

The OEO fostered welfare rights and facilitated the spirit behind the rights revolution. Meanwhile, the welfare advocates thought that the SRS, with its ideas of rehabilitating the poor, was hopelessly outdated. The poor people's movement laid the blame on society, whereas social rehabilitation put it on the people themselves. Switzer and the rehabilitation experts rejected this approach for welfare and rehabilitation, opposing the notion of client rights. To them, rehabilitation experts must retain their expertise in judging the physically, mentally, socially, economically, or culturally disadvantaged. Discretion was essential. Rehabilitation experts screened out 90 percent of the 10 percent that Social Security sent them. In large part, this could be attributed to the fact that they would accept those with the least debilitating impairments as a means of ensuring that the vocational rehabilitation program maintained its high success rates. At the same time, however, they emphasized the importance of attitude and authority. If patients did not have the right attitude, rehabilitation counselors must wield their authority and deny them services.

While Switzer would not take urban leaders seriously, she did try to bridge the gap between the advocates of rehabilitation and the advocates of rights by bringing experts—social workers and rehabilitation experts —together in a series of conferences. Switzer's efforts, however, went for naught. One conference, for example, showed just how far apart these two fields were, as sixty groups from the public, private, and consumer sectors met to discuss social and economic disabilities.[85] The SRS had sponsored conferences on this subject before, but this one was planned carefully to avoid the usual problems that social workers in welfare and rehabilitation experts encountered. Rusk, who served as the general chairman of this conference, with Switzer herself as a cochair, scheduled no speeches. Instead, they relied on informal presentations and films to portray the needs of people in poverty and with disabilities. Then, the participants were to talk out their differences and come to an understanding about social rehabilitation.

This conference was intended to bridge the gap between the welfare social workers, who knew little about rehabilitation, and the rehabilitation providers, many of whom had never become familiar with the problems associated with poverty. The rehabilitation experts thought those dealing with poverty were "too militant."[86] Being unaccustomed to the bitterness of the minority groups, they were offended by the social workers' behavior. The sentiment of the rehabilitation experts was not entirely genuine, however, since patients who were not grateful probably had been denied rehabilitation. The difference between the rehabilitation experts and the social workers also could be attributed to the power that the former expected to wield. If persons with a physical or mental disability lacked a "positive" attitude, they could not be treated. This fundamental difference about treatment could not be bridged by any conference that simply brought together social workers and rehabilitation experts.

Not surprisingly, the conference was no more successful than Switzer's attempts to bring her notion of social rehabilitation to the press or the public. Switzer knew, moreover, that the "big gulf between the administrators of public welfare and the restrictions is a frightening one. . . . The thing that has really happened in describing Resurrection City and so on that differentiates welfare in the 1960's from the 50's and 40's is the legitimation of the concept of client power, a different position of the client vis-à-vis the services which he's receiving."[87]

By early 1969, it was apparent that Switzer's attempts to build a constituency or a coalition in support of social rehabilitation had failed. Both the poor people's movement and the social workers who worked with the poor opposed social rehabilitation. Neither could accept the view underlying social rehabilitation that professed the poor were not just lacking funds, but that the condition of their lives showed that they were inferior.

Before Switzer could finish the battle over social rehabilitation, President Richard M. Nixon took office. Rather than supporting her side or taking that of the welfare rights advocates, Nixon added yet another dimension to the debate about rehabilitation, planning to scale down both its vision and scope. To Switzer, this new dimension meant that her retirement was imminent and that there was little she could do to persuade members of the new administration about the value of social rehabilitation.

Under the Nixon administration, HEW was to become an entirely different type of department. It forged a new path that could be distinguished both from the welfare rights advocates and from the old epistemic community with its patronizing attitude. This path reflected Nixon's position that money, not rights or the advice of psychologists and social workers, pulled someone out of poverty. Nixon thought that the poor could be motivated or rehabilitated as they furthered their rational economic interests with money.

Beginning in 1969, Switzer had nowhere to turn for support. Social rehabilitation had alienated the liberal community, and now she discovered that it no longer appealed to the new conservative community. Nixon's administration of New Federalism would share little with Eisenhower's administration of welfare capitalism, which became apparent immediately when the new president proposed that the SRS be abolished.

It was the task of Secretary Robert Finch, who replaced Secretary Cohen on January 22, 1969, to create a plan that would replace the SRS.

Once this task was accomplished, Switzer was asked to step down. This time, Howard Rusk could not help her keep her position, and in February 1970 Switzer retired.[88]

With her retirement, the rehabilitation movement ended.[89] As Herbert Rusalem, a rehabilitation expert, expressed it, the pioneer days of rehabilitation were over.[90] Physicians in the rehabilitation movement still controlled the rehabilitation center, but the movement lost its vitality. What is more, social rehabilitation, one of the grand schemes associated with the Great Society, had failed.

Ironically, the failure of social rehabilitation would mean more to rehabilitation than to the poverty movement, because this movement showed disabled people that rights could be extended, not simply to African Americans and women but to all those disadvantaged in society. Although a fledgling disability rights movement was organized in the late 1960s, just as Switzer was launching social rehabilitation, this movement had little impact on the formation of disability policy, particularly the policy about vocational rehabilitation, until after the passage of the Rehabilitation Act of 1973. At that time, more and more disabled people began looking for help by turning outward, not inward as the rehabilitation movement had long advocated, launching a full-scale disability rights movement.

4

An Accident of History:
Rights and the Passage
of the Rehabilitation Act

Switzer's death in 1970 marked the end of rehabilitation and the rehabilitation movement.[1] In addition, the vocational rehabilitation program lost its emphasis on disabled people themselves and began to explore the societal determinants of discrimination. If employers were reluctant to hire disabled people, what was the point of throwing money at vocational rehabilitation?

What accounted for this fresh approach to vocational rehabilitation was the new spirit about rights. By the 1970s, few social problems were cast in individual or subjective terms.[2] It was no longer thought, as Switzer once expressed, that "a society, if you please is no healthier, no happier than its individual citizens."[3] In 1973, when the Rehabilitation Act was passed despite the Nixon administration's opposition, the old vocational rehabilitation program was reinvigorated with a new perspective on rights. As one policy expert observed, "Future historians of American social policy will look back to 1973 as a year which separates one epoch of disability policy from another."[4]

Although the fledgling disability rights movement had begun to demand rights, it did not mastermind this legislative transformation. The rights orientation, which was embodied by Section 504, was an unanticipated consequence of the passage of the Rehabilitation Act of 1973. Legislative aides working for Senators Alan Cranston and Harrison Williams, among others, included this section during the last stage of the policymaking process, and, surprisingly, it almost went unnoticed.

Nonetheless, the moment the rehabilitation bill became law, the disability rights movement recognized the significance of Section 504. Activists used Section 504 to advance their movement's fundamental principle that societal attitudes obstructed disabled people, not their physical or mental impairments. This section helped build and bolster the movement, giving it the legal ammunition to wage a full-fledged attack on the psychoanalytic approach underlying the postwar vocational rehabilitation program.

The first struggle the disability rights movement undertook was with the rehabilitation experts. Although the rehabilitation movement had lost its vibrancy by 1970, the antirights emphasis it had inculcated from the 1940s onward lived on in the Department of Health, Education and Welfare (HEW), particularly in the Social and Rehabilitation Service (SRS) that housed the vocational rehabilitation program. The antirights legacy became evident when Section 504 and other rights provisions in the Rehabilitation Act were penned. For the first time, neither the federal bureaucrats nor rehabilitation experts took interest in helping to shape the new disability policy.

The SRS officials maintained their earlier position despite Switzer's retirement and unexpected death. To these officials, disabled people were patients, whereas the disability rights movement emulated the poor people's movement and the civil rights community by insisting that they were clients who had a right to rehabilitation. Meanwhile, rehabilitation experts were still comfortable in their old epistemic community, championing the values and beliefs that Rusk, Kessler, and the Menningers had formulated in the 1940s, which the disability rights activists now perceived as demeaning toward disabled people.

Throughout the 1970s, the disability rights movement, the SRS officials, and what was left of the rehabilitation movement would lock horns. While the disability rights movement had the benefit of having the momentum of a new movement, the fact that its members had not helped shape Section 504 of the Rehabilitation Act would be to its detriment. When it came time to enforce this antidiscrimination provision, the movement encountered resistance from the Nixon, Ford, *and* Carter administrations.

Unlike the rehabilitation movement's campaign for the whole man theory of rehabilitation during the 1950s, the disability rights movement lacked any governmental spokesperson who championed its cause. None of the officials who ran the vocational rehabilitation program during the Nixon, Ford, or Carter administrations advanced the new rights orientation as Switzer had promoted the psychoanalytical orientation. Without federal bureaucrats, either political appointees or senior executive civil servants, pushing for a strong antidiscrimination perspective, the rights provisions in the Rehabilitation Act remained vague and were open to manipulation during their implementation.

Nowhere was the manipulation of the rights perspective more conspicuous than in the federal courts. Despite the overwhelming bipartisan majorities that rehabilitation programs received, Congress left the enforcement of Section 504 up to the federal courts. Instead of building a new administrative agency, like the National Labor Relations Board, or using an existing agency, such as the Equal Employment Opportunity Commission (EEOC), Congress decided that Section 504 could be enforced with litigation. The federal courts, however, could not be described as strong proponents of promoting disability rights, particularly in the workplace. Hence, while the Rehabilitation Act of 1973 represented a significant departure from the vocational rehabilitation program founded in the 1950s, it did not wipe out the prevailing prejudices against disabled people that the first program had helped inculcate.

First Attempts at Rights

Neither the rehabilitation movement nor Switzer's SRS helped mobilize the disability rights movement. This movement, while being a product of the 1960s, did not fully mature until the 1970s. The disability rights movement was developed after other rights movements, in part because of the interference of the rehabilitation movement. Unlike the civil rights movement, the rehabilitation movement was not a social movement since it was composed of professionals who treated disabled people. Although Rusk first developed the term "independent living," and the rehabilitation movement had long fought to release people with disabilities from institutions, physicians in the movement still held patronizing attitudes about them. This attitude influenced not only disabled people but also their families, who represented their primary source of emotional support, and it did not engender the spirit of outrage that usually accompanies group mobilization.

The disability rights movement also had difficulty organizing because people with disabilities shared no common social position and had little reason to interact with each other socially. People with physical and mental disabilities often deliberately distanced themselves from those who shared the same problems. The disability rights movement, therefore, unfolded slowly over the course of the 1960s and 1970s, coming into its own in the wake of black power, feminism, and other movements that not only fought for rights but bolstered the self-image of their members.[5] The first fight that engaged the disability rights movement was against the caregivers of people with severe disabilities. In the mid-1960s, Edward Roberts started the movement, eventually founding the Center for Independent Living (CIL) in Berkeley, California, in 1972. Roberts and other students from Berkeley who became active in the movement fought for the self-determination of people with disabilities and made it into a coherent philosophy of self-determination.

Roberts's disability rights movement challenged the fundamental principles behind the psychoanalytical approach. Rejecting custodial help in favor of innovative self-help groups, the disability rights movement concluded that disabled people had a better understanding of what they needed for daily living than all the doctors, physical therapists, and rehabilitation counselors combined.[6] Echoing the views of the poor people's movement in the 1960s, the disability rights movement advocated that people with disabilities were "clients" who had the right to determine their own treatment. Hence, this movement demoted the caregivers in rehabilitation from experts to program managers.

Forced to fight first for autonomy over their minds and bodies, the disability rights movement started by Roberts paid scant attention to employment rights.[7] Similarly, the disability law projects that sprang up across the country concentrated on providing basic needs for people with disabilities. The Public Interest Law Center of Philadelphia, for instance, worked on deinstitutionalization, the right to treatment, and education before it tackled employment rights.[8]

In 1971, the disability rights movement won its first victory when a federal court judge, Frank Johnson, limited the indiscriminate institutionalization of people with mental disabilities, offering them the "right to treatment."[9] Johnson ruled that patients involuntarily committed to an institution had been denied their constitutional rights to "receive such individual treatment as [would] give each of them a realistic opportunity to be cured or to improve his or her mental condition."[10] The opinion Johnson wrote established the doctrine of the "least restrictive setting," which was based on the equal protection clause of the Fourteenth Amendment.[11]

Shortly after Johnson's opinion, another federal court rendered a decision which found that disabled people could not be warehoused in institutions that had "inhumane conditions."[12] Together, these decisions established the trend that people with mental disabilities deserved medical treatment, not just custodial care.[13] What constituted this treatment, however, was still undefined.

While some disability law projects fought for this basic right, others fought for guaranteeing children with disabilities a public education. Even after the passage of the Education for All Handicapped Children Act of 1975, almost one-third of all children with disabilities were still denied a public education.[14] This situation existed, in part, because it was not until 1969 that a federal court ruled that disabled children had the right to attend public school.[15]

Another federal court carried this principle one step further, holding that the state owed children with mental disabilities an "appropriate" program of education and training under equal protection of the laws. Disabled children could no longer be excluded on the grounds that they were less than the mental age of five. Professionals persuaded the court that the idea that children with mental disabilities were "unable to profit" was spurious. The federal court heeded what became known as the "zero reject concept," which stipulated that everybody, including children with mental disabilities, had the capacity to learn.[16]

Still another federal court shored up the zero reject concept when Judge J. Skelly Wright ruled that denying children with disabilities a public education violated their right to equal protection and due process under the Fourteenth Amendment.[17] Ironically, the attorneys for this disability law project made a decision that had furthered the rights of the poor people's movement, the centerpiece of the project's case.[18] Applying the same rationale about rights, the lawyers representing the disabled children argued that the local school board denied their right to due process under the Fourteenth Amendment by excluding them from publicly supported education and training.[19] Cost, the federal court judge ruled, was not a justifiable reason for denying a student an education.[20]

This decision carried the same weight for disabled children that *Brown v. Board of Education* carried for African American children, at least until it reached the Supreme Court which, to the dismay of disability activists, overturned it.[21] Following the precedent it set in *San Antonio v. Rodriguez,* the Court refused to acknowledge that children, with or without disabilities, had a right to public education.[22] No one, the Court had decided, had a fundamental right to public education. Having established this principle, the Court did help the children in Pennsylvania on the grounds that they had been arbitrarily labeled. While children with disabilities had no constitutionally guaranteed rights, they did benefit from public education and, therefore, could not be deprived of it.[23] Although the disability rights movement celebrated its victory about the zero-reject principle, the Court's position about rights would continue to haunt it.

Rights and Rehabilitation

The public interest law firms helped advance the disability rights movement by capitalizing on the judges' rulings and the experts' testimony, which reflected a new attitude about people with mental and physical disabilities.[24] Without the zero-reject concept, lawyers could never have claimed that children with physical and mental disabilities had been victims of discrimination. This principle undergirded the most basic precept of equal protection by demonstrating that *all* children profit from education. These cases represented a benchmark, not just for public education but for disabled people in all settings, establishing a new tone about disability that was present when Congress initiated the proceedings to renew the VRA.

Instituting rights for people with disabilities had not been Congress's intent when Section 504 was introduced. The legislation, however, had come before Congress simply because the funding for the vocational rehabilitation program was up for renewal. What was telling was that the most significant provision—Section 504—was not proposed by either the public law firms engaged in disability rights or any other members of the disability rights movement. While the fledgling disability rights movement championed "equal rights for the disabled," it had no hand in drafting this section.[25] Nor did it provide the initiative for this employment rights provision. In fact, most disability activists did not perceive the significance of Section 504 until shortly after its passage.

Activists, however, did influence another aspect of the rehabilitation bill. Participating in the disability rights movement founded by CIL, they convinced Congress to abandon the paternalistic position that rehabilitation experts took. They challenged the authority that the vocational rehabilitation counselors wielded over them. Hence, in the first rehabilitation bill a new relationship between the client and the counselor was proposed. The bill provided that the client be involved in the "design and delivery of vocational rehabilitation services." An "individualized" written rehabilitation program was required that would be developed "jointly by the rehabilitation counselor and the handicapped individual."[26] Although the final bill did not include these provisions, it set the agenda for future amendments that would.

The disability activists had their position shored up by the general political climate in the early 1970s. The politics behind the passage of rehabilitation legislation represented not just the rights revolution but also the shift from the Great Society to New Federalism. Waging a battle against

Richard Nixon's New Federalism reform program, the Democratic Congress was no longer prepared to spend money on large "do good" programs like those in the Great Society. The debate about funding rehabilitation revolved around the issue of federal versus state spending and the cost-cutting device that captured the spirit of the 1970s cost-benefit analysis. The legislative debate also became a means of thwarting Nixon's attempt to decrease federal spending on all social programs.[27]

While the Democrats led the campaign for maintaining a strong rehabilitation program, the Nixon administration took a completely different path toward privatization. Thinking that Nixon's plan would not have public support, someone in HEW leaked an internal memorandum exposing it. As Herbert Rusalem, a rehabilitation expert, explained, this memorandum indicated that the Nixon administration "recommended that the painstakingly developed, professionally staffed Federal-State Vocational Rehabilitation Program be replaced with a system of grants, which people with disabilities could use to purchase local rehabilitation services."[28] The Nixon administration wanted to give people with disabilities vouchers for vocational rehabilitation.

Thus, the SRS officials were attacked from both sides: disability rights activists demanded independent living, eroding the power of rehabilitation experts, whereas Nixon wanted to dismantle the institution that housed these experts. The Nixon administration's idea about vouchers reflected the president's personal disdain for social workers. Nixon himself "abhorred snoopy, patronizing surveillance by social workers which made children and adults on welfare feel stigmatized and separate. . . . What the poor needed to help them rise out of poverty," Nixon said, "is money."[29]

The Nixon administration was ready to forge a fresh path for vocational rehabilitation, making vouchers—not rights and not social rehabilitation—the heart of the new program. Quite simply, Nixon insisted that the poor could be motivated or rehabilitated as they furthered their rational economic interests with money. This, more than counseling, would help them alter their "unproductive and immoral lifestyles."[30]

Dismayed by the Nixon administration's attack on vocational rehabilitation, the subcommittee members responsible for the legislation challenged his attempt to privatize the program. By so doing, they also interjected the issues of rights and employment discrimination for the first time. Despite their conscious attempts to defeat Nixon, however, these members included Section 504 without any forethought or fanfare. They would only later become aware of its import.

The Closed Doors of the Civil Rights Movement

In 1971 and 1972, Senator Hubert Humphrey, a Democrat from Minnesota, and Representative Charles Vanik, a Democrat from Ohio, proposed that the Civil Rights Act of 1964 be amended to include disability.[31] Vanik initially introduced legislation in December of 1971 to amend Title VI, which prohibited discrimination in federally assisted programs, by simply adding physical and mental health to the grounds for discrimination.[32] Vanik also brought a separate piece of legislation before the House to amend Title VII of the Civil Rights Act to end employment discrimination against disabled people.

Sixty members of the House were listed as cosponsors of Vanik's legislation. Humphrey and Senator Charles Percy, a Republican from Illinois, introduced legislation to this end that twenty other members of the Senate cosponsored.[33] Despite this tremendous show of support for antidiscrimination rehabilitation legislation, no hearings were held in 1972.

The lack of legislative momentum came not so much from Congress as it did from the civil rights community. Civil rights leaders feared that amending the Civil Rights Act could weaken its protection of women and minorities. The civil rights community was also afraid of associating civil rights with disability rights; it was concerned that providing for disabled people would be costly, whereas the antidiscrimination provisions for minorities and women bore no cost.[34] Opposition from the civil rights community, combined with that of the Nixon administration, was enough to pull this bill off the committee's table. The antidiscrimination legislation died in 1972 and was not resurrected until the next Congress convened.[35]

The battle for rights began anew when legislation for the vocational rehabilitation program came up for reauthorization. In the fall of 1972, John Brademas, a Democrat from Indiana, brought a rehabilitation bill before the Education and Labor Committee.[36] This bill contained none of the provisions prohibiting discrimination against disabled people that the Vanik bill had. It followed all other renewals before it in that it contained no references to disability rights.

The Vocational Rehabilitation Amendments of 1972 were designed to expand and improve the existing vocational rehabilitation program.[37] As Representative Albert Quie, a Republican from Minnesota who helped Brademas draft the bill, explained, "The devoted experience and wisdom of the late Mary E. Switzer is inextricably woven into the many constructive changes that have been made in this rehabilitation legislation over the years."[38] Switzer's influence was not surprising, since a long-time ally of hers, E. B. Whitten, the head of the National Rehabilitation Association (NRA), had helped draft the legislation.[39]

Brademas's rehabilitation bill did, however, contain a new emphasis on helping people with severe disabilities, something that Switzer, Rusk, and other members of the rehabilitation movement had been lobbying for since the mid-1960s. This bill indicated that self-esteem is derived not just from "self-support and contributions to the national economy, but through acceptance in the community and being viewed as a complete human being with rights equal to [those of] all other citizens."[40] Brademas and Quie included these provisions because they were concerned for "those handicapped individuals who have not been accepted for services because of the severity of the case or terminated as 'unrehabilitated' after the initial evaluation because of the severity of their handicaps." The provisions for independent living for people with severe disabilities would have created what Quie called the "first new comprehensive program" in fifty-two years of vocational rehabilitation.[41]

Administrators from HEW reacted to the renewal proposal with no new plans and little enthusiasm. By this time, those in the SRS, which housed the vocational rehabilitation program, thought that associating it with the Great Society welfare programs had been a grave mistake. As explained in Chapter 3, in 1967 Secretary of HEW John Gardner founded the SRS, which brought welfare, vocational rehabilitation, and other services together under one large roof. Under Switzer's direction, this program had been expanded to include the socially, culturally, and economically disabled. Rehabilitation, in other words, had been made available to welfare recipients.

Although the SRS was built to correct the problems of the war on poverty, when President Lyndon Johnson left office HEW was blamed for the welfare crisis.[42] Without Switzer at the helm of SRS, the vocational rehabilitation program was buried in this large bureaucracy. It was criticized by its own officials who did not like being associated with welfare.[43] The SRS, moreover, had never had a supportive constituency. Disabled people resented being linked with welfare, and welfare recipients resented being rehabilitated.

The SRS was vulnerable, therefore, to the Nixon administration's charges that, given the escalating costs, rehabilitation did not best serve people with physical and mental disabilities.[44] It came under attack for treating "everyone from the blind to the criminal offender as a single homogeneous population."[45] Again the SRS was put in an awkward position with disability rights activists attacking it from one side and the Nixon administration from the other.

What is more, members of the Nixon administration concurred with the disability rights activists that the vocational rehabilitation model gave too much power to the vocational rehabilitation counselor. A report prepared by the Office of Program Planning and Evaluation stated that "since the cost participation rules and formulas appear fairly harsh and rigid the client is placed in the position of being beholden to the counselor if he wishes the rules to be softened in their application. This dependent status in which the client is placed makes it possible for the counselor to treat clients inequitably without the knowledge of the client. Even if the clients do feel unfairly treated, they are probably reluctant to complain for fear the rules would be even more rigidly applied in retaliation for their complaint."[46]

The clearest indication of the failure of the SRS, however, was that neither the federal bureaucrats in HEW nor the liberal Democrats in Congress proposed that vocational rehabilitation be used to extend the liberal do-goodism underlying social rehabilitation. The officials themselves gave up, putting up little opposition when the Brademas bill replaced the SRS with a more narrow institution, the Rehabilitation Services Administration (RSA). The new program dropped the term "vocational" and simply provided rehabilitation for people with physical and mental disabilities. Rehabilitation was no longer solely about one's identity as a worker. There were other means of being a productive citizen.

Like the officials who ran the program, the rehabilitation experts raised few objections to Brademas's legislative proposal. These experts were either apathetic or inattentive to the whole legislative process. When the Nixon administration suggested that the vocational rehabilitation program be privatized, they mounted no campaign to save it. Few objected when the administration also reduced spending on training rehabilitation experts.[47] As Rusalem explained, "With few exceptions rehabilitation agency administrators accepted the new order."[48] Notable leaders, like Mary Switzer and Jim Garrett, who were identified with a specific approach to rehabilitation, were no longer around to lead HEW. Vocational rehabilitation was no longer at the cutting edge of either "the new scientific frontier" or the "humanists in the field of rehabilitation."[49]

Professional organizations, like the NRA, also led "no campaigns to save the program." While Whitten helped draft the Brademas bill, he did little to mobilize his membership in opposition to Nixon's proposal. To be sure, several rehabilitation experts raised concerns about it. The president of the Delaware chapter of the NRA, for instance, wrote a letter advocating that Nixon sign the rehabilitation bill.[50] Nonetheless, there were no pioneers like Switzer and Rusk who, as Rusalem described, "did not fear to confront deleterious entrenched dogmas and power structures."[51] "The history of rehabilitation is the history of its leadership," and, he added, "few such leaders are now among us."[52]

No More Creaming

Once the House introduced its legislation, the Senate sent another version of the rehabilitation bill to committee. Senator Harrison Williams, a liberal Democrat from New Jersey who chaired the Committee on Labor and Public Works, was a leading proponent of the rehabilitation legislation. Strengthening his own position, Williams appointed another proponent, Senator Alan Cranston, a liberal Democrat from California, to chair the subcommittee.

Cranston went into the legislative process thinking that this bill was an extension of the fifty-three-year-old VRA. Upon learning that people with severe disabilities received little treatment from the vocational rehabilitation centers, Cranston, however, changed his mind about extending the existing legislation. He agreed with the disability activists who came before his subcommittee that the practice of "creaming," that is, rehabilitating the people who were the least impaired and, therefore, stood a greater chance of being employed, constituted a problem. Cranston thought all disabled people should have the right to vocational rehabilitation, which included the right to question the authority of the rehabilitation experts who oversaw the vocational rehabilitation process.[53] Therefore, he helped draft legislation that provided "due process for rehabilitation clients."[54]

Given this new perspective on independent living, Cranston's bill would have fundamentally altered the balance of power between disabled people and the rehabilitation counselors who directed the vocational rehabilitation program. It mandated an annual plan for vocational rehabilitation services and provided for periodic review. Moreover, it proposed that the vocational rehabilitation program give the most help to those with severe disabilities. The Cranston bill tried to eliminate the process of creaming by proposing that an "individualized written rehabilitation plan" be signed by both the counselor and the client to ensure the latter's satisfaction.[55] It also created client assistance programs, which further protected clients and client applicants by ensuring that special counselors or ombudsmen inform and advise them all about the opportunity to devise individualized plans. Initially, seven pilot client assistance projects were initiated to explore whether the ombudsmen would be effective. If these were completed successfully, the bill mandated that programs had to have client assistance projects.

To eliminate the institutional incentive to serve the people with the least debilitating disabilities, the Cranston bill no longer made a rehabilitation center or a facility responsible for how many people it rehabilitated. Previously, these facilities had helped people who had the slightest impairments as a means of increasing their odds for finding employment.

Despite alleviating this institutional pressure, Cranston's bill put disabled people on a collision course with rehabilitation counselors. These two groups often disagreed about the limitations physical and mental disabilities imposed upon people and the question of where the failures of society began.[56] Counselors valued their professional autonomy, whereas disabled people valued their right to self-determination. This relationship would change under the Cranston bill since the individualized written rehabilitation plan meant that a counselor would no longer "dominate" a client.

Knowing that the success of the rehabilitation movement could be attributed to its ability to shape the field of rehabilitation medicine, the disability rights movement wanted to do the same. For this reason, it convinced Cranston to establish the Council for Rehabilitation Education, Inc. (CORE), which gave disabled people themselves the ability to weigh in on how rehabilitation experts should be trained. The CORE was an accrediting body for all Rehabilitation Education Training Programs, including Rehabilitation Counselor Training and Rehabilitation Administration programs.[57]

Antidiscrimination Focus

Under both the Brademas and the Cranston bills, vocational rehabilitation underwent a transformation. Services changed their emphasis from rehabilitating patients to having clients help design and direct their own recovery with individual plans. During the postwar period, vocational rehabilitation had emphasized restoring the subjective conditions of the patient's mind and body. It also argued that disabled people could by working become productive citizens again. By contrast, this new legislation rehabilitated people who had little chance of employment. For those who could work, it emphasized the objective conditions that inhibited them. Cranston and other members of the subcommittee recognized that discrimination in employment had an especially detrimental effect on programs. As Cranston explained, "Such problems as unfounded discrimination in employment and in housing, difficulties of access to centers, and duplication and fragmentation of services across program lines were voiced repeatedly to the Committee."[58]

Cranston understood that this new antidiscrimination perspective would reconfigure the vocational rehabilitation program. He said that "discrimination in placement, hiring and advancement continue to limit vocational rehabilitation program's ability to affect successful rehabilitation. . . . the expenditure of money on vocational rehabilitation programs is not well spent if we do not . . . provide substantial accomplishments in employment for handicapped individuals."[59] Senator Robert W. Taft Jr., a conservative Republican leader, agreed. "In spite of the relatively high success of this program," he declared, "we still have a long way to go. . . . we must devote more of our head toward the elimination of the most disgraceful barrier of all—discrimination."[60]

To eliminate discrimination at the workplace, Cranston's bill included Titles V and VI. Of particular importance was Section 501, which instituted affirmative action hiring practices for federal agencies, departments, and instrumentalities, including the United States Postal Service. It proposed that annual written affirmative action plans that specified goals for employing and advancing applicants be mandated from these offices.[61]

Section 503 required businesses that received governmental contracts to have a plan for affirmative action. This section differed from affirmative action plans for women and minorities in that it was not based upon specific goals. This section did not mandate that employers hire a specific number of people with disabilities as laws in Great Britain, Germany, and France had. Again, the idea of instituting a quota system, which most European nations had established as part of their social welfare states after World War II, did not constitute a real policy option.[62] Hence, Section 503 did not deviate from the American ideal that the federal government should interfere as little as possible with the employers' right to manage. This section sanctioned "a working relationship in which the employer will take the handicapped person's condition into account, and facilitate employment wherever possible."[63] It mandated that employers reach out and recruit people with disabilities, but it never gave them the right to employment. As proponents of the Cranston bill described it, this section created a *facilitative* approach to affirmative action.[64]

The bill also created two administrative bodies to ensure the good faith implementation of the rights provisions. Section 601 created the Interagency Committee on Handicapped Employees, and required every federal agency to develop and implement affirmative action for the hiring, placement, and advancement of disabled workers. Section 602 enforced the Architectural and Transportation Barriers Compliance Board (ATBCB) as a means of enforcing the Architectural Barriers Act passed in 1968.

The breakthrough in the Rehabilitation Act, however, was not embodied by any of these plans for affirmative action. It was Section 504, the provision against discrimination, that gave the Rehabilitation Act its most comprehensive rights provision. Section 504 stipulated that "no otherwise handicapped individual in the United States, as defined in section 7 (6), shall, solely by reason of his handicap, be excluded from participation in, be denied the benefits of, or be subjected to discrimination under, any program or activity receiving Federal financial assistance."[65] This one sentence gave approximately 800,000 disabled people protection from employment discrimination.[66]

Section 504 was conceived by the legislative assistants who worked for Cranston; Williams; Randolph Jennings, a Democrat from West Virginia; Jacob Javits, a liberal Republican from New York; and Robert Stafford, a moderate Republican from Vermont.[67] As Richard Scotch, a political scientist, has explained, the Labor and Public Welfare Committee incorporated it, with little or no thought, as a goodwill gesture. "Section 504," he stated, "began as an inconspicuous segment of routine legislation."[68] According to Scotch, the staff modeled Section 504 on Title VI of the Civil Rights Act, which had been used to integrate public schools.[69]

Despite sensitivity about rights in the early 1970s, few people recognized the significance of Section 504. Only one comment was recorded about it during the hearings, when John Nagle, director of the National Federation of the Blind, said that Section 504 had "major significance." Yet, Nagle's comment went unnoticed.[70] Section 504 was neither discussed in any hearings nor considered on the House or Senate floor. The House reports, moreover, made scant reference to it.[71]

Even more telling about Section 504's heritage was how Cranston and Vanik justified prohibiting discrimination against disabled people. They relied on the very same logic that the rehabilitation movement had used: if disabled people could work, they could become productive members of society. Discrimination should be prohibited, in other words, not because disabled people should have this right but because it was cost-effective for the state and society. Not only could disabled people be dropped from the rolls that gave them subsistence, but they would become taxpayers. As Switzer said years earlier, disabled people could become taxpayers rather than "taxeaters."[72]

The consequence of relying on this cost-effective rationale rather than on an antidiscrimination rationale was that only those who the rehabilitation experts deemed employable were eligible for vocational rehabilitation. A rehabilitation counselor would determine if someone could "benefit from rehabilitation services."[73] Hence, Congress was not ready to help disabled people help themselves, and all the provisions that the disability rights movement advanced were not part of the final bill.

Nonetheless, both bills placed rehabilitation in a new context. Without their emphasis on vocation, rehabilitation became associated with the rights of disabled people. Rehabilitation experts now had to take into account the wishes of their constituents, the people with disabilities themselves. Most important, the main rights provision—Section 504—would bolster the disability rights movement.

Nixon's Opposition

With unanimous approval from the Senate Committee on Public Works and Labor, no one in the Senate was surprised that the rehabilitation bill passed with a strong majority.[74] What was surprising was Nixon's opposition.[75] Neither Randolph nor Cranston had anticipated this reaction; first, because of the bipartisan support for the rehabilitation bill; and second, since key members of Nixon's administration had worked closely with Cranston's subcommittee. Nixon's position caught even some members of his administration by surprise who "thought the President would sign the legislation sent up in November."[76]

In his veto message, Nixon explained his position by citing costs. He also found fault with the new programs created by the rehabilitation, and the new advisory structure, which gave disabled people a voice in the operation of the vocational rehabilitation program. All of these things, Nixon insisted, would unduly constrain the executive branch.[77]

Disappointed by Nixon's veto, the disability rights movement and many members of Congress reintroduced the rehabilitation legislation shortly after the 1972 election. It was passed by an overwhelming bipartisan majority. Maintaining his position, Nixon vetoed the legislation again.

Thinking that it had the votes, the Senate immediately moved to override the veto. Between midnight and 2 A.M. on April 3, 1973, the Senate deliberated. Hugh Scott, a Republican from Pennsylvania, led the successful campaign against the rehabilitation bill. Four votes shy of the two-thirds vote necessary to override it the move failed, and Nixon's veto prevailed.[78]

Not everyone on Nixon's White House staff had favored that second veto.[79] William Timmons, the assistant to the president for congressional relations, argued, "We should try to avoid such an early and potentially disastrous confrontation with the Congress which could possibly fuel Congressional confidence in opposing Administration efforts" in the future.[80] Thinking that another veto was a lost cause, Timmons recommended that, instead, "we try to remove the most pernicious features of these bills."[81]

Nixon justified his second veto by arguing that vocational rehabilitation was part of the Great Society. He insisted that, like other policies in Lyndon Johnson's program, it was "simply throwing money at problems," which "does not solve anything." The new vocational rehabilitation legislation, he argued, would "open the floodgates on the federal budget."[82]

One part of the bill that Nixon did not express any objection to was Section 504. He had no more foresight about the heart of the new rights orientation than anyone else. Rather, he thought social programs like welfare should simply offer work.[83] As explained earlier, Nixon derided the patronizing attitude of social workers who, within their spirit of do-good-ism, assisted the poor. Trying to please Nixon, Daniel Moynihan, then a White House aide, promised that his social program would "wipe out" social workers. The Nixon administration argued that "monetary transfers . . . could also counter habitual dependency as the welfare poor reacted to financial incentives to alter their immoral or unproductive lifestyle."[84]

Despite Nixon's explanation, opposition was mounting against his position. Representative Carl Perkins, a Democrat from Kentucky who chaired the committee, said, "[I]n my judgment, the vetoes of these bills were among the most unjustified and unwarranted this country has ever experienced."[85]

This opposition, however, did not come from the professionals in rehabilitation. As Rusalem explained, "This encounter, coupled with the Nixon administration's cavalier handling of many other HEW rehabilitation programs, unfortunately failed to generate the widespread professional indignation that it deserved." While the administration made move after move to undermine the program, many rehabilitation leaders stood by passively." Rusalem added, "All too many rehabilitation leaders tacitly acquiesced or took to the sidelines while a few of them participated in concerted counterattacks." Instead, Nixon's position mobilized many disabled people who began fighting for independent living and rehabilitation for the first time. "One bright spot was that this prevailing passivity was recognized by disabled persons . . . some of whom helped to organize and lead grass roots client-directed movements that forcefully spoke out for the disabled at a time when their interests were in grave peril."[86]

Hoping to break this legislative impasse, key members in the House and Senate worked with the Nixon administration on a new bill. The legislation introduced on May 23, 1973, which was sponsored by Brademas, reduced the amount of funding the Cranston bill had initially requested, making expenditures "consistent with the administration's budget request." This bill also secured the autonomy of the RSA, and eliminated advisory boards that "the administration objected to" when it vetoed the rehabilitation bills. It was most important that "the committee deleted that entire title (Title II, which would have given the severely disabled services) and mandated instead a special comprehensive study including research and demonstration projects to determine the feasibility of working with those individuals."[87] Associating these provisions with the 1960s Great Society ethic, Nixon insisted that the independent living provisions be eliminated.[88]

Once these compromises were made, and the legislation passed both chambers, Nixon signed the Rehabilitation Act on September 26, 1973.[89] This law provided for the continuation of the vocational rehabilitation program, first established by the Smith-Fess Act of 1920, giving federal financial assistance to states for vocational and other services. Similarly, it gave additional funding and a number of new services. What few foresaw, however, was that Section 504, still contained within it, would provide the basis for the disability rights revolution.

State Capacity and Recalcitrance

When the bill became law, the significance of Section 504 was not readily apparent. What was evident, however, was how uncooperative top level officials at HEW were. The secretary was not prepared to cooperate with Congress by promptly drafting the regulations necessary to implement the Rehabilitation Act of 1973.

Anticipating this problem even before the bill became law, Brademas and other members on the Committee of Education and Labor had made the highly unusual request that the RSA consult with them about the regulations. Just two months after the Rehabilitation Act was passed, the Select Subcommittee on Education held hearings that put James S. Dwight Jr., the administrator of SRS, and Corbett Reedy, the acting commissioner of the RSA, on the defensive about the regulations for the Rehabilitation Act. During the hearings, Brademas said to Dwight, "I am asking when you intend to consult us. Now surely you can give me an answer to that question." He also conveyed his dissatisfaction when he said that "to put it as bluntly as I can, we have strong reservations about the extent to which you intend to obey the law." Brademas elaborated, "We are not happy about what you are doing." He continued, "We think in many instances you are in violation of the law. We think in many instances you have not placed uppermost the purpose of the law, which is the provision of effective services for the rehabilitation of handicapped Americans."[90]

Although he went to great lengths to convey this message, Brademas also expressed his disapproval in personal terms. HEW, he noted, had not responded appropriately to its own disabled employees. One employee fell and broke a hip in an agency bathroom, Brademas recounted, because a grab bar had not been installed properly. A year lapsed, however, before the bar installation was repaired.[91]

Brademas also used the hearings to give the "leaders in the rehabilitation community" an opportunity to express their "alarm" over the RSA. Now that the vocational rehabilitation program had been changed, members of this community realized the consequences and were upset. As Craig Mills, the director of the Florida Division of Vocational Rehabilitation, said, "I wish it would be possible to come to you today and tell you there is the same bright enthusiasm of moving forward that took place in 1943 and 1954 and when other milestones of rehabilitation legislation were passed. I cannot. . . . Instead I think there is a serious concern being expressed throughout the breadth of the land with regard to the lack of prompt implementation of the wonderful new opportunities presented in this new piece of legislation."[92]

Although the hearings put the RSA on the spot, this is not to say that the subcommittee understood how vital Section 504 would become to the disability rights movement. During these first months, the import of Section 504 was still open for discovery. Ignoring it, the rehabilitation experts who were brought before the subcommittee relayed their disappointment with the Nixon administration for limiting the existing program. Quie went so far as to offer his support of the whole man theory, which still dominated rehabilitation. "To laymen," he said, "rehabilitation sometimes looks just like teaching a person skills. Rehabilitation is more than that. There are medical services. People who are handicapped have emotional problems. I always look at Dr. Rusk as the expert heading the kind of consolidated service where they try and provide the medical help, the emotional help, or you can call it psychological help and then the occupational training, to try to do them all at once." Mills agreed with Quie:

"Getting these pieces you describe together is the most effective way for a client."[93] No one spoke on behalf of Section 504.

The rehabilitation movement's ideas were still embraced by some notable experts. For instance, Carl Hanson of the Department of Special Education at the University of Texas, and a past president of the National Rehabilitation Counseling Association, emphasized that it was crucial to continue funding graduate programs for rehabilitation counselors. Although senators like Cranston had been critical of these counselors for exercising too much power and authority over who they chose to rehabilitate, Hanson wanted to ensure that rehabilitation counselors would not be shortchanged under the new law.

Brademas's subcommittee was not the only one to push the RSA. The Senate had also anticipated problems. The Subcommittee on the Handicapped requested that HEW comply with the Rehabilitation Act as soon as possible.[94]

Stalled Regulations

Advocates of the rehabilitation bill in Congress could do only so much in taking HEW to task through hearings. Just one year after the Rehabilitation Act had been passed, Congress amended it again. Now, the Senate had come to understand Section 504's great potential for protecting the employment rights of disabled people. When HEW would not draft the regulations for Section 504, the Senate demanded that it do so. The Rehabilitation Act Amendments of 1974 acknowledged the difficulty that disabled people had with HEW and the vocational rehabilitation program, and it gave them a private right to action.[95]

The 1974 amendments also expanded the definition of *disability*. Previously, the Office of Vocational Rehabilitation's definition had been geared toward those who could profit from vocational training and counseling, not serving those who could not work like children, the elderly, or severely disabled people. Moreover, people who had lived with a disability in the past, like a nervous breakdown, or those with a perceived disability, such as diabetes or epilepsy, could not receive rehabilitation. Earlier, the people who secured services were those the vocational rehabilitation counselors expected would benefit.[96] The 1974 amendments changed all that by extending the definition of a disability to include these three groups.

Although Congress passed these amendments with ease, the secretary of HEW still refused to issue regulations prohibiting employment discrimination. While the words of HEW officials did not necessarily convey their opposition to Section 504 and the new rights emphasis in rehabilitation, their actions did. Believing that HEW officials would never act in good faith alone, in June 1975 the Action League for Physically and Mentally Handicapped Adults brought suit against Secretary David Matthews to force him to draft the regulations that would make Section 504 enforceable.[97]

Another year lapsed, however, before any action was taken. On April 28, 1976, President Gerald Ford issued an executive order creating a government-wide enforcement scheme. Secretary Matthews was directed to coordinate the government's efforts in implementing the statute. HEW would issue standards to define who was covered by the Rehabilitation Act of 1974 and to establish guidelines for determining the existence of discriminatory conduct. The secretary was also to include specific enforcement procedures and sanctions patterned after those of Titles VI and IX of the Civil Rights Act.

Anticipating that HEW might stall again, the Senate Subcommittee on the Handicapped requested that HEW draft regulations the very next month. When HEW officials were called before the subcommittee, they blamed the delay on the absence of a substantive legislative history that provided greater insight about congressional intent. Senators like Harrison Williams, sitting on the subcommittee, were not impressed with this reasoning. They had passed the 1974 amendments specifically for the purpose of showing congressional intent.

Finally, on May 17, 1976, Secretary Matthews published a notice of intent to issue regulations. These rules and regulations would apply to all programs and activities funded by HEW. Of particular importance for the disability activists were the series of questions concerning Section 504, a draft of the proposed regulation, and analysis of the potential inflationary and economic impact of the regulation.[98]

Setting the rules was scheduled for July 1977. Before the public hearings had convened, the federal court issued an order mandating just that.[99] The Office of Civil Rights (OCR) also held hearings.[100] More than 850 pages of written comments flooded into HEW. Yet, in January 1977, Secretary Matthews still had not signed the regulations. Using one last stalling tactic, he took the unprecedented step of forwarding to the Senate Committee on Labor and Public Welfare a request for verification that the regulations reflected legislative intent. Matthews left office before implementing the regulations.

More Foot-Dragging

On January 20, 1977, the Carter administration came into office. Joseph Califano, as the newly appointed secretary of HEW, took responsibility for issuing the Section 504 regulations. Since President Carter had made what members of the White House staff described as a "major commitment to citizens with disabilities," the disability rights movement thought that the new HEW secretary would sign the regulations that the OCR had drafted.[101] When Califano announced that he wanted time to "study" the regulations, these activists were astounded.[102] Califano was ignoring "virtually everyone consulted," wrote one activist, all of whom had "recommended that the January 21 version of the regulations be signed."[103]

What caused the delay was what Dr. Frank Bowe, head of the American Coalition of Citizens with Disabilities Inc., and other disability rights activists feared.[104] "Not only has he not signed," said Bowe, "but he is now making sweeping changes that will drastically weaken their effectiveness."[105] "By late March," Bowe added, " . . . it had become unmistakably clear that 60 days of 'study'" had in fact been used to introduce waivers, exemptions, and loopholes through which recipients could escape compliance" of Section 504.[106]

What disturbed Bowe was that Califano proposed that disability rights should be counterbalanced by questions about cost. "Secretary Califano wholly ignores," wrote Bowe, "the fact that section 504 nowhere allows for exemptions and waivers, but, rather calls for an end to discrimination."[107] Senator Williams echoed Bowe's sentiment about cost. In a letter counseling Califano to issue a strong set of regulations, the senator urged him "to reject reasoning which would build in any greater balancing of the questions of cost or burden on the recipient vis-a-vis the right of the individual to be free from discriminatory treatment."[108]

After two months of Califano's "foot-dragging," Bowe and a coalition of disability rights advocates decided to stage a public protest.[109] On March 18, Bowe sent the president the message that, unless the regulations were signed by April 4, "a peaceful protest would be staged by the coalition of handicapped organizations."[110] When the Carter administration let the deadline lapse with no action, the disability rights movement staged sit-in demonstrations in the vocational rehabilitation offices of eleven cities.[111]

The occupation of the disability rights movement of HEW's regional offices called public attention to Secretary Califano's refusal to enforce the Rehabilitation Act of 1973.[112] In nine cities the demonstrations ended quietly. Califano himself stopped the demonstrations in Washington, D.C., after twenty-eight hours by cutting off the phone service and not allowing the demonstrators to have any food or medicine.[113] The situation was different in San Francisco, however, where the disability rights movement had a strong political foothold and enjoyed broad public support. In the Bay area, the sit-in received a tremendous amount of media attention with some politicians, among them Congressman Philip Burton, a Democrat from San Francisco, and George Moscone, the mayor of San Francisco, visiting the demonstrators as a show of support.[114] For twenty-five days, more than 100 demonstrators occupied the San Francisco HEW office, leaving only on April 28 when Califano announced that he would sign the regulations.[115]

Regulations at Last

Once the regulations were signed, as Mary Lou Breslin, a disability rights activist, described it, "[T]he disability community had sustained a profound and historic victory."[116] In celebration of this victory, Breslin and other disability rights activists marched to the Federal Building in Washington, D.C. By so doing, these activists called attention not only to the new regulations, but also to the fact that they were part of a well-organized, national movement which had the capacity to bring together people with all different types of physical and mental disabilities, and which could no longer be ignored.

Breslin's characterization of Section 504 was apt. For the first time, people with disabilities had civil rights. Disabled people now had the statutory right to public accommodations, which most notably included transportation. They could no longer be refused admittance to colleges and universities that accepted public funding. Finally, the work force that dealt with the public was prohibited from discriminating against people with disabilities. Employers who accepted governmental funds and contracts, moreover, were obliged to do the same.

The disability rights movement, however, did not bask in the limelight of its victory for long. Like most activists, disability rights activists understood that having rights committed to paper constituted only the first step. Enforcing these rights, they knew, would constitute the next battle in the fight for disability rights.

Just after the regulations were issued, disability rights activists scored a number of victories regarding public accommodations. Enforcing protection against discrimination in the workplace, however, presented a much more difficult challenge. The biggest stumbling block facing the disability rights movement was that the regulations drawn up by the Carter administration were self-enforcing, like the proposals for Section 504 regulations drawn up by the Nixon and Ford administrations that preceded Carter.[117] Since Section 504 was almost a copy of Title VI of the Civil

Rights Act, Califano decided that HEW's regulations could simply follow the Federal Procedural Requirements instituted for the civil rights title.[118] Just as with the implementation of Title VI, the federal agencies that gave funding to public and private programs would issue their own antidiscrimination regulations. Section 504, in other words, would have no enforcement arm.

With disabled people having to sue for compliance, one of the trickiest courtroom battles affected disabled people who were seeking employment or accommodations in the workplace. The regulations provided no consistent definition of the qualifications of people with disabilities. The Carter administration issued regulations that people with disabilities purported that they must be "otherwise qualified," yet without providing a clear idea of what "otherwise" referred to. Did this mean in spite of a disability, or in spite of a disability after the reasonable accommodations had been made by employers?

What is more, the burden under the section enforcing affirmative action was more onerous than the one for employment discrimination. Under Section 503, "essential functions" meant that a person must be capable of performing a particular job after he or she had been given reasonable accommodations. For Section 504, HEW regulations specified that "otherwise qualified" meant that an individual could perform the essential functions of the job.

HEW regulations also cast doubt on the meaning of "reasonable accommodation." Section 503 gave employers more flexibility in determining if financial costs and impacts on business created hardship, and thus it eliminated reasonable accommodation requirements.[119] But Section 504 stipulated that reasonable accommodations must be made unless they caused an employer undue hardship. This qualification gave employers a reason not to accommodate workers with disabilities. While cost could not be addressed in determining what discrimination is, HEW determined that it could be used to fashion a remedy.[120]

To be sure, Sections 501, 503, and 504 had been written without much thought being given to implications, so that HEW had little legislative history to build on. Nonetheless, Califano could have used the regulatory process to make the Section 504 antidiscrimination provision clear by giving employers more direction about how to determine if a person with a disability was qualified and what reasonable accommodations could be made.[121] Most important, the archives show that some people within the administration had suggested that Califano take the opportunity to develop a legally enforceable statute.

A year after the regulations were drafted, Albert Hamlin, assistant general counsel, Civil Rights Division, revealed that "perhaps the most novel issue concerning the content of the regulations is whether they should establish administrative remedy. Since neither Title VI nor Title IX cover federally conducted programs, there is no existing administrative procedure pursuing the government for discrimination that could serve as a model for Section 504." Califano could have followed the precedent set by Title VII of the Civil Rights Act, Hamlin added, which "establishes a procedure whereby the Office of Personnel Management enforces nondiscrimination requirements covering federal employees." As Hamlin observed *"In principle, there is no reason why the Department could not establish a process for dealing with complaints alleging discrimination in its federally conducted programs."*[122]

Section 504 would have profited from having such an enforcement agency because "such a remedy can be more flexible," Hamlin elaborated, "and considerably less cumbersome than the present due process procedures used." Califano and other members of the Carter administration dismissed the idea that an "administrative remedy be included in the regulations." Califano decided that Section 504 should be enforced the same way that Title VI of the Civil Rights Act was, which meant that all the parties involved had, in Hamlin's words, "to resort to expensive and time-consuming litigation."[123]

A Politically Unattractive Fight

Since the Carter administration issued regulations that offered less protection than some disabled people and disability rights activists sought, Senators Williams and Randolph, along with Congressman Brademas, spearheaded another campaign to augment the rights orientation underlying the Rehabilitation Act when the legislation was up for renewal in 1978.[124] With these amendments, they rendered a broader definition of eligibility for rehabilitation than was available with the 1973 legislation. They also funded independent living services and gave disabled people input on how to make public accommodations accessible.

Behind the scenes, the Carter administration immediately registered its opposition to these amendments, insisting as James McIntyre, director of the Office of Management and Budget (OMB), did, that they were "seriously flawed in fundamental respects."[125] In a letter trying to dissuade Williams regarding the merits of this legislation, Califano explained that the administration did not want to expand and enlarge the rehabilitation program. It also opposed giving disability rights activists more of a voice on accessibility issues, as the Williams bill proposed by increasing the number of public members on the Architectural and Transportation Barriers Compliance Board.[126]

Meanwhile, within the White House, Carter's advisors began exploring whether the president could sustain a veto without causing too much damage to his relationship with liberal Democrats in Congress or eroding his support among constituents who backed programs for disabled people. On one hand, McIntyre; Bob Libshutz, counsel to the president; Jack Watson, White House cabinet secretary; and Dick Pettigrew, assistant to the president for reorganization, all counseled the president to veto these amendments.[127] Pettigrew put a cynical twist on his recommendation, explaining that disability rights activists could not cause the president too much grief since "the handicapped interest group coalition is basically held together by the funding contained in the bill."[128]

On the other hand, Califano; Stuart Eizenstat, assistant to the president for domestic affairs; Max Cleland, director of the Veterans Administration; and Patricia Roberts Harris, secretary for HUD, recommended that the president sign the amendments. While these officials also thought the Rehabilitation Act was "far from acceptable," they advised Carter to sign it for tactical reasons.[129] Eizenstat thought it was an "unwinnable and politically unattractive fight."[130] "A similar bill will pass next year if this bill is vetoed," he explained, "and a nasty confrontation will be set up on an issue [on] which is difficult to mobilize public or congressional opinion."[131] What is more, Carter could "use the threat of the veto to make the Act more 'desirable,'" said Califano.[132] In the worse case scenario, he told Carter, the administration could achieve the same ends by instructing key members of the House and Senate Appropriations Committees not to fund the pivotal programs, most notably the independent living program.

While Eizenstat and Califano gained the leverage they sought with Williams's office, which indicated that there was "some room for negotiations," Brademas refused to sit down and discuss any legislative compromises with them. Despite this setback, Eizenstat and Califano maintained their position that a veto was politically unwise because "what is worse" than the negotiations failing was that "we see little chance of improving the legislation when it comes back next year without the cooperation of Brademas and Randolph."[133] "Congress is likely to pass the same bill again next session and override a subsequent veto. The view," Eizenstat's office added, "will buy us nothing but the enmity of a highly sympathetic constituency."[134]

Just as Eizenstat and Califano had predicted, the Rehabilitation Act Amendments passed with overwhelming majorities. The Senate bill passed by a vote of 81 to 1, whereas the House bill received a vote of 382 to 12 under a suspension of the rules. When both legislative chambers voted for the Conference Report, little had changed. The Senate accepted the amendments by voice vote, and the House passed it by a margin of 365 to 2.[135] When it came before Carter, he had little choice but to sign it.[136]

A Civil Rights Approach

Still dissatisfied with the protection from employment discrimination that the Rehabilitation Act provided, Senator Cranston introduced the Equal Employment Opportunity for the Handicapped bill.[137] With neither Sections 503 nor 504 enforceable under Title VII's rules and regulations, Cranston decided to amend this title to protect people with disabilities from discrimination.[138] This legislation, which was backed by the disability rights movement, inserted the term "handicapping condition" each time the other affected classes, namely, race and gender, were mentioned in Title VII of the Civil Rights Act of 1964.

Harold Russell, chair of the President's Committee on Employment of the Handicapped, in his testimony summed up the sentiment about protecting disabled people from workplace discrimination. "Handicapped people had jobs," he purported, "but they did not have job rights." He explained, "Before this time, his committee, which has been around since 1947, was to promote more jobs for handicapped people, by encouraging employers to hire them voluntarily. I underline that word 'voluntarily.' Nobody could tell employers what they had to do."[139]

While this legislation required no spending, the Carter administration gave three reasons why it could not throw its support behind it. First, Drew Days, assistant attorney general from the Civil Rights Division, said that officials in their department did not subscribe to the disability rights emphasis on rights, asserting that there were "conceptual and practical differences" between it and civil rights for race and gender.[140] Elaborating what this difference was, Days said, "The basic premise underlying Title VII is one of equality, namely the persons are able to perform the duties of a job equally well, without regard to race," whereas "this premise would not be applicable to those individuals who are in fact suffering from a handicap." Days insisted that "such persons are not equal in abilities." Hence, Days did not take the disability rights activists' argument about the societal roots of discrimination seriously "because," as he explained, "the handicapped are impaired in some abilities and functions."[141]

Second, the Justice Department raised the concern that "merely inserting the term 'handicap in condition' each time the other affected classes are mentioned, the bill may well result in court decisions limiting the protections afforded the other classes."[142] This was the position that the civil rights movement had adopted when the idea had been raised initially in 1972. Civil rights leaders argued that employment rights for people with disabilities "should be attempted through separate legislation, if at all."[143]

Finally, Days thought this amendment to Title VII would be for naught. He insisted that "the absence of specific language requiring employers to make reasonable accommodation to the impairment of qualified handicapped persons jeopardizes the effectiveness of the bill and is not remedied by language in the Committee Report." He continued, "In the absence of specific language providing for reasonable accommodation, the bill might well result in judicial rulings that no substantial action is required."[144]

So as not to confuse the civil rights of disabled people with those of women and minorities, the Justice Department recommended that the senators interested in strengthening the antidiscrimination provisions try "attempting to achieve the bill's goal by amending the Rehabilitation Act." They could amend the Civil Rights Act so that it included a separate section for people with disabilities."[145] Williams, however, must have questioned the sincerity of this suggestion since, after all, he had just gone head-to-head with the Carter administration when he attempted to strengthen the Rehabilitation Act.

Cranston and Williams, therefore, chose the latter, although they took heed of the Justice Department's advice, including a provision about reasonable accommodation in his legislation to amend Title VII. Their attempt to amend the Civil Rights Act did not go far since the bill was never reported out of committee.[146] This legislation was also hindered by a backlash that was brewing against disability rights. According to Berkowitz, the media underscored what many Americans viewed as ridiculous accommodations requests. Journalists picked up on stories such as the one in Iowa, where a rural community was asked to spend over $6,000 making its public library accessible although no one in the community used a wheelchair.[147] The death of the civil rights amendments and the backlash against Section 504 showed that the spirit of reform that gave rights to people with disabilities was receding.

Section 504 transformed disability law, freeing disabled people from discrimination in the public arena. "Section 504 more than any other single section of law," said one official in the Carter administration, "is perceived as a Civil Rights statute for the handicapped."[148] To be sure, the new rights orientation changed the direction, not just of vocational rehabilitation but of disability law. Disabled people won the distinction of being considered one of the last minority groups in need of rights.

The battles would continue since the American state and society was not willing to see disability rights as equivocally as the disability rights movement had hoped. This was demonstrated by the public support generated for HEW's regulations, which conferred specific threshold requirements on a person with a disability. That person had to satisfy these requirements before he or she could be granted protection. Not only did disabled people have to demonstrate that they were otherwise qualified, they also had to show that their requests for accommodation were reasonable.

On face value these requirements, particularly the first one, seemed essential. How could a person be hired for a position if he or she lacked the qualifications? Racial minorities and women also had to be qualified for a position before they could claim discrimination. (Indeed, all persons must be qualified before they can receive a job.) Unlike Section 504, Title VII of the Civil Rights Act of 1964 did not have a similar threshold requirement that minorities and women must first demonstrate that they were qualified for a position before they could receive protection under law. Unless the matter was litigated, it was assumed that they were qualified. No special test was devised that every employer could use to determine if a minority person or a woman was qualified. So why did Section 504 make a special provision for articulating the obvious: that disabled people must be qualified for a job?

The difference between disability rights and civil rights was that Section 504 assumed that disabled people were not qualified until they showed otherwise. This section sustained the stereotype that disabled people cannot work except in special circumstances. While civil rights placed the burden on the employer to show that minorities or female candidates were not as qualified as their white or male counterparts, disability rights imposed this burden on those persons with a disability.

The assumption about qualifications also betrayed a stereotypical fear about disabled people: that they might seek unsuitable positions. What if a person with eye impairment problems wanted to be an air traffic controller? Federal court judges expressed the concern that disabled people thought that they should be exempt from the normal rules of society.

Hence, the qualifications provision showed that the rights orientation of the Rehabilitation Act was still influenced by the psychoanalytical model. The stipulation that persons with a disability must be otherwise qualified protected the employer, not those with a disability, from all the disabled people who considered themselves exempt from the rule that nondisabled persons must be qualified for the particular position they seek.

Aside from the provision about qualifications, disability rights also departed from civil rights for minorities and women in that it posed a limit such as reasonable accommodations. The difference between civil rights and disability rights with reasonable accommodations stemmed from the fact that providing accommodations cost employers money, whereas respecting civil rights did not. Section 504 imposed an affirmative obligation on an employer, and for this reason a limitation was put upon this right. Realizing that rights are rarely accompanied by such limitations, HEW provided in its regulations that the issue of reasonable accommodations could be brought into play only when a person with a disability sought a remedy and not simply the right to freedom from discrimination. Critics of this limitation quickly pointed out that a right is not of much use without a remedy.

Overall, these two threshold questions of qualifications and reasonable accommodations meant that the individual with a disability carried the initial burden of proof. This notion of rights fell far short of the view that society constituted the biggest stumbling block to people with disabilities. It gave no voice to what the disability rights movement believed: that societal prejudice, not the actual physical or mental impairments, constituted the greatest problem to people with disabilities. Underlying Section 504 and HEW's regulations for implementing this section was the idea that differential treatment of people with disabilities depended on who was the target of this treatment.

There was still a larger issue behind proof of qualifications and reasonable accommodations that Congress did not address. The most significant problem with the fact that Section 504 was influenced by both the psychoanalytical model and the rights model was not that this section required that persons with a disability must prove that they are qualified and then must request only reasonable accommodations. Instead, the problem lay in the question of who ascertained this proof. Section 504 did not recognize the conflict of interest facing the employer. The regulations were presented as if the threshold questions could be asked with impartiality. Who was to say that an employer determining qualifications or the cost of an accommodation (or fear of future costs associated with accommodations) could remain impartial in making this assessment? The employer might very well assess the worth of the individual from a position of prejudice. By not fully addressing these issues, Congress and HEW left them to the Supreme Court to decide.

5

Court Constraints
on Disability Rights

Disability activists made great use of the antidiscrimination provisions in the Rehabilitation Act to bolster the disability rights movement. Yet, these activists were caught off-guard by a Supreme Court decision less than two years after the Department of Health, Education and Welfare (HEW) had finished drafting the regulations for the Rehabilitation Act. As an official in the Carter administration wrote, "The recent Supreme Court decision "has been viewed by some as a severe psychological blow to the handicapped."[1]

While this first decision proved disappointing, more time would not necessarily have made the Supreme Court receptive to disability rights. This became evident when the Court outlined its position on disability law in a series of cases involving other federal, state, and local statutes in the 1970s and 1980s. All but one of these decisions proved disheartening to the disability rights community, in part because the Supreme Court was influenced by the whole man theory of rehabilitation.

On one level, the whole man theory underscored the accomplishments of disabled people, not their limitations. On another level, it judged these accomplishments in context with what "normal" people could do, measuring disabled people against the able-bodied to arrive at an understanding of normality. Society made room for people who were differently abled, provided that these people could compensate for their limitations. Likewise, the Supreme Court ruled that disabled people could work as long as they could prove that their qualifications were as strong as those people who faced no physical or mental limitations. If such could be proved, the disability per se could not be held against them.

The Supreme Court found, however, that assessing the qualifications of disabled people was no simple matter. Disabled people had to show their employers and their prospective employers that they were "otherwise qualified." The Court was unclear about what was meant by this term. Did otherwise mean in spite of an impairment? Or could someone be qualified if he or she had a reasonable accommodation that compensated for the problem associated with the disability?

Before settling these questions, the Supreme Court also ruled that, even if disabled people supplied ample evidence of their qualifications, the extent to which employers needed to make room for them was limited on other grounds. In a decision about college admissions, which was also applicable to employers, the Court ruled that a college must offer a student reasonable accommodations as long as these accommodations did not change the "fundamental nature" of its program.

The Supreme Court further muddied the legal waters by initially holding that reasonable accommodations were similar to affirmative action plans. This explains why schools were not obliged to offer any accommodations that changed the fundamental nature of an educational program. But when the Court changed this ruling—declaring that the concept of reasonable accommodations was different from affirmative action—it rendered a restrictive interpretation of the former. Although reasonable accommodations were attempting to redress less of a wrong than affirmative action plans were, the Court made its application more narrow, imposing less of a burden on schools and employers to provide them.

The Court came to this reasoning regarding reasonable accommodations because it argued that they should not be extended for retributive reasons. Unlike affirmative action, reasonable accommodations came with no acknowledgment of what injustices society had committed against disabled people in the past. Nor were the existing biases against disabled people recognized by the Supreme Court. Not only did the Court distinguish reasonable accommodations from affirmative action in this way, but it never afforded disabled people as much protection as minorities received from other civil rights legislation. Antidiscrimination legislation, unlike affirmative action policy, did not level the playing field. It gave minorities and women equal access or equality of opportunity. The Supreme Court ruled, however, that disability law had not mandated that disabled people be given equality of opportunity.

Underlying this interpretation of the idea of reasonable accommodation was the Court's perception not just that disabled people faced hardship, but that their hardship could be accounted for by their inferiority. Whereas civil rights legislation in the 1960s had been based on the understanding that minorities and women should enjoy equal standing with the rest of society, this was not the case for disabled people. The Supreme Court widely viewed people with disabilities as inferior to those without them, and expressed this view by having them shoulder the initial burden of proof in disability law. Only after disabled people demonstrated that they could work were any demands placed on employers.

The Supreme Court's rejection of the rights model, and the accompanying belief that disabled people were second-class citizens, became most apparent when it rejected the disability rights movement's bid for constitutional rights. Disabled people were not part of a protected class, the Court ruled, because they satisfied only two of the three characteristics of such a class. Although they had a long history of discrimination and most of them suffered from an immutable characteristic, the Supreme Court held that they were not powerless. The Court was satisfied by the existence of a disability policy. It had no interest in determining whether those who supposedly benefited from this policy abhorred or preferred it. Vocational rehabilitation could undermine disability rights, and yet, because it was a federally funded program, the Court concluded that the government had fulfilled its obligation of caring for disabled people who could, therefore, not be considered powerless.

The Supreme Court's determination that disabled people did not deserve equal protection under the Fourteenth Amendment revealed how little regard it had for two of the basic principles of the rights orientation: equality of opportunity and individual autonomy.[2] While American civil rights law rarely recognized equality of impact underlying affirmative action policy, it had provided equality of opportunity for minorities and women. The Court's interpretation of disability law was based on neither equality of impact nor equality of opportunity. According to a majority of justices on the Supreme Court, society had *reason* for prejudice because disabled people were "different."

A Suspect Society

Since 1954, when the Supreme Court handed down *Brown v. Board of Education,* African Americans had been guaranteed equal protection under law. Although the Court had not ruled that any legal reference to race was unconstitutional per se, it applied the strict scrutiny test to determine if legislation violated the equal protection clause of the Fourteenth Amendment. The Court relied on this test for three reasons. First, African Americans had endured a long history of discrimination. Second, race was an immutable characteristic. Third, both the state and society had rendered African Americans powerless by depriving them of the ability to change their situation. Laws that made reference to race, while not unconstitutional, were strictly scrutinized by the courts.

The Supreme Court extended what became known as the scrutiny test to legislation not only directed at African Americans, but also to indigent criminal suspects, illegitimate children, and the disenfranchised.[3] To do so, the Court developed two more levels for determining violations of the equal protection clause: the rational basis and the heightened scrutiny test. First, the rational basis test relied on a more relaxed standard than the strict scrutiny test.[4] Laws about gender, for instance, were examined under the rational basis of a scrutiny test.[5] It offered less scrutiny because, while nothing distinguished people of different races from one another, a woman's capacity for reproduction made her different from a man. Laws that made reference to gender, therefore, could be justified. Moreover, legislation about women did not demand the judiciary's strict scrutiny, because women had not endured the same degree or type of state-sanctioned discrimination that African Americans had.[6]

Second, the Supreme Court devised the heightened scrutiny test so that it could offer a middle level of scrutiny that would be less rigorously applied than the rational basis test.[7] This test stipulated that while a statute need not rest on a rational basis, a substantial governmental objective was required. A child's right to support from his parents, for instance, while not fundamental, did warrant the Court to invalidate statutory classifications that eroded this right. A standard of reasonableness had to be established that had a fair and substantial relation to the object that a piece of legislation sought to achieve.[8]

Disability activists watched with great interest as the Warren and Burger Courts produced these three levels of scrutiny for the protection of a group's right to equal protection under the Fourteenth Amendment. While they realized the strict scrutiny test would probably not be applicable to laws about disability—given the difference between disabled people and the able-bodied—they hoped that either the rational basis or the heightened basis would. The disability rights movement was particularly encouraged about this prospect in 1974 when a judge in North Dakota in a state court applied a "compelling state interest" test to a statute about public education.[9] The judge used this test to show that a statute discriminated against disabled people for reasons that had nothing to do with their actual limitations.

The disability activists were optimistic that disabled people would be guaranteed constitutional rights one step further when Congress passed the

Developmental Disabilities Assistance and Bill of Rights Act. This act also included a "bill of rights" for students with disabilities. The Supreme Court's response to their bid for constitutionally guaranteed rights of equal protection, however, was disappointing.[10] In 1981, the Court ruled, in *Pennhurst State School and Hospital v. Halderman,* that the bill of rights in the Developmental Disabilities Act (DDA) had not given them any constitutional guarantees. While Terri Lee Halderman, a child with mental retardation, lived in less than ideal conditions, the Court held that she had no substantive right to better conditions in this state-operated school and hospital.[11]

Because the DDA was only a federal-state funding statute, wrote Justice William H. Rehnquist for the majority, its bill of rights granted disabled people no constitutional rights. Congress had not planned for this statute to provide these rights. He argued that the statute only encouraged states to improve their programs by giving them financial assistance.[12] Congress had not articulated its intent, Rehnquist insisted, in "plain meaning."[13]

Rehnquist's decision rested on his interpretation of legislative intent. Yet, according to Justice Byron R. White, Rehnquist ignored the fact that Congress had modeled this law after the Civil Rights Act of 1964 and the Fourteenth Amendment.[14] White agreed that the DDA had not been drafted solely pursuant to the Fourteenth Amendment. It was a statute that was meant primarily to provide funding. But unlike the majority, he still found "substantive significance" in the bill of rights.

As evidence that Congress had intended that the bill of rights would provide disabled people with just that—rights—White quoted what representatives and senators had said during the legislative process. Initially, the House version of the act had stipulated that funds be used to eliminate improper institutionalization. Money had been set aside to help create and run community-based facilities.[15] White also interpreted the 1978 amendments to the DDA as having specified that the bills of rights was "in addition to any constitutional or other rights."[16] According to White, the Court's majority had transformed the bill of rights into an empty expression of legislative policy. They had done so by ignoring these declarations of legislative intent.[17]

Four years later, the Court again took up the question of the constitutionally guaranteed rights of disabled people, with the same result. In this case, the City of Cleburne in Texas had denied Jan Hannah a building permit because she was going to construct a residential group home for the mentally retarded.[18] The city did this in response to the property owners in the area who had voiced their opposition to the Cleburne Living Center (CLC). Interpreting the zoning board's decision as discriminatory, Hannah challenged the denial of her building permit, making the argument that the zoning scheme itself was a violation of the equal protection clause under the Fourteenth Amendment.[19]

When the Court handed down the *Cleburne* decision in 1985, the disability rights movement was disappointed again. In this decision, White, who had been the lone dissenting voice in *Pennhurst*, not only joined the majority, but he drafted the opinion that provided that neither strict scrutiny, rational basis scrutiny, nor heightened scrutiny should be applied to laws targeted at disabled people.

Reviewing the three requirements for such protection, White first argued that the mentally retarded were vulnerable to discrimination. He also thought they lacked the power to change their situation through the political process. Yet, White did not concede that disabled people satisfied the powerlessness category. As he saw it, the mentally retarded profited from legislation that recognized them as a group.[20] "The legislative response, which could hardly have occurred and survived without public support, negates any claim that the mentally retarded are politically powerless in the sense that they have no ability to attract the attention of the lawmakers."[21] Hence, disabled people were empowered simply because Congress had passed legislative programs and policies that were supposed to help them.

Finally, White stipulated that the mentally retarded could not be placed in the quasi-suspect classification of deserving protection because they were different from those who were not. "Because mental retardation is a characteristic that the government may legitimately take into account in a wide range of decisions, and because both State and Federal Governments have recently committed themselves to assisting the retarded, we will not presume that any given legislative action, even one that disadvantages retarded individuals, is rooted in considerations that the Constitution will not tolerate." As evidence of their differences, he cited their "reduced ability to cope with and function in the everyday world."[22] Although he knew that 90 percent in this group were only mildly retarded, White argued that they still had less ability than the able-bodied.[23] The City of Cleburne, therefore, had every right to prohibit the CLC from moving into a specific neighborhood.

After offering this painstakingly careful analysis of why the mentally retarded did not deserve equal protection under law, White struck down the actual zoning law anyway. He simply said it was unfair.[24] The zoning law failed to meet what White described as the minimal requirement of rationality required of any law.

In a dissenting opinion, Thurgood Marshall expressed his opposition, not to White's result but to his reasoning.[25] To Marshall, White had not identified the real interests at stake, which involved the property owners' prejudice against people with mental retardation. White was insincere, Marshall claimed, in ruling against the zoning ordinance. Marshall suggested that White was really relying on the heightened scrutiny test.[26] White's refusal to acknowledge that he had done so caused two interrelated problems. On one hand, it encouraged the judiciary to conduct a searching inquiry of all laws affecting disabled people. On the other hand, legislative bodies would keep trying to exclude disabled people, because the Court had not given the real reason for its decision. White's ruling gave future legislation what Marshall called a "presumption of constitutionality."[27]

Marshall offered his own explanation about why the zoning law violated the rights of the mentally retarded. First, the right to establish a home was fundamental. Second, group homes were not just homes for the mentally retarded; they were also the primary way that this population could enter the community. Third, the mentally retarded had a long history of being discriminated against by mainstream society. Fourth, Marshall argued, the rational basis test perpetuated false stereotypes about the retarded. Finally, Marshall rejected the notion that the mentally retarded had political power.[28] The idea that they needed no protection because remedial legislation had been passed to care for them obscured the relationship between those who had power and those who did not.

Discussing power relations, Marshall argued that White's interpretation of people with mental disabilities echoed some of the basic precepts behind Social Darwinism. He also drew an analogy between the mentally retarded and women and African Americans. To Marshall, the zoning ordinance was tantamount to segregation, because it placed people with mental disabilities in social isolation. The mentally retarded, he argued, must be integrated into the community, as deinstitutionalization advocates proposed. To socially isolate women or African Americans would not be accepted, whereas it was with the mentally retarded. Marshall insisted that "mental retardation *per se* cannot be a proxy for depriving retarded people of their rights and interests without regard to variations in individual ability."[29]

Precisely because the legislative process had already failed the mentally retarded, Marshall thought the Court should not use the legitimate state interest argument as a means of justifying judicial restraint.[30] In Marshall's mind, disabled people satisfied all three characteristics of people deserving strict scrutiny under the equal protection clause. They had immutable characteristics, they had a history of discrimination, and they were powerless to affect political change. The Court, therefore, should do nothing less than offer them the most rigid scrutiny test to protect their constitutionally guaranteed rights. As Marshall explained, the heightened scrutiny review had been applied to gender and illegitimacy; why not to disabled people? After all, women and those who cared for illegitimate children, who were protected, did not suffer from the same level of political powerlessness that the retarded did.[31]

The Demands of Organized Society

Marshall had cause for suspicion about how the legislative process affected disabled people. Three years before the *Cleburne* decision, the Court had ruled that legislative bodies should balance the needs of disabled people with the "demands of organized society." That is, society could offer people with mental and physical disabilities less than it gave the able-bodied. The Court, moreover, had explicitly stipulated that legislation need not offer disabled people equality of opportunity. Hence, it had built this understanding about remedial legislation and the power of those who had disabilities upon the premise that the needs of disabled people must be balanced with those of the able-bodied.[32]

The case that balanced the so-called demands of an organized society against disabled people involved Nicholas Romeo, who at the age of thirty-three had the mental capacity of an eighteen-month-old.[33] Romeo's IQ was between eight and ten. As a result, he was unable to talk and lacked the most basic skills to care for himself. When Romeo's mother could no longer care for him, she had her son involuntarily admitted to Pennhurst, the Pennsylvania state institution for people with physical and mental disabilities. After discovering that her son had injured himself and had been hurt by other residents at least sixty-three times since his institutionalization, Mrs. Romeo became concerned about his welfare. She became increasingly distressed when Romeo's arm was broken and, instead of returning him to the ward once it healed, the doctor kept Romeo restrained to a hospital bed. Ostensibly, these restraints were used to protect him and others in Pennhurst. Mrs. Romeo objected to the restraints, insisting that the best way to help her son was to teach him self-help skills and provide a behavior modification program that might reduce his aggressive behavior. She was also concerned that her son had been "shack-led" in retaliation for the complaint she had lodged against the hospital.[34]

Although the trial court cleared the hospital of any wrongdoing and decided that the hospital was not obligated to provide Romeo with a self-help program, the Court of Appeals for the Third Circuit relied on the Fourteenth Amendment and found that people who had been involuntarily committed "retain[ed] liberty interest in freedom of movement and in personal security." The Court of Appeals described the question of whether Romeo could be shackled to a bed as an example of one of the "fundamental liberties" that can be limited only "by an 'overriding, non-punitive' state interest." Was it necessary to restrain Romeo to protect the state interest? The Third Circuit could not agree, however, on whether Romeo's rights had been violated.[35]

Hearing the case, the Supreme Court, with Justice Lewis J. Powell writing for the majority, decided that Romeo's liberty under the Fourteenth Amendment had not been violated. Powell ruled that Romeo had the right to safe conditions and freedom from bodily restraint, but that these interests were by no means absolute. Powell balanced the interests of disabled people against the interests of the able-bodied because of the "demands of an organized society."[36]

To do so, Powell weighed the utility of not accepting a constitutional right against the utility of accepting one. Juxtaposing the state's interests and the individual's interests, he ruled in favor of the state. Order, unity, normality, and objectivity—the state's interests—were more important than the individual's interests.[37] Romeo, Powell argued, had a constitutional right to only the minimal care that hospital experts could determine.

Relatively few people protested Powell's conclusion that Romeo could secure a constitutional right to only minimal care. The Supreme Court sustained exactly what Mary Switzer had fought for in her opposition to the poor people's movement—the use of the Fourteenth Amendment. The Supreme Court concluded that disabled people deserved no protection under this amendment.

Just as Switzer and the rehabilitation movement believed that disabled people should have no constitutionally guaranteed rights, the Supreme Court found that society had no obligation to offer them equality of opportunity. The Court ruled that Romeo did not need the self-help and behavior modification program; this program went beyond what hospital experts described as a minimum of care. What is more, the standard for what was the minimum was not influenced by disabled people or their guardians looking after their best interest. Only the professionals who treated them could determine their treatment. Rehabilitation experts, Powell maintained, not his mother, could best decide what was "minimally adequate habilitation" for Romeo. Powell got rid of the least intrusive means doctrine, replacing it with the doctrine of substituted judgment. That is, he called for experts to determine the minimum that the hospital needed to offer Romeo. He concluded that professionals "are entitled to a presumption of correctness."[38]

Although diagnoses of people with mental disabilities had always been tenuous at best, Powell deferred to psychiatric experts for this determination. He paid little heed to the fact that psychiatrists practicing in mental institutions had once judged people like Romeo to be diseased and deviant.[39] Minimally adequate care would undoubtedly be different for people judged to be this way than it would be for other people. Yet, from Powell's standpoint, the Court should not interfere with expert judgment unless there was "a substantial departure from accepted professional judgment, practice, or standards as to demonstrate that the person responsible actually did not base the decision on such a judgment."[40] The Supreme Court did not recognize Mrs. Romeo's complaints about her son's treatment as valid.

With these three decisions, the Supreme Court made it clear that disabled people had no constitutional rights under the equal protection clause of the Fourteenth Amendment. Nor did national, state, or local legislative bodies need to provide them with the same opportunities that it gave able-bodied members of society. These legislative bodies could take into account "the demands of organized society" when they developed their policies and programs for disabled people.[41] The Court provided the means to justify why it was not necessary to treat disabled people like the able-bodied. Legislative bodies had to offer them only a minimum of care. This minimum of care, however, was further diminished by the Supreme Court's ruling about reasonable accommodations. For someone trying to enter mainstream society by receiving an education or seeking employment, school officials and employers did not have to provide even a minimum of access if they could show that to do so interfered with the fundamental nature of their program or place of employment.

Unreasonable Accommodations

In the first decision after the passage of the Rehabilitation Act of 1973, *Southeastern Community College v. Davis,* the Supreme Court argued that reasonable accommodations were similar to provisions instituting affirmative action.[42] Frances Davis sought admission to a vocational training program for nurses at a state community college. Although Davis had already received training as a nurse, she wanted to become a state-certified registered nurse. But Davis had a congenital hearing impairment in both ears, and the college ordered a medical evaluation to determine whether it would interfere with her studies. Upon finding that a hearing aid offered Davis some assistance, but that she could not understand normal speech without lipreading, the college denied her application. It did so, first, because Davis would require individualized faculty supervision to finish her degree. Second, because the college officials believed she could not ensure a patient's safety either during the temporary training or in practice. Third, they doubted that state authorities would license her under these circumstances. All told, the college denied Davis entrance because she could not profit from her education.[43] A unanimous Supreme Court concurred. Writing again for the Court, Powell underscored what Davis could not do instead of distinguishing what she could do.

Powell argued that the individualized faculty supervision that Davis would require was analogous to an affirmative action policy. Because affirmative action and reasonable accommodations gave someone special treatment, whoever provided this treatment—a school or employer—was expected to do less than if they provided equality of opportunity.[44] Reasonable accommodations, like affirmative action, imposed less of a burden on an institution than programs that had to be changed because they had initially denied a student equality of opportunity. Since reasonable accommodations imposed an affirmative obligation on a school or an employer, it must be exercised with caution. The Court ruled that affirmative action should be applied only if it did not fundamentally alter a program.[45]

Powell, then, defined what he meant by a fundamental alteration or a substantial modification.[46] He framed the issue of accommodations cautiously, asking if the physical qualifications demanded were necessary for participation in the program. When the school officials answered affirmatively, he agreed that a nurse must have the capacity to understand speech to ensure patient safety. At the same time, Powell recognized that the college would have to provide Davis with more clinical supervision than it did other students. More extensive modifications would require "fundamental changes" in the "nature of [the] program" and would alter her basic course of study to permit her to "receive even a rough equivalent of the training a nursing program normally gives." The Court defined the necessary accommodation as the elimination of the entire clinical program. This could not be demanded, as Powell explained, because Congress had not intended Section 504 "to limit the freedom of an educational institution to require reasonable physical qualifications for admission to a clinical program."[47] The college was, therefore, not obliged either to provide Davis with individualized faculty supervision or to change the clinical orientation of the program.

As Powell saw it, Davis could not protest that she had been discriminated against, unless she proved that the program had been designed specifically to exclude her among other disabled people.[48] Causation must be found. If the Court established that criteria for admission to the program were neutral, then the person with a disability could not protest discrimination. Powell went out of his way to embrace the type of analysis found in Title VII disparate impact cases, which required that selection criteria that excluded members of a protected class be justified by a showing of necessity. Disabled people must prove that the exclusionary criteria were unnecessary and, therefore, illegitimate.

The Supreme Court distinguished its decision in *Davis* from an important lower court decision, in which a judge had decided that all the barriers to equal treatment for disabled people were wrong. The lower court judge had stipulated that barriers could be separated into three categories: social bias, disparate impact from neutral surmountable barriers, and insurmountable barriers. Powell ruled that Davis faced insurmountable barriers, whereas the disabled people in the lower federal court case had not. His reasoning was because their employers complained about the cost of accommodations, and cost, he said, was not an insurmountable barrier. Powell used the 1978 Rehabilitation Act amendments to gain this insight into congressional intent.[49]

Powell also held that the college had no obligation to extend accommodations to Davis if she was unlikely to "benefit from any affirmative action that the regulation reasonably could be interpreted as requiring."[50] Unlike civil rights cases about racial prejudice, in *Davis* the Court had what could be described as a paternalistic card to play that proved detrimental to a person with a disability fighting discrimination. Whether someone benefits from education was determined not by disabled people themselves but by experts. Powell did not rule, however, on who should choose the experts and whether those experts should be trained in education or in disability.

Finally, Powell ruled that Davis could be denied entrance if her presence endangered public safety.[51] Again, Powell deferred to experts and the institution to determine public safety. A refusal could be justified if it were backed by the professional judgments of the institution concerning significant health risks to third parties.[52] Just as in the situation with the experts who determined whether Davis would benefit from her education, Powell did not give this prospective student the opportunity to challenge the institutions' experts with disability experts.

Powell gave school officials and employers three reasons for not providing accommodations: no fundamental changes in programs, the person with a disability will not benefit, and the safety defense. Powell's decision, however, ignored what had really been behind the case: the expense of accommodations. The college feared that it would have to shoulder this burden.[53] But instead of making the college face this issue, Powell placed the burden back upon Davis. Even more maddening to Davis was that, while this burden was imposed on her, she was not permitted to present her own defense. Experts provided her defense. Just as he would rule in the *Romeo* decision, Powell sought the experts' opinions to determine reasonable accommodations.

Powell's determination about experts not only robbed Davis of her own voice, but it also skirted the issue of who would choose the so-called impartial experts and what training would make them eligible to make judgments. Different experts have different findings. The Court not only listened to the expert that Southeastern College had hired from Duke University Medical Center, but it also heeded the majority opinion of the entire nursing staff at the college. No questions about the staff's motives were raised when they acted as experts and voted to deny Davis's entrance. Meanwhile, no experts had been appointed by or for Davis herself to contest the opinion of these experts.[54]

Recognizing the discrepancy in expert determination, the workers' compensation scheme, for instance, allows both the injured worker and the employer to have input into who will offer expert opinion. This scheme recognizes that employers and injured workers are entangled in an antagonistic relationship, and it attempts to provide an impartial expert by allowing each side to help choose the expert. Powell made no such allowance. He accepted experts chosen by the school officials, who determined that Davis would not benefit from the program and that her work as a nurse might jeopardize public safety. Powell did not address the school's motivation for having the experts come to this conclusion: the cost of providing accommodations for Davis and other students with disabilities.

Neither Affirmative Action nor Equality of Opportunity

Although the Supreme Court never reversed its narrow construction of reasonable accommodations, in 1984, in *Alexander v. Choate,* it *did* modify the *Davis* ruling by differentiating the definition of reasonable accommodations from that of affirmative action.[55] The Court decided that unlike affirmative action, which helped those who had been victimized in the past, reasonable accommodations were designed to eliminate only the barriers that disabled people presently faced.[56] Instead of increasing the burden of schools and employers, because reasonable accommodations lacked any element of compensation or retribution, the Court decreased it. Whereas affirmative action provided more relief for victims of racial discrimination than did the antidiscrimination provisions in the Civil Rights Act, reasonable accommodations gave disabled people less relief, in failing to secure for them the equality of opportunity offered by the antidiscrimination provisions.

Alexander v. Choate resolved whether the Tennessee Medicaid Office's decision to reduce coverage for in-hospital days from twenty days to fourteen days had a discriminatory impact on disabled people. Thurgood Marshall, writing for a unanimous Court, argued that, while it did hurt disabled people, Medicaid had to give them only "equal access" to healthcare, not "meaningful care."[57] To reach this conclusion, Marshall distinguished reasonable accommodations from affirmative action, arguing that the former imposed less of a burden on institutions than the latter.

Reasonable accommodations were different from affirmative action in that disabled people needed tools to practice equal opportunity. Affirmative action, by contrast, gave preference to minorities and women if they were as qualified as white male candidates for a job. The tools, Marshall decided, did not have to level the playing field so that disabled people could compete equally with people who did not have disabilities. The Court relied on what was called the *de minimus* doctrine. That is, persons with a disability could receive minimum help, not help that would give them the opportunity to compete on an equal basis with other members of society. Reasonable accommodation did not provide preferential treatment as affirmative action did, or equality of opportunity as antidiscrimination laws did.

More important, Marshall's idea that an educational facility or an employer must provide the minimum help to a person with a disability stemmed from an earlier Supreme Court decision, which maintained that this minimum did not have to be applied equally to all cases. If persons overcompensated for a disability, the institution could give them less than the minimum. The minimum, in other words, was determined as the Court examined each case individually, taking into account the specific talents and problems of the person with a disability. One who could partially compensate for a hearing problem because of a sharp intellect could be given less help than someone with a similar problem and a different intellect.

The decision that entrenched the *de minimus* doctrine was *Hendrick Hudson District Board of Education v. Rowley.*[58] With Justice Rehnquist writing for the majority, the Court held that a free appropriate public education, or FAPE, does not require a state to maximize the potential of each handicapped child commensurate with the opportunity provided to nonhandicapped children. The Education for All Handicapped Children Act of 1975 (EAHCA), the Court held, did not give children with disabilities the same rights to an educational opportunity that nonhandicapped children received.[59] "We think . . . provid[ing] specialized educational services to handicapped children generates *no* additional requirement that the services so provided be sufficient to maximize each child's potential 'commensurate with the opportunity provided other children.'"[60]

According to Rehnquist, Congress passed this legislation to provide federal assistance to those states which had a policy assuring that all handicapped children had the right to a free appropriate education. The key word in this phrase was *appropriate,* not *equality.* "The theme of the Act is 'free appropriate public education,'" Rehnquist articulated, "a phrase which is too complex to be captured by the word 'equal.'"[61] This legislation ensured that children with disabilities could be mainstreamed, or placed into classrooms with able-bodied children. It also extended the logic underlying the least restrictive environment theory about medical and psychological treatment of the physically and mentally disabled.[62] Rehnquist insisted that Congress never meant to provide children with disabilities equality of opportunity, which he saw as inconsistent with the phrase "basic floor of opportunity" found in the House Report for the EAHCA.[63]

If a student excelled, Rehnquist held, a school could provide this student with less help than other students.[64] In the case at bar, Amy Rowley's above-average intelligence offset her hearing impairment. The lower court had found that this eight-year-old "performs better than the average child in her class and is advancing easily from grade to grade," although it was recognized that "she understands considerably less of what goes on in the classroom than she would if she were not deaf." Amy was "not learning as much, or performing as well academically, as she would without her hand-icap." Despite a "disparity between Amy's achievement and her poten-tial," Rehnquist decided that the school had no obligation to provide her with a sign language interpreter.[65]

The reason given for not offering Amy a sign interpreter was that she heard 59 percent of what happened in her classroom. This was sufficient, according to Rehnquist, because it was above the median for Amy's class.[66] Amy, moreover, had received an individualized educational pro-gram (IEP). That this program did not maximize her potential, or even level the playing field with other children, was not the school's burden. The Court's interpretation of public education was simply that it must be available to all school-aged children. There was no guarantee that public education should be geared to any particular level. "We think, however, that the requirement that a State provide specialized educational services to handicapped children generates no additional requirement," Rehnquist wrote, "that the services so provided be sufficient to maximize each child's potential 'commensurate with the opportunity provided other children.'"[67]

Justice Harry Blackmun concurred with the holding but not with the rationale underlying the majority opinion. He argued that Rehnquist had relied on a misreading of the legislative history of the EAHCA. First, he said, Rehnquist had reasoned that congressional intent showed that this legislation never defined a free appropriate public education. Second, Rehnquist had misinterpreted that the legislation required that educa-tional services be offered first to those children receiving no education and then to those who had been receiving an inadequate education. Third, Rehnquist had improperly concluded that the EAHCA was adopted to open the door to public education, not to be a guarantee of it.[68]

What Rehnquist missed, Blackmun argued, was that Amy's perfor-mance must be compared to that of children without disabilities. Just as Brown v. Board of Education had drawn comparisons between education for African American children and education for white children, so should a decision about disability rights draw some comparison. Without such a comparison, the school could not discover what is appropriate for any child. According to Blackmun, Rehnquist should have argued that the act was designed so that children could develop their maximum self-suffi-ciency, not merely receive some education. Blackmun purported that chil-dren with disabilities should be entitled to the same level of education that the rest of the children received. He insisted that a self-sufficiency stan-dard was appropriate and consistent with the legislative history of the act, and he quoted the Senate Report's statement that children should have "equal educational opportunity."[69]

Blackmun also thought that determining the "adequacy of educational benefits" should not be left up to school officials or rehabilitation experts. Lower federal courts, he purported, had acknowledged this potential for bias.[70] To avoid the possibility that society's aversion to disabled people would color their determination, *Mills v. Board of Education of District Columbia* had provided a scheme for equitable spending: if money was a factor in determining what type of education should be provided, the school had to reduce spending on everyone, not just the children with disabilities. This scheme created a level of comparison between the able-bodied and students with disabilities that the Supreme Court majority in *Rowley* had not.

The Supreme Court not only rejected this scheme for equitable spending, it also failed to acknowledge that prejudice could bias the so-called experts' determination that a certain level of education was adequate. Rehnquist relied only on Amy's grades and general academic progress to determine if the school had met an adequate standard. Without any general standard for comparison, Amy's intelligence acted as a compensating factor that reduced the school's burden for her education. This meant that the Court did not give children with disabilities equality of opportunity, but rather expected them to conform to society.[71] Amy could aim for the middle of the bell curve, nothing more.

Justices White, Brennan, and Marshall dissented from the majority opinion. Like Blackmun, they insisted that children with disabilities were to receive "full educational opportunity." They also insisted that children with disabilities must be compared to children without disabilities in order to provide some sort of measure of equality. Unlike Rehnquist, this trio of justices did not believe that Amy had been given "an equal opportunity to learn." White wrote, "Amy Rowley, without a sign-language interpreter, comprehends less than half of what is said in the classroom—less than half of what normal children comprehend. This is hardly an equal opportunity to learn, even if Amy makes passing grades."[72]

The *Rowley* decision was not a total defeat for disabled people. Just as *Youngberg v. Romeo* gave disabled people a minimum standard of treatment, so too did this case. With its *Rowley* decision, the Supreme Court instituted some educational benefit standard, even if that standard was not on par with the one that existed for the rest of the children. It concocted what was called a multifactor test for determining the meaning of "appropriate education." This test discerned the nature and severity of disability, ascertained the local level of resources and results, and sought an evaluation by educational experts and an impartial hearing officer.[73] A minimum, the disability activists concluded, was better than nothing.

Generating Resentment and Antagonism

Society's obligation to disabled people appeared to be minimal. Neither Congress nor the Supreme Court ruled that disabled people were entitled to equal protection under law. They deserved only a minimum of care, be it in a hospital, an institution, or a school. The Court did not oblige members of mainstream society to provide disabled people the same equality of opportunity that the able-bodied population enjoyed. Because disabled people were different, legislation on their behalf could contain specific provisions that were not necessarily to their liking or to their advantage. At the same time, since society provided for them at all, they were not powerless. They should be grateful for any disability policy. The Court also ruled that society should not be made to face too heavy of a burden with reasonable accommodations. Programs for disabled people should not conflict with the demands of an organized society.

What is more, the room reserved for people with physical and mental disabilities was in large part dependent upon them. If disabled people could not profit from their education or perform their job in accordance with guidelines determined by their employers, society had no obligation to help them fit into the mainstream. To be sure, the state had to clothe, feed, and shelter disabled people. But protection from discrimination in school and at the workplace was not called for unless a person individually proved that he or she was worthy of such a placement. The Supreme Court's ruling on *Davis* not only narrowly construed what accommodations were reasonable, it also established the precedent that before a school or an employer had to make these accommodations for someone with a disability, that person had to show that he or she was "otherwise qualified."

In 1978, when HEW issued its regulations for implementing Section 504, it coined the term "otherwise qualified." Yet, because the Supreme Court had no obligation to follow departmental guidelines, it could have defined this term in three different ways when it ruled in the *Davis* case. First, it could have held that Davis should be able to accomplish all that the college required, despite her handicap. This interpretation placed the burden on disabled people. Also, it only protected them from prejudice about their disability. Second, the Court could have held that, in order to be considered otherwise qualified, Davis needed to show that she would profit from an education with the accommodation. Finally, Davis had to show that she could perform all the duties other than those her disability inhibited her from doing. Unlike the first two, this last interpretation made the employer shoulder the burden of providing accommodations. It guaranteed that employers would take their procedural duties seriously.[74]

Writing a unanimous opinion, Justice Powell chose the second interpretation and decided that "otherwise qualified" meant that persons with a disability must prove that they could profit from the education despite their handicap.[75] This meant that the Court protected Davis only from the perception that her disability hindered her ability to learn; it did not protect her from any actual limitation placed upon her from the outside. Powell's interpretation could be equated with the anatomical view of disabled people that Dr. Howard Rusk and the rehabilitation movement had abandoned in the 1940s. What Powell's interpretation meant was that if Davis could not complete any one aspect of the program, she could rightfully be denied entrance.[76]

Powell arrived at this definition of "otherwise qualified" because the Rehabilitation Act did not have "plain meaning." It was ambiguous. Congress had never included similar phrases in other antidiscrimination laws, argued Powell. Hence, the Court had no guide for interpreting the qualifications of a person with disabilities. Congress might have meant "qualified other than with regard to the handicap" or "qualified notwithstanding the disability." Taking into consideration how a handicap influenced an individual's abilities was necessary and inevitable, Powell argued, and the Court was merely recognizing the policy decision Congress had already made. Powell concluded that Davis must prove that she was capable of being educated *despite* her deafness.[77]

Powell's position on "otherwise qualified" reflected what has been described as the equal treatment model, and not the equal impact model, of discrimination. That is, all people were evaluated by neutral rules and standards regardless of personal characteristics. Powell stipulated that the term "otherwise qualified" meant that a person with a disability must be as qualified as an able-bodied person. To compete successfully for a job, this person with a disability would have to be more qualified than the person without one.

By contrast, the equal impact model found discriminatory practices if a protected group suffered an adverse impact. It leveled the workplace playing field and allowed disabled people to compete on an equal basis *with* accommodations. This model would rely on empirical evidence, questioning, for instance, how many disabled people there are in comparison to how many were employed at a company. The evidence revealed the impact that enough, or not enough, disabled people were employed. There was no need to prove that the company had purposely excluded disabled people from employment.

Before the Supreme Court ruled on *Davis,* a number of federal courts had relied on the equal impact model to deem how a person with disabilities was otherwise qualified.[78] These courts examined the qualifications of the person with disabilities in context with what were the essential functions of a job. The Pennsylvania Department of Public Welfare (DPW), for instance, had to provide three blind income maintenance workers with part-time readers so that they could perform their job duties. The federal court forced the DPW to pay for the services of these readers. The court arrived at this conclusion by determining that, while reading without aid was helpful, it was not an "essential function" of the job. Instead, the position required dedication, mature judgment, and experience.[79] Thus, the maintenance workers were qualified, since their positions could be restructured so that readers could complete the one task of reading.

By being more concerned about equaling the positions of social groups than promoting neutral treatment, this lower federal court had followed some semblance of the equal impact model.[80] The Pregnancy Discrimination Act of 1981 constituted another example of this model. Here, Congress mandated that the competitive disadvantage at the workplace that resulted from women bearing children could not be cause for termination. The employer must pay for the inconvenience associated with the birth. Laws preventing discrimination because of religious practice followed the same logic.[81]

More important, the essential functions interpretation of some lower federal courts held that employers should provide reasonable accommodations while determining if someone was qualified. It did not provide a sequential threshold where the employer would first insist that someone was not qualified so that the employer would then not need to provide accommodations. This position alleviated the employers' temptation to show that an applicant or worker with a disability was not qualified so that they need not provide accommodations. Some critics claimed that the emphasis on essential functions undermined the very notion of qualifications. While this might be an overstatement, it was true that the judicial determination of essential functions deprived employers of their absolute discretion over qualifications.

Once the Court handed down *Davis,* some lower federal courts navigated around the issue of qualifications by determining that the essential functions of the position were different.[82] Still, most workers with disabilities could not meet the high threshold of being otherwise qualified. The irony about Davis herself was that she was already a licensed practical nurse with some experience. In denying her entrance to the program, the Court said, in effect, that if she could not perform every duty of a nurse she could not be trained to be one. It ignored the possibility that not all nurses took positions in operating rooms, for instance, where their inability to hear would endanger a patient. Davis could have practiced nursing in a doctor's office, where she could have understood all the patients' needs.

With the *Davis* decision, the Court placed the burden of proof squarely on disabled people. They had to prove that they were otherwise qualified. This decision gave school officials and employers a means of raising a roadblock against disabled people that would not disguise their intent. They could raise the issue of qualifications in the beginning; then they would not have to fight about accommodations.[83] In addition to "professional autonomy," "inability to benefit," and "public safety," the college hid behind the issue of "otherwise qualified" to avoid having to pay for the accommodations.[84]

Most important, the *Davis* decision determined that the first threshold question in disability law was qualifications. Placing this question first cultivated an antagonistic relationship between disabled people and the able-bodied. Employers scrutinized the persons to determine if they were otherwise qualified. In this sense, disability law has encouraged employers to either make light of employees' or applicants' disabilities or emphasize their incompetence. The discussion about the qualification rested on the issue of capability. The Court's ruling in *Davis* encouraged school officials and employers to emphasize that disabled people were not "differently-abled," but rather they were *un*able to work or learn in school.

The Question of Disability

Trying to prove that someone with disabilities was better suited for a position than all the other able-bodied candidates for that position was complicated by one last factor. From the outset, people had to disclose their disabilities in order to receive protection under the law. Proof of a disability, in combination with the issue of qualifications, put disabled people, especially those with invisible disabilities, in a dilemma. Workers with disabilities had to reveal their differences at the same time they were making the case that these differences posed no problem for them. They shouldered the burden of proving that their disabilities did not limit their ability to work. Nowhere was this dilemma more true than with a person who had a debilitating disease.

The issue of which disabilities gave people protection under Section 504 of the Rehabilitation Act was addressed in the 1987 *School Board of Nassau County, Florida v. Arline* decision.[85] Gene Arline, who had been dismissed from her position as an elementary school teacher when her tuberculosis (TB) flared up, protested that her dismissal had been based on discrimination. Arline had first been hospitalized for TB in 1957. The disease went into remission for twenty years; then she suffered relapses in 1977 and 1978.[86] The question before the Supreme Court was not whether Arline was a danger to her students because the disease was contagious. The Court refused to rule on this without medical documentation. Instead, the question was whether TB could be considered a disability even though Arline had no diminished capacity as a result of it. Was an asymptomatic disease considered a disability and, therefore, covered under the jurisdiction of the Rehabilitation Act?

Writing for the majority, Justice William J. Brennan relied on the three-pronged definition of a *disability* established by HEW to determine if Arline had a disability. He decided that this disease was in fact a disability. Although Arline's TB might not have affected a major life activity, which was the first prong of the definition, it fulfilled the second prong. That is, Arline clearly had a history of an impairment. The disease also satisfied the third prong of the definition—that she could be "regarded as" having a disability. Brennan, therefore, rejected the argument that Arline could be dismissed simply for having the disease. Nor could the decision be dropped because she had no disability. Brennan wrote that "such an impairment might not diminish a person's physical or mental capabilities, but could nevertheless substantially limit that person's ability to work as a result of the negative reactions of others to the impairment."[87]

When Arline brought suit in a federal district court, the judge dismissed her case, ruling that Arline's handicap did not protect her. Even if Arline did not suffer from diminished capacity, the judge wrote, the fact that TB was contagious prevented her from being otherwise qualified. Arline was caught within a Catch-22: this judge ruled that her disability was not serious enough for her to be protected by Section 504 of the Rehabilitation Act but that it was severe enough to cost her her job.

The Supreme Court refused to distinguish between the contagiousness of Arline's disease and the level of her impairment. Brennan decided that the underlying conditions were the same. He then faulted the district court for inadequate discovery of factual findings about Arline's disease. He ruled that the district court needed to determine the duration and severity of Arline's disease: Was the TB contagious when the board dismissed Arline? Could she have transmitted TB to her students? And had the school board reasonably accommodated Arline? The Supreme Court had no means of determining if Arline was otherwise qualified until these questions had been answered. Brennan remanded the case back to the lower federal court for the determination that Arline was or was not putting her students at risk.

To arrive at the answers, Brennan decided that experts, not the judiciary, should submit medical evidence.[88] The school board, not Arline, had to provide evidence of her limitations. Once the board had this information, it could assess what were the essential functions of Arline's position and whether it could reasonably accommodate her.[89]

While the disability community was pleased by the Court's ruling in the *Arline* decision, it was disturbed by one aspect of Brennan's ruling. He gave credence to the fear and apprehension that society had about Arline's disease. This acknowledgment resembled the *Cleburne* decision, where White had highlighted the idea that the retarded are not capable of caring for themselves.

Rehnquist and Scalia disagreed with the majority's decision that a person with a contagious disease had a disability under Section 504 of the Rehabilitation Act. Rehnquist, writing the dissent, argued that the Court had established a precedent in offering a narrow interpretation of this legislation with both *Rowley* and *Alexander v. Choate*. He believed that "there was no doubt that Arline was discharged because of the contagious nature of tuberculosis, and not because of any diminished physical or mental capabilities resulting from her condition." Yet, Congress never answered the question of "whether discrimination on the basis of contagiousness constitutes discrimination 'by reason of . . . handicap.'"[90] He concluded that the Court could not render such an "expansive" interpretation of the Rehabilitation Act and decide that a contagious disease was a disability.

Overall, disability activists applauded the Court's findings in the *Arline* decision. Within this series of decisions that the activists thought had narrowed either Section 504 or limited disability rights, it was the one exception. Rendering an expansive definition of *disability* had an impact not only for TB and other contagious diseases like the HIV virus, but it also meant that any asymptomatic disease might be considered a disability. When Congress passed the Americans with Disabilities Act (ADA), this decision would help it formulate what constituted a disability. More important, it provided the federal courts with guidance about how to interpret this definition of *disability* when they interpreted the ADA.

The rights orientation of the Rehabilitation Act proved not nearly as strong as the disability activists had hoped. Neither HEW's regulations nor the Supreme Court's rulings conveyed support for disability rights unambiguously. Section 504 had not been anticipated in 1973, and despite modifications to the Rehabilitation Act with the amendments of 1974 and 1978, Congress still made no strong commitment about employment rights of disabled people. While Congress elaborated its position about these rights by making references to civil rights law, the federal courts immediately interpreted disability rights differently than civil rights for minorities and women.

To be sure, the discrimination leveled at disabled people and at minorities and women shared many of the same characteristics. Discrimination was based on fear, false stereotypes, and social animus. The Court, however, concentrated little on the myths surrounding disability, emphasizing instead the intractable problems caused by the physical and mental impairments of disbled people. The Supreme Court justices emphasized that minorities faced no physical or mental impairments and that women faced only a few physical ones, like the capacity to bear children, that could prevent them from qualifying for a position, whereas disabled people encountered many.

To minimize the problems associated with the federal courts' interpretation and, therefore, strengthen disability employment rights, Congress needed to tailor the provisions about the terms "otherwise qualified," "essential functions," "reasonable accommodations," and "undue hardship" specifically to the problems of disabled people. Congress did not resolve this confusion with the Rehabilitation Act amendments of 1974 or 1978, however, because it left these issues up to the federal courts. When the Supreme Court resolved these questions, it arranged them in a way that required disabled people to prove their qualifications before the issue of reasonable accommodations could be raised, thereby weakening the rights granted under Section 504.

By the time the disability rights movement succeeded in influencing the passage of the Americans with Disabilites Act of 1990, these threshold questions had become entrenched in disability law. Not only did they become the centerpiece of this antidiscrimination legislation, but again Congress gave the federal courts great latitude in defining the limits of the threshold determinations. The federal courts decided who had a disability and if a person with a disability was qualified for a position. In effect, federal court judges became the experts who decided whether people had impairments or disabilities. Acting as state experts, the federal court judges were the gatekeepers of the ADA, determining who warranted statutory protection and who did not.

6

Two Horns of a Dilemma: The Americans with Disabilities Act

In 1990, Congress enacted the Americans with Disabilities Act (ADA). Scores of members of Congress crowded onto the list of legislative sponsors hoping to claim credit for this humanitarian law. Like so many pieces of disability legislation before it, the ADA transcended partisan lines. With President George H. W. Bush's avid support, Congress passed it by an overwhelming majority, and the ADA was signed into law with great panoply.

The passage of ADA was heralded as the most meaningful law since the Civil Rights Act of 1964. Members of the disability rights movement thought they had great cause for celebration. "It's the first declaration of independence and equity for people with disabilities," said Justin Dart, a disability activist. "It's like the Berlin Wall coming down."[1] Another person with a disability succinctly conveyed her enthusiasm by declaring, "I'll be human again."[2]

Other disability activists extolled specific provisions in the ADA. In particular, Robert Burgdorf described the public accommodations provisions as "innovative" and "unprecedented [in] scope."[3] He went so far as to suggest that the civil rights community, long seen as the role model for the disability rights movement, might profit from using the public accommodations provisions in the ADA as a model for changing the Civil Rights Act. These provisions banned discrimination against disabled people, not only in hotels and restaurants but in every "mom and pop" store that civil rights legislation failed to reach.[4]

Disability activists also viewed the provisions for protection from discrimination at the workplace—Title I—as a tremendous accomplishment. While the disability rights movement was exhilarated, employers voiced fears of being buried under an avalanche of lawsuits. In preparation for the enactment of the ADA in 1992, employers had their legal counsel trained in disability law and set up workshops to help them understand it.[5] Some employers expressed the concern that the new disability law would erode their rightful control over the workplace.

Contrary to the business community's forecast, disabled people have found the provisions for protection from employment discrimination have been profoundly disappointing.[6] Few disabled people have gained employment as a result of the antidiscrimination provisions in Title I. An even smaller number of disabled people, who already have employment, have not had their suits thrown out by the federal courts on summary judgment. And just a handful of people have won suits against employers, forcing them to provide reasonable accommodations. These conclusions are substantiated by the fact that 80 percent of all Title I cases have been thrown out on summary judgment, and that 94 percent of the remaining 20 percent have been decided in the employer's favor.[7]

Few people with disabilities have received relief from discrimination, for the most part because the federal courts have interpreted the ADA so that those people seeking employment or trying to maintain their positions confront a Catch 22: either they have such a severe disability that they are not qualified to work, or their disability is not serious enough to warrant statutory protection. What disability activists have found even more alarming is that some people have discovered that while their impairment provides them with no protection under law, it does give their employer grounds to terminate them. The federal courts have upheld an employer's right not to hire someone with a history of cancer, for instance, whose condition, this employer fears, might increase a company's health insurance costs.

In mid-1999, the Supreme Court went even further than most of the lower federal courts. The Court limited who warrants statutory protection, with the holding that persons must have a disability that substantially limits their daily life activities which cannot be mitigated by medication or equipment. People who control their epilepsy or diabetes with medication, for example, do not have a disability that entitles them to protection. What is more, the Supreme Court affirmed the lower federal courts' position that some people with limiting, but not substantially limiting, disabilities expose themselves to termination when they request accommodations.

Oddly enough, this legal bind was not anticipated by either the advocates or the opponents of the ADA. One activist had been concerned that "the bill's key phrase, 'undue hardship,' is its undoing."[8] Meanwhile, the business lobby put most of its energy into diminishing the strength of the legislation on the same grounds, insisting that the provisions about reasonable accommodations and undue hardship be made less stringent.[9] Few cases before the federal courts, however, have been dismissed on summary judgment because of these issues. Most cases are dismissed, since disabled people have had difficulty proving that they do indeed have a substantially limiting impairment that does not interfere with their ability to work.

Neither the disability activists nor business lobbyists could have anticipated this battle over definitions for two reasons. First, the three-pronged definition of a disability that Congress included in the ADA was not new. This definition had been included in the Rehabilitation Act, though neither the federal courts nor employers contesting requests for accommodations had made it into a significant issue. Second, in House and Senate Committee Reports and on the floor of both chambers, Congress spent a great number of words clarifying what constituted a disability. The idea that medication or assistive devices, like a prosthesis, mitigated a condition had been discussed and dismissed by Congress.

In rendering these three decisions, the Supreme Court clearly departed from the administrative and legislative precedents. What changed between the 1970s and the 1990s was that the lower federal courts and the Supreme Court switched their emphasis from the threshold about qualifications to the one about coverage. That is, the federal court judges and justices stopped referring to medical experts and started acting like these experts themselves.

Acting as such experts, these judges and justices have turned themselves into gatekeepers. Instead of adjudicating if people with disabilities have encountered discrimination, they have concentrated on who deserves protection. The federal court judges and justices essentially have said "enough," and limited statutory coverage under Title I.

Although critics of antidiscrimination legislation often have leveled the charge that this type of protection produces frivolous lawsuits that waste the time and money of all parties involved, the Supreme Court's rulings on Title I constitute the second time this charge has not been dismissed. Barring one exception, the Supreme Court has been expansive about these jurisdictional issues, deciding that the Civil Rights Act of 1964, for example, included Hispanics, though Congress only discussed African Americans during the legislative process.

What accounts for this type of reasoning is that vestiges of the psychoanalytic rehabilitation model remain in the minds of the lower federal court judges and a majority of Supreme Court justices. On one hand, the lower federal court judges have expressed themselves in terms of this model, because the few people they have ruled as deserving of accommodations could be characterized as "super crips," or people who more than compensate for their impairments. On the other hand, most of the federal court judges and a majority on the Supreme Court have incorporated the ideas underlying the psychoanalytic model by ruling that employers cannot be expected to meet the needs of employees who are impaired, though not substantially impaired, because it would undermine their managerial prerogatives.

Requests for accommodation have been characterized by the federal courts as if disabled people thought they were exempt from the rules and regulations that govern the workplace. As a result, when disabled people pursue litigation, they put their credibility on the line. In most cases, the credibility of these people has been questioned, since the federal court judges have ruled that most of them do not have disabilities. In questioning the legitimacy of their claims, they are exposing these people with "boutique" disabilities for what they are—cheaters, shirkers, or frauds—who are unjustly attempting to circumvent the rules and regulations that all employees must abide in the United States.

Public attention is drawn from the prejudice of the employer or the barriers within the workplace, which constitutes the crux of the disability rights model, to the person with a disability. The federal courts have not held employers or the workplace up for scrutiny because their decisions do not go beyond examining people with disabilities. Thus, the federal court judges and Supreme Court justices have taken it upon themselves to safeguard employers from being overrun by employee demands for accommodation. They have been, in effect, disciplining them for bringing cases to court that attempt to disrupt workplace normalcy. Attempting to modify the behavior of these employees, these judges and justices have limited their statutory access.

Rights and Worth

Beginning in the early 1980s, the disability rights movement campaigned for the ADA. This movement wanted legislation that would strengthen the antidiscrimination provisions in the Rehabilitation Act and be applicable to disabled people who worked in the private sector. It was estimated that more than 8 million people with disabilities who wanted to work had not landed a position.[10] With the hope of employing these people, the disability rights movement lobbied Congress to broaden and strengthen the rights of disabled people.

Unlike the psychoanalytical approach embraced by the pioneers in rehabilitation medicine and the officials who ran the vocational rehabilitation program, the rights perspective put forth by the disability rights movement focused on discrimination in society. Workers with disabilities should not accommodate society, as the people behind vocational rehabilitation had initially propounded. On the contrary, society had an obligation to accommodate them. In terms of employment, the disability rights movement suggested that the workplace should be reconfigured so that people with disabilities could work. The legislation, therefore, concentrated on eliminating the restraints and restrictions that society imposed on people with disabilities. Unlike the traditional approach advocated by the rehabilitation movement, the rights approach never tried to increase the physical and economic impact of people with disabilities by correcting or compensating for their impairments. As Harlan Hahn characterizes this approach, or what he calls the minority group perspective, it rejects the idea of "encouraging disabled individuals to strive to approximate standards set by the nondisabled majority."[11]

This movement also advocated changing the external environment through collective action. First, it maintained that the biases and unfavorable attitudes of the able-bodied represent the primary problem associated with having a disability. "Being paralyzed has meant far more than being unable to walk," proclaimed Arlene Mayerson, a disability activist. "It has meant being excluded from public schools, being denied employment opportunity and being deemed an 'unfit parent.'"[12] An antidiscrimination disability law was intended to fight what was seen as a pervasive prejudice in American society against people with disabilities.

Activists wanted society to take full responsibility for its prejudices and fears about people with disabilities. The rights model propounded by the disability rights movement took issue with the attitude expressed by Justice Thurgood Marshall in the 1985 Supreme Court decision *Alexander v. Choate.* Marshall claimed that discrimination stems from "apathy not animus." He implied that the "unconscious aversion to illness and injury" should be treated less harshly under law than other forms of prejudice. The disability rights movement, by contrast, demanded that society tackle these fears head-on. Members of this movement underscored the need to combat the stigma and prejudice that people without disabilities held against those with disabilities. There was no need to discover whether their prejudice was conscious and malicious or if it sprang from what

Hahn calls existential anxiety, an unconscious source of prejudice that people without disabilities have because of their fears about having a disability themselves. Prejudice is prejudice, and the disability rights movement thought that the state and society should make the same commitment to its eradication that it had for women and minorities.[13]

Second, the rights orientation of the disability rights movement maintained that the environment or the public arena was shaped by public policy. During the public hearings for the ADA bill, one person explained how a policy can simply entrench a discriminatory attitude against people with disabilities. As an illustration, this witness described how he discovered that some airlines had a policy mandating that all people who used wheelchairs had to sit on a blanket placed over their seat. Supposedly, this policy had been instituted "to help evacuate [people with disabilities] in likelihood of a crash." But this witness believed that "it was a policy that airlines had invented to make sure that I, as a wheelchair user, a paralyzed person, did not soil their upholstery." Fed up with complying with humiliating policies like this one, this person protested and was arrested for refusing "to sit on an airline blanket." Neither private nor public policies, he vigorously maintained, can be accepted at face value, because they have the capacity to "rob people of their dignity and . . . their humanness."[14]

Finally, the rights approach furthered by the disability rights movement contended that policies reflect pervasive social attitudes and values. Dart explained that "our society is still infected by the ancient, now almost subconscious assumption that people with disabilities are less than fully human and therefore are not eligible for the opportunities and services and support system which are available to others as a matter of right."[15] Dart and other disability rights activists recognize the prejudice born from the stigma associated with disability. For this reason, disability rights activists demanded that American society accept responsibility for its fears about the prospect of having a disability. Part of this responsibility meant that it would have to face prejudice resulting from what Hahn calls "aesthetic anxiety, which betrays a deep sense of discomfort about the presence of persons with physical characteristics that are perceived as deviant or unappealing."[16] Underscoring society's attitudinal bias, one witness during the public hearings for the ADA insisted that it should no longer be acceptable to exclude a class of children with Down Syndrome from a zoo, as a zookeeper in New Jersey had done, because "they would upset the chimpanzees."[17] Switching the burden from people with disabilities to the society they live in, the rights model underscores how society has created a disabling environment. This model also calls into question the stigma that so many people associate with disability.[18]

Yet, despite the lobbying efforts of the disability rights movement, the ADA is a hodgepodge of both the rights approach and the traditional psychoanalytical approach. On one hand, the legislation provides people with strong statutory rights. It ascribes much of the joblessness of people with disabilities to employment discrimination, not their inability to work. On the other hand, the legislation gave the federal courts the discretion to interpret these rights, knowing that the courts might make it difficult for people with disabilities to obtain them. And indeed, this is what has happened. The lower federal courts have followed the Supreme Court's notion that society's prejudicial attitudes about people with disabilities should not be highlighted. The Court's perception has been that these attitudes do not stop disabled people from securing employment. Rather, it is their actual physical or mental impairments that limit job performance and, therefore, their ability to find and maintain work.

At the same time, the Court has decided that people with disabilities should be kept from flooding the courtrooms with their requests for reasonable accommodations. Interpreting the employment provisions for the first time, the Supreme Court decided against disabled people, not because they could not perform a job, or their requests were unreasonable, or even that they caused an employer undue hardship. Instead, the Court held that they should not be protected by the ADA. Given the strength of the statute, the Court insisted that the employers needed protection from being overrun by all the disabled people who were wrongly seeking legal redress.

Legislative Beginnings

In the late-1980s, it was widely acknowledged in Congress that the Rehabilitation Act had two interrelated problems. First, the broad language made congressional intent unclear, giving the federal courts free reign to interpret the legislation. Second, the Rehabilitation Act protected only people working in the public sector or under a governmental contract. Disability rights activists insisted that legislation that would prevent discrimination in the private sector was needed.[19]

Between 1981 and 1988, discrimination against people with disabilities had become more pronounced. In 1988, only 23.4 percent of men with disabilities worked full-time, down from 29.8 percent, and only 13.1 percent of women, up from 11.4 percent. Salaries for men fell from 77 percent to 64 percent of what other workers made, and from 69 percent to 62 percent for women. A study of the cost of accommodations in 1982 by federal contractors pursuing Section 503 reported that only 22 percent of the people with disabilities working for them required any accommodations. Of that 22 percent, 51 percent were achieved at no cost, and 30 percent cost $500 or less. Also, workers with disabilities were often found to be just as productive as, or more productive than, their able-bodied coworkers. The employers' cost of workers' compensation, moreover, did not rise as a result of employing disabled people. The disability rights movement often referred to these figures as evidence that refusing to hire people with disabilities occurred not as a result of an employer's expense but because of either his or her ignorance or prejudice.[20]

Disability rights activists initially persuaded the legislative authors of the first bill that disability rights should be treated differently than civil rights. In 1983, the United States Commission on Civil Rights observed that civil rights legislation should apply to people with disabilities "only when, and to the degree that, they are equally relevant." The commission quoted a judge as writing that "attempting to fit the problem of discrimination against the handicapped into the model remedy for race discrimination is akin to fitting a square peg into a round hole."[21] The 1986 National Council on the Handicapped devoted thirty-four pages of its report to the problem of modeling disability rights law on civil rights.[22]

The primary distinction between civil rights and disability rights rests on the fact that people with disabilities must demonstrate that they belong in the class or category of people with disabilities. Racial minorities and women have no need to submit proof. To compensate for this difference, the first piece of legislation—the Weicker bill—proposed that disabled people not have to show that they had been victims of workplace discrimination.

Senator Lowell Weicker, a Republican from Connecticut, introduced a disability rights bill in April 1988 that was premised on the assumption that people with disabilities regularly encountered discrimination in the workplace.[23] While these people had to prove that they had disabilities, once this had been demonstrated they did not have to show that their employer or potential employer had consciously discriminated against them.[24]

The Weicker bill derived this perspective on discrimination from the Supreme Court's decision in *Alexander v. Choate*. Here, Justice Marshall had written for the Court that intentional and unintentional discrimination in the workplace should be actionable. This was not that discrimination could be proven solely through the disparate impact test, which discovered discrimination as a result of an impact. In other words, if only

1 percent of a company's employees had disabilities, whereas 5 percent of all potential employees lived with disabilities, a person with a disability could show that the company was discriminatory. Contrary to Weicker's belief, Marshall had not discarded the question of intent. Rather, he had tried to balance the disparate impact test with the need to prove discriminatory intent. The Weicker bill carried Marshall's idea one step further, using only the disparate impact test.

The prohibition against discrimination in the Weicker bill was vast and far-reaching. While Weicker defended the bill by arguing that he drafted these provisions after considering the Supreme Court's position in *Alexander v. Choate,* it might be more appropriate, albeit more controversial, to suggest that he had simply extended to employment the same logic that underlay the public accommodations provisions. That is, employment, like public accommodations, cannot be exclusionary. The motivation behind the exclusion was irrelevant. Just as there was no need to show that a building had been constructed to keep people with disabilities out, it was not necessary to prove that employers purposely excluded people with disabilities from their work force.[25] For this reason, the Weicker bill also required that employers make "outreach and recruitment efforts" to increase the work force representation of individuals with physical or mental impairments, or records of impairments.[26] Employers not only had to make the workplace more inclusive of people with disabilities, they also were required to publicize that they had done so.

The Weicker bill included a "broad-scoped prohibition" against discrimination of people with disabilities in the work force as well as in public accommodations and transportation. It focused on what the disability movement called the disabling environment. Kenneth Clark's findings about the psychological damage that segregation did to African American schoolchildren in *Brown v. Board of Education* was also applied to people with disabilities.[27] The segregation of people with disabilities contributed to a disabling environment.

Weicker's emphasis on the disabling environment came as no surprise to disability activists. After all, the bill had been the product of the National Council on the Handicapped. Although all the members on this council had been appointed by President Ronald Reagan, who was not a strong defender of disability rights, these members believed first and foremost that they represented the interests of people with disabilities.[28]

Weicker's bill also included no provision for employers to claim that making a reasonable accommodation for a person with a disability would cause them undue hardship. Employers could not protest about the cost of accommodating disabled people. The only way they could be absolved from providing an accommodation was if it altered the essential nature, or threatened the existence, of a program, activity, business, or facility.[29]

Another measure of the Weicker bill's strength stemmed from the fact that Senator Alan Cranston had reservations about supporting it. Cranston, a liberal Democrat from California, who had been responsible for the path-breaking antidiscrimination provision, Section 504, in the Rehabilitation Act of 1973, was concerned that Weicker's bill had no undue hardship provision for employers.[30] Cranston disagreed with Weicker, arguing that employers should not be required to provide reasonable accommodations that caused them financial hardship. Not surprisingly, the business community was also alarmed that no provision for undue hardship had been included in the Weicker bill; it labeled the reasonable accommodations provision the "bankruptcy provision."[31]

Finally, the Weicker bill was criticized because of its strict enforcement measures. Weicker modeled the enforcement mechanism on Title VII of the Civil Rights Act. It provided people with disabilities administrative action, a private right to action, monetary damages, injunctive relief, and attorney's fees. It also gave Congress the capacity to cut off federal funds from programs.[32] By contrast, Section 504 had been enforced by relying on Title VI, which was a much weaker enforcement mechanism than Title VII. For this reason, even some of the legislation's supporters maintained that the enforcement provisions in the Weicker bill were too strong.

Despite these complaints, the Weicker bill passed the Senate by a large majority of seventy-six to eight. It never became law, however, because the Speaker of the House referred it to four separate committees for consideration, and it lost legislative momentum. It was stalled also when "a rumor began to circulate that the administration was no longer in favor of the bill."[33]

Passage of the Americans with Disabilities Act

Senator Weicker left office after the 1988 election, and Senator Tom Harkin, a Democrat from Iowa, and Representative Tony Coelho, a Democrat from California, reintroduced the Americans with Disabilities bill. This piece of legislation, however, no longer rested on the assumption that the low number of employed people with disabilities indicated that discrimination was pervasive in the work force.[34] Weicker's notion that people with disabilities should be accommodated because the design of the workplace excluded them was dropped from the new ADA bill.[35] This provision had been set aside, supplanted by what its new primary Senate sponsor, Harkin, deemed more important: reporting the bill to the Senate floor without amendments.[36]

The employment discrimination provision was also weakened by the House Judiciary Committee. The term "essential functions" was modified so that the employer's definition of these functions was given consideration. As Representative Steny H. Hoyer, a Democrat from Maryland, described, "Consideration must be given to an employer's determination as to what job functions are essential."[37] A federal court would take into account both the employee's and the employer's ideas about what constituted the essential functions of a job and then make its own determination.

Finally, the ADA bill no longer gave people who protested discrimination a private right to action or punitive damages. It relied on the administrative remedy that the Equal Employment Opportunity Commission (EEOC) provided. If people with disabilities believed that their employers or prospective employers had discriminated against them, they could file a complaint with the EEOC. This change was viewed as a compromise. As Senator Theodore Kennedy, a liberal Democrat from Massachusetts, said, he would have preferred to include an "adequate remedy." He noted, "We have seen in the past that where we do not provide an adequate remedy we do not get compliance."[38] Yet Kennedy, among other supporters, did not think the bill's proponents had the strength to fight for a stronger enforcement mechanism.

Giving a person with a disability a right to private action had been opposed by some of the legislation's opponents. Although the bill's opponents preferred this administrative remedy to the right to private action and punitive damages, they were still concerned that, as Senator David Pryor, a Democrat from Arkansas, said, "This is a bill that is going to create thousands of court cases." In part, this came from the view that the ADA bill gave an "extremely loose" definition of a *disability*.[39]

Although some of the legislation's supporters disagreed, they had not thought it necessary to include a private right to action or punitive damages. For instance, Senator Robert Dole, a Republican from Kansas, said, "Those who would suggest that the ADA will unleash a mountain of litigation, I believe, are simply missing the point." Dole never explained what "the point" was, other than to offer his support for people with disabilities relying on the EEOC to file complaints against employers. Kennedy's response was more puzzling. He tackled this issue with the argument that "if you look back at the history of Section 504, you do not find many individuals who have mental and physical disabilities that have the time or the resources to go down to the court house to be able to get that injunction and bring the case." Kennedy's two statements make his motivation unclear. On one hand, he was dissatisfied with "the balance that we struck" in providing the less effective remedy. On the other hand, he had few fears that people with disabilities would have the energy or the resources to pursue litigation. "What we have seen in the areas of the disability movement," he observed, "is a different pattern in terms of litigation than has been the case of some of the other violations of the basic civil rights."[40]

Once these changes were made, the Senate passed the ADA with a great majority. Senator Orrin Hatch, a Republican from Utah, called it "the most sweeping piece of civil rights legislation possibly in the history of our country."[41] The House Education and Labor Committee reported the Senate version of the bill to the House floor two months later, on November 14, 1989.[42] On May 22, 1990, the House version of the Americans with Disabilities bill also passed with a majority of 403 to 20.[43]

Some Legislative Guidance

Although the Senate and House versions of the ADA bill had a few discrepancies, none of these addressed the fundamental provisions within the legislation.[44] They involved either minor jurisdictional points or politically sensitive issues, such as whether HIV, drug addiction, or sexual problems should be considered disabilities.[45] Once concessions were made on these points, the House passed the final version of the ADA bill with a vote of 377 to 28 on July 12. The following day it passed by a vote of ninety-one to six in the Senate.[46] On July 26, 1990, Bush signed the Americans with Disabilities bill into law.[47] Although some disability rights activists were disappointed that the final provisions about workplace discrimination no longer made the assumption that employment practices excluded people with disabilities, they applauded the legislation because it tried to establish constitutional rights for them. The ADA pieced together an amalgam of phrases to denote the qualifications of a constitutionally suspect classification for equal protection purposes. Disability activists fought for a congressional endorsement that people with disabilities should have heightened judicial scrutiny under the equal protection clause of the Fourteenth Amendment.[48]

By not following the Weicker assumption about a disabling environment, however, the employment relations provisions were modeled on the rationale underlying the Supreme Court decisions in *Davis, Alexander,* and *Arline.* As a result, the ADA replicated the Catch-22 situation embodied by Section 504. First, individuals must prove that they deserve protection because of their disability. For this reason, the definition of who has a disability was cast in extremely broad terms. Second, if deserving of protection, people with disabilities must show that they are not so disabled that they cannot perform the essential functions of a position.

Unlike Section 504 of the Rehabilitation Act, which originally gave almost no guidance about implementation, the ADA saw Congress articulating what it meant by the threshold requirements. While in the legislative debate it was not clear that members of the Senate or the House understood the legal complexities that these definitions would instill in the federal courts, the Senate Report issued by the Committee on Labor and Human Resources, chaired by Kennedy, elaborated the meaning of these requirements.

First, in an attempt to provide greater relief for people with disabilities, the Senate Report offered the extremely broad definition of a *disability* that had been included in the Rehabilitation Act Amendments of 1974. A *disability* was "a physical or mental impairment that substantially limits one or more of the major life activities." It also covered someone like a cancer survivor, for example, who had a record of having such an impairment and, although no longer impaired by it, would not be hired by an employer who feared high insurance premiums. Finally, it covered a person who had no impairment but was regarded as having one. This category was included so that a burn victim, for example, could be protected. This third prong of the definition was "particularly important for individuals with stigmatic conditions that are viewed as physical impairments but do not in fact result in substantive limitations of a major life activity."[49]

Second, the Senate Report specified what it meant for a person with a disability to be qualified for a position with or without a reasonable accommodation. This provision differed from Section 504 by getting rid of the notion that a person must be "otherwise qualified." It was believed that the word "otherwise" made the issue more confusing.[50] Moreover, the means of judging qualifications were to be determined, not by examining every aspect of the job but by scrutinizing its essential functions. The term "essential functions" was used so that people with disabilities would not be fired for failing to perform what the Senate Report called "marginal tasks" or "functions."

For further clarification, Congress specified that the EEOC should develop regulations that would discern what the term "essential functions" meant.[51] The balance between professional autonomy and employee power was to be decided, not by the employer but by this administrative agency. Employers can still require a test for a position, such as a test to ascertain whether someone can lift 100 pounds, provided that it pertains to the essential functions of a job. The tests themselves are open to question. The ADA necessitates that, to eliminate a test, people with disabilities must prove that the criteria are unnecessary and, therefore, illegitimate.[52] A test can also be changed to accommodate someone. The Senate Report gave an example from a federal court case in which a truck lifter, who had dyslexia, could not pass the written test that gave him the qualifications to operate the lift machinery. The federal court held that the company should accommodate this job candidate with an oral, instead of a written, exam.[53]

Third, the Senate Report gave guidelines about what the legislation meant by the term "reasonable accommodations." Some of the accommodations offered as examples were job restructuring, part-time or modified work schedules, and reassignment to vacant positions. The stipulation about reassignment was particularly important, since it meant that a person with a disability who could not complete the essential functions of one position in a company could request a transfer to another position.[54]

Finally, Congress made it clear that a more rigorous standard than the *de minimis* approach was needed to determine if an accommodation was reasonable. Thus, the ADA included a new term called "undue hardship."[55] A reasonable accommodation had to be made for a person with a disability unless it caused a company or firm undue hardship. The House Judiciary Committee stipulated that, in addition to the Senate Report, the federal court case *Thornburgh v. Nelson* should serve as a guide for what caused an employer undue hardship. In this case, maintenance workers who were blind had been assigned readers to help them complete the paperwork necessary for their job. This case held that employers would have to provide extensive accommodations before they could protest along the lines of hardship.

Given how difficult it would be for a company to turn down an accommodation, two amendments had been proposed during the debate on the House and Senate floors. First, it was suggested that employers should never spend more than 5 percent of their business's annual net profit on accommodations. This amendment failed by a large majority. Second, an amendment proposed that an accommodation could only cost 10 percent of employees' annual wage. This amendment was also defeated. The ADA bill contained no concrete definition or formula for determining what constituted an undue hardship.[56]

Proponents of the legislation concluded that a fixed standard could not be applied with any consistency.[57] The federal courts, it was decided, could do better defining the term on a case-by-case basis. During the debate on the House and Senate floors, members of Congress from both sides of the aisle repeatedly claimed that the federal judiciary had interpreted disability law appropriately.

Not everyone, however, agreed with the expansive role that Congress gave the federal courts. As one critic commented, why Congress believed that the federal courts had presented a "uniform and coherent interpretation of undue hardship is a complete mystery." Another law review author exclaimed that "Congress' failure in this regard was nothing short of an abdication of its responsibility."[58] As he explained, "The assumption that the courts will adequately clarify what Congress did ignores both history and reality."[59]

In the ADA, Congress gave a good deal of power to the federal courts. Although Kennedy indicated, as explained earlier, that he would have preferred to provide their own remedy to people with disabilities, this was the deal that was struck for its passage. Complaints would be lodged at the EEOC, which would also issue mandates to provide the owners of public accommodations and employers, for instance, with regulations by which to implement the ADA. If there was any contest over the enforcement of the regulations, the final interpretation was left to the federal courts. These courts, moreover, were not obliged to follow the EEOC's guidelines or mandates. This administrative body acted as an advisory body only.

For the most part, the federal courts have ignored the guidance provided by the Senate Report. Many of the courts have paid scant attention to it. For instance, some courts have ignored the directive that shift changes or job reassignments that represent reasonable accommodations. The courts have also often ignored the EEOC's mandates. Instead, these courts have taken their cue from the body of law established by the Supreme Court. Like the Supreme Court, many of the federal courts have combined the substantive issue about employment discrimination with the procedural issue of determining whether someone has a disability.[60] This has made it difficult for people with moderate disabilities, who constitute the bulk of complainants, to receive protection from discrimination in the workplace.

A Narrow Window of Opportunity

Senator Pryor's concern that the ADA would cause an explosion of litigation has not held true. To be sure, the act has produced more litigation than the Rehabilitation Act, but, as one report shows, "[T]he ADA has resulted in a surprisingly small number of lawsuits—only about 650 nationwide in five years.[61] That is tiny compared to 6 million businesses, 666,000 public and private employers, and 80,000 units of state and local governments that must comply."[62]

This is not to say that what Pryor characterized as the "extremely loose" definition of a *disability* has been free of controversy. As these complaints have begun to wind their way through the judicial system, disability activists claim that employers, not people who sought protection under the ADA, have profited from this definition. Almost 80 percent of the cases filed in the federal courts have been dismissed on summary judgment in favor of the employer. The Disability Compliance Bulletin has reported that 209 of the 261 decisions in the federal appeals courts have not been in favor of the people with disabilities.[63] Although the number of decisions has risen, this percentage has stayed constant.

People with disabilities, who thought that the new law would protect them from discrimination, have been greatly disappointed. To use the word of one disability activist, the federal courts have expressed great "hostility" toward people with disabilities.[64] This hostility has manifested itself as the federal courts render such a narrow interpretation of what it is to have a disability that few people fall within the protective scope of the ADA. If people have too much of an impairment, the federal courts have ruled that they are not qualified for a position. If they do not have what these courts consider a significant impairment, they have been excluded from coverage under the ADA. People with disabilities must demonstrate that their disabilities are so severe they dramatically hamper their daily life, yet do not impede their job performance.

Defining a Disability
A Physical or Mental Impairment that Affects a Major Life Activity

The most difficult hurdle a person with a disability confronts in the courtroom is establishing that he or she does in fact have a disability.[65] Proving that someone belongs to a protected class of people is unique to disability law. This has been complicated all the more by the fact that Congress left the determination of this all-important definition to the EEOC and the federal courts, which do not see eye-to-eye on it.

In the minds of many federal court judges, the EEOC has issued mandates—which provide concrete examples of what physical and mental conditions might be considered a disability—that are too broad. According to one legal analyst, "[I]n response to initial concerns that too many people with minor conditions were qualifying as disabled," the federal courts have issued a narrow interpretation of a disability.[66]

Indeed, the EEOC has advised that diseases like epilepsy and diabetes, along with nontraditional physical impairments like back problems and carpal tunnel syndrome, are disabilities, provided they affect "a major life activity" like walking, standing, seeing, breathing, caring for oneself, or working."[67] To provide more guidance about the term "major life activity," the EEOC stipulates that it must determine, first, the nature and severity of the impairment; second, the duration or expected duration of the impairment; and third, the permanent or long-term impact, or the expected permanent or long-term impact of the impairment.

The EEOC developed these guidelines, in part, because the bulk of the complaints of discrimination filed between August 1992 and March 1997 have not involved traditional disabilities. From the pool of 81,595 complaints, approximately 18 percent were for back impairments, and 13 percent were for emotional or psychiatric impairments. Only 9.2 percent involved a person's extremities, which included people in wheelchairs. Less than 3 percent of the complaints were expressed by people with severe hearing and visual loss disabilities.[68]

While there has been resistance in the federal courts, the EEOC issued mandates stipulating that traditional *and* nontraditional disabilities should be under the jurisdiction of the ADA because it believed that that was the intent of the people who drafted the legislation. The Senate Report discussing the Americans with Disabilities bill presented a long list of nontraditional disabilities as examples of what it means to have a disability. Moreover, the disability rights movement so involved in the legislative process has long advocated that "for employment, the expansive definition of disability is especially appropriate." Employment discrimination, this movement argues, affects people with severe, moderate, and perceived disabilities alike. "A person with a history of epilepsy or severe facial scars may not fit the traditional or popular image of a 'handicapped' person. When an employer, however, rejects them because of their condition for a job for which they are qualified, the effect is the same as if they had been blind, deaf, or quadriplegic."[69]

Whether it is despite, or in response to, the EEOC mandates, most federal courts have refused to categorize a nontraditional impairment as a disability. The courts have done so either by ignoring the EEOC, which judges note they are not legally obliged to follow, or by applying the major life activity test so narrowly that few people with disabilities are covered.[70] One reporter noted that "the ADA has been applied narrowly by the courts over the seven years since its inception, providing no more than minimal protection against disability discrimination."[71] As a result, the federal courts have created what one legal analyst describes as "an unreasonable burden for people with disabilities." He suggests that "it has led to an unbalanced process in favor of employers and left many disabled individuals unprotected."[72]

Recognizing the reluctance of the federal courts to accept the EEOC-mandated definition of a disability, employers increasingly have begun to challenge whether an employee who is not in a wheelchair, for example, even has a disability.[73] The most successful legal strategy has been to acknowledge that an employee may indeed have an impairment that prevents him or her from housekeeping, for example, and hinders but does not affect a major life activity. Then the employer suggests that this impairment does hinder the employee's ability to perform the job, thereby providing grounds for terminating the employee. Whereas the difficulty associated with receiving protection from Section 504 of the Rehabilitation Act revolved around the question of qualifications and reasonable accommodations, most people have had their cases dismissed on summary judgment under the ADA, because the federal courts do not perceive them as having an impairment worthy of protection.

While the federal courts have been reluctant to accept nontraditional disabilities, some people have convinced judges that their disabilities do affect a major life activity. There has been no clear line of reasoning, however, about why one impairment is a disability and another is not. The people who have succeeded thus far, which is to say that their cases have not been dismissed on summary judgment, have had depression, HIV, diabetes, and infertility. The people who lost, and consequently had their cases dismissed, have had disabilities like paranoid thought disorder, asthmatic bronchitis, carpal tunnel syndrome, back injuries, high blood pressure, skin condition psoriasis, and degenerative arthritis.

Why a court decides that a back injury is not debilitating enough to be considered a disability, but that infertility is, remains a mystery. For instance, one federal court ruled that a police officer who had a form of depression that required medication did have a disability.[74] Another police officer in Chicago, who shared the same diagnosis of depression, also belonged to the protected class of people with disabilities.[75] A supervising clerk who worked for Alameda County, California, and had posttraumatic stress disorder was also viewed as living with a disability.[76] Yet a computer programmer who had paranoid thought disorder did not have a disability. The court ruled that paranoid thought disorder may be an impairment, but because the programmer claimed that it did not affect any major life activities he had no disability.[77] What the programmer meant was that his mental condition in no way hindered him from performing his job. Nonetheless, the federal courts, without offering clear reasoning, perceive some mental illnesses as constituting a disability and others as not.

The federal courts also developed no coherent pattern of thought about whether a disease should be classified as a disability. An electrician with diabetes, for instance, was ruled as having a disability.[78] It was not the disease per se that warranted the federal court's conclusion, but the fact that management at a Chrysler plant regarded him as having such a significant impairment that he could not perform a whole range of jobs. The EEOC, moreover, had listed diabetes as a disability. Yet, in another case involving diabetes, a federal court ruled that this disease was not a disability. This court also noted that "the EEOC's guideline [about diabetes being regarded as a disability] is not binding on the court."[79] The court held that it concurred with the employer that "the 'mere use' of a medicine such as insulin does not establish a per se disability."[80] Similarly, in a case involving epilepsy, which again the EEOC had categorized as a disability, a state court did not accept that the person had a disability.[81] The judge "found it to be an open question whether the nurse's epileptic condition would rise to the level of such an impairment," or, in other words, an impairment that affected a major life activity.[82] The federal court justified its action with the explanation that it had no obligation to follow the EEOC, an administrative agency. And while epilepsy was a serious disease, in this case it did not affect one of the major life activities of the litigant.

Some of the courts have held that a disease is not a disability if it is controlled by medication. "If the problem is remediated by medication, then disability isn't substantially limiting any longer," explained Laura Rothstein, a law professor at the University of Houston. "One of the biggest challenges of the medical community," a journalist wrote, "is to get people to take their medicine. But to get protection under the act, an employee would have to forgo treatment." As Jim Sacher, an attorney for the EEOC of Houston, said, this "seems medieval in its impact."[83]

The argument against the federal courts has been difficult to challenge, because these courts have recognized that people bringing suits have impairments. It is just that they do not think the impairment is severe enough to be categorized as a disability. A university professor who had difficulty breathing when her asthmatic bronchitis was aggravated by the air quality in her office and the classrooms where she taught was not viewed as having a disability.[84] The professor had an impairment, the court ruled, that affected but did not substantially limit the major life activity of breathing.

Similarly, a person whose vision in his left eye was impaired did not have a disability.[85] Although this person was fired for not being able to drive, the court ruled that the fact that this person's vision could not be corrected enough so that he could get behind the wheel of a car was insufficient proof of a disability. By contrast, a woman who had difficulty procreating, and sought infertility treatment to remedy the situation, did have a disability.[86] Infertility, the court ruled, substantially limited the major life activity of reproduction. Of course, this woman still had the possibility of procreating: otherwise the clinic would have refused her treatment. The infertility defense also worked for someone with HIV. This person had a disability, not because he was living with a terminal disease, but because, in good conscience, he could not procreate.[87]

Some people who brought suits against employers have found themselves in a predicament worse than just losing discriminatory protection from the ADA. Evidence of a disability has given some employers grounds for terminating their employees. A woman with degenerative arthritis of her hip was also not perceived as having a disability for two reasons.[88] First, surgery could "cure" her of the disability. Second, her ability to stand for four hours, but not eight hours, might be considered an impairment. As the federal judge considered it, however, it did not substantially limit or affect any of her major life activities. The bitter irony for this person was that having the strength to stand for only four hours provided her employer with the grounds for her termination.[89] A janitor was placed in a similar position: The fact that he was missing one hand and had sustained permanent back injuries did not mean that he had a disability, but it did give his employer cause to let him go.[90]

A Disability Working

An even more arduous way of proving that a major life activity is affected by a physical or mental impairment is to say that the impairment affects the major life activity of working. While a disability cannot interfere with work performance, people must show that their disabilities are so severe as to "generally foreclose" them from a whole class of jobs or an occupation. This notion has been developed into what the federal courts refer to as the "general foreclosure test."

This test has been a great source of confusion, however, because "anyone who is 'generally foreclosed' from a line of work is, almost strictly by definition, unqualified" for a particular position. This test aptly describes the Catch-22 position that confronts people with disabilities who seek freedom from workplace discrimination.

What makes the general foreclosure test unique is that it is not based on establishing whether a disability to work is a medically recognized impairment. Instead, it is a review of what tasks a person making this claim can and cannot perform. Yet, the EEOC decided that it was not necessary to examine each job and how many tasks one can perform within a particular job, but rather to check how many tasks within a category or class of jobs.[91] It is not enough, in other words, to fail to perform the tasks in one particular job. The person must show that he or she is precluded from employment in a whole category of jobs that require the same level of training, skills, and abilities.

To arrive at this determination, the EEOC created a quantitative analysis.[92] After conducting a job search in a specific geographical area, working people with disabilities must show that their unemployability exceeds their employability.[93] While these people must prove their employability, according to the EEOC, they do not have to conduct actual failed job searches to provide evidence of unemployability.

The federal courts have made good use of this quantitative method. Unlike the EEOC, however, some federal courts have demanded proof of unemployability.[94] An assembly worker was fired, for instance, because of an injury she had sustained in the factory. Given the fact that this worker had only a high school education, she qualified for a myriad of unskilled jobs.[95] According to the court, she could find employment in sales, in an office as a helper, or as an information clerk or answering clerk. Because she failed to produce the evidence that she was unqualified for all these positions, the court denied this assembly worker's request to be transferred to another position within the factory.

Similarly, the professor with asthmatic bronchitis mentioned earlier tried to show workplace discrimination by claiming not only that her breathing affected a major life activity, but that it restricted her ability to work. Dismissing the case, the federal court ruled that the professor was not barred from practicing her occupation. It was only that she could not work at *this* university, the court held, without debilitating her health.[96] Thus, the professor was restricted from working at a particular job in a particular location.

A welder who had a seriously injured arm faced the same problem as the professor, because her injury prevented her from climbing involved in a welding assignment.[97] The welder's case, in which she had requested a transfer to an assignment that required no climbing, was thrown out on summary judgment. Although the welder had an impairment, the court decided that it made no limitations on her ability to work. The fact that she could not complete this job, and could be terminated because of it, did not mean that she had a disability. She failed to perform only the climbing aspect of her job. The skill of welding per se, the court ruled, required no climbing, and the welder could, therefore, find other welding jobs that did not require climbing.[98] Similarly, a person in the body-weld division who had carpal tunnel syndrome and muscle inflammation was not limited in the major life activity of working.[99] She, too, could find other employment that did not require the type of movement that exacerbated her injury.

This argument about working affected people with impairments differently, depending greatly upon their level of education and skill. An order selector, who had injured himself on the job, did not need to be rehired in a different capacity, according to one federal court, because he did not have a disability that affected the major life activity of working.[100] Although the order selector could not return to his particular job without accommodation, the court ruled that this demonstrated no substantial limitation in the major life activity of working. This person could still perform a class of jobs or a broad range of jobs in various classes.[101] Since no skills were necessary to be an order selector, a whole array of unskilled jobs were available to this man.

The assembly worker, the professor, the welder, and the order selector had impairments that prevented them from adequately performing their jobs. This is not to say that these four people could not work. Theoretically, the assembly worker could find another job, since her dearth of education and lack of skills made her eligible for a number of positions. The professor could teach at another university that did not aggravate her condition. The welder could find a position that did not require her to climb. And the order selector, who had very few skills, could find employment in many other factories.

While the federal courts rendered such a strict view of how a disability affected working, it did not at first take into account whether these people could compete for jobs better than able-bodied applicants. According to disability activists, the ADA has not been effective in helping people with disabilities find work.

The federal courts expected workers with disabilities to make a thorough survey of what jobs in the area were available to them. What is more, some federal courts have used post-termination job searches as evidence of employability, despite the fact that a job application reflects nothing more than the worker's desire for employment.[102] The federal court in the welder's situation, for instance, insisted that she should look until finding a job that did not require climbing or any other activity she could not do because of her arm injury. This worker, however, would need to take a position before she disclosed her limitations. Underscoring any limitations at a job interview would put her in a less competitive position than a worker without a disability. The employer might hire someone with the same qualifications who had no visible impairment. Similarly, neither the order selector nor the professor would want to disclose any impairments at job interviews, since it might weaken their bargaining positions.

According to one legal analyst, only one court has exposed how this interpretation of the definition of a *disability* gives employers an inequitable advantage over any employee who has a moderate or severe impairment.[103] The advantage is best illustrated by the view that the federal courts could have just as easily ruled that persons with a disability could maintain their jobs on the grounds that the activities they could not do were not essential to the position. The term "essential functions" had been included in the ADA so that workers with disabilities could keep their positions despite failing to perform marginal duties. Relying on this term, it would seem that the welder was qualified to practice the essential function of welding, but not the secondary function of climbing to the place for welding. Or, the professor had the capacity to do research and teach, but not just in any classroom or office. These problems, too, could have been seen as secondary duties rather than essential ones and would, therefore, not have disqualified these people from employment. The result, in fact, would have been the opposite. Title I, when interpreted from the essential functions vantage point, could have meant that their jobs were protected. Few cases, however, were decided on the issue of essential functions. The burden of proof was thrown not on the employer but on the employee.

Having a "Record of Such an Impairment," or Being "Regarded as" Having a Disability

Despite the difficulty associated with showing that a person has a disability working, demonstrating that a person should be protected for having a "record of such an impairment," or being "regarded as" having a disability, is even more problematic. When the ADA had been formulated, Congress decided that people who have no functional, physical, or mental limitation could also be covered by the statute. "Regarded as" was included to protect a person, for instance, who had a facial scar and might not be hired because of the concern that customers might be repelled. Meanwhile, cancer survivors, for example, were protected by the legislation because they had a history of an impairment and might be fired because of concerns about high insurance rates.

People who fell under these last two categories of the definition of a *disability* were, therefore, to be protected from employers. These last two prongs of the definition of a *disability* were included in the ADA to ensure that people who were perceived as having a disability were protected from false stereotypes and prejudices. As such, these two prongs of the definition were fundamentally different from the first prong of having a disability, which stipulated how a physical or mental impairment affected a major life activity.

The federal courts have almost totally ignored this definition of a disability.[104] An operator who worked for Ameritech, for instance, sought protection on the grounds that her boss responded to her disability—a skin condition called "psoriasis"—by cultivating a hostile work environment.[105] Instead of defending this supervisor before the federal court, legal counsel for Ameritech contended that upper management had not been properly informed about the supervisor's actions and were, therefore, not culpable. The federal court, however, took a different point of view and ruled that the employee did not have a disability, since no major life activities were affected by her skin condition.

The federal courts have required that people with disabilities provide evidence of a substantial limitation.[106] As one disability activist described, "Ironically, the more likely a plaintiff is able to perform the job, the more likely it is that he or she will not be seen as disabled enough to be protected by the ADA." She added that "these restrictive judicial interpretations of the ADA reflect, at best, a lack of understanding of the statute and, at worst, a blatant hostility towards the profound goals of the ADA."[107]

Otherwise Qualified

The few people who clear this first threshold of having a disability must then surmount the second threshold of being qualified for a position. Here again, the federal courts have not formulated a coherent doctrine or a consistent line of argumentation to account for why one worker is qualified and another is not. A truck driver who had a heart attack and could no longer drive was considered qualified enough for the court to compel the company to maintain a job for him in the company, although the job had no relationship to his trucking position.[108] Other people with disabilities who requested similar transfers were told that not being qualified for one job meant that their employer need not transfer them.[109]

An electrician also succeeded in calling a question of fact about his qualifications.[110] The court did not dismiss his case on summary judgment, because he was perceived as qualified. One year after Chrysler denied the electrician the job because of his epilepsy, they hired him for the same job at another facility.[111] The court regarded the electrician as qualified and as posing no "direct threat" to himself or anyone else on the job. It was pure speculation, ruled the court, for the managers to argue that this electrician threatened safety at the Chrysler plant.

Similarly, a nonfoods specialist, working for Allied-Sysco Food Services, was fired for being unavailable to work because she had a bad back and knee.[112] The company had a "return to work policy" that implied no accommodation for cases like the plaintiff's by stating an "unrestricted return to work" policy. The court found evidence indicating that the company may have violated the ADA.

Other courts have discovered that a person with Chronic Fatigue Immune Deficiency Syndrome was not qualified.[113] In another case, a chemical process operator who became an insulin-dependent diabetic was considered not to have a disability.[114] When he was fired for not following proper procedures the court, instead of upholding the employer's contention that this operator was let go for negligence, held that he lacked the qualifications for this position. An executive director who suffered from terminal cancer had the same problem; the court ruled that he was not qualified for his position, because the illness hindered him from attending all the functions associated with the position.[115]

Reasonable Accommodations

Once someone made it over these two thresholds—having a disability and being qualified—he or she had a greater chance of success in the courtroom. Despite all the fears employers expressed during the passage of the ADA, it has been less difficult for persons with a disability to find a reasonable accommodation than it has been for them to provide proof of a disability and qualifications despite this disability.[116]

A registered nurse who had a chronic obstructive lung disease that prevented her from working in extreme temperatures, a requirement of her job, did not have her case dismissed despite her request for the accommodation of working inside.[117] Some police officers in Denver faced a similar situation. After being placed on light duty, these officers were terminated, allegedly on the basis of their disabilities.[118] The court rejected the department's claim that reassigning injured police officers who could not use a firearm or make arrests with force was an unreasonable request.

The greatest victory for a reasonable accommodation thus far was won by an attorney when her employer had to pay for a space in a New York City parking garage so that she could work. After surviving a near-fatal automobile accident, this attorney walked with walkers, canes, and crutches. Wearing a brace, she could not stand for extended periods or climb or descend stairs without difficulty.[119] Instead of using public transportation, as she had before the accident, she now drove into the city. She made a request for a parking spot near her office and the courts. The city rejected her request, insisting that she was asking for preferential treatment. The court, however, found that parking near her office and the courts was an essential prerequisite for her position.

A data entry operator who suffered from depression and sleep disorder was seen as having a disability. His request for the day shift was viewed by the court as reasonable.[120] For this court, the central issue was to what extent the company was obligated to reassign an employee to a different position. The court found that reassignment was not beyond the scope of reasonable accommodations required by ADA.[121] Indeed, this is what the Senate Report had concluded. A precedent had been established that, while it was not necessary to reassign workers, an employer who already had a regular practice of reassigning able-bodied workers upon request should also reassign those with disabilities.[122]

Similarly, a truck driver who had a heart attack and could no longer continue driving won the right to contest that he be reassigned to a vacant position in his company.[123] It was questionable whether Congress intended "reassignment to a vacant position" as a reasonable accommodation when the new job has no relationship to, and is in no way connected to, the job for which the plaintiff was employed when he became disabled. The court held that the case could not be dismissed, because there was a jury question as to whether the truck driver should have been given another position after his heart attack.

There is no consensus in the federal courts, however, about reassignment. A part-time carrier for the United States Post Office who had severe foot pain, hallux rigidas limites, which prevented him from doing the extensive walking required of a mail carrier, was refused reassignment.[124] Until his foot condition could be determined, the post office gave him a "casing" position. But once it was established that the disability was permanent, he was laid off. The court held that the Rehabilitation Act of 1973 did not require the employer to create an alternative position for an employee with a disability, which the post office had done temporarily in creating the "casing" position.

A railroad worker who had epilepsy requested that his company ac-commodate this disability by changing his shift assignment. To do so, however, would have conflicted with the seniority system established by a collective bargaining agreement, and it was thrown out of court for that reason.[125] The court ruled that Title I of the ADA was not supposed to in-terfere with a seniority system established by collective bargaining. Able-bodied workers could not be "bumped" from their position by a worker with a disability.[126]

A buyer who had bronchial asthma and worked in the purchasing de-partment of an electric and power company requested that a smoke-free work environment be created. He was turned down.[127] The company provided smokeless ashtrays and moved all the smokers who had been seated near the buyer, but it refused to make the office smoke-free. Here, rather than arguing that the buyer was not qualified, the company argued that the accommodations were unnecessary since his job performance demonstrated that he could perform the essential functions of his position. The federal court concurred; the company had no obligation to prohibit smoking in the office.

Employers may also offer reasonable accommodations that do not keep the employee at the same pay level or at the same number of hours.[128] To keep their jobs, employees might be required to change from a full-time to a part-time position, which would result not only in less pay but also in a loss in benefits. A person who stocked shelves, for instance, who asked for a daytime position rather than the night shift because a se-vere head injury prevented him from driving at night, was given the choice of a part-time day shift or no position at all.[129] He needed to work during the day so that his wife could drive him to work or he could take public transportation.

As cited earlier, fewer than 20 percent of people with disabilities have won suits preventing their employers or potential employers from dis-criminating against them.[130] The federal courts' interpretation of the law has helped employers defend themselves from accusations of discrimina-tion. Despite the fact that no coherent line of argumentation has been es-tablished about Title I, the Supreme Court decided to hear a case about public accommodations before employment discrimination.

An Unaccommodating Dentist

In 1998, the Supreme Court, in *Bragdon v. Abbott,* handed down its first decision about the ADA.[131] This case involved a dental patient, Sidney Abbott, who had been infected with the HIV virus.[132] While Dr. Randon

Bragdon agreed to treat her for a cavity, he refused to do so in his office. An outspoken critic of the "universal precautions" approach advocated by the American Dental Association, which advised dentists and hygienists to create an environment in their offices that would prevent the transmission of HIV and other contagious diseases, Bragdon maintained that treating Abbott in his office would have put him in "direct threat" of getting an HIV infection.[133]

Instead of taking universal precautions, Bragdon proposed that Abbott drive two hours to the nearest hospital to be treated. Abbott protested, arguing that Bragdon's suggestion for treatment was discriminatory. Not one patient had been documented as having transmitted this disease to a dentist or a hygienist. Bragdon's action, therefore, was not founded on a realistic fear that filling her cavity would infect him with HIV, said Abbott's attorneys, Bragdon, thus, was sued for violating the public accommodations provisions of the ADA.

Despite the fact that *Bragdon v. Abbott* settled a public accommodations case, it gave the disability rights community the first inkling of how the Supreme Court would handle employment discrimination, because the issue at bar was who had a *disability*. Does a person with an asymptomatic disease have a disability? Are other diseases, contagious or not, and some moderate physical impairments, disabilities worthy of coverage under the ADA? One reporter described it as "far from being an anomaly, this case brings to the fore an important unresolved issue under the disability law: the definition of disability."[134]

As shown above, most of the people bringing suits against their employers are living with moderate impairments or diseases such as epilepsy and diabetes. Making the case that these impairments and diseases should be classified as disabilities, Bennett Klein, who made the arguments before the Supreme Court for Abbott, insisted that the ADA is "not the Social Security Act where being disabled means you can't work." Klein insisted that "the assumption of Congress was that what was preventing them from doing that was discrimination-based."[135]

In a five-to-four decision, the Supreme Court accepted Klein's argument. The majority decided that an asymptomatic illness or disease could be considered a disability that substantially limited Abbott's life, and, as a consequence, she deserved statutory protection from the dentist's discrimination. Anthony Kennedy delivered the Court's opinion with John Paul Stevens, David Souter, Ruth Bader Ginsburg, and Stephen Breyer joining. The minority was composed of Chief Justice William Rehnquist, who presented an opinion that dissented in part and concurred in part with Antonin Scalia and Clarence Thomas joining. Sandra Day O'Connor also joined the minority, writing her own mixed opinion.

Despite the mixed decisions, what clearly divided the Court was the threshold issue of who had a disability that was accompanied by a substantially limiting impairment. To both the majority and the minority, three questions were raised to make the determination. First, was the HIV infection a physical impairment? Second, the Court had to identify the life activity that could be affected, which in this case was reproduction and child-bearing. Finally, "tying the two statutory phrases together, we ask whether the impairment substantially limited the major life activity."[136] Did the HIV infection affect Abbott's capacity for reproduction?

While all the justices agreed that HIV was a disability, they disagreed about, first, whether reproduction was a major life activity; and, second, if Abbott had been substantially limited by its absence. Writing for the majority, Kennedy answered both of these questions affirmatively. Reproduction limited Abbott first, he explained, because simply trying to conceive a child would impose a 20 percent risk that her partner would contract the infection. For this reason, some states "forbid persons infected with HIV from having sex with others, regardless of consent," reported Kennedy. Second, Kennedy maintained that there was a 25 percent chance that Abbott's child would be born with the infection. While Kennedy did not dispute that Abbott had the capacity to both conceive and bear a child, he emphasized that "the Act addresses substantial limitations on major life activities, not utter inabilities. Conception and childbirth are not impossible for an HIV victim but, without doubt, are dangerous to the public health." For Kennedy these facts were enough for him to decide that the HIV infection, whether symptomatic or not, "meets the definition of a substantial limitation."[137]

Providing further evidence of why reproduction was a major life activity that had been substantially impaired by the HIV infection, Kennedy emphasized that all the federal regulatory agencies and executive departments administering the ADA had come to the same conclusion. What is more, the agencies administering Section 504 of the Rehabilitation Act had included symptomatic or asymptomatic HIV on their list of what constituted a disability. While the Supreme Court was not bound to abide by the precedent that these federal agencies and departments had established, Kennedy argued that "we find the uniformity of the administrative and judicial precedent construing the definition significant."[138]

The minority also recognized the three steps the Court must follow to determine if Abbott had a disability that gave her protection from the

ADA's statutory shield. Writing a dissenting opinion that Scalia and Thomas joined, Rehnquist argued that although Abbott had a disability, it did not substantially limit *her* life. The HIV infection imposed no limitations on Abbott because "there is absolutely no evidence" that she "would have had or was even considering having children."[139] The minority argued that since the definition of a disability was written "with respect to the individual," Abbott's individual goals and desires must be taken into account.[140] Not having expressed any desire for procreation, Abbott had not lost anything. The HIV infection, therefore, had not substantially limited Abbott's life, and the dentist would not be liable for discrimination.

Further, Rehnquist argued that Abbott did not need statutory protection since reproduction was not a major life activity. Citing Webster's Collegiate Dictionary, Rehnquist noted that the word "major" has two alternate definitions: first, "of comparative importance"; and, second, "greater in quantity, number, or extent." Rehnquist then dismissed the majority's emphasis on major as meaning of comparative importance. To him, the definition of major that was bound by numbers, or simply repetition, was the "most consistent with the ADA's illustrative list of major life activities." While reproduction is important, Rehnquist reasoned, it is not one of the activities that "are repetitively performed and essential in the day-to-day existence of a normally functioning individual."[141]

Finally, Rehnquist challenged the majority's argument that a substantial limitation need not be an "utter inability." If this limitation was not deemed an utter inability, he suggested, the Court would have to show that someone's ability had been diminished. Reproduction, according to Rehnquist, was not something that a person could do in moderation. How could Abbott "engage" less "in those activities," he wondered.[142]

Writing her own dissenting opinion, O'Connor agreed with the minority that Abbott was not substantially limited by her disability. Reproduction, she purported, was not the "same as the representative major life activities of all persons: caring for one's self, performing manual tasks, walking." It was not an essential, daily task which was how she interpreted what Congress had meant by the phrase "a major life activity." Unlike Rehnquist, O'Connor saw no need to pursue the question. She dismissed discussing it if "HIV status would impose a substantial limitation on one's ability to reproduce if reproduction were a major life activity."[143]

Although a narrow decision, *Bragdon v. Abbott* was important because it gave disability rights activists and employers an idea about how the Court would define a disability. Calling the *Bragdon* decision a victory, many disability rights activists were cautiously encouraged. Arlene May-erson, directing attorney for the Disability Rights and Education Defense Fund (DREDF), said, "It is bizarre and ironic that as medical technology has improved and people can now live their lives fully, which was the intent of the ADA, that they would lose their civil rights protection and the courts would condone discrimination. . . . It made no sense."[144] The victory that Mayerson and other disability rights activists celebrated was short-lived. Just one year later, she would voice the same concerns.

Creating Legal Dams

In June of 1999, the Supreme Court handed down a trio of decisions about the employment provisions of the ADA that would "send a shock wave," as Senator Tom Harkin described it, "through the disability commu-nity."[145] What came as such a surprise was that, on the heels of the *Brag-don* decision, the Court went beyond most of the lower federal courts, creating a more restrictive view of who warranted statutory protection than these conservative courts had. Under Title I, the Supreme Court held that a person did not have a disability if his or her condition could be mitigated with medication or equipment, like a prosthesis. "These kind of judges seem to say, 'If you lose an arm, but you get a replacement arm,'" said Hallie Kirkingburg, one of the plaintiffs involved, "'you no longer have a handicap.'"[146]

While Kirkingburg may have overstated the Court's position, taking into account mitigating factors means that being treated by a dentist was not the same as working for one. The Court's decisions showed that, in ef-fect, there was a distinction between being discriminated against in public places and at the workplace. Moreover, in what one reporter character-ized as "an unusual move," the Court had gone to great lengths to make itself clear about this distinction, handing down not one but *three* deci-sions about who should be protected in the workplace.

In the first decision, which was also the lead case, the twin sisters Karen Sutton and Kimberly Hinton, who both had severe myopia—a condition that approximately 2 percent of the population shares—which was fully corrected by their eyeglasses, challenged United Airlines' decision that they could not be considered for employment. Already pilots for regional airlines, Sutton and Hinton met the federal vision standards required to become global airline pilots. Both of their applications for United were re-jected, however, because barring these standards, in addition to the other requirements about age, education, experience, and FAA certification qualifications, they fell short of fulfilling this airline's standard of having uncorrected vision of 20/40.

Ignoring the issue of essential functions, where safety concerns would have been addressed, the Court focused exclusively on determining who fell under the shield of the statute in the *Sutton* decision. In a seven-to-two majority, the Court argued that since Sutton and Hinton had impairments that were mitigated by glasses, they could not be considered disabled enough to receive statutory protection. O'Connor, who wrote the majority opinion, presented three reasons why the twin sisters did not fall within the statute's definitional guidelines.

First, analyzing the definition presented in the ADA's text, which stipulated that a disability is an impairment that substantially limits one or more of the major life activities, O'Connor resolved that this statement was written in the "present indicative verb form." As she interpreted this verb form, it is "properly read as requiring that a person be *presently*— not potentially or hypothetically—substantially limited in order to demonstrate a disability." Neither Sutton nor Hinton had a disability, O'Connor expounded, because their glasses fully corrected their vision. If either one of them lost or misplaced their glasses, they "might," "could," or "would" have a disability, but until that moment their impairments imposed no substantial limitations.[147]

Second, the Court cited *Brandon*, which specified that who had a disability must be made on a case-by-case basis. "The determination of whether an individual has a disability," O'Connor quoted from the text of the ADA, "is not necessarily based on the name or diagnosis of the impairment the person has, but rather on the effect of that impairment on the life of the individual." Guidelines could not be rendered without lumping people together, she warned, and the Court opposed treating people "as members of a group of people with similar impairments, rather than as individuals . . . ," which she maintained was "inconsistent with the individualized approach of the ADA."[148]

Finally, O'Connor argued that Sutton and Hinton could not be considered disabled people, since she thought neither one of them could be included in the 43 million disabled persons figure contained in the ADA's text. To her, "[T]he 43 million figure reflects an understanding that those whose impairments are largely corrected by medication or other devices are not 'disabled' within the meaning of the ADA." O'Connor came to this conclusion after examining the two different means of ascertaining who had a disability—the functional and nonfunctional approaches.

What disability experts meant by the nonfunctional approach, she reported, was that an impairment alone, which would include the 160 million people, did not define someone as having a disability. By contrast, the nonfunctional approach the legislative authors of the ADA had relied on included over 32 million people.[149]

After concluding that the twin sisters' vision was not debilitating enough to be considered a disability, the Court ruled on the next relevant plank of the definition of a disability: the "regarded as" plank. Did United regard Sutton and Hinton as having substantially limiting impairments? To O'Connor, the burden of proving that someone was "regarded as" having a disability was met if an employer "mistakenly believes" that this "individual has a substantially limiting impairment." This mistake, O'Connor added, must be "based on myth."[150]

Applying this logic to the case at hand, United, she decided, could not have mistakenly regarded either twin as having an impairment, since the mitigating equipment—glasses—were ubiquitous. Moreover, the officials at this airline had not rejected their applications on the basis of a myth that people with glasses could not fly airplanes.

Interpreting the one other way that United could have regarded the twins as having a disability—as having a disability working—O'Connor again ruled in favor of the employer. She affirmed United's position that the officials interviewing them had rightfully concluded that Sutton and Hinton were qualified to fly planes regionally but not globally.[151] Having made this distinction meant that United had not regarded the twin sisters as having an impairment that substantially affected their ability to work.

By offering this definition, O'Connor upheld the lower federal courts' notion that to be regarded as having a substantial limiting impairment of working meant that an employer decided an employee cannot fulfill the requirements of a whole array of jobs rather than those of one particular position. "To be substantially limited in the major life activity of working, then," O'Connor wrote, "one must be precluded from more than one type of job, a specialized job, or a particular job of choice."[152] Sutton and Hinton must show, in other words, that United had told them they were not qualified to fly *any* planes.

Finally, O'Connor used her explanation about being "regarded as" having a disability to discuss managerial prerogatives in the hiring and firing process. "An employer," she emphasized "is free to decide that physical characteristics or medical conditions that do not rise to the level of an impairment—such as one's height, build, or singing voice—are preferable to others." To her, an employer had every right not to hire (or fire) people who had limiting impairments as long as these impairments were not substantially limiting. An employer "is free to decide that some limiting, but not *substantially* limiting, impairments make individuals less than ideally suited for a job."[153]

Applicants for employment could be rejected if they had epilepsy or a vision problem as long as the employer saw their physical condition as limiting, but not necessarily substantially limiting. With this point, O'Connor went beyond what all but a few of the lower federal courts held. Emphasizing managerial prerogatives meant that O'Connor turned the ADA on its head. She gave employers the right to discriminate or, as she put it, the freedom to decide, against hiring people who had limiting impairments. Whether employers could discriminate or, conversely, be sued for discrimination all depended on how a federal court interpreted the word "substantial."

O'Connor understood just how much this perspective represented a departure from other administrative and legislative interpretations of the ADA. For this reason, she presented a detailed explanation about what gave the Court the authority to do so. Neither the EEOC, with its Interpretative Guidelines, nor the Department of Transportation's and the Architectural and Transportation Barriers Compliance Board's regulations took into account mitigating measures. As far as the Court was concerned, these guidelines were irrelevant. "No agency," the Court majority decided, had "been given authority to issue regulations implementing the generally applicable provisions of the ADA." With the definition of a disability being the "most notable applicable provision," the Court was obligated to render its own interpretation. By so doing, it found that evaluating people in their hypothetical uncorrected state" was an "impermissible interpretation" of the definition of a disability.[154]

O'Connor also explained why the Supreme Court had no reason to abide by the ADA's legislative history. Like the federal agencies administering the ADA, the House and Senate Committee Reports had indicated that mitigating measures, like medicine or equipment, could not be taken into consideration when an employer or a federal court decided if a person with an impairment had a disability. Again, O'Connor emphasized that the Court had the authority to interpret generally applicable provisions listed in the ADA. She concluded that the "ADA cannot be read in this manner" of excluding mitigating measures. As a result, she said that "we have no reason to consider the ADA's legislative history."[155]

Offering almost a point-by-point response to the majority opinion, Stevens and Breyer dissented. To begin with, Stevens challenged O'Connor's explanation about why the Court should dismiss the EEOC's Interpretative Guidelines and the Committee Reports, which both had indicated that mitigating measures must not be factored into the calculation about a disability.

To confront the majority on its explanation about why it was unnecessary to refer to the ADA's legislative history, Stevens cited an opinion authored by Rehnquist. Stevens quoted the Chief Justice as writing that "we have repeatedly stated that the authoritative source for finding the Legislature's intent lies in the Committee Reports on the bill." If the majority had taken these reports into account, Stevens argued, it could not have justified its ruling about mitigating measures because "the Committee Reports on the bill that became the ADA make it abundantly clear that Congress intended the ADA to cover individuals who could perform all of their major life activities only with the help of ameliorative measures."[156]

Aside from challenging the Court's authority to render an opinion far afield from the administering federal agencies and the legislative authors, Stevens disputed how O'Connor arrived at the idea that the twin pilots did not have a disability that deserved protection from discrimination. To his mind, O'Connor had regarded each of the three prongs as discrete categories, whereas Congress had drafted them as overlapping categories. The first prong may have been written in the present, but the second and third prongs were not, claimed Stevens. "If we apply customary tools of statutory construction," Stevens declared, "it is quite clear that the threshold question whether an individual is 'disabled' within the meaning of the Act—and, therefore, is entitled to the basic assurances that the Act affords—focuses on her past or present physical condition without regard to mitigation that has resulted from rehabilitation, self-improvement, prosthetic devices, or medication."[157]

Stevens also suggested that O'Connor had adopted a broad literal interpretation of the functional definition of a disability to further her own argument. This definition was so broadly cast that it penalized those who could compensate for their deficiencies more than those without them. "With the aid of prostheses, coupled with courageous determination and physical therapy, many of these hardy individuals can perform all of their major life activities just as efficiently as an average couch potato."[158] Indeed, O'Connor's interpretation was reminiscent of the *de minimus* doctrine that Rehnquist had established for disabled school children.[159] If children with disabilities could compensate for an impairment, they were not entitled to help in the classroom simply because of their disabilities. Similarly, Stevens held, "If the Act were just concerned with their present ability to participate in society, many of these individuals' physical impairments would not be viewed as disabilities."[160]

Addressing O'Connor's final concern about the definition of a disability, Stevens contested her interpretation of the numbers of those who had substantially limiting impairments. For the sake of who is counted as having a disability, the Court again used a broad definition, which included 160 million people, and neglected to delineate the individual medical condition that Sutton and Hinton had. According to Stevens, the visual problems that these two woman had could not be accounted for with the argument that they, like 100 million other people, wear glasses. Only 2 percent of the population had the same level of myopia, he argued, that these women had.[161]

Most important, Stevens's dissenting opinion explored how the Court's action, in general, would affect disabled people in the future. Presenting such a narrow interpretation of what constitutes a disability, he maintained, made the Court a gatekeeper. As Stevens said, the case revolves around whether or not "the ADA lets petitioners in the door in the same way as the Age Discrimination in Employment Act of 1967 does for every person who is at least 40 years old, and as Title VII of the Civil Rights Act of 1964 does for every single individual in the work force." Disability rights should be placed in context with other statutory rights. Someone can already file for race, gender, age, or religion, he said, making it "hard to believe that providing individuals with one more antidiscrimination protection will make any more of them file baseless or vexatious lawsuits."[162]

Trying to explain why the Court adopted this role, Stevens said, was that it was responding to the business community's concerns that the federal courts would be flooded with lawsuits. Stevens, however, characterized this as "misguided."[163] "Congress has never seen this," he added, "as reason to restrict classes of antidiscrimination coverage."[164] How many people pursued legal redress, he argued, should have been irrelevant to the Court.

Restricting legal access, moreover, marked a significant departure from Supreme Court past precedents. "When faced with classes of individuals or types of discrimination that fall outside the core prohibitions of antidiscrimination statutes," he said, "we have consistently construed those statutes to include comparable evils within their coverage, even when the particular evil at issue was beyond Congress' immediate concern in passing the legislation." As evidence, Stevens highlighted that Hispanic Americans, Asian Americans, and, "ironically," Caucasians in one instance had been interpreted by the Court as entitled to protection under the Civil Rights Act, although the Committee Reports only referred to African Americans. Rendering such a generous definition of who could pursue legal action, he added, was not limited to antidiscrimination laws. After all, the Racketeer Influenced and Corrupt Organization Act (RICO) had applied to organized *and* nonorganized crime alike.[165]

In offering such a restrictive definition of a disability, Stevens said, the Supreme Court has become a gatekeeper for employers, ensuring that few people would receive requests for accommodations. What is more, they could be punished for making these requests. The requests exposed the limitations of disabled people whose employment could lead to termination if a judge decided their limitations were not *substantial.* As Stevens explained, this approach was not only "misdirected," it was also "perverse" because it set the precedent that "permits any employer to dismiss out of hand every person who has uncorrected eyesight worse than 20/100 without regard to the specific qualifications." Ironically, he noted that the Court's approach "would seem to allow an employer to refuse to hire every person who has epilepsy or diabetes that is controlled by medication, or every person who functions efficiently with a prosthetic limb."[166]

To Stevens, the case of the twin sisters should not have been decided on the basis of coverage or access. "Inside that door lies nothing more than basic protection from irrational and unjustified discrimination because of a characteristic that is beyond a person's control." Instead, the Court should have examined "regarding employers' affirmative defenses."[167] Had United decided that the twin pilots should not be hired because of safety concerns, he might not have dissented. Indeed, both Stevens and Breyer joined the majority in one of the cases that followed *Sutton* for precisely that reason.

In *Albertsons, Inc. v. Hallie Kirkingburg,* the second decision about employment discrimination, the Court rendered a unanimous decision about a truck driver with amblyopia, an uncorrectable condition that left the driver with 20/200 vision, giving him monocular vision, thus making him not qualified for the job. The decision resulted from the discovery that Hallie Kirkingburg, a truck driver in Portland, Oregon, did not meet the Transportation Department's basic vision test, and he was fired from Albertsons.[168] When Kirkingburg found out that he qualified for a waiver from this test, he asked Albertsons to rehire him. After this grocery store rejected his application, the Ninth Circuit Court found that Kirkingburg had a disability. Since the waiver program was a legitimate part of the Department of Transportation's regulatory scheme, they believed he should be rehired.

Writing a unanimous decision, Souter concluded that there was one controlling issue. Does this grocery store, he asked, "have to justify enforcing the regulation solely because its standard may be waived experimentally in an individual case?"[169] If Kirkingburg could get a waiver from the Transportation Department's standard for vision, in other words, was Albertsons obliged to accept it? Souter and the other eight justices decided that Albertsons was not so obliged.

The Department of Transportation's waiver, Souter explained, had been instituted on an experimental basis as a means of gathering data. The Court, therefore, concluded that "the regulatory record made it plain that the waiver regulation did not rest on any final, factual conclusion that the waiver scheme would be conducive to public safety in the manner of the general acuity standards." Further, Souter decided that employers could not be expected to abide by such a regulation, because they would be "required in effect to justify in *de novo* an existing and otherwise applicable safety regulation issued by the Government itself." The federal government could not oblige employers to follow every change in standards, particularly since the Department of Transportation had granted this waiver as part of "an experiment to provide data."[170]

Distinguishing this decision from the *Sutton* decision, Stevens and Breyer joined the majority on the grounds that Kirkingburg was not qualified to perform his duties as a truck driver. Stevens and Breyer, however, disagreed with the majority about the noncontrolling issue of whether the truck driver had a disability. As a result, Stevens and Breyer wrote a concurring opinion that deferred to their opinion in the *Sutton* decision. Why had Souter analyzed this issue again? they wondered.

Souter himself wrote that "we need not speak to the issue whether Kirkingburg was an individual with a disability." Nonetheless, he thought the issue should be reviewed "to correct three missteps the [N]inth [C]ircuit made in its discussion of the matter."[171] Souter added this dicta, in other words, to show the lower federal courts how to determine who had a disability.

To Souter, Kirkingburg was not substantially impaired. Although this truck driver's vision constituted a significant "difference" between the manner in which he saw and the manner in which most people see, because his brain had compensated for this difference he was not substantially impaired and, therefore, worthy of statutory protection under Title I of the ADA. Any mitigating factors, Souter explained, must be taken into account "whether the measures taken are with artificial aids, like medications and devices, or with the body's own systems" when a lower federal court decided if someone had a disability.[172]

The last case in the trio of Title I decisions was *Vaughn L. Murphy v. United Parcel Service* where, again writing for the same seven-to-two majority behind the *Sutton* ruling, O'Connor affirmed the Tenth Circuit Court decision that mitigating measures disqualify a person with an impairment from receiving protection from the ADA.[173] In this decision, Vaughn Murphy, a mechanic who had very high blood pressure, was not considered substantially impaired because, when medicated, he functioned normally.

The Court also held that Murphy's employer had not regarded him as having a disability because he did not terminate him on the basis of "an unsubstantiated fear that he would suffer a heart attack or stroke." The mechanic had been fired because "his blood pressure exceeded the Department of Transportation's requirements for commercial vehicle drivers." Just as the twin sisters found themselves in a quandary, so, too, did Murphy. He functioned too well to be thought of as having a disability, and yet he was too sick to perform the job.

With Breyer joining, Stevens wrote another dissenting opinion.[174] Like the twin sister pilots, Stevens noted, many people may suffer "from his category of ailments." The Court, he argued, should not construct such a liberal interpretation when looking at his ailment because "taken individually, Murphy had an unusually severe case of hypertension." Without medication, Murphy's hypertension was so severe that he would "likely be hospitalized," wrote Stevens. Indeed, Stevens distinguished Murphy's physical condition from that of the twin sister pilots, arguing that "this case scarcely requires us to speculate whether Congress intended the Act to cover individuals with this impairment." Murphy's severe hypertension "easily falls within the ADA's nucleus of covered impairments," said Stevens.[175]

Lawsuits Unlimited?

When the Supreme Court handed down these three employment decisions, many a business spokesperson gave a great sigh of relief.[176] The employment provisions of the ADA, as Stephen Bokat, general counsel for the United States Chamber of Commerce, said, were "very, very scary for employers."[177] Yet, Bokat did not base this fear on fact, since the legal record showed that employers had little chance of having a federal court order them to accommodate an employee. Instead, he expressed a largely unsubstantiated fear that, armed with Title I, disabled people would find a way to storm the Bastille. "'Give an inch, take a mile' is the best way to describe the explosion of claims under the ADA," wrote one business advocate.[178]

For this reason, most spokesmen did not characterize the three Supreme Court decisions as a victory for employers. Beleaguered by what they depicted as frivolous lawsuits, many businessmen and women were relieved that these three decisions might restore a balance. As one journalist wrote, these decisions returned "balance to an area of U.S. law exploited for too long by opportunistic lawyers and in danger of running quite out of control."[179]

What disabled people stood to gain from Title I, these employers feared, was that their demands for reasonable accommodation would erode managerial prerogative power. Encouraged that the Supreme Court had taken a position behind an employer's rightful power, Bokat said that the Court "went with the business community right down the line." To him, "the most significant aspect of the opinions makes clear that employers can consider physical conditions and attributes and prefer some over others for that reason."[180] Another person called attention to the dilemma that negotiating over accommodations put managers under, succinctly stating that "the question becomes: When does accommodation become capitulation?"[181]

The business community, however, did not carry its concerns about managerial control to the extent that they thought no employees should be accommodated. Employers were careful to make a distinction between the deserving and undeserving. Who they opposed accommodating were those with what became known as "boutique disabilities" or disabilities that embodied what one reporter depicted as "every type of personal failing, character flaw and academic problem." To them, some disgruntled employees found experts who gave their problems "a scientific-sounding syndrome," which could then be turned into leverage at the workplace. As Jim Pugh, a spokesperson for Wisconsin Manufacturers & Commerce, maintained, the ADA was to protect employees who had "legitimate disabilities that can't be corrected."[182] The trio of decisions handed down by the Court respected this distinction. "The Supreme Court, in whacking back the definition of disability," said Christopher Bell, a lawyer who represented employers in disability cases, "may have saved the ADA, like whacking back a bush will help it grow."[183]

The disability rights movement was well aware of the problem with boutique disabilities. A year earlier, Tony Coelho, who chairs the President's Committee on Employment of People with Disabilities, said, "The law has prompted some frivolous suits, such as a claim by brewery workers that the company's offer of free beer exacerbated their alcoholism. But such suits filed under the law have routinely been thrown out by the courts."[184] To disability rights advocates, the legal record—with 80 percent being dismissed on summary judgment and 8 percent of the remaining 20 percent being decided in favor of a person with a disability—said it all.

Not surprised that the business community would misconstrue the Supreme Court's rulings about the employment provisions, disability rights activists were nonetheless alarmed that the Court's restrictive definition of who could seek legal redress under the ADA stood in contrast to what they perceived as legislative intent. People with diseases like diabetes, epilepsy, and conditions such as missing one foot could not be described as "boutique disabilities" unworthy of protection against discrimination, the disability rights activists argued. Instead of restoring balance between employers and employees, they described the Supreme Court's decisions as a "profound setback," which would make it all but impossible for most disabled people to work.[185] Lisa Rau, a disability rights attorney, said that the Court's decisions had "gutted" the ADA.[186] Chai Feldblum, a law professor who helped draft the legislation, also said, "Where it leaves the ADA is with a huge gaping hole right at its heart."[187]

Disability rights activists were dismayed both by how the Court arrived at this interpretation of who had a disability and what the consequences would be. They demonstrated that the high court had gone beyond most of the lower federal courts, which could hardly be described as liberal in their interpretations of Title I. Eight of the circuit courts did not take into account mitigating measures.[188] Further, the Supreme Court ignored the EEOC's Interpretative Guidelines and decided that it had no reason to read the ADA's Committee Reports, which specifically included disabilities like epilepsy and diabetes that were mitigated by medication.

Ignoring mitigating measures, disability rights activists proclaimed, would put most people in a Catch-22. "You're damned if you don't medicate," said Michael Greene, a lawyer for the American Diabetes Association, "but you're damned if you do because you loose your legal rights."[189] Or as Mayerson explained, "It's just so completely contrary to that notion that if someone takes something that mitigates the disabling effects of their impairment, which enables them to participate more, that they're then cut out of protection under the act."[190]

The disability rights advocates also condemned the Court's interpretation of being "regarded as" having a disability. It set a standard, they claimed, that was out of reach to most people with a history of having substantially limiting impairments. The Court's interpretation placed some disabled people, particularly those with invisible disabilities, in danger of being fired. Worse yet, the "regarded as" provision gave employers the "freedom" to discriminate against people with impairments that might be limiting, but were not deemed "substantially" limiting. In a friend of the court brief, Guy Phelan, an attorney for the National Employment Lawyers Association, wrote that "the employer is saying the disability isn't serious enough to rise to the level of coverage under the ADA, and at the same time, they are saying we don't hire people with this condition."[191]

Finally, disability rights advocates echoed Justice Stevens's concerns about the gatekeeping role the Supreme Court was playing. As Stevens observed, the Court could have taken issue in all three cases with job performance, reasonable accommodations, or undue hardship. Deciding on these grounds would have meant that the Court was not discouraging people with impairments to pursue legal redress. Accepting people's rights to seek legal redress, however, did not mean that they would win. Referring again to the Supreme Court's gatekeeping role, Judith Heumann, the assistant secretary of education, who oversees all the disability programs, conveyed that the decisions would have a "chilling" effect on all people with disabilities.[192]

What disability rights attorneys foresee is that the Court's position of affirming an employer's right to discriminate will have devastating consequences. As one attorney predicted, the Court's decisions give "employers the right to fire or to refuse to hire any employee with an expensive medical condition such as diabetes, epilepsy or cancer survivors." This will leave "legions of workers without health coverage."[193]

The institution that has taken the greatest role in shaping the ADA has been neither Congress nor the EEOC but the federal courts. Unlike the EEOC, which has provided guidelines to help advise both employers and employees about discrimination against disabled people in the work force, these courts have focused primarily on the activities of the employee or potential employee. The controversy about the legislation has not been centered on reasonable accommodations or undue hardship as the business community initially feared. Instead, the two points of contention involve the person with a disability, not the employer.

The federal courts have asked, first, whether the person has a disability and, second, whether he or she is qualified for a position? A majority of the courts have used these threshold questions to determine if a person warrants protection. In most decisions, disabled people are knocked out once the first two threshold questions have been determined. They rarely reach the third question about the substantive requirement—the accommodation—that the employer would provide.

The federal courts' interpretation of the ADA has not, therefore, revolved around the affirmative obligation that the state has imposed on employers. That is, the courts have not questioned if the federal government has the capacity or the constitutional authority to demand that employers provide special equipment or conditions for their workers with disabilities. Nor have the federal courts decided most cases by scrutinizing an employer's behavior. Most of the Title I cases, particularly the three precedent-setting Supreme Court decisions, were resolved before the nature of the accommodation or undue hardship was raised.

While undoubtedly it must be established that a person has a disability, the qualifications threshold question is a red herring. As explained in Chapter 4, no court—state or federal—has ever compelled an employer to hire an unqualified person. Hence, the qualifications threshold determination has given employers another mechanism that underscores the linkage between a disability and job qualifications or performance, which rests on the underlying assumption that most disabled people are not qualified to work.

Most important, the federal courts have ruled in favor of employers on an overwhelming number of the Title I decisions, most notably, the Supreme Court, because a person has a limiting, but not a substantially limiting, disability. By so doing, the federal courts have taken on a new role—that of the medical expert. Instead of deferring to experts, as the federal court judges did with the doctrine of substituted judgment, these judges have become, in effect, experts themselves.[194]

Evaluating each person individually, federal court judges and justices have become gatekeepers for employers, keeping most disabled people from receiving statutory protection. Yet, few people outside the disability rights community have issued any public outcry for excluding them. On a theoretical level, the visibility of power, as Foucault delineated, has been switched from the institution—the judiciary—or those who operate it—the judges and justices—to the plaintiff, who is seeking justice.

Reversing power relations, the judges and justices have focused on the smallest details of persons with an alleged disability, making them the object of power. Disabled people are not subjects to be heard as they challenge discrimination, but are rather objects of power that the federal court judges scrutinize. Taken to task by the federal courts, the plaintiffs serve as examples for disabled people. Just as the rape victim's sexual history is put on trial to determine if she should have been protected from the case at bar, so, too, is a person's disability. Hence, the federal courts, particularly the Supreme Court, have wielded their precedent-setting capacity to mold the behavior of disabled people by showing them the risks associated with questioning workplace normalcy.

Judges and justices, however, have reversed power relations not because disabled people are weak. In his dissenting opinion, Justice Stevens wonders why the Supreme Court went to such great lengths to restrict antidiscrimination coverage to people with disabilities. One can seek protection from discrimination because of race, gender, age, or religion, so what would be the harm of including disability? The federal courts could have taken on this new gatekeeping role because the administrative agencies, which usually fulfill this role, have not. As the Supreme Court views it, the EEOC and other federal agencies have given disabled people too much statutory power.

The difference between Title I and other civil rights statutes is precisely that—it gives disabled people the power to negotiate with their employers or prospective employers. This power for negotiation also gives them the capacity to question workplace normalcy as disabled people question work rules and regulations, whereas an African American cannot use the Civil Rights Act to challenge, for example, a Caucasian corporate culture. Prohibiting discrimination because of fixed categories like race, gender, or age, by contrast, only eliminates one reason a person cannot be fired. Accommodating disabled people, by contrast, changes the relationship between the employer and the employee. Only disabled people have the capacity to challenge the natural hierarchy between an employer and an employee.

Thus, the federal court judges and justices have rendered a narrow interpretation of Title I because, like many employers, they perceive disabled people as threatening. Title I gave people with disabilities the capacity to negotiate with their employers about work conditions and challenge the norms and values of this workplace. The federal courts have essentially acknowledged that disabled people disturb the autonomy of their employers and their colleagues, showing that American society does not extend the able-bodied as much freedom as they initially believed. This is a power the federal court judges and justices think the American state and society can ill afford.

AFTERWORD

People with disabilities seeking employment have gone from being subjects of medicine to subjects of law. During the 1940s, physicians established the new field of rehabilitation medicine which, by the 1950s, gave birth to the psychoanalytical approach underlying vocational rehabilitation. From newly built rehabilitation centers, teams of experts overseeing the vocational rehabilitation process thought they could adjust and normalize the so-called maladjusted people with disabilities, making those who compensated for their impairments with other parts of their minds and bodies "whole" and, therefore, ready for work.

Relying on the same assumptions and applying the same type of reasoning and logic, the federal courts have followed the precedent established by the Supreme Court's employment decisions and turned this situation around. Quite simply, the federal court judges have substituted the term "mitigation" for what rehabilitation experts called "compensation." In the year that has lapsed since these rulings, many lower federal court judges have followed the Supreme Court in asking if people with disabilities "mitigate" their impairments. They utilize this term as a means of sorting out who does, and who does not, deserve statutory protection under Title I of the Americans with Disabilities Act (ADA). Only those whom federal court judges view as not "whole" because of their physical or mental impairments should be protected from employment discrimination.

By handing down the employment decisions, the majority on the Supreme Court opened all the possible doors for federal court judges to begin scrutinizing the lives of people with disabilities. The federal court judges query not only what medication or equipment disabled people have used to mitigate their impairments, but also what they *could use,* or have *chosen not to use.* Further, some judges have affirmed the Supreme Court's idea that mitigation should not be examined solely from a medical, scientific, or technological perspective. It appears that people with disabilities can mitigate their physical or mental impairments because of their personal or societal situation. The lifestyles or the education of disabled people can make them compensate for the effects of their respective impairments. Since the *Sutton* decision, federal court judges have started examining the whole spectrum of the disabled person's life history. As a result, people with disabilities have fallen increasingly under what Foucault might describe as the objectifying gaze of these judges.

What makes the federal court judges gazing so similar to that of the postwar rehabilitation experts is that it is grounded in the same type of functional view of disability that their predecessors employed. Functionalism has informed the federal courts, since the judges are defining people not by who they *are* but by what they can *do.* A hammer is not a hammer, a functionalist would explain, because of its physical nature—that it has a wooden handle with an iron head. It is a hammer if it knocks nails into boards. Similarly, federal court judges do not recognize that persons have a disability because they have a specific impairment, but rather if this condition substantially interferes with a significant aspect of their lives. The court identifies people with disabilities because of their experience, not the essence of their impairments. While activists from the disability rights movement also embrace a nonessentialist definition, they have expressed outrage at how the federal court judges have used a broad experiential definition of people with disabilities, which limits their access to antidiscrimination legislation.

What is more, the federal court judges' determination of a disability is normative, just as the rehabilitation physicians' notion of the whole man theory was. The value of what a person with a disability can and cannot do, federal court judges have maintained, is shaped and determined by societal considerations. A person with only a moderately limiting impairment, yet who has less of an education than someone with a more debilitating one, could be identified as "disabled" in the eyes of the court. Society rewards a person with more education, federal court judges have suggested, and the person who benefits from this reward may well use it to counterbalance the restrictions of his or her impairment. It is only by scrutinizing the "whole man"—the gamut of the plaintiff's entire life history—that federal court judges can determine if a plaintiff should profit from Title I's protective shield.

Finally, the precedent the Supreme Court set was teleological in that it took into account when and why society *should* protect some people with disabilities from discrimination and not others. Disabled people who compensate for their impairments should not be safeguarded, the majority ruled, because such protection would undermine an employer's right to manage. This is not to say that the Court weighed an employee's rights against an employer's rights. Nor did it overturn the authority of the legislative and executive branches to grant this right. Instead of questioning its constitutionality, the Supreme Court has given the lower federal courts great definitional latitude, ensuring that few people could exercise the right to accommodations at the workplace.

Recognizing the Supreme Court's view of accommodations, the federal courts have been ruling that protection from employment discrimination should be awarded, not because disabled people have rights but because they have needs and vulnerabilities. What makes this perspective reminiscent of the attitude of the rehabilitation medical pioneers is the belief of courts that the vulnerability encountered by people with disabilities cannot simply be derived from a value-free scientific or medical definition of what constitutes a physical or mental impairment. Like the rehabilitation experts, the federal court judges have juxtaposed medicine, science, and technology with personal life experiences, morality, and knowledge from disciplines in social science.

Just as the rehabilitation physicians were explicit that the whole man theory of disability should be associated with a larger worldview, so, too, the federal court judges have been open about how their belief that only the un-whole persons—those who are truly deserving, given their vulnerabilities—should have disability rights is part of a larger ideological perspective. While the physicians maintained that rehabilitation could advance democratization, the judges have promoted one of the essential values underlying capitalism—that employers should have tight, if not total, control over the workplace. What is more, these judges know that this battle over a definition represents only the first part of the Catch-22 that many people with disabilities experience. Once inside the courtroom, disabled people must still demonstrate that, despite their vulnerabilities, they can perform the essential functions of their respective jobs.

Normalizing Judges

Contrary to what the business community had initially anticipated when the Supreme Court made its rulings, the number of lawsuits about employment discrimination has diminished little. The number of people filing suits, however, does not arise from the fact that the lower federal courts have distinguished themselves from the Supreme Court. Although most cases are still dismissed in favor of employers, the amount of litigation may remain constant because of the inconsistencies in the federal court rulings.

The Supreme Court's ideas about mitigation have given the lower federal courts so much discretion to decide who has a disability that a situation has arisen whereby people with traditional disabilities, for example, hearing impairments or multiple sclerosis, are no more likely to succeed or fail than those with nontraditional impairments, like back problems. Relating and evaluating how parts fit in with an organic whole, federal judges have recognized that a person with a mild impairment might be classified as having a disability, whereas someone with a severe one might not. Hence, lawyers will continue having difficulty advising prospective clients about the chance of success against an allegedly discriminatory employer.

Since *Sutton,* the discretion that accompanies a functionalist interpretation has manifested itself in decisions that raise a number of distinct issues. One of the issues that has arisen is that some judges suggest that personal factors can mitigate someone's impairment. A person's age, education, experience, and/or employment history helps or hinders his or her ability to compensate for an impairment. Essentially, the federal court judges have been issuing what Foucault characterized as normalizing judgments. That is, the judges consider how people cope with their impairments by measuring them to the "average" person. If people with disabilities are more successful than the average, not just at work but in life in general, some judges have maintained that they should not be protected from employment discrimination. It is a metric mode of thinking that explains how judges can view some people with minor impairments as having a disability, whereas others with more limiting ones have not. The following two cases are examples of normalizing judgments.

First, there was a case involving a meat grinder, whose physical impairment was that he could not lift over fifty pounds because of a back injury. The court noted that he had a sixth-grade education, was in his fifties, and had worked at only one job at Pathmark for thirty-five years.[1] Combining these factors, a rehabilitation expert gave evidence that the meat grinder would have great difficulty finding employment. He would be qualified for very few jobs. As a result, the court concurred with the expert, deciding that this person had a disability working.

Clearly, the meat grinder's physical limitation was not what made this court rule in his favor. In several cases, those with lifting restrictions even up to ten pounds have not been regarded as having a disability working. One court ruled that anything up to twenty-five pounds is not considered a substantial physical limitation, nor even fifty pounds.[2] Rather, it was the combination of factors about the meat grinder's employability—the mixture of the physical, the personal, and the societal factors—that compelled this judge to rule that he had a disability warranting statutory protection.

Second, another federal court held that a pharmacist with cerebral palsy, who claimed that King Soopers, a supermarket, discriminated against her during the hiring process, did not have a disability working that qualified her for protection under the ADA.[3] In the case at bar, the federal court judge acknowledged that this woman lacked coordination, had an intention tremor that produced a scissors gate, and had great difficulty with rapid or fine movement. Nonetheless, he concluded that she could not be defined as having a disability working. "The fact that a person with an impairment performs her major life activities 'differently' than the rest of the population will not suffice to establish disability under the ADA."[4] This pharmacist seeking employment compensated for her physical limitations and could practice her profession without any accommodations.

Analyzing the situation further, the federal judge explained that this pharmacist "is a commendable example of a person with an impairment." She "has succeeded in accommodating her impairment to achieve many successes in both her personal and professional life. She walks, talks, and performs manual activities differently from the average person. No doubt, as she contends, she has to use focus, concentration, and energy to control her muscles when walking, speaking, and using her hands." Declaring that he was bound to follow the Supreme Court, which "requires that I consider mitigating measures," the judge said "that she herself has taken, whether consciously or not, with her own body systems." On almost a congratulatory note, the judge further suggested that "she defies restrictions in her daily life," noting that this "mother of three boys, lives in a two-story house with the master bedroom on the second floor." Unlike the meat grinder, the pharmacist compensated for her impairments and could operate as a whole person, given her good education and a busy and fulfilling personal life. In fact, applying what he called a societal standard of success, the judge concluded that this pharmacist was a successful person. Why, he asked, should the court protect such a person from employment discrimination?[5]

In addition to education and overall employability, another court took into account how a lifestyle choice mitigated an impairment. In this case, the judge ruled that a person with asymptomatic HIV did not have the major life activity of reproduction affected because he expressed no interest in having children. This court distinguished its ruling from the Supreme Court's decision in *Bragdon v. Abbott,* where the higher Court had decided that someone with asymptomatic HIV had a disability because it interfered with reproduction. "While HIV positivity clearly is a disability under the ADA when it limits a major life activity," the judge wrote, "it is apparent here that reproduction is not a major life activity." As the judge put it, this plaintiff "admits he does not currently, nor has he ever, desired to father children. In contrast, the plaintiff in Bragdon testified that her HIV status dictated her decision not to have children." The judge ruled essentially that the plaintiff mitigated his own impairment by expressing his wish not to procreate. "His decision not to have children," wrote the judge, "was a personal one, not caused by his HIV positive status."[6]

Not all judges agreed that the federal courts should issue decisions that rested on such a loose interpretation of functionalism that brought personal and societal factors into play. One judge lamented that the ADA "expressly requires analysis of whether an impairment substantially limits a major life activity, not whether the individual is highly functional as a general matter." To take into account "general matters," like a person with a disability's education, job experience, and lifestyle choices, this judge said, would undermine the intent of this antidiscrimination law. "To conclude otherwise," he said, "would eviscerate the ADA by excluding from coverage all individuals, who, though possessing an impairment substantially limiting a major life activity, remain highly-functional overall." Underscoring the painful irony of this situation, he elaborated that "such an interpretation would render the ADA inapplicable to those individuals most likely to have the capacity to perform various jobs capably if provided with reasonable accommodation."[7]

This judge's perspective, however, is reflective of a small minority of federal court judges. What is more, while the judge cast aside the idea that personal and societal factors should be used, he still extended the Supreme Court's precedent about mitigation. This judge was one of the federal court judges who helped escalate the overall scrutiny of people with disabilities by examining how medicine, science, and technology gave people with disabilities special equipment and medication that dampened the effects of an impairment. To do so, these judges began asking about the mitigation itself. Is a mitigating device or medication corrective or compensatory?

Ruling that only corrective devices can mitigate a condition, one federal court examined if lipreading and telephone lights actually improve the hearing of a plaintiff with a serious impairment or compensate for it. Comparing this equipment to glasses, the federal court reasoned that "lipreading is even unlike corrective measures taken by the body to improve the ability of a person with monocular vision to see both range and depth." This judge decided that lipreading is "more akin to use of a wheelchair or braille—all are devices that assist an impaired individual to remain functional, even highly so, but do not alter the status of the impairment." For this reason, the federal court judge thought that if a piece of equipment only compensated for, but did not correct an impairment, the person should be classified as having a disability.[8]

Taking a different perspective about the mitigating effects of medication, another judge decided that the fact that dilantin, a drug for epilepsy, controlled but did not fully correct this disease was enough to disqualify persons for coverage under the ADA.[9] This stance, however, differed from another judge's ruling that if people with epilepsy limit but do not eliminate seizures, they should be viewed as having a disability. In the latter case, the judge accepted the treating doctor's opinion that there was no possibility that the medication would eliminate the risk of seizures altogether and rendered this opinion.[10] This judge also distinguished his ruling with the argument that his plaintiff had more severe seizures than the other plaintiffs.

Adding another twist to the mitigation debate, a federal court judge ruled that he could not speculate about a specific type of medication because its effects were in the future. In the case at bar, the judge ruled that he could not decide if a teacher's use of medication for Attention Deficit Hyperactive Disorder (ADHD) would affect her in the future. "If medication controls ADHD such that it enables [Patty] Schumacher [the plaintiff] to think, sleep, and otherwise function as would the average person, just as corrective eyewear enables a person with myopia to attain 20/20 vision, Schumacher would not have a disability. . . . However, this court is unable to say, at this stage, that ADHD, controlled by medication, still does not substantially limit Schumacher's ability to perform these major life activities and still does not render her disabled within the meaning of the ADA."[11] Unlike the first case presented about epilepsy, the judge's uncertainty about the effects of medication worked in the disabled person's favor.

In addition to looking at whether a mitigating device is corrective or compensatory, some federal court judges questioned further if the device itself is debilitating. Put simply, some judges asked if a medication had negative side effects. In answering this question, again, the lower federal courts have established no consistent line of legal reasoning. One court ruled, for instance, that when a president of a small steel pipe, valves, and tube company was demoted to vice president when the owner, his employer, discovered he had a form of blood cancer, this executive could not protest employment discrimination before trial, because his treatment—chemotherapy—was not debilitating. Scrutinizing what toll chemotherapy might take on this person's life, the court decided that it would not substantially impair his ability to work. The chemotherapy treatment meant that this executive "would have to be away from the job for one to three days of an ordinary work week each month." Yet, because he was an executive, he had the flexibility to complete this treatment without it affecting his work. It was the "flexibility [that] most executives have in scheduling professional obligations," which mitigated his situation.[12]

By contrast, another federal court judge decided that the lithium that a school district's secretary took to mitigate her bipolar disorder was debilitating enough to suggest that she should be identified as having a disability. "Even though lithium has improved her condition and has reduced the risk of full-blown psychotic episodes, the drug has not perfectly controlled her symptoms, leaving her still substantially limited in her ability to think." The judge's reasoning in this case, moreover, went against the expertise offered by a psychiatrist provided by the school district, who had written, "If she continues to take her medications as instructed, she will be able to work. She is now not at all disabled from a psychiatric point of view."[13]

With both the chemotherapy and the lithium cases, the federal court judges carefully explained that their decisions rested not on the type of treatment each patient was receiving, but rather on how each one of them coped with it. They followed the same logic that the Supreme Court and the lower federal courts had in determining if someone had a disability, only now they were examining how a person with a disability *coped* with the mitigating treatment. At the same time, the judge, dismissing the suit filed by the executive recovering from cancer, based his decision on a normalizing judgment. Had this executive not climbed so high above the average person in business, he might have been seen as having a disability working.

The precedent established by the *Sutton* decision also led some federal courts to question what role persons with a disability could play in ascertaining what was in their best interests. Could federal court judges speculate if someone would profit from a different course of treatment? Should they respect someone's right to choose his or her own treatment? One court, for example, explored whether an employee with a substantial hearing impairment, who chose not to wear a hearing aid, should receive antidiscrimination protection. After all, she *could* have used a hearing aid which might have mitigated her condition. In fact, the head of otolaryngology at a local state university said, "I think that [plaintiff] would benefit from hearing aids." Nonetheless, the judge rejected this doctor's opinion, suggesting that the court should not speculate about "the limitation a plaintiff would face if she used a corrective measure she presently does not use, and, with respect to the former, speculation about the limitations a plaintiff would face if she stopped using a corrective measure she presently uses."[14]

While the court ruled in favor of the employee, the federal court judge scrupulously maintained that it was not because he respected this employee's choice. The court had not accepted the employee's own explanation for rejecting hearing aids, that she found the background noise annoying. "Of greater importance," the judge argued, was that "the mitigating measures or devices that must be considered are those employed by the individual claimant, such as hearing aids or blood pressure medication, not those provided by, and within the control of, the employer."[15] It was not a matter of choice, and certainly not a choice dictated by an employer, but rather the facts involved with the current situation. How did employees mitigate their condition *now?*

The idea that the person with an impairment should not be awarded this discretion was the subject of another case when an interior designer at Johns Hopkins Hospital, who had asthma, chose not to use steroids. Asthma, the court noted, is controlled by medication. Yet, the interior designer believed this medication would affect another medical condition that she had, pituitary adenoma, although several physicians told her the contrary. Elaborating further, one of the physicians treating her explained that he had "a difficult time treating plaintiff's asthma because of her reluctance to take steroid drugs." After weighing the evidence, the federal court judge dismissed the case against the hospital on the grounds that the designer's "asthma is correctable by medication and since she voluntarily refused the recommended medication, her asthma did not substantially limit her in any major life activity." Interjecting his own sense of morality, the judge concluded that the interior designer "is not a 'qualified individual' under the ADA." To him, a person who refuses the benefits of medical treatment cannot also have the benefit of legal protection.[16]

Finally, the Supreme Court's rulings about employment discrimination led to an ironic twist. While the majority rendered an extremely narrow construction of who has a disability, many attorneys began emphasizing not that their clients were disabled, but that they were "regarded as" having a disability and should be protected on this basis. Ironically, people with disabilities have had more success with these cases. Given the discretion that the idea of mitigation afforded in the *Sutton* decision, people with traditional *and* nontraditional impairments have prevailed against summary judgment on these grounds. The federal court judge deciding the pharmacist's case, for example, spurned the notion that she had a disability working, but he did accept the idea that a reasonable jury might think that King Soopers regarded her as having a disability. Juries hearing the cases, moreover, have found more decisions in favor of employees than employers, awarding large settlements.

Nonetheless, the decisions involving the "regarded as" clause of the ADA's definition since *Sutton* have not all helped people with disabilities avoid summary judgment. Disability activists had lobbied to maintain this clause, which had been included in the Rehabilitation Act, thinking that it addressed the subjective issue of prejudice against people with disabilities. One court, however, made no distinction between the subjective nature of prejudice and how the term "a broad class of jobs" was empirically demonstrable when it ruled on a case where a physician was allegedly regarded as having a disability. Intermixing the two categories, the judge decided that the anesthesiologist, who had had a major depression and a panic disorder and yet was fully recovered through medication, had not been regarded as having a disability working by the hospital. While the physician had been terminated because hospital administrators thought that his medication interfered with his work, these administrators had not claimed that he was unfit to practice medicine. No one in the hospital ever said he could not be a doctor anywhere, which would have been tantamount to saying that this anesthesiologist was incapable of doing a broad class of jobs.[17]

Furthermore, the judge indicated his support for the teleological undertones of the Supreme Court's decisions by citing Sandra Day O'Connor's majority opinion: that "employers" have the right "to prefer some physical attributes over others."[18] Following her position in *Sutton,* the judge proclaimed that the hospital should have the prerogative to fire people because of an impairment as long as it did not rise to the level of being, or being regarded as, a substantially limiting impairment. The federal court turned the intent of the employment relations provisions on their head. Rather than protecting the anesthesiologist, it gave the hospital the right to fire that person for having a mental impairment that had been mitigated by medication.

Holism Gone Haywire

The federal court decisions rendered since the Supreme Court handed down *Sutton* thus far have produced an idiosyncratic body of law. While almost all the suits still revolve around the identity issue, the Court's concept of mitigation has put the lives of people with disabilities under more scrutiny than ever before. This is not to say that the judgments have followed a consistent line of reasoning. Whereas 94 percent of the cases were decided in the employers' favor, only 71 percent were decided in their favor after the Supreme Court's rulings.[19]

What has been the most consistent aspect of these cases is how the federal court judges have used the term "mitigation" to gain leeway to assess the identity of a person with a disability. The lower federal courts have enhanced their power and knowledge and, in effect, become the modern-day experts of vocational rehabilitation because of the idiosyncratic nature of disability. Further, what makes this discretionary power similar to the postwar period is that the federal judges have not reverted back to what the disability rights movement once called "the medical model of disability." Instead of using medical categories, the judges have employed a medley of personal, social, and environmental categories. It is their reliance on an organic mix—an examination of the parts in relation to the whole—that grounds the federal court judges in a 1950s perspective about functionalism. It is this functionalist understanding that makes the actions of the judges reminiscent of the rehabilitation counselors, who scrutinized the attitudinal as well as the medical condition of people with disabilities to see if they were deserving of vocational rehabilitation.

While opening people with disabilities to more scrutiny has not all been to their detriment, these cases rest on reasoning that, nevertheless, reveals how reluctant the federal courts are to perceive the employment provisions in Title I as statutory rights. The federal courts have essentially stripped down the meaning of employment relations provisions to one based not upon rights but upon vulnerabilities and needs. People with disabilities must demonstrate that they have done all that can be done to mitigate their condition. If they cannot compensate for it, as the meat grinder failed to do, then and only then will the federal court rule that they have a disability and allow them to proceed to trial.

Basing a definition of disability on needs, however, indicates how resistant the federal courts have been to accepting the rights orientation of the

ADA's employment provisions. If people with impairments are not more vulnerable than their coworkers, the reasoning goes, providing them with an accommodation is tantamount to giving them a "leg up." Such a leg up constitutes an advantage, these federal courts have decided, that disturbs the balance of power between employers and employees. This is not to say that the courts are juxtaposing the rights of employers to that of employees. The rights that constitutional, common, or statutory law grants different groups are often balanced. Rather, the federal courts have assessed the needs of persons with disabilities to determine if they should have access to protection with this statutory right. If a person with a disability is qualified to receive this right then, at trial, it will be balanced against an employer's right to manage.

Rights, or even access to rights, however, can hardly be based on an employee's vulnerability in the employment market. A right, according to an apt definition offered by Karen Orren, involves a "moral attachment." This is to say, a right must represent "any violation [which] constitutes an assault on the latter's dignity, and to varying degree, a wrong to the social order as a whole."[20] The cases under Title I described above, by contrast, indicate that persons with disabilities are only afforded this dignity if they need help. Most important, the federal courts' preoccupation with mitigation places the identity of disabled people in flux. It also leaves little room for questioning the social order. How can people proclaim that their rights have been violated only after a judge has gone through their medicine cabinets to make sure that they have not, could not, or chose not to, mitigate their impairments?

Moreover, rights cannot be based on needs because they do not fulfill the second category of Orren's definition that they be fact-independent. As she explains it, rights serve as *a priori* standards against which particular facts in litigation may be evaluated. In the United States, these standards can arise from the Constitution, from statutes, or from common law.[21] Even access to a statutory conception of rights, which is what the ADA establishes, cannot be based on terms like "need," "vulnerabilities," or "weakness," because they are fact-*dependent*. Depending on someone's present situation, judges assess if they should exercise their rights. A rights-oriented view of persons with disabilities should rest on a more stationary conception of their identity and not fluctuate on the basis of need.

Toppling Workplace Hierarchies

Few people with disabilities have exercised their rights. In the cases where they did, however, the federal courts have placed a very significant burden on employers to accommodate their employees. They have done so by arguing that requests for accommodation trigger an "interactive process" between an employer and an employee. First, the courts have ruled that an employer must accommodate persons with whatever tools, equipment, or schedule they need to fulfill their jobs. A federal court judge ruled that an attorney could start working one hour later than all the other attorneys because epilepsy affected her sleep.[22]

Second, if persons with a disability can no longer perform the essential functions of a position, an employer must reassign them to a new position.[23] As long as a reassignment does not mean that disabled persons receive a promotion or that a job was created specifically for them, an employer must retain them. Then, it is up to the employees whether or not to accept the new job. This move could also involve a demotion in terms of pay or status. Some employees, for instance, might decide to work only on a part-time basis.

Third, the federal courts have ruled that it is up to the employer, not just the employees, to anticipate the employees' needs. While the employer can only act on the basis of information, a company must help accommodate employees. Federal court judges assume that employers are much more knowledgeable about what kind of accommodations could be made.[24]

Once initiated, the interactive process created by a quest for a reasonable accommodation makes employers provide significant changes in work conditions and work rules. It is these changes that have the capacity to undermine one of the most fundamental rules in capitalism—that employers should not take into account an employee's needs. Providing for needs, moreover, does not merely help the person with a disability, it can also alter the workplace environment for the coworkers, because most employers provide different work conditions for purposes of control. The best employees receive the best conditions on the basis of merit. With the interactive process instituted because of need, it could inhibit an employer from maintaining an entirely merit-based workplace.

Workers receiving accommodations, moreover, would not only disturb this notion of workplace hierarchy for themselves, but their accommodations might raise questions for other workers about their conditions. Providing different conditions for one set of workers might show just how shackled the other set is. Indeed, this is the point of merit-based differences, providing an incentive to employees who do not produce the most into producing more, so they will receive better conditions. This is not the case, however, with reasonable accommodations based on needs. Whereas not all employees are equally talented, all employees have needs.

If an employer favors one set of needs over another, this might well generate resentment. The resentment could then be transformed into workplace demands that employers must decide, or not decide, to grant. From an employer's perspective, demands, let alone concessions, erode the power that he or she has to manage the workplace.

Gazing and Gatekeeping

Examining all the issues that the battle over disability rights raises makes it clear that if accommodations were perceived as statutory rights, available to the large number of people in the United States with disabilities, the employment relations provisions in Title I of the ADA would have a major impact on employment relations. The power behind this right will stay dormant, however, as long as the federal courts remain the gatekeeper for so many employers. The situation will not change if the courts continue protecting employers from the burden of even facing, let alone losing, suits from employees or prospective employees who request reasonable accommodations.

The federal courts' interpretation of the disability rights in the workplace has, therefore, enacted what could be called a Foucauldian state—that is, a state in which the federal court judges scrutinize the everyday rituals and practices of citizens who maintain that they have debilitating physical and mental impairments. Acting as state experts, the federal court judges control what each individual should receive, be it a reasonable accommodation or termination as a result of exposing a limiting, but not substantially limiting, impairment to his or her employer.

Nonetheless, making the federal courts become so involved in essentially implementing the employment relations provisions of the ADA is exceptional. While one of the primary functions of the federal government is gatekeeping, this role does not often fall to the federal courts. Gatekeeping is usually performed by either an administrative agency or an executive department that is given the authority to implement a public policy or program. In this instance, the Supreme Court has taken on its new gatekeeping role as a last resort. Its interpretation of Title I stands in stark contrast to the federal bureaucracy's interpretation of a disability.[25]

Given its exceptional nature, the federal court judges' gatekeeping role could always change. Since their interpretation of who should be considered disabled is culturally bound, the federal courts could alter their view about what impairments substantially limit people with disabilities. Or, public outcry might induce Congress and the president to make this definition more concrete, thereby limiting the role of the federal courts. Finally, these courts also could have reservations about exercising their discretionary power and simply stop dismissing so many cases on summary judgment, leaving the decisions to juries.

If any of these scenarios happen, more people would receive accommodations at the workplace, and the employment provisions of the ADA thereby would transform employee-employer relations. Requests for accommodation could upend the idea of workplace normalcy and make employers soften the edges of capitalism, an economic system that denies any notion of need. These accommodations might well offer those with and without disabilities more control over their lives at work.

NOTES

Introduction

1. The Americans with Disabilities Act (ADA) has a broad definition which includes, first, that a person has a "physical or mental impairment that substantially limits one or more of the major life activities . . . ; second, a record of such an impairment; or third, as being regarded as having such an impairment." The major life activities are: "Functions such as caring for one's self, performing manual tasks, walking, seeing, hearing, speaking, breathing, learning, and working." That a major life activity is limited is not self-evident. Proof of a limitation is necessary. A physical impairment is a "physiological disorder or condition, cosmetic disfigurement, or anatomical loss affecting any of a list of body systems." A mental impairment is "any mental or psychological disorder, such as mental retardation, organic brain syndrome, emotional or mental illness, and specific learning disabilities." Analysis of the definition by the Department of Health, Education and Welfare regulations indicated that it was not feasible to list all the specific conditions. See Robert L. Burgdorf Jr., "The Americans with Disabilities Act: Analysis and Implications of a Second-Generation Civil Rights Statute," *Harvard Civil Rights–Civil Liberties Review* 26 (1991): 445–51.

2. Ibid. A person who is "regarded as" having an impairment, like someone who has a mild limp or is rumored to have a mental illness, yet has no such impairment, is also protected under the ADA.

3. This surpasses the number of elderly (33.2 million) and African Americans (32.7 million), according to the American census in 1995. Quoted from *Achieving Independence: The Challenge for the 21st Century* (Washington, D.C.: National Council on Disability, July 26, 1996), 14.

4. Justin Dart, *Washington Post,* July 18, 1995, quoted from *Achieving Independence,* 13.

5. See Robert Murphy, *The Body Silent* (New York: W. W. Norton, 1990). He borrows this notion from Lévi-Strauss's idea that people with disabilities represent humanity.

6. See John Gliedman and William Roth, *The Unexpected Minority: Handicapped Children in America* (New York: Harcourt Brace Jovanovich, 1980), who write about the self/other distinction. Also see Ingunn Moser, "Against Normal-

izaton: Subverting Norms of Ability and Disability," *Science as Culture* 9 (2000): 201–41.

7. Robert Murphy, "Encounters: The Body Silent in America," 140–57 in *Disability and Culture*, edited by Benedicte Ingstad and Susan Reynolds Whyte (Berkeley: University of California Press, 1995), 143.

8. Quoted from *Achieving Independence*, 13. See Irving K. Zola, "Disability Statistics: What We Count and What It Tells Us," *Journal of Disability Policy Studies* 4 (1993).

9. "It is said that witnessing a disabled person," wrote Albert B. Robillard in a memoir about living with a disability, "is equivalent to seeing one's own mortality." Robillard, *Meaning of a Disability: The Lived Experience of Paralysis* (Philadelphia: Temple University Press, 1999). Robillard is a sociology professor at the University of Hawaii, Manoa. Also see Leonard Kriegel's book *Flying Solo: Reimaging Manhood, Courage and Loss* (Boston: Beacon Press, 1998), for a powerfully written memoir about living with a disability.

10. "People with disabilities are very resourceful, and they figure out ways to do things," maintains Paul Longmore, a historian and a disability cultural studies expert at San Francisco State University. See Peter Monaghan, "Pioneering Field of Disability Studies Challenges Established Approaches and Attitudes," *Chronicle of Higher Education* (January 23, 1998).

11. A journalist wrote a story showing how inventions that were designed for people with disabilities became essential to those without. The phonograph, for instance, had been designed by Thomas Edison to read to blind people. The typewriter was also created for people with visual problems. Eric A. Taub, "The Blind Leading the Sighted," *New York Times*, October 28, 1999.

12. The effect of this power ranges from chasing someone off a sidewalk who is afraid of bumping into a person using a white cane to restructuring a job. As Stephen Kuusisto relayed about a friend with a severe vision impairment: "What I like to do is lurch toward the people who are doing everything they can to get off the sidewalk so I can pass . . . they're afraid that you'll bump them, and then they'll be blind too." Kuusisto, *A Planet of the Blind: A Memoir* (New York: Delta Trade Paperbacks, 1998).

13. According to *Black's Legal Dictionary*, employment-at-will "provides that, absent express agreement to the contrary, either employer or employee may terminate their relationship at any time, for any reason." Aside from private agreements like a collective bargaining agreement, there are a number of federal laws that prevent employers from firing employees without cause. The Civil Service Reform Act has a provision for whistle blowers that *Black's Legal Dictionary* states are "designed to protect employees from retaliation for a disclosure of employer's misconduct. State and federal antidiscrimination statutes also prohibit wrongful discharge."

14. Quoted from *Criscione v. Sears Roebuck Co.*, 384 N.E.2d 91 (Ill. App. Ct. 1978). The American courts developed employment-at-will from English master-servant law, which had been established by the British to deal with yearly hirings of agricultural and domestic workers. Unlike the American version of the doctrine, the original interpretation of the doctrine created an equitable relationship between the employer and the employee. "[I]njustice would result," explained William Blackstone, the famous eighteenth-century jurist, "if . . . masters could have the benefit of servants' labor during planting and harvest seasons but dis-

charge them to avoid supporting them during the unproductive winter." Quoted from Andrew D. Hill, *Wrongful Discharge and the Derogation of the At-Will Doctrine,* Labor Relations and Public Policy Series, no. 3 (Philadelphia: University of Pennsylvania Press, 1987), 2. According to legal historians, the American conception of employment-at-will also imposed duties on employers until the industrial revolution, when Wood's rule was adopted by the judiciary. This rule was taken from Horace Wood's treatise on master-servant relations law that was written in 1877. See Deborah A. Ballam, *American Business Law Journal* 33 (1995): 1–50.

15. Jay M. Feinman, "The Development of the Employment at Will Rule," *American Journal of Legal History* 20 (1976): 132–34.

16. See Amartya Sen, *The Standard of Living* (New York: Cambridge University Press, 1987); and David Levine, *Needs, Rights, and the Market* (Boulder: Lynn Rienner Publisher, 1988).

17. See Arlene B. Mayerson, "Restoring Regard for the 'Regarded As' Prong: Giving Effect to Congressional Intent," *Villanova Law Review* 42 (1997): 591–93. A person who is "regarded as" having an impairment, like someone who has a mild limp or is rumored to have a mental illness, yet has no such impairment, is also protected under the ADA.

18. *Karen Sutton and Kimberly Hinton v. United Air Lines, Inc.,* 527 U.S. 471 (1999) (Note: "Air Lines," as in United Air Lines, is listed by the Supreme Court as two separate words, whereas the company name considers it one word); *Vaughn L. Murphy v. United Parcel Service, Inc.,* 527 U.S. 516 (1999); and *Albertsons Inc. v. Hallie Kirkingburg,* 527 U.S. 555 (1999).

19. See Sigmund Freud, *Character and Culture,* edited by Philip Rief (New York: Macmillan Books, 1960).

20. Michel Foucault, *Discipline and Punish: The Birth of the Prison,* translated by Alan Sheridan (New York: Vintage Press, 1979), 170–94.

21. Elizabeth Lunbeck, *The Psychiatric Persuasion: Knowledge, Gender, and Power in Modern America* (Princeton: Princeton University Press, 1994), 5.

22. Unlike individualism, individuality places the individual within a specific context—namely, within a community. One person's relationship with another constitutes the primary means of judging one's uniqueness and originality. Measures are not instruments used for conformity but rather for understanding how people differ.

23. Michel Foucault, *Ethics: Subjectivity and Truth,* vol. 1, edited by Paul Rabinow (New York: New Press, 1994): 202.

24. Ibid., 203.

25. *Thalos v. Dillon Companies, Inc.,* 86 F. Supp. 2d 1079 (D.Colo. 2000), 1084.

26. Joseph P. Shapiro, *No Pity: People with Disabilites Forging a New Civil Rights Movement* (New York: Times Books, 1993), 52–53.

27. See Edward D. Berkowitz, "Professionals as Providers: Some Thoughts on Disability and Ideology," *Rehabilitation Psychology* 29 (1984): 211–16, for an excellent article that captures the difference between the two approaches.

28. Ibid., 26.

29. Two other projects were the National Center for Law and the Handicapped in South Bend, Ind.; and the Children's Defense Fund Institute for Public Interest Representation at Georgetown University. See Richard K. Scotch, *From Good Will to Civil Rights* (Philadelphia: Temple University Press, 1984), 37.

30. Richard K. Scotch, "Disability as the Basis for a Social Movement: Advocacy and the Politics of Definition," *Journal of Social Issues* 44 (1988): 159,161.

31. See Harlan Hahn, "Introduction: Disability Policy and the Problem of Discrimination," *American Behavioral Scientist* 28 (1985): 310. Not all scholars view this as merely an organizational problem. As James I. Charlton sees it, "The failure of most people with disabilities to identify with other people with disabilities is, I believe, the principal contradiction that limits the DRM's [Disability Rights Movement's] potential influence and power." Charlton, *Nothing about Us without Us: Disability Oppression and Empowerment* (Berkeley: University of California Press, 1998), 78.

32. See H. Dirksen, L. Bauman, and Jennifer Drake, "Silence Is Not without Voice," 307–14 in *The Disability Studies Reader*, edited by Lennard J. Davis; Sue Schwarz, editor, *Choices in Deafness: A Parents Guide* (Rockville, Md.: Woodbine House, 1987).

33. See Shapiro, *No Pity*, 126–27, for a good description of the sectarian battles within what he calls the "disability movement."

34. Interview with Beverlee J. Stafford, director, Planning, Policy & Evaluation Staff, U.S. Department of Education, July 1999, Washington, D.C.

35. Unlike other organizations that served people with specific disabilities, the National Federation of the Blind had fought for its constituents' rights long before the 1960s. See Scotch, "Disability as the Basis for a Social Movement," 163.

36. Jean Flatley McGuire, "Organizing from Diversity in the Name of Community: Lessons from the Disability Civil Rights Movement," *Policy Studies Journal* 22 (1994): 119.

37. Simi Linton, *Claiming Disability: Knowledge and Identity* (New York: New York University Press, 1998), 4.

38. Lennard J. Davis, *Enforcing Normalcy: Disability, Deafness, and the Body* (New York: Verso, 1995), 13. Also see Marta Russell, *Beyond Ramps: Disability at the End of the Social Contract* (Monroe, Maine: Common Courage Press, 1998), 17, who writes that "'normal' demands political conformity as well as physical conformity, and as such can be used as a tool for social control."

39. Quoted from Linton, *Claiming Disability*, 2. Within the field of disability studies, some work takes a global view, documenting how disabled people have experienced a "human rights tragedy of epic proportions," and examining how "disability based consciousness is emerging throughout the world and has begun to contest the oppression of these people." See Charlton, *Nothing about Us without Us*. Other disability studies projects have focused on one particular culture. See the essays in *Disability and Culture*, edited by Ingstad and Whyte. While this book does not dispute the political, social, and cultural oppression of people with disabilities worldwide, it examines a much smaller issue—why American policymakers developed the particular policy they did, and how it cultivated a culture of resistance to the disability rights model that has become manifest in the federal courts.

40. John Hockenberry, *Moving Violations: A Memoir, War Zones, Wheelchairs, and Declarations of Independence* (New York: Hyperion Press, 1995), 33.

41. Quoted from Shapiro, *No Pity*, 24.

42. Hockenberry, *Moving Violations*, 34.

43. "History Making Ride for Winning Golfer," *New York Times*, January 12, 1998.

44. Burgdorf Jr., "The Americans with Disabilities Act," 420–21.

45. Mitchell P. LaPlante, Jae Kennedy, H. Stephen Kaye, and Barbara L. Wenger, "Disability and Employment—#11," Disability Statistics Abstract, University of California, San Francisco, September 8, 1997, 2.

46. For a good historical analysis of how the American state defines disability as an inability to work, see Deborah A. Stone, *The Disabled State* (Philadelphia: Temple University Press, 1984).

47. Interview with Arlene Mayerson, Disability Rights Education and Fund, Berkeley, Calif., December 1997. Colker came up with this figure after conducting a survey of cases from 1992 to 1998. See Ruth Colker, "The ADA: A Windfall for Defendants," *Harvard Civil Rights–Civil Liberties Law Review* 34 (1999): 99–163. The American Bar Association conducted a study of 700 Title I cases between 1992 and 1997 in which employers won 92 percent. Quoted from Michael Doyle, "Disability Law Keeping Courts Busy," *Sacramento Bee,* November 26, 1998.

48. *Sutton v. United Air Lines; Murphy v. United Parcel Service;* and *Albertsons v. Kirkingburg.*

49. The number of people with severe disabilities being employed has gone from 23.3 percent in 1991 to 26.1 percent in 1994. The number of all people with disabilities has increased less. It has gone from 52 percent in 1991 to 52.3 percent in 1994. The President's Committee on Employment of People with Disabilities derived these figures from the Census Bureau's Survey of Income and Program Participation conducted by the U.S. Census Bureau. See President's Committee on Employment of People with Disabilities, "Basic Facts," l.

50. *Sutton v. United Air Lines,* 490–91.

51. Ibid., 510.

52. John Hockenberry, "Disability Games," *New York Times,* June 29, 1999. Hockenberry added that "someone should tell the doctors working on a cure for spinal cord injury they are wasting their time. The Supreme Court just beat them to it."

53. Linda Greenhouse, "High Court Limits Who Is Protected by Disability Law," *New York Times,* June 23, 1999.

54. *Sutton v. United Air Lines,* 505. As Stevens wrote, "When faced with classes of individuals or types of discrimination that fall outside the core prohibitions of anti-discrimination statutes, we have consistently construed those statutes to include comparable evils within their coverage, even when the particular evil at issue was beyond Congress' immediate concern in passing the legislation."

55. Patricia Yeager, "Not a Free Ride," Letter to the Editor, *New York Times,* June 30, 1999.

56. Burgdorf Jr., "The Americans with Disabilities Act," 420–21.

57. Peter Hall, *Governing the Economy: The Politics of State Intervention in Britain and France* (New York: Oxford University Press, 1986). Also see Judith Goldstein and Robert O. Keohane, eds., *Ideas and Foreign Policy* (Ithaca: Cornell University Press, 1993).

58. Judith Goldstein, "The Impact of Ideas on Trade Policy: The Origins of U.S. Agricultural and Manufacturing Policies," *International Organization* 43 (1989): 32.

59. Ibid. Not every group of experts, however, belongs to an epistemic community. Aside from sharing a set of ideas and beliefs, these experts must cultivate a

common practice or a standard means of exercising their ideational framework. They also have a preordained notion of validity. Finally, members of an epistemic community help shape policy only if their ideational framework fits within the confines of the institutions implementing it.

60. Theda Skocpol, *Protecting Soldiers and Mothers: The Political Origins of Social Policy in the United States* (Cambridge: Harvard University Press, 1992), 41, 47.

61. Quoted from Dorothy Ross, "The Many Lives of Institutionalism in American Social Science," *Polity* 28 (1995): 121.

62. Karen Orren, "Ideas and Institutions," *Polity* 28 (1995): 97; Stephen Skowronek "Order and Change," *Polity* 28 (1995): 91–96.

63. Orren, "Ideas and Institutions," 99.

64. Sven Steinmo, "American Exceptionalism Reconsidered: Culture or Institutions?" 106–31 in *The Dynamics of American Politics: Approaches and Interpretations*, edited by Lawrence C. Dodd and Calvin Jillson (Boulder, Colo.: Westview Press, 1994), 107.

65. Ellen Immergut, "The Theoretical Core of New Institutionalism," *Politics & Society* 26 (1998): 19.

66. Goldstein, "The Impact of Ideas on Trade Policy," 32.

67. Foucault, *Discipline and Punish*, 7–9.

68. Foucault's work isolates the rituals of power, like punishment, disclosing both how power works and precisely what it does. Power itself seeks invisibility, and the object of power—on whom it operates—becomes more visible. To Foucault, the small details of everyday life and the most mundane activities become a focus of study as the state determines what is appropriate for individuals, particularly those in the mainstream. Ibid., 187–93.

69. Ibid., 22.

70. See Hugh G. Gallagher, *FDR's Splendid Deception* (New York: Dodd Mead, 1985).

71. Harlan Hahn, "Civil Rights for Disabled Americans: The Foundation of a Political Agenda," 181–203 in *Images of the Disabled: Disabling Images*, edited by Ian Gartner and Tom Joe (New York: Praeger, 1987), 181–82.

Chapter One

1. Margaret Mead, "Applied Anthropology: The State of the Art," 142–61 in *Perspectives on Anthropology, 1976*, edited by Anthony F. C. Wallace, J. Lawrence Angel, Richard Fox, Sally McLendon, Rachel Sady, Robert Shoner (Washington, D.C.: American Anthropological Association, 1977), 142.

2. Howard A. Rusk, "A Community Rehabilitation Service and Center," *Archives of Physical Medicine* 28 (1947): 583.

3. Rusk was the most prominent doctor in the rehabilitation movement. Senator Douglas said Dr. Rusk "is certainly one of the greatest authorities on rehabilitation, if not the greatest, in the country." U.S. Congress Hearings before the Subcommittee of the Committee on Labor and Public Welfare in the U.S. Senate, 81st Cong., 2d sess., May 22, 1950, 501. Kessler also played a large role. In addition, Drs. Frank Krusen, Dean Clark, and William G. Lennox were important participants in this movement. D. H. Dabelstein, assistant director of the Office of Vocational Rehabilitation (OVR), to Oveta Hobby, secretary of Health, Education and Welfare, July 30, 1953, Box 28, General Subject File, Rehabilitation Ser-

vices Administration, Record Group 363, Records of Social and Rehabilitation Service, Department of Health, Education and Welfare, National Archives, College Park, Md.

4. Harlan Hahn, "Civil Rights for Disabled Americans: The Foundation of a Political Agenda," 181–203 in *Images of the Disabled: Disabling Images,* edited by Alan Gartner and Tom Joe (New York: Praeger, 1987), 181.

5. "Rehabilitation Centers, Report of the Committee on Rehabilitation Centers, States' Vocational Rehabilitation Council," October 23, 1950, Advisors Council of the Office of Vocational Rehabilitation, Box 126, Record Group 468, General Records of the Department of Health and Human Services, National Archives, College Park, Md.

6. John A. Millet, "Psychoanalysis in the United States," 546–96 in *Psychoanalytic Pioneers,* edited by Franz Alexander, Samuel Eisenstein, and Martin Grotjahn (New York: Basic Books, 1966), 555.

7. One psychiatrist, who recognized William Menninger as one of the leaders of psychodynamic therapy, called him a "militant missionary." See Bernard H. Hall, *A Psychiatrist for a Troubled World: Selected Papers of William C. Menninger* (New York: Viking Press, 1967), 563.

8. "S. 1066, S. 2273, S. 3465, Bills Relating to the Vocational Rehabilitation of the Physically Handicapped," U.S. Congress, Hearings before the Subcommittee of the Committee on Labor and Public Welfare in the U.S. Senate, 81st Cong., 2d sess., 1950, 506.

9. See Marta Russell, *Beyond Ramps: Disability at the End of the Social Contract* (Monroe, Maine: Common Courage Press, 1998), 25–27. Russell reports that approximately 280,000 disabled people were exterminated (including 5,000 children) in Nazi Germany before the Roman Catholic Church helped put an end to the official euthanasia program in 1942.

10. Michel Foucault, *Discipline and Punish: The Birth of the Prison,* translated by Alan Sheridan (New York: Vintage Press, 1979), 185.

11. Henry H. Kessler, *The Principles and Practices of Rehabilitation* (New York: Arno Press, 1980), 3. Also see Henri-Jacques Stiker, *A History of Disability,* translated by William Sayers (Ann Arbor: University of Michigan Press, 1999), 123–24, 131, who argues that the notion of rehabilitation emerged during World War I. He defines rehabilitation as what "the war has taken away, we must replace." To Stiker, the "maimed person is someone missing something precise, an organ or function." What is striking is the development of the "pro-sthesis," which is "not only the pieces of wood, iron, now plastic that replace the missing hand or foot. It is also the very idea that you can *replace.*" By contrast, I suggest that the American version of rehabilitation was cultivated during World War II. And while I agree with Stiker's larger argument that "the concept of rehabilitation (=the demand to be like the others)," this book emphasizes the compensatory aspect of rehabilitation. It was not the prosthesis, but the well-adjusted personality that supposedly represented the key to rehabilitation.

12. Howard A. Rusk, "The Broadening Horizons of and Physical Medicine," *Archives of Physical Medicine* 30 (1949): 27.

13. Glenn Glitzer and Arnold Arluke, *The Making of Rehabilitation: The Political Economy of Medical Specialization, 1890–1980* (Berkeley: University of California Press, 1985), 42. Also see Howard A. Rusk, Mary E. Switzer, and Eugene J. Taylor, "International Programs in Rehabilitation," 527–48 in James F.

Garrett and Edna S. Levine, eds., *Rehabilitation Practices with the Physically Disabled* (New York: Columbia University Press, 1973).

14. Gertrude G. Johnson, "Manpower Selection and the Preventative Medicine Program," 1–13 in *Preventative Medicine in World War II: Personal Health, Measures and Immunization,* edited by Colonel John Boyd Coates Jr. (Washington, D.C.: Office of Surgeon General, Department of the Army, 1955), 1.

15. E. W. Rowe, "Tuberculosis of the Kidneys from the Roentgen Standpoint," *Journal of Radiology* (1920), 83–89; Henry Schmitz, "The Modern Treatment of Cancer of the Uterus with the Combined Surgical and Radiological Methods," *Journal of Radiology* (1920), 90–106; George E. Pfahler, "Radiotherapy in Carcinoma of the Larynx, with Special Reference to Radium Needs through the Thyroid Membrane," *Journal of Radiology* (1922), 511–16. Also see Gritzer and Arluke, *The Making of Rehabilitation,* 50. According to Gritzer and Arluke, the key physical therapy journal, *Archives of Physical Therapy* (formerly, *Journal of Radiology*) had only two articles which referred to from 1920 to 1940, and neither was written by a physical therapy physician.

16. Gritzer and Arluke, *The Making of Rehabilitation,* 63, 68–69.

17. Ibid., 40.

18. Oscar M. Sullivan and Kenneth O. Snortum, *Disabled Persons: Their Education and Responsibility* (New York: Arno Press, 1980), 482–83.

19. Quoted from Gritzer and Arluke, *The Making of Rehabilitation,* 43.

20. Ibid., 41. In May 1916, the American Orthopedic Association had a committee represent their interests in the expanding military market. By July of the same year, this association offered its members services to the surgeon general.

21. Gritzer and Arluke, *The Making of Rehabilitation,* 41–42, 44.

22. Ibid., 46–48. The Federal Board for Vocational Education began its own study of vocational rehabilitation in August 1917. It questioned the surgeon general's plan for the wounded.

23. Ibid., 49.

24. Lennard J. Davis, *Enforcing Normalcy: Disability, Deafness, and the Body* (New York: Verso, 1995), 5.

25. Donald K. Pickens, *Eugenics and the Progressives* (Nashville: Vanderbilt University Press, 1968); and Daniel J. Kevles, *In the Name of Eugenics: Genetics and the Uses of Human Heredity* (New York: Alfred A. Knopf, 1985); and Richard Hofstadter, *Social Darwinism in American Thought,* rev. ed. (Boston: Beacon Press, 1970), 165.

26. See Robert Burgdorf Jr. and Marcia Pearce Burgdorf, "The Wicked Witch Is Almost Dead," *Temple Law Quarterly* 50 (1977): 1000.

27. Kevles, *In the Name of Eugenics,* 100.

28. See Burgdorf Jr. and Burgdorf, "The Wicked Witch Is Almost Dead," 996–98.

29. *Buck v. Bell,* 274 U.S. 200 (1927). As Judith Baer explains, the *Buck* decision meant that the Court decided that "There is a group of people whose rights do not much matter, because they only sap the state, and anyway, they hardly notice what is being done to them." See Judith A. Baer, *Equality under the Constitution: Reclaiming the Fourteenth Amendment* (Ithaca: Cornell University Press, 1983), 198.

30. Pickens, *Eugenics and the Progressives,* 138. Rationalism has been criticized for its overestimatation of benevolence. It underestimates the destructive im-

pulses in motivation and importance of nonrational factors such as tradition and faith in human economy; reason praised in opposition to faith, traditional authority, fanaticism, and superstition.

31. Greta Jones, "Eugenics and Social Policy between the Wars," *Historical Journal* 25 (1982): 728.

32. Lee D. Baker, *From Savage to Negro: Anthropology and the Construction of Race, 1896–1954* (Berkeley: University of California Press, 1998), 90.

33. When the stock market crashed in 1929, throwing 25 percent of workers out of the work force, the eugenics movement lost public appeal. See Pickens, *Eugenics and the Progressives,* 202–10.

34. Elizabeth Lunbeck, *The Psychiatric Persuasion: Knowledge, Gender, and Power in Modern America* (Princeton: Princeton University Press, 1994). Also see David B. Truman, "The Impact on Political Science of the Revolution in the Behavioral Sciences," 38–67 in *Behavioralism in Political Science,* edited by Heinz Eulau (New York: Atherton Press, 1969).

35. See Fred Eggan, "The History of Social/Cultural Anthropology," 1–13 in *Perspectives on Anthropology, 1976,* edited by Anthony F. C. Wallace, J. Lawrence Angel, Richard Fox, Sally McLendon, Rachel Sady, and Robert Sharer (Washington, D.C.: American Anthropology Association, 1977), 4–6; and Melville Herskovits, *Franz Boas: The Science of Man in the Making* (New York: Charles Scribner's Sons, 1953).

36. Judith Schachter Modell, *Ruth Benedict: Patterns of a Life* (Philadelphia: University of Pennsylvania Press, 1983), 196.

37. Ibid.

38. Studying a myriad of cultures and societies, anthropology made the most use of functionalism. See A. R. Radcliffe-Brown, "The Methods of Ethnology and Social Anthropology," *South African Journal of Science* 20 (1923): 124–47; Bronislaw Malinowski, "Culture," *Encyclopedia of the Social Sciences* (New York: Macmillan Books, 1938), 621–45; Edward Sapir, "Cultural Anthropolgy and Psychiatry," 509–21 in *Selected Writings of Edward Sapir in Language, Culture, and Personality,* edited by David G. Mandell (Berkeley: University of California Press, 1949); and Robert F. Spencer, "The Nature and Value of Functionalism in Anthropology," 1–17 in *Functionalism in the Social Sciences* (Philadelphia: American Academy of Politics and Social Science, 1965).

39. Ian Whitaker, "The Nature and Value of Functionalism in Sociology" 127–43 in *Functionalism in the Social Sciences* (Philadephia: American Academy of Politics and Social Science, 1965), 127.

40. Edward D. Berkowitz, *Disabled Policy: America's Programs for the Handicapped* (New York: Cambridge University Press, 1987), 203.

41. Ute Gacs, Aisha Khan, Jerrie McIntyre, and Ruth Weinberg, *Women Anthropologists: A Biographical Dictionary* (Westport, Ct.: Greenwood Press, 1988), 3.

42. Modell, *Ruth Benedict,* 198. Benedict read Freud, borrowed from Gestalt psychology, and knew the popular Freudian book, Kurt Koffka's *The Growth of the Mind* (1924). From these three sources, she derived a notion about the concept of wholeness of personality. Also see Solomon W. Ginsburg, *A Psychiatrist's Views on Social Issues* (New York: Columbia University Press, 1963), 106.

43. Ginsburg, *A Psychiatrist's Views on Social Issues,* 108–9.

44. A. L. Kroeber, *An Anthropologist Looks at History* (Berkeley: University of California Press, 1966), 177.

45. Roscoe C. Hinkle, *Developments in American Sociological Theory, 1915–1950* (Albany: State University of New York Press, 1994), 202; Robert Hunt, editor, *Personalities and Culture: Greetings in Psychological Anthropology* (New York: Natural History Press, 1967), ix–xv.

46. Hunt, editor, *Personalities and Culture,* ix.

47. Ibid., xiii.

48. Spencer, "The Nature and Value of Functionalism in Anthropology," 15; and Mark C. Smith, *Social Science in the Crucible: The American Debate over Objectivity and Purpose, 1918–1941* (Durham: Duke University Press, 1994), 35.

49. Smith, *Social Science in the Crucible,* 7, 36–37, 39–40. In order to judge whether values could be verified, purposive social scientists followed the philosophy of pragmatism founded by John Dewey and William James, which traced the relationship between action, knowledge, and belief, and searched for verifiable knowledge.

50. Ibid., 7. Also see Dorothy Ross, *The Origins of American Social Science* (New York: Cambridge University Press, 1991), 8.

51. Smith, *Social Science in the Crucible,* 253, 255. Realizing the significance of the academic community's commitment to the fight for democracy, President Franklin D. Roosevelt helped sustain their support by removing any overt ideological references. He made the overall value—the fight for democracy—into what could be described as a "generic" ideology. Social scientists, doctors, and scientists knew who they were fighting—the Germans, the Italians, and the Japanese—and that they must defeat fascism. What type of democracy would or should prevail, be it representative or participatory, with a strong or weak welfare state, was not at issue.

52. See Kroeber, *An Anthropologist Looks at History,* 175. The anthropologists were so dedicated that 295 of the 313 anthropologists in the United States gave their services to the war effort.

53. Rosemary Stevens, *American Medicine and the Public Interest* (New Haven: Yale University Press, 1971), 179–80. Typhoid fever, dysentery, and diphtheria, among other contagious diseases, were no longer such a grave threat. Also, diseases like those connected to blood vessels, diabetes, arthritis, and various allergies were controlled.

54. Major Edgar L. Coke and John E. Gordon, "Accidental Trauma, Nonbattle Injury," 233–70 in *Preventative Medicine in World War II: Personal Health, Measures and Immunization,* edited by Colonel John Boyd Coates Jr.(Washington, D.C.: Office of Surgeon General, Department of the Army, 1955), 233.

55. Edward D. Berkowitz, *Rehabilitation: The Federal Government's Response to Disability, 1935–1954* (New York: Arno Press, 1980), 107.

56. Stevens, *American Medicine and the Public Interest,* 183–84.

57. Berkowitz, *Rehabilitation,* 91, 110.

58. Ibid., 111.

59. Mary Lenz Walker, *Beyond Bureaucracy: Mary Elizabeth Switzer and Rehabilitation* (Lanham, Md.: University Press of America, 1985), 119.

60. See "Baruch Committee on Physical Medicine," *Archives of Physical Therapy* 25 (1941): 199–201; and Charles F. Behrens, "Activities of the Subcommittee on Rehabilitation of the Baruch Committee," *Archives of Physical Therapy* 25 (1941): 581–86.

61. Berkowitz, *Rehabilitation,* 109.

62. Quoted from ibid., 112. Albee set up a reconstruction hospital for wounded soldiers during World War I. He borrowed the principles established by a German orthopedic surgeon who stressed utilizing medicine to develop the person's occupation potential.

63. Kessler, *The Principles and Practices of Rehabilitation*, 5.

64. Memorandum titled "Resources for Rehabilitating and Employing More Handicapped Workers," Director's Letters, Box 125, Record Group 468.

65. Toynbee also is influenced by anthropological and social-psychological thinking of the 1920s. See Kenneth W. Thompson, *Toynbee's Philosophy of World History and Politics* (Baton Rouge: Louisiana State University Press, 1985), 48–49.

66. C. Esco Obermann, *A History of Vocational Rehabilitation in America* (Minneapolis: T. S. Dennison and Co., 1965), 25.

67. Ibid., 27.

68. Rusk, Switzer, and Taylor, "International Programs in Rehabilitation," 529.

69. Ibid., 528. Also see Arnold Toynbee, *A Selection from His Works*, edited by E. W. F. Tomlin (Oxford: Oxford University Press, 1978), 183.

70. Rusk, "A Community Rehabilitation Service and Center," 585.

71. Lawrence J. Friedman, *Menninger: The Family & the Clinic* (Lawrence: University of Kansas Press, 1990), 66–68. Teamwork, however, was not democratic. The team had a distinct hierarchy, with the psychiatrist or doctor taking the lead. The Menningers went so far with this idea that their conference table reflected this hierarchy.

72. Switzer's speech before the National Rehabilitation Association, 1951, Box 16, Mary Elizabeth Switzer Papers, Schlesinger Library, Radcliffe College, Cambridge, Mass.

73. See Berkowitz, *Disabled Policy*, 202; and Smith, *Social Science in the Crucible*, 217.

74. Lunbeck, *The Psychiatric Persuasion*, 68. Lunbeck describes how the word "personality" originally meant "the quality of being a person and not a thing." By the eighteenth century, it took on a different meaning, referring to a person's character or individuality and distinctiveness. Character made references to an ideal, and in this way it also was elitist. It was associated with a degree of respect that only few could achieve. By contrast, everybody had a personality. It was not until the twentieth century that the idea of personality came into common usage, supplanting character as a designation for individual nature. Not only did the term "personality" carry a lighter moral load than character, but it also had a different, less exalted set of values. The personality gave the possibility of turning to the everyday because, unlike character, it was malleable.

75. Harold I. Kaplan and Helen S. Kaplan, "An Historical Survey of Psychosomatic Medicine," *Journal of Nervous Mental Disorders* 124 (1956): 546–68.

76. Eric D. Wittkower, "Historical Perspective of Contemporary Psychosomatic Medicine," 3–13 in *Psychosomatic Medicine'Current Trends and Clinical Applications*, edited by Z. J. Lipowski, Don R. Lipsett, and Peter C. Whybrow, (New York: Oxford University Press, 1977); Kaplan and Kaplan, "An Historical Survey of Psychosomatic Medicine," 546–68.

77. Gerald N. Grob, *The Mad among Us: A History of the Care of America's Mentally Ill* (Cambridge, Mass.: Harvard University Press, 1994), 131, 142.

78. Ibid., 142, 150.

79. Lunbeck, *The Psychiatric Persuasion,* 117. Those practicing the new psychiatry—people like Adolf Meyer and William Allen White—also referred to it as "psychodynamic" psychiatry. William Menninger, Karl Menninger, and Franz Alexander, who were part of the second generation practicing the new psychiatry, also practiced "psychodynamic therapy." These psychiatrists coined this term as a means of juxtaposing their "dynamic" approach with the prevailing, descriptive psychiatry, which White and Menninger, among others, portrayed as static and hopelessly outdated. Emil Kraepelin, who many doctors considered the father of modern psychiatry, had created this scheme.

80. Lunbeck, *The Psychiatric Persuasion,* 222; Friedman, *Menninger,* 30, 90, and 123; and Grob, *The Mad among Us,* 222. In Karl Menninger's critique of Alfred Kinsey's book on female sexuality, he argued that you could reconcile psychoanalytic psychiatry with Judeo-Christian traditions and values.

81. Millet, "Psychoanalysis in the United States," 577–78. According to Millet, the appointment of Menninger "signaled very important improvements in Army psychiatry." The medical profession began to realize the large percentage of disorders encountered in civilian life were from emotional stress, which promoted the study and treatment of psychoneurosis. Menninger and his counterparts John M. Murray in the air force; Ralph Kaufman, Henry Brosin, and Roy Grinker in the army; Howard Rome in the navy; and Daniel Blain in the marines were analysts who practiced the American version of psychoanalysis during World War II.

82. Friedman, *Menninger,* 214–15.

83. William C. Menninger, "Psychiatry and the Practice of Medicine," *Bulletin of the Menninger Clinic* 17 (1953): 170–72, 178.

84. Quoted from "Self-Diagnosis," *Time* (May 3, 1948), 68. Also see Karl Menninger, "The Contribution of Psychoanalysis to American Psychiatry," *Bulletin of the Menninger Clinic* 18 (1954): 85–91.

85. John R. Stone, business manager, Menninger Clinic, to Laura G. Jackson, director of Public Relations, American College of Surgeons, Chicago, December 28, 1944, Box 75, Mary Elizabeth Switzer Papers.

86. Millet, "Psychoanalysis in the United States," 578–79. In June 1946, General William C. Menninger retired. Lieutenant Colonel Elwood W. Camp, *Adventure in Mental Health: Psychiatric Social Work with the Armed Forces in World War II,* edited by Henry S. Maas (New York: Columbia University Press, 1951), 202.

87. Hall, *A Psychiatrist for a Troubled World,* 563–64.

88. Quoted from Sigmund Freud, *Character and Culture,* edited by Philip Rief (New York: Macmillan Books, 1960), 160.

89. Ibid.

90. Edith Jacobson, "The 'Exceptions': An Elaboration of Freud's Character Study," *Psychoanalytic Study of the Child* 14 (1959): 143.

91. Freud, *Character and Culture,* 161.

92. Jacobson, "The 'Exceptions,'" 136.

93. Freud, *Character and Culture,* 159.

94. Ibid.

95. Jacobson, "The 'Exceptions,'" 136.

96. Joseph Levi, "The Rorschach Pattern in Neurodermatitis," *Psychosomatic Medicine* 14 (1952): 48.

97. Malcolm Brown, T. J. Bresnahan, F. C. R. Chalke, Barbara Peters, E. G.

Poser, and R. V. Tougas, "Personality Factors in Duodenal Ulcer," *Psychosomatic Medicine* 12 (1950): 1, 5.

98. Lee Meyerson, "Experimental Injury: An Approach to the Dynamics of Disability," *Journal of Social Issues* 4 (1948): 75–77.

99. Ibid., 88.

100. See E. D. Wittkower, "Studies of the Personality of Patients Suffering from Urticaria," *Psychosomatic Medicine* 15 (1953): 117, 125.

101. See Joseph Levi, "The Rorschach Test in Rehabilitation," *Journal of Rehabilitation* 19 (1953): 13–15, 29; Nathan Nelson, "Rehabilitation Centers—an Appraisal," *Journal of Rehabilitation* 23 (1957): 4–5, 21.

102. Friedman, *Menninger,* 76–77.

103. Barbara Goldberger and Jacques Goldberger, "Psychosomatic Concepts in Physical Medicine," *Archives of Physical Medicine* 27 (1946): 5–11.

104. Dunbar founded the American Psychosomatic Society and its *Journal of Psychosomatic Medicine* in 1934. The movement's first best-seller was Helen Flanders Dunbar, *Mind and Body: Psychosomatic Medicine* (New York: Random House, 1947). Also see Robert C. Powell, "Helen Flanders Dunbar (1902–1959) and Holistic Approaches to Psychosomatic Problems. I. The Rise and Fall of a Medical Philosophy," *Psychiatric Quarterly* 49 (1977): 134.

105. See Dunbar, *Mind and Body.* Dunbar's project included 1,600 psychosomatic patients and their families who suffered from one of eight illnesses: fracture, coronary occlusion, hypertensive cardiovascular disease, anginal syndrome, rheumatic fever, rheumatoid arthritis, and diabetes.

106. See Chase Patterson Kimball, "Conceptual Developments in Psychosomatic Medicine, 1939–1969," *Annals of Internal Medicine* 73 (1970): 309. For instance, patients with hypertension were observed as having a need to keep peace and having conflicts over seeking satisfaction with themselves or devoting themselves to achievement of external, long-range goals.

107. Frederick Josep Rattner, *Alfred Adler,* translated by H. Zohn (New York: F. Ungar Publishing Co., 1983), 50–51.

108. Rubin Klein, *A History of Psychoanalysis* (New York: Columbia University Press, 1979), 224.

109. See Kaplan and Kaplan, "An Historical Survey of Psychosomatic Medicine," 557–58. Alexander, working in collaboration with T. M. French, studied seven diseases, like bronchial asthma and hyperthyroidism, that other physicians reverently called the "holy seven." Specificity means that specific causes lead to specific diseases.

110. Kaplan and Kaplan, "An Historical Survey of Psychosomatic Medicine," 557–58; Powell, "Helen Flanders Dunbar," 133; Bernard Bandler, "Some Conceptual Tendencies in the Psychosomatic Movement," *Psychosomatic Medicine* 38 (1958): 36, read at the American Psychiatry Association, Chicago, Ill., May 13–17, 1957; and Wittkower, "Historical Perspective of Contemporary Psychosomatic Medicine," 6.

111. Bandler, "Some Conceptual Tendencies in the Psychosomatic Movement," 38.

112. "More than any one man, Alexander stands out as the most prominent contributor of our time to psychosomatic medicine." Wittkower, "Historical Perspective of Contemporary Psychosomatic Medicine," 6.

113. Friedman, *Menninger,* 29–30. Also see J. E. Carney, "The Psychoanalytic

Education of the Dean of American Psychiatry: Karl Menninger and Smith Ely Jel-liffee," *Psychohistory Review* 19 (1990): 5.

114. Friedman, *Menninger,* 122. Karl Menninger defended the legitimacy of Freud's focus on sexuality, but he argued that sexuality usually represented a mix-ture of death and life instincts—hate and love.

115. Memorandum by the OVR in collaboration with Social Security Admin-istration, Office of Education, Public Health Service, "Report of Study of Pro-grams for Homebound Physically Handicapped Individuals," Box 299, Record Group 235. Records of the Federal Security Administration, National Archives, College Park, Md.

116. Ibid.

117. U.S. Congress Hearings before the Subcommittee of the Committee on Labor and Public Welfare in the U.S. Senate, 81st Congress, 2d sess., May 22, 1950, 519.

118. Alfred Adler, *A Study of Organ Inferiority and Its Psychical Compensa-tion* (New York: Nervous and Mental Disease Monographs, 1917).

119. Adler was an early follower of Freud. He eventually left the group in order to develop his own approach toward emotional problems. See Adler, *A Study of Organ Inferiority;* Adler, *Individual Psychology* (New York: Humanities Press, 1951); Adler, *The Practice and Theory of Individual Psychology* (London: Kegan Paul, 1925); Adler, *Social Interest* (London: Farber and Farber, 1940); F. G. Crookshank, *Organ Inferiorities,* Individual Psychology Medical Pamphlet, no. 16 (London: C. W. Daniel Co., 1936); F. McKinney, "Concomitants of Adjust-ment and Maladjustment in College Students," *Journal of Abnormal Social Psy-chology* 31 (1938).

120. Just four years after Adler broke with Freud in 1911, he wrote *A Study of Organ Inferiority and its Psychical Compensation,* which was a pathbreaking book that laid the foundation for psychosomatic medicine in the United States. Rattner, *Alfred Adler,* 4–5.

121. Kaplan and Kaplan, "An Historical Survey of Psychosomatic Medicine," 555–56. Sandor Ferenczi and Smith Ely Jellife followed a similar approach as Groddeck in explaining psychosomatic symptoms as conversion reactions. Mel-anie Klein and Felix Deutsch were also early followers.

122. Rattner, *Alfred Adler,* 36–42.

123. Ibid., 5–6, 26–29, 41. Quoted from 43.

124. See Rudolf Dreikurs, "The Socio-Psychological Dynamics of Physical Dis-ability: A Review of the Alderian Concept," *Journal of Social Issues* 4 (1948): 39–54. Also see Adler, *A Study of Organ Inferiority;* Adler, *Individual Psychology;* and Adler, *The Practice and Theory of Individual Psychology.*

125. Dreikurs, "The Socio-Psychological Dynamics of Physical Disability," 40; and Rattner, *Alfred Adler,* 19–21. Adler never mentioned it, but he was also in-spired by Wilhelm Dilthey's Gestalt psychology and Wilhelm Stern's differential psychology. Adler also embraced J. C. Smuts's perception about holism or the phi-losophy of totality.

126. Also see Rattner, *Alfred Adler,* 42–44.

127. Ibid., 7, 43.

128. Ibid., 23–25, 36–41.

129. Deikurs, "The Socio-Psychological Dynamics of Physical Disability," 39.

130. Kessler, *Principles and Practices,* 3. According to Kessler, the word "reha-bilitation" means restoration.

131. Rattner, *Alfred Adler,* 50–51; Dreikurs, "The Socio-Psychological Dynamics of Physical Disability," 39.

132. Gerald N. Grob, "Psychiatry and Social Activism: The Politics of a Specialty in Postwar America," *Bulletin of Medical History* 60 (1986): 492.

133. Grob, "Psychiatry and Social Activism," 487–501. Organized in 1946, the Group for the Advancement of Psychiatrists (GAP) was composed of some of the most renowned psychiatrists in the United States. The prominent members who assembled before the American Psychoanalytical Association (APA) conference in 1946 included William C. Menninger, Karl Menninger, Daniel Blain, M. Ralph Kaufmann, Marion Kenworthy, Robert Felix, Douglas Bond, Henry Brosin, Norman Brill, Laurence Smith, Roy Grinker, John Romano, Thomas A. C. Rennie, and Wilfred Bloomberg. Three years after its founding, 177 individuals joined GAP. Between mid-1947 and 1948, fifty-three of the psychiatrists held seventy-two committee positions in the APA. Also see Hall, *A Psychiatrist for a Troubled World,* 563–66. Crediting William Menninger with its founding, one psychiatrist described the GAP as a "unique" medical organization.

134. Grob, "Psychiatry and Social Activism," 565.

135. Characterized as neither liberal nor conservative, psychiatry pledged its support to help democratize the world. This is not to say that psychiatrists had a hazy conception. Ginsburg, and others, were very clear about what they meant by social issues, to the point that they made a distinction between, as the cultural anthropologist Herskovits noted, "[A] culture is the way of life of the people, while society is the organized aggregates of individuals who followed a given way of life." In simpler terms, "[T]he society is composed of people; the way they behave is their culture." Quoted from Ginsburg, *A Psychiatrist's Views on Social Issues,* 107.

136. According to Stiker, the notion that a sick individual causes a society illness can be traced to classical antiquity. To document this, Stiker cites the work of Marie Delcourt, a historian of classical Greek, who shows that deformed infants were killed by exposure "because they are *harmful, maleficent.* They implicate the group." Delcourt suggests, "If they were exposed, it is because they caused fear: they were the sign of the gods' anger and they were also the reason for it. This is symptomized by a concomitance where the untrained mind distinguishes poorly between cause and effect." Given the gravity of the concern about becoming a sick society, the decision of whether children are exposed or not, Stiker explains, was "not usually [made by] the parents . . . but the social body, the state" to ensure that what was best for the collective would be done." See Stiker, *A History of Disability,* 40.

137. Seminar Report, published by Menninger, April 11, 1947, Box 75, Switzer Papers.

138. Ibid. The GAP stated that "the individual becomes a healthy, productive adult not only by having his physical sustenance assured from infancy on, but also by establishing constructive relationships with the various groups of people with whom he comes in contact through the normal course of development."

139. Halliday's work was well received in the United States. His book, *Psychosomatic Medicine: A Study of the Sick Society* (New York: W. W. Norton, 1948), was reviewed in *Time.* See "At the Mental Seams," *Time* (March 22, 1948), 63–64.

140. "A Sick Society," May 5, 1947, Box 75, Switzer Papers.

141. Halliday had the support of the Menninger Clinic. He addressed the Men-

ninger Clinic on the topic of "A Sick Society" in 1947. Switzer to John F. Stone, May 5, 1947, Box 75, Switzer Papers.

142. Rusk, Switzer, and Taylor, "International Programs in Rehabilitation," 529.

143. Halliday also wrote directly about rehabilitation. See James L. Halliday, "Psychologic Implications of Physical Therapy," *Archives of Physical Therapy* 22 (1941): 261–65.

144. Karl Menninger, "Psychiatric Aspects of Physical Disability," in *Psychological Aspects of Physical Disability* (Washington, D.C.: Office of Vocational Rehabilitation, 1952).

145. "The Social Responsibility of Psychiatry, a Statement of Orientation," formulated by the Committee on Social Issues of the Group for the Advancement of Psychiatry, July 1950, found in the Switzer Papers, Box 74.

146. Ibid.

147. Ibid. "The Social Responsibility. . . ." The GAP recognized that "the beginnings of such a science are already evident . . . but that the sociology, social psychology, and cultural anthropology could provide tangible help."

148. Clara Thompson with collaboration from Patrick Mullahy, *Psychoanalysis: Evolution and Development* (New York: Hermitage House, 1950), 131.

149. Ibid., 152.

150. Ginsburg, *A Psychiatrist's Views on Social Issues,* 108–9. Also see the introduction of Ginsburg's book by William Menninger, xv. Menninger wrote, "It is questionable whether any psychiatrist played a larger role in fundamental research and social psychology than Sol Ginsburg during the decades of the 1940s and 1950s."

151. Smith, *Social Science in the Crucible,* 233. Just as anthropology had applied anthropology, so did psychiatry. In the 1930s, Harold Laswell came up with the term "political psychiatrist," which Arnold Rogrow later termed "applied psychoanalysis." Members of the GAP prescribed that psychiatrists should start practicing "social psychopathology" or applied psychoanalysis.

152. Davis, *Enforcing Normalcy,* 24. According to Davis, the norm was used in the modern sense since around 1855 and normality and normalcy in 1849 and 1857, respectively.

153. Ibid.

154. Lunbeck, *The Psychiatric Persuasion,* 5.

155. See Ingstad and Whyte's introductory essay in *Disability and Culture,* 7.

156. "Introduction," 1951, Box 16, Switzer Papers; H. Bond, "Rehabilitation —American Style," *Journal of Rehabilitation* 16 (1950): 17–19; and Arthur Bierman, "Toward a Philosophy of Employment of the Handicapped," *Vocational Guidance Quarterly* (1957–58): 72–73.

157. Quoted from Bierman, "Toward a Philosophy of Employment of the Handicapped," 73.

158. Ingstad and Whyte, introductory essay in *Disability and Culture,* 7.

159. Stiker, *A History of Disability,* 134.

Chapter Two

1. Resources for Rehabilitating and Employing More Handicapped Workers, Box 125, Director's Letters, Record Group 468, General Records of the Department of Health and Human Services, National Archives, College Park, Md.

2. Switzer to Jean Menninger, July 18, 1944, Box 75, Switzer Papers, Schlesinger Library, Cambridge, Mass.

3. Switzer to William Menninger, April 5, 1943, Box 75, Switzer Papers; Switzer to Karl Menninger, March 14, 1945, Box 73, Switzer Papers.

4. Mary E. MacDonald, *Federal Grants for Vocational Rehabilitation* (New York: Arno Press, 1980), 51–54, 57; and "The State-Federal Program for Vocational Rehabilitation—Historical Background," Box 1, Division of Research and Statistics, General Correspondence, Record Group 47, Records of Social Security Administration, National Archives, College Park, Md. This legislation was criticized for being too paternalistic and humanitarian. The Vocational Rehabilitation Act (VRA), which passed Congress on July 11, 1919, with bipartisan support, was modeled on the Smith-Sears Act in 1918, which helped veterans. The program carried appropriations for four years, $750,000 the first year, $1 million thereafter, and was up for renewal in 1924.

5. Edward D. Berkowitz, *Disabled Policy: America's Programs for the Handicapped* (New York: Cambridge University Press, 1987), 153.

6. Michael J. Shortley, director of the Office of Vocational Rehabilitation (OVR), wrote a memorandum titled "The Administration of War and Post-war Rehabilitation of Handicapped Persons," February 10, 1944, Box 299, Record Group 235, Records of the Federal Security Administration, National Archives, College Park, Md. Also see Hans von Hentig, "Physical Disability, Mental Conflict and Social Crisis," *Journal of Social Issues* 4 (1948): 21.

7. Edward D. Berkowitz, *Rehabilitation: The Federal Government's Response to Disability, 1935–1954* (New York: Arno Press, 1980), 85–86.

8. Ibid., 87. Between 1925 and 1941, over 91 percent of the rehabilitated were white, and few were women.

9. MacDonald, *Federal Grants for Vocational Rehabilitation,* 44. See Berkowitz, *Rehabilitation,* 83.

10. Quoted from Berkowitz, *Rehabilitation,* 84–85.

11. Ibid., 92; Edward D. Berkowitz and Kim McQuaid, *Creating the Welfare State: The Political Economy of Twentieth Century Reform* (New York: Praeger Press, 1988), 138; Chrisann Shiro-Geist and William A. Calzaretta, *Placement Handbook for Counseling Disabled Persons* (Springfield, Ill.: Charles C. Thomas, 1982), 31. The people responsible for including it were W. F. Faulkes, the Wisconsin bureau chief, and Tracy Copp, a regional field agent for the vocational rehabilitation program.

12. In 1938, the vocational rehabilitation program, in the Office of Education, became a charter member of the Federal Security Agency (FSA). See Berkowitz, *Rehabilitation,* 92–93.

13. Quoted from Berkowitz, *Rehabilitation,* 238, 242–43.

14. Berkowitz and McQuaid, *Creating the Welfare State,* 149.

15. The Barden-LaFollete Act passed the 78th Congress on July 6, 1943, becoming Public Law 113. See House Report, no. 426, 78th Cong., 1st sess., 1943, 4. Also see Mary Lenz Walker, *Beyond Bureaucracy: Mary Elizabeth Switzer and Rehabilitation* (Lanham, Md.: University Press of America, 1985), 127. The head of the OVR reported directly to the Federal Security administrator, just as the heads of the Public Health Service and the Social Security Board did.

16. Berkowitz, *Rehabilitation,* 101.

17. Oscar R. Ewing, Federal Security administrator, opposed S. 1066 and S.

3465 because they proposed that the administration of Vocational Rehabilitation be removed from the FSA. Ewing supported S. 2273, which his agency drafted.

18. "S. 1066, S. 2273, S. 3465, Bills Relating to the Vocational Rehabilitation of the Physically Handicapped," U.S. Congress, Hearings before the Subcommittee of the Committee on Labor and Public Welfare in the U.S. Senate, 81st Cong., 2d sess., 1950, 386–87.

19. Berkowitz, *Rehabilitation*, 95, 135. For the first time, amendments extended services to the mentally ill and the mentally retarded. The number of people who received rehabilitation increased 60 percent from the previous year.

20. See Berkowitz, *Rehabilitation*, 141–42; and Timothy M. Cook, "Nondiscrimination in Employment under the Rehabilitation Act of 1973," *American University Law Review* 27 (1977): 38. Although the rehabilitation movement reconfigured the vocational rehabilitation program so that it involved reconditioning, neither Rusk, Kessler, nor officials from the FSA suggested that rehabilitation cover people who had little chance of employment. Also see Jonathon Drimmer, "Cripples, Overcomers, and Civil Rights: Tracing the Evolution of Federal Legislation and Social Policy for People with Disabilities," *UCLA Law Review* 40 (1993): 1368–74. Drimmer sees this as saying the problem is not prejudice but the disability itself. The dominant social assumption about disability was that the individual is inferior, has low self-esteem, and "saps the strength of the nation."

21. "S. 1066, S. 2273, S. 3465, Bills Relating to the Vocational Rehabilitation of the Physically Handicapped," U.S. Congress, Hearings, 501; and Berkowitz, *Rehabilitation*, 170.

22. Walker, *Beyond Bureaucracy*, 127, 140. Shortley succeeded John Kratz, who had been the director while it was in the Office of Education.

23. Arthur Hess was the social security official in charge of the disability program. Berkowitz, *Disabled Policy*, 81.

24. "Report of a Study of Programs for Homebound Physically Handicapped Individuals," OVR in collaboration with the SSA and the Office of Education, Box 1, Record Group 47, Policy Records of the Department of Health, Education and Welfare (HEW), SSA, no date. Arthur E. Hess, assistant director, Division of Disability Operations, Bureau of Old Age and Survivors Insurance, Report titled: "Some Practical Aspects of the Recently Enacted Disability Insurance Provisions of the Social Security Act." Declaring it an important year in a report titled, "A Look Ahead," Hess wrote that the bureau was not only interested in "a program of income maintenance . . . we are interested in the *WHOLE MAN*—and in the constructive preparation for that man's return to industry through whatever means."

25. Director Michael Shortley to State Boards of Vocational Education; Divisions of Vocational Rehabilitation; Commissions and other Agencies for the Blind, December 14, 1949, Box 124, Director's Letters, Record Group 468. The letter was about the address by Dr. Wilma Donahue, director of Psychological Services of the Institute for Human Adjustment, University of Michigan (see n.27 below).

26. Ibid.

27. Address of Dr. Wilma Donahue, "Needs and Developments in Psychological Research for the Blind," presented at the States' Rehabilitation Council Meeting, San Antonio, Texas, November 7, 1949, found in Box 124, Director's Letters, Record Group 468.

28. It was Freud, according to Donahue, who developed this notion of depth psychology and discovered "how psychosomatic medicine could further clarify

the close relationship between the physical and mental aspects of personality." Also see Helton McAndrew, "Rigidity in the Deaf and Blind," *Journal of Social Issues* 4 (1948): 72–77.

29. Donahue, "Needs and Developments in Psychological Research for the Blind."

30. The early years of vocational rehabilitation coincided with the rise of psychiatric social work and the use of tests. Psychological tests were so prevalent that large corporations used them to understand industrial problems like absenteeism and labor turnover. The number of people using it grew from 14 percent in 1939 to 50 percent in 1947 and 75 percent in 1952, according to Berkowitz and McQuaid, *Creating the Welfare State,* 136.

31. Mrs. Jewell W. Swofford, commissioner, Special Services, to Michael J. Shortley, director of the OVR, November 13, 1947, Box 2, General Subject File, Record Group 235, Records of FSA, National Archives, College Park, Md.

32. Berkowitz, *Rehabilitation,* 140.

33. H. Dabelstein, acting director, OVR, to Representative Samuel K. McConnell, July 26, 1953, Box 28, General Subject File, Rehabilitation Services Administration, Record Group 363, Records of Social and Rehabilitation Service, Department of Health, Education and Welfare, National Archives, College Park, Md.

34. Berkowitz, *Rehabilitation,* 126.

35. Walker, *Beyond Bureaucracy,* 114.

36. Jewell W. Swofford, commissioner, Special Services, to Oscar Ewing, administrator, November 24, 1947, Box 2, General Subject File, Record Group 235.

37. Memorandum to the president from Dr. Rusk, April 23, 1947, Box 2, General Subject File, Record Group 235.

38. Berkowitz, *Rehabilitation,* 132.

39. "S. 1066, S. 2273, S. 3465, Bills Relating to the Vocational Rehabilitation of the Physically Handicapped," U.S. Congress, Hearings, 501, 506, 508.

40. Ibid., 503, 504. For example, Rusk illustrated that "we say to industry: 'here is a package; this is our finished product; here is what we can do physically, here are his limitations; here is his personality.'"

41. Ibid., 516. The OVR and the FSA also reflected the influence of Rusk.

42. Rehabilitation Centers, Report of the Committee on Rehabilitation Centers, States' Vocational Rehabilitation Council, October 23, 1950, Box 126, Record Group 468.

43. Michael J. Shortley to State Boards of Vocational Education; Divisions of Vocational Rehabilitation and Other Agencies for the Blind, September 13, 1950, Box 124, Record Group 468. Senator Paul H. Douglas, a Democrat from Kansas, introduced it on August 15. By August 29, Labor and Public Welfare issued "The Nation's Health: A Report to the President by the Federal Security Administrator," which was supported unanimously.

44. Summary of S.4051, Box 124, Record Group 468. S. 4051 passed with no recorded vote. See *Congressional Record,* 81st Cong., 2d sess., 1950, 96, pt. 11: 14682 and 14691. The six titles of the legislation were (1) technical and fiscal amendments to the VRA, (2) vending stands for the blind, (3) social programs for the blind and other severely disabled persons, (4) establishment of workshops and rehabilitation centers, (5) research and adjustment centers for the blind and other severely disabled, (6) revolving loan funds.

45. Berkowitz, *Rehabilitation,* 219.

46. Ibid., 245; Press Release, November 10, 1950, Box 2, Switzer Papers; Mary E. Switzer and Howard A. Rusk, *Doing Something for the Disabled,* Public Affairs Pamphlet, no. 197 (Washington, D.C.: Government Printing Office, 1952).

47. Switzer met influential doctors who served in this service and were the "who's who" in medicine, such as Frank Lahey; Harold Diehl, who headed the Mayo Clinic and was later vice president of the American Cancer Society; Max Lapham, later dean of Tulane College of Medicine; James Paullin, University of Georgia Medical School dean; Allen Gregg of the Rockefeller Foundation; Theodore Klumpp and George Merck from the pharmaceutical industry. Switzer was also impressed with Franz Alexander and his "crowd" of psychoanalysts from the University of Chicago. Switzer to Charles F. Ernst, Menninger Clinic, August 27, 1947, Box 75; and Press Release, November 10, 1950, Box 2, Switzer Papers; memorandum titled "Highlights on Experience in Health and Medical Work of Miss Mary E. Switzer," Box 1, Switzer Papers.

48. Berkowitz, *Rehabilitation,* 241.

49. Walker, *Beyond Bureaucracy,* 126.

50. Ibid., 248–49.

51. Berkowitz, *Rehabilitation,* 24. By 1947, Switzer wrote Rusk regularly about rehabilitation matters, such as asking him to suggest names to staff the Bell Grave's rehabilitation center.

52. Walker, *Beyond Bureaucracy,* 125–26, 247.

53. Switzer speech to the National Rehabilitation Association (NRA), 1951, Box 16, Switzer Papers.

54. William Menninger not only thought that psychoanalysis should play an important role in vocational rehabilitation, but he also thought occupational therapy should. Memorandum titled "Note on Occupational Therapy Research, Box 75, Switzer Papers.

55. Quoted from Walker, *Beyond Bureaucracy,* 137. Switzer described William Menninger's psychiatric program as "a thrilling oasis in a pretty dry field." Switzer to L. Laszlow Ecker-Racz, economic advisor to the Minister, United States Mission, September 24, 1946, Box 75, Switzer Papers.

56. Walker, *Beyond Bureaucracy,* 112–13. Some of the other witnesses were Captain Frank Braceland, chief of the Neuropsychiatry Division of the U.S. Navy, and Edward Strecker, vice president of the American Psychiatric Society. Switzer introduced Karl Menninger to Paul McNutt.

57. Walker, *Beyond Bureaucracy,* 112–14. David Rapaport, a clinical psychologist at the Menninger Clinic, helped draft the technical sections of the act. Rapaport not only worked at the Menninger Clinic, but he had made an important contribution to psychodynamic therapy in his own right with psychological tests, which essentially quantified Freudian thought and made the subjective field of psychoanalysis more scientific. David Rapaport to Switzer, July 24, 1945, Box 73, Switzer Papers. When the bill was drafted, Switzer had members of the FSA tutored, namely, Dr. Felix, chief of the Mental Hygiene Division of the FSA and Surgeon General Thomas Parran. Percy Priest introduced the legislation. Switzer then guided the legislation through congressional hearings. Here, Switzer asked key members of the medical community to be witnesses, for example, William Menninger, chief of the Neuropsychiatric Division of the U.S. Army, and Daniel Blain, of the Neuropsychiatric Division of the Veterans Administration. The National In-

stitute of Mental Health (NIMH) received $9 million in 1950 and $400 million by 1970. The psychiatry community was so indebted to Switzer that she was made an honorary member of the American Psychiatry Association. She was only the second layperson to receive this honor. James G. Townswell, acting chief, Division of Publications and Reports, OVR, to Dean Russell, director of Vocational Rehabilitation Services, Arkansas, August 29, 1958, Box 45, Switzer Papers.

58. Karl Menninger to Switzer, August 14, 1945, Box 73, Switzer Papers. Karl Menninger wrote to Switzer about "a definite and immediate service that you can do for psychiatry and the Foundation . . . to support the National Neuropsychiatric Institute Bill." Switzer also helped strategize how the Menninger Clinic could increase its influence. Switzer to Stone, June 14, 1946, Box 75, Switzer Papers. Stone asked Switzer to "have your secretary send us a list of important bill or bills that we should take an interest in, that might provide funds for our work." Stone to Switzer, June 3, 1947, Box 75, Switzer Papers.

59. Switzer also supported psychological testing or projective tests that were used by David Rapaport, a psychologist at the Menninger Clinic. Switzer to William Menninger, December 23, 1946, Box 75, Switzer Papers.

60. Switzer to William Menninger, April 5, 1943, Box 75, Switzer Papers; Switzer to Karl Menninger, March 14, 1945, Box 73, Switzer Papers; speech by Switzer titled "Attacking Dependency through Rehabilitation," for the Institute Day at the Institute for the Crippled and Disabled, New York, May 16, 1953, Box 29, Switzer Papers.

61. Switzer to William Menninger, November 19, 1948, Box 45, Switzer Papers.

62. Karl Menninger to Switzer, March 29, 1943, Box 75, Switzer Papers.

63. Ibid. Switzer also agreed with the goals of the Group for the Advancement of Psychiatry. Twenty years later, Switzer said, "[I]n that exciting period . . . there has always been for me a sense of responsibility for helping psychiatry play its full role in human affairs."

64. Switzer to William Menninger, September 27, 1943, Box 75, Switzer Papers. Switzer also lobbied for a "combined program between Vocational Rehabilitation and the [National Institute of Mental Health]." Switzer to R. H. Felix, director, NIMH, May 17, 1951, Box 45, Switzer Papers.

65. Switzer to R. H. Felix, director of the NIMH, June 10, 1952, Box 45, Switzer Papers; Switzer to R. H. Felix, director, NIMH, May 17, 1951, Box 45, Switzer Papers; and Switzer to John L. Thurston, assistant administrator, FSA, July 28, 1952, Box 45, Switzer Papers.

66. Switzer's address was titled "New Horizons in Rehab," and presented at the meeting of the State Advisory Committee to Florida Center of Clinical Services, March 26, 1954.

67. Quoted from Berkowitz, *Rehabilitation*, 121.

68. Switzer's speech delivered to the NRA, 1951, Box 16, Switzer Papers.

69. Switzer, address to American Congress of Physical Medicine and Rehabilitation, titled "The Role of the Federal Government in Vocational Rehabilitation," August 30, 1955, Box 18, Switzer Papers.

70. The idea of advisory councils initially had not been supported by President Truman. Switzer to Representative James E. Murray (D-Montana), September 21, 1945, Box 73, Switzer Papers; Harry N. Rosenfield, assistant to administrator of OVR to Watsona B. Miller, also assistant to administrator of OVR, August 27,

1945, Box 73, Switzer Papers. The Public Health Service also did not endorse it initially. Alanson W. Willcox, assistant general counsel, FSA to Switzer, June 8, 1945, Box 73, Switzer Papers.

71. See Walker, *Beyond Bureaucracy,* 116.

72. Ibid., 115-16. Switzer's other success was the creation of the National Science Foundation (NSF) in 1950. Switzer's penchant for psychoanalysis again was reflected by the fact that Rapaport became the first representative for social sciences at the NSF. Also see Berkowitz, *Rehabilitation,* 129. The act relied on "a mixture of federal funds, local initiative, and professional control to build hospitals."

73. Walker, *Beyond Bureaucracy,* 117.

74. According to Mary Lasker, it had not been apparent to many doctors that the government could take this role of funding medical research. The idea came from a few medical leaders such as the Menningers. Mary Lasker to Switzer, March 6, 1946, Box 73, Switzer Papers.

75. Memorandum titled "Biographical Sketch of Warren P. Draper, Box 59, Switzer Papers; and speech by Draper to President's Committee on National Employ the Physically Handicapped Week, October 12, 1951, Box 59, Switzer Papers. Draper's approach differed from Rusk and Switzer in that he did not rely on psychoanalysis in rehabilitation despite Karl Menninger's urging. Draper to Karl Menninger, November 17, 1952, Box 59, Switzer Papers; and Draper to Rusk, December 4, 1952, Box 64, Switzer Papers.

76. Berkowitz, *Rehabilitation,* 239.

77. Switzer, address to American Congress of Physical Medicine and Rehabilitation, titled "The Role of the Federal Government in Vocational Rehabilitation," August 30, 1955, Box 18, Switzer Papers.

78. Berkowitz, *Rehabilitation,* 165. Rusk opens his own rehabilitation center with funds, in part, from Baruch, on March 1, 1948, on 38th Street in New York City.

79. Walker, *Beyond Bureaucracy,* 119.

80. See Colin Barnes, *Disabled People in Britain and Discrimination: A Case for Anti-Discrimination Legislation* (London: Hurst & Co., 1991), 85-88, for a good description of the quota system in Britain. Also see Edward D. Berkowitz, "Professionals as Providers: Some Thoughts on Disability and Ideology," *Rehabilitation Psychology* 29 (1984): 212. Berkowitz writes that Paul Strachan, a disability activist, lobbied for quotas.

81. Werner Sombart, *Why Is There No Socialism in the United States?* (New York: M. E. Sharpe, 1976), for the classic interpretation of American exceptionalism. For the modern debate see Karen Orren, *Belated Feudalism: Labor, the Law, and Liberal Development in the United States* (New York: Cambridge University Press, 1991); Byron Shafer, editor, *Is America Different? A New Look at American Exceptionalism* (New York: Oxford University Press, 1991); and Stephen Skowronek, *Building a New American State: The Expansion of National Administrative Capacities, 1877–1920* (New York: Cambridge University Press, 1982).

82. See Victoria C. Hattam, *Labor Visions and State Power: The Origins of Business Unionism in the United States* (Princeton: Princeton University Press, 1993); and Ruth O'Brien, *Workers' Paradox: The Republican Origins of the New Deal Labor Policy, 1886–1935* (Chapel Hill: University of North Carolina Press, 1998).

83. Memorandum by Leonard Cohen, October 4, 1940, Box 198, Commissioner's Correspondence, Record Group 47. S. 4238 required that an applicant successfully complete a course of vocational training directed by an agency, which was financed or directed by the U.S. government and had been certified by such agency as competent in the work for which the applicant applies. It provides for a fine of $1,000 "contractual relations with the U.S. and engaged in the sale to the U.S. of supplies."

84. Leonard Cohen to Elbert D. Thomas, chair, Committee on Education and Labor, regarding S. 4328, October 1, 1940, Box 198, Commissioner's Correspondence, Record Group 47.

85. Ibid.

86. Wayne Coy, acting administrator, to Senator Elbert D. Thomas, chairman of the Senate Committee on Education and Labor, November 25, 1940, Records of the SSA, Box 198, Commissioner's Correspondence, Record Group 47. Coy wrote Thomas that "in the first place, the approach of the bill [S. 4328] is thought to be unwise in its interference directly with the employer's choice of his employees." He emphasized the voluntary approach that "has made reasonable progress in selling employers on the productive capacity of the rehabilitated." A. J. Altmeyer, chair of the Social Security Board, to Leonard J. Calhoun, assistant general counsel, February 11, 1941, Box 198, Commissioners Correspondence, Record Group 47.

87. The memorandum said, "Dr. Storms, for instance, felt that there was real value in compulsory features which although they may not be used would be available and which would, to some extent, motivate the individual to undertake the rehabilitation." George F. Rohlich to Robert M. Ball, April 25, 1952, Box 2, Division of Research and Statistics, General Correspondence, Record Group 47. The memorandum was about the report by the Public Health Service and the OVR relating to the Lehman and Dingell bills of 1952 (S. 2705 and H.R. 6750) in the handling of individual cases; failure to bring some pressure to bear upon those among the disabled who are adjudged capable of being rehabilitated would, very probably, lay us open to even more severe criticism of undermining the basis for successful rehabilitation. Switzer objected to this as well.

88. See Berkowitz, *Rehabilitation*, 246.

89. George F. Rohlich to Robert M. Ball, April 25, Box 2, Division of Research and Statistics, General Correspondence, Record Group 47.

90. Walker, *Beyond Bureaucracy*, 128.

91. Berkowitz, *Disabled Policy*, 211.

92. Walker, *Beyond Bureaucracy*, 111–12, 116–17.

93. Ibid., 136.

94. Switzer's speech delivered at the NRA 1951, Box 16, Switzer Papers.

95. South Korea had been invaded six months before Switzer became director in June 1950. See Robert J. Donovan, *Tumultuous Years: The Presidency of Harry S. Truman, 1949–1953* (New York: W. W. Norton, 1982), 204–13.

96. Executive Office of the president, Office of Defense Mobilization, for release to papers on January 25, 1952, Box 13, Switzer Papers. These letters indicated that 250,000 people were in need of rehabilitation, with a backlog of 2 million. I. H. Borgen to Perrin Lowrey, October 21, 1949, Box 4, Record Group 47.

97. Berkowitz, *Rehabilitation*, 254.

98. Walker, *Beyond Bureaucracy,* 137, 140, and 227.

99. Berkowitz and McQuaid, *Creating the Welfare State,* 139–40. By 1951, sixty-eight boards had been created. Two years later, the total was 554.

100. Walker, *Beyond Bureaucracy,* 139.

101. Quoted from Berkowitz and McQuaid, *Creating the Welfare State,* 139. Stephen E. Ambrose, *Eisenhower: The President* (New York: Simon and Schuster, 1984), 115. Ambrose writes that Eisenhower described himself as "liberal on issues, conservative on economic ones." According to Berkowitz and McQuaid, the term "security" in social security took on a new meaning during the Cold War. In the 1930s, Social Security meant security for shelter and food, whereas in the 1940s it was connected with the military.

102. Berkowitz and McQuaid, *Creating the Welfare State,* 140–41.

103. Berkowitz, *Rehabilitation,* 254.

104. See Walker, *Beyond Bureaucracy,* 132–35, 137, and 255.

105. Walker, *Beyond Bureaucracy,* 111, 142–43. Switzer had become a civil servant during Hoover's administration, yet Walker labeled her a "baby Brain Truster." Mrs. Hobby had been instructed to appoint a woman from California who had been active in Nixon's campaign.

106. A day-by-day account, including analysis of what was said during the public hearings, is contained in Box 28, General Subject File, Record Group 363. Russell J. N. Dean to D. H. Dabelstein, memorandum titled "Hearings, House Education and Labor Subcommittee: Tuesday morning, 28 July 1953"; J.H. Gerber to Switzer, memorandum about legislative proposals, 1953, Box 28, General Subject File, Record Group 363; Cecile Hillyer to Gerber, memorandum titled "DMS Proposed Legislation, 1953," April 8, 1953, Box 28, General Subject File, Record Group 363.

107. In July 1945, Dr. Vannevar Bush prepared a report called "Science, the Endless Frontier." See Berkowitz, *Rehabilitation,* 121–23.

108. Some officials in the FSA concurred with Truman about the autonomy issue. Willcox to Switzer, June 8, 1945, Box 73, Switzer Papers.

109. Berkowitz and McQuaid, *Creating the Welfare State,* 135.

110. Eisenhower was distant from Congress and relied on his advisors. See Stephen Hess, *Organizing the Presidency* (Washington, D.C.: Brookings Institution, 1976), 65.

111. Eisenhower was still casting about for a program that would dispel the image that Secretary Hobby was the "Secretary of Not-Too-Much Health, Education and Welfare." See Walker, *Beyond Bureaucracy.* 149.

112. Quoted from Berkowitz and McQuaid, *Creating the Welfare State,* 144. Marion Folsom became the head of HEW in 1956. He was a prominent welfare capitalist who had been an executive at Eastman Kodak.

113. Berkowitz and McQuaid, *Creating the Welfare State,* 142–43. They argue that business did not mind disability as long as the federal government was not directly involved and allowed for local control.

114. Quoted from Berkowitz, *Rehabilitation,* 146, 263. The ranking Republican on the Labor and Public Welfare Committee told Hobby to find a program

115. Walker, *Beyond Bureaucracy,* 141–42; and Berkowitz, *Rehabilitation,* 143. On April 11, 1953, HEW was established under the Reorganization Plan #1 of 1953, the first executive department instituted since the Labor Department in 1913.

116. S. 2759 reported June 22, 1954, in Senate Report, no. 1626. Hearings were held on April 6, 1954. In the House, hearings had been held in 1953. H.R. 9640 reported by the House Education and Labor Committee June 28, 1954. House Report, no. 1941. It passed the House by a 347 to 0 vote. S. 2759 passed by an 82 to 0 vote. After a conference report was written (House Report, no. 2286), it was agreed to by voice vote in both chambers. Gerber to D. H. Dabelstein, assistant director of OVR, April 9, 1953, Box 28, General Subject File, Record Group 363.

117. "S. 1066, S. 2273, S. 3465, Bills Relating to the Vocational Rehabilitation of the Physically Handicapped," U.S. Congress, Hearings, 513. The act is administered by the secretary of HEW and by the Welfare Department through the existing OVR.

118. Mary E. Switzer, "Rehabilitation—A Public Trust," *Journal of Rehabilitation* 18 (1952): 3.

119. Switzer convinced Rockefeller to include this provision. She thought that an advisory council, like the NIMH, "would be highly desirable." Nelson Rockefeller to Representative Samuel K. McConnell, chairman of the Committee on Education and Labor, June 17, 1954, Box 28, General Subject File, Record Group 363. Switzer thought highly of Rockefeller. She thought he had a "delightful personality" whose role "gave great promise" to vocational rehabilitation. Switzer to George Merck, August 14, 1953, Box 61, Switzer Papers.

120. She was present at the Executive Sessions with Rockefeller and Reginald Conley from HEW. See Walker, *Beyond Bureaucracy,* 149–52.

121. Walker, *Beyond Bureaucracy,* 145–47.

122. Switzer to D. H. Dabelstein, assistant director of the OVR, June 25, 1954, Box 46, Switzer Papers.

123. Henry Redkey, consultant, Rehabilitation Centers, to Switzer, July 21, 1953, Box 28, General Subject File, Record Group 363.

124. Berkowitz and McQuaid, *Creating the Welfare State,* 147. They supported the 1954 amendments because they amounted to a public assistance program rather than the direct insurance opposed by the AMA, whose secretary described it as the first step toward national health, or a "total national compulsory sickness program."

125. Switzer to Lois Wheelwright, August 20, 1953, Box 80, Switzer Papers.

126. Memorandum from Switzer to Secretary Hobby, January 21, 1954, Box 4, Switzer Papers.

127. Whitten, president of the NRA, was present at the ceremony. Neither Whitten nor the NRA lobbied for the legislation. Switzer and members of the Eisenhower administration sought its support, and the NRA obliged. Berkowitz, *Rehabilitation,* 27.

128. Switzer's speech before the NRA, 1951, Box 16, Switzer Papers; "New Federal Legislation for the Handicapped," *Journal of Rehabilitation* 21 (1954): 4–6.

129. Berkowitz and McQuaid, *Creating the Welfare State,* 146.

130. Dr. Frank Krusen, Also Dr. Klumpp who chaired the 1951 Task Force on the Handicapped, Henry Viscardi, and Mrs. Spencer Tracy. The state directors were represented by Scurlock from Oklahoma. See Walker, *Beyond Bureaucracy,* 160.

131. Switzer, address to American Congress of Physical Medicine and Rehabil-

itation, titled "The Role of the Federal Government in Vocational Rehabilitation," August 30, 1955, Switzer Papers, Box 18; and Switzer to Arthur A. Kimball in a memorandum about "Organization and Staffing Recommendations for the Office of Vocational Rehabilitation," June 23, 1954, Box 1, Switzer Papers.

132. Walker, *Beyond Bureaucracy,* 157, 160.

133. Ibid., 156, 161. Because of Eisenhower's enthusiasm, the VRA was to increase the number of persons rehabilitated from 60,000 to 200,000 by 1959. This would be as many in one year as had been rehabilitated since the creation of the OVR in 1943.

134. Switzer to OVR regional representatives, June 7, 1954, Box 45, Switzer Papers.

135. The budget breakdown was as follows: $24,500,000 for rehabilitation services, and $1,500,000 for improvement and extension. There was also $1,900,000 for special projects, of which $900,000 was for training of personnel. Walker, *Beyond Bureaucracy,* 159–60.

136. "Mobilization and Health Manpower, Report of the Subcommittee on Paramedical Personnel in Rehabilitation and Care of the Chronically Ill," January 1956, Report to the director of the Office of Events Mobilization by the Health Resources Advisory Committee, Box 13, Switzer Papers; and "S. 1066, S. 2273, S. 3465, Bills Relating to the Vocational Rehabilitation of the Physically Handicapped," U.S. Congress Hearings, 513.

137. Walker, *Beyond Bureaucracy,* 162.

138. The American Board of Physical Medicine and Rehabilitation totals 300, an increase of twenty-five over the past few years. There were 500 vacant positions requiring a qualified physician. By 1970, Switzer hoped to see 250 trainees in physical medicine instead of 125. Switzer's statement before the House Special Education Subcommittee, July 1, 1957, Box 21, Switzer Papers.

139. Walker, *Beyond Bureaucracy,* 167.

140. Arthur Duning, "Rehabilitation: A New Specialization?" *Social Work* (1957), 3–9; Walker, *Beyond Bureaucracy,* 167.

141. Walker, *Beyond Bureaucracy,* 170. Dabelstein was Switzer's closest associate in Washington, D.C.

142. Ibid., 167–70. Dabelstein and Garrett both had written articles or textbooks dealing with the psychological aspects of rehabilitation. Before working at the OVR, Garrett was the chief of psychosocial and vocational services at Rusk's Rehabilitation Center at Bellevue–NYU Hospital. Switzer to all regional representatives, Headquarters News Notes, November 2, 1951, Box 45, Switzer Papers.

143. Quoted from Walker, *Beyond Bureaucracy,* 166.

144. Berkowitz, *Rehabilitation,* 173–74.

145. Rehabilitation Centers, Report of the Committee on Rehabilitation Centers, States' Vocational Rehabilitation Council, October 23, 1950. This is an Advisors Council of the OVR, FSA, Box 126, Record Group 468.

146. Edward M. Litin, "Emotional Aspects of Chronic Physical Disability," *Archives of Physical Medicine and Rehabilitation* (1957), 140. Also see J. Edward Conners, "A New Step in the Rehabilitation of the Chronic Mental Patient," *Journal of Counseling Psychology* 5 (1958): 115–19.

147. Berkowitz, *Rehabilitation,* 157.

148. Oscar M. Sullivan and Kenneth O. Snortum, *Disabled Persons: Their Education and Responsibility* (New York: Century, 1926), 187.

149. Berkowitz, *Rehabilitation,* 158.

150. Mary E. Switzer to State Boards of Vocational Education; Divisions of Vocational Rehabilitation; and Other Agencies for the Blind, March 3, 1953, FSA, Director's Letter, no. 42, Box 125, Record Group 468.

151. Berkowitz, *Disabled Policy,* 171–72. Academics between 1958 and 1968 wrote 1,413 documents relating to rehabilitation counselors and have more than 2,000 represent rehabilitation counseling and service delivery.

152. Walker, *Beyond Bureaucracy,* 156–58. Referrals were sent to rehabilitation centers because of the VRA and the SSA Amendments of 1954.

153. "Partial List of Research and Demonstration Projects, U.S. Office of Vocational Rehabilitation," Box 126, Record Group 468.

154. Berkowitz, *Rehabilitation,* 257.

155. Address by Donahue, "Needs and Developments in Psychological Research for the Blind."

156. Switzer to Dr. Robert H. Felix, director of the National Institutes of Health, June 10, 1952, Box 45, Switzer Papers.

157. Interview with Dr. Fredric K. Schroeder, commissioner of Rehabilitation Services Administration, July 1999.

Chapter Three

1. *Brown v. Board of Education of Topeka,* 347 U.S. 483 (1954).

2. The evidence of the success of the rehabilitation movement was seen in what it had achieved in collaboration with the government. By 1960, a total of 154 rehabilitation facilities had been established or were being constructed. The training program, which made its first grant in 1955, awarded 150 grants to institutions and 1,500 traineeship grants a year. Memorandum titled "Background," Box 1, Mary Elizabeth Switzer Papers, Schlesinger Library, Radcliffe College, Cambridge, Mass.; and Director's Letter, no. 176, Box 126, Record Group 468, General Records of the Department of Health and Human Services, National Archives, College Park, Md.

3. "Presentation to the Social and Rehabilitation Service," National Medical Advisory Committee, November 4, 1968, Box 42, Switzer Papers.

4. Switzer's address titled "The Disabled Poor: How Do We Reach Them," presented at the Jewish Guild for the Blind, September 26, 1968, Box 40, Switzer Papers.

5. Oscar Lewis, *Children of Sanchez* (New York: Random House, 1961).

6. Michael Harrington's book *The Other America* (New York: Macmillan Books, 1962) presented a powerful argument about the many cultures of the poor, all of which were not taken into account by the polis. Also Harry Caudill offered a fictionalized account of Appalachian poverty in his best-selling novel *Night Comes to the Cumberlands* (Boston: Little, Brown, 1962).

7. Irving Bernstein, *Guns or Butter: The Presidency of Lyndon Johnson* (New York: Oxford University Press, 1996), 89.

8. See Sar A. Levitan, *The Great Society's Poor Law* (Baltimore: Johns Hopkins University Press, 1969), 282; and John A. Andrew III, *Lyndon Johnson and the Great Society* (Chicago: Ivan R. Dee, 1998), 28.

9. Tip Sheet for Switzer called "Challenges in Social Rehabilitation," Foundry Methodist Church, October 2, 1968, Box 40, Switzer Papers.

10. Switzer's address titled "Rehabilitation—an Act of Faith," Box 38, Switzer Papers.

11. Address by Mary E. Switzer, at Assumption College, Worchester, Mass., March 13, 1969, Box 41, Switzer Papers.

12. Address by Switzer titled "Our Nation's Commitment to Children," attached to a Tip Sheet, Southwest Regional Conference, Child Welfare League of America, St. Louis, Mo., April 22, 1968, Box 39, Switzer Papers.

13. Address by Switzer titled "Attacking Dependency through Rehabilitation," delivered at the Institute Day at the Institute for the Crippled and Disabled, New York, May 16, 1953, Box 29, Switzer Papers.

14. David Malikin, "Rehabilitating the Socially Disabled," 121–31 in *Contemporary Vocational Rehabilitation,* edited by Herbert Rusalem and David Malikin (New York: New York University Press, 1976), 121–22.

15. Tip Sheet for Switzer, Southwest Regional Conference, Child Welfare League of America, St. Louis, Mo., April 22, 1968, Box 39, Switzer Papers.

16. Samuel Bernstein, "Vocational Rehabilitation and the War on Poverty," *Vocational Guidance Quarterly* (1966), 178.

17. Robert M. Ball, commissioner of the Social Security Agency, memorandum regarding "Discussions on Advance Policy Items," July 15, 1964, Box 6, Record Group 47. Records of Social Security Administration, National Archives, College Park, Md.

18. Mary Lenz Walker, *Beyond Bureaucracy: Mary Elizabeth Switzer and Rehabilitation* (Lanham, Md.: University Press of America, 1985).

19. Address by Switzer titled "Rehabilitation—an Act of Faith," Box 38, Switzer Papers.

20. Ibid.

21. Switzer to secretary of the Department of Health, Education and Welfare (HEW), August 11, 1965, Box 5, Switzer Papers.

22. Walker, *Beyond Bureaucracy,* 212. These amendments also included a provision for rehabilitating the severely disabled who cope with daily living. This provision reflected the emergence of the movement for independent living.

23. Irving Bernstein, *Guns or Butter,* 103–4; Andrew, *Lyndon Johnson and the Great Society,* 59; and Robert Dallek, *Flawed Giant: Lyndon Johnson and His Times, 1961–1973* (New York: Oxford University Press, 1998).

24. Kathleen Arneson, program consultant, legislation and public affairs to Switzer, August 4, 1964, Box 33, General Subject Files, Record Group 363, Records of Social and Rehabilitation Service, HEW, National Archives, College Park, Md.

25. This term resonated with the same type of resentment that Switzer had harbored against the old establishment of state rehabilitation officials who she had called the "Rehab Boys." See Walker, *Beyond Bureaucracy,* 212.

26. Frances Fox Piven and Richard A. Cloward, *Regulating the Poor: The Functions of Public Welfare* (New York: Pantheon Books, 1971), 260–61.

27. See Martha F. Davis, *Brutal Need: Lawyers and the Welfare Rights Movement, 1960–1973* (New Haven: Yale University Press, 1993), 40–55.

28. Piven and Cloward, *Regulating the Poor,* 270–72.

29. Ibid., 277–79.

30. Programs in the war on poverty were spread out over the Labor Department, HEW, and the Office of Economic Opportunity. Vaughn Davis Bornett,

The Presidency of Lyndon Johnson (Lawrence: University of Kansas Press, 1983), 61.

31. Address by Switzer, Brandeis University, Florence Heller Graduate School, April 1, 1969, Box 41, Switzer Papers.

32. Gardner succeeded Anthony Celebrezze. See Bornett, *The Presidency of Lyndon Johnson,* 349.

33. Eric Goldman, *The Tragedy of Lyndon Johnson* (New York: Alfred A. Knopf, 1969).

34. "Between unrest over urban upheaval, the war, and the need to raise taxes," an article in *Time* expounded, "the President's popularity has shriveled almost to a vanishing point." "The Presidency," *Time* (August 18, 1967), 18.

35. "Big Stick, Small Carrot," *Time* (August 25, 1967), 11.

36. "Sparks and Tinder," *Time* (July 21, 1967), 15.

37. Theodore J. Lowi, *The End of Liberalism: The Second Republic of the United States* (New York: W. W. Norton, 1969), 219–20.

38. "Urbanologist," *Time* (July 28, 1967), 11. Johnson first incorporated some of the ideas of Moynihan's 1965 address at Howard University. Initially, when the Moynihan report had been published, he was accused of being a racist.

39. "The Cities," *Time* (August 11, 1967), 11.

40. "Urbanologist," *Time* (July 28, 1967), 11. The urbanologist was "not just a city planner, not just an educator, not just a politician, he is something of each— and something more."

41. Walker, *Beyond Bureaucracy,* 232–33.

42. Ibid., 224, 227.

43. John W. Gardner, secretary to Lyndon B. Johnson, June 1966, Box 4, Switzer Papers.

44. Switzer's address titled "Implementation of the New Opportunities," National Rehabilitation Association, October 4, 1966, Box 36, Switzer Papers.

45. Walker, *Beyond Bureaucracy,* 218.

46. Joseph Hunt, commissioner to Switzer, April 23, 1969, in a memorandum about "Issues and Answers Session," Box 41, Switzer Papers.

47. Memorandum titled "Plan for a National Citizens Conference on Rehabilitation of the Disabled and Disadvantaged," January 6, 1969, Box 42, Switzer Papers.

48. See Lee Rainwater, "Crucible of Identity: The Negro Lower Class Family," 244–70 in *Children and Poverty: Some Sociological and Psychological Perspectives* (Chicago: Rand-McNally, 1969).

49. See Malikin, "Rehabilitating the Socially Disabled," 124–25, for a good review of this literature. Also see Walter S. Neff, *Work and Human Behavior* (New York: Atherton Press, 1968).

50. Quoted from Malikin, "Rehabilitating the Socially Disabled," 124. See Joseph T. Kunce and Corrine S. Cope, *Rehabilitation and the Culturally Disadvantaged* (Columbia: University of Missouri, Rehabilitation Research Institute Series, no. 1, 1969).

51. Malikin, 125–26.

52. Edward D. Berkowitz, *Disabled Policy: America's Programs for the Handicapped* (New York: Cambridge University Press, 1987), 162.

53. Briefing memorandum about "Public Employment Programs and the VRA," May 17, 1967, Box 6, Switzer Papers.

54. Ibid.

56. Worth Bateman to Bill Gorham, May 3, 1967, Box 6, Switzer Papers. Among other things, Switzer argued that "the VRA is experienced in administering such a program."

56. Ibid.

57. Warren E. Whipple, program analysis officer, memorandum, May 3, 1967, Box 6, Switzer Papers; and Joel Cohen, assistant general counsel to Switzer, October 30, 1968, Box 42, Switzer Papers.

58. Address by Switzer titled "Priorities and New Directions," presented at the Social and Rehabilitation Service Conference, February 19, 1968, Box 12, Switzer Papers; and address by Switzer titled "Administration and the Concept of Social Service," presented before the National Conference on Public Administration, March 29, 1968, Box 38, Switzer Papers.

59. Switzer to executive staff, regional representatives, in a memorandum titled, "Secretary's Statement before the House Committee on Education and Labor," September 8, 1966, Box 2, Switzer Papers.

60. Switzer, Bateman, and Gorham finalized plans for the OVR to become the Social Rehabilitation Service (SRS) between February and August 1967, which had been enacted with the passage of the Vocational Rehabilitation Act (VRA) Amendments of 1967 and 1968. Worth Bateman to Bill Gorham, May 3, 1967, Box 6, Switzer Papers.

61. "Organization Woman," *Time* (August 1, 1967), 14.

62. Ibid.

63. Garrett, assistant commissioner, research and training, OVR, to Switzer, November 16, 1966, in a memorandum regarding "HEW Reorganization," Box 2, Switzer Papers.

64. Walker, *Beyond Bureaucracy*, 235. With 1,900 employees Switzer was responsible for 4 percent of the population in 1967.

65. The secretary's enthusiasm for Switzer became publicly evident when he was quoted as calling her a "dynamo." See "Organization Woman," *Time* (August 1, 1967), 14. Not everyone was as generous in their description of Switzer. This article reported that "to Washington's surprise, Gardner went over the heads of the HEW's brightest young men and selected as the first boss of SRS a 67 year old spinster." Leaving nothing to chance, Rusk had also spoken to Gardner on Switzer's behalf. Rusk had told Gardner that he would not attempt such a comprehensive organization unless Switzer headed it.

66. Tip Sheet for Switzer called "Challenges in Social Rehabilitation," Foundry Methodist Church, October 2, 1968.

67. Walker, *Beyond Bureaucracy*, 235.

68. Remarks by John W. Gardner, October 2, 1967, Box 37, Switzer Papers. Chrisann Shiro-Geist and William A. Calzaretta, *Placement Handbook for Counseling Disabled Persons* (Springfield, Ill.: Charles C. Thomas, 1982), 37–38.

69. Briefing memorandum titled "Public Employment Programs and the VRA," May 17, 1967, Box 6, Switzer Papers.

70. Walker, *Beyond Bureaucracy*, 240.

71. Tip Sheet for Switzer about "The Meeting of the Associate Regional Commissioners for Rehabilitation Services," September 19–20, 1968, Box 40, Switzer Papers.

72. Lowi, *The End of Liberalism*, 229.

73. Jill Quadagno, *The Color of Welfare: How Racism Undermined the War on Poverty* (New York: Oxford University Press, 1994), 120.

74. Switzer's address titled "New Directions in Rehabilitation," presented before the International Society for the Rehabilitation of the Disabled and the Workmen's Compensation Board of Ontario, Toronto, Canada, March 5, 1969, Box 41, Switzer Papers.

75. Quoted from Walker, *Beyond Bureaucracy,* 238.

76. Tip Sheet for Switzer titled "Year of Urgency—Our Joint Commitment," April 3, 1968, Box 38, Switzer Papers; and address by Switzer titled "The Image of Welfare—1968," before the American Public Welfare Association, December 8, 1967, Box 38, Switzer Papers.

77. Transcript of address by Switzer, February 28, 1969, Box 41, Switzer Papers.

78. Address by Switzer at Assumption College, Worchester, Mass. March 13, 1969, Box 41, Switzer Papers.

79. "Insurrection City," *Time* (June 14, 1968), 24–25.

80. Piven and Cloward, *Regulating the Poor,* 88–90, 295, 303. Approximately 15 percent of the expenditures of community action agencies were given to neighborhood service center programs, which in 1965 amounted to $24 million and by 1968 to $132 million. Public firms brought thousands of voluntary groups into different organizations to help the poor gain welfare rights. The National Welfare Rights Organization was formed in the spring of 1966. The result was dramatic with applications for Aid to Families with Dependent Children (AFDC) that rose from 90,000 to 998,000 in 1967 to 1,099,000 in 1968.

81. *King v. Smith,* 392 U.S. 309 (1968); *Shapiro v. Thompson,* 394 U.S. 618 (1969); and *Goldberg v. Kelly,* 397 U.S. 254 (1970). These three landmark cases were won in the Supreme Court between 1968 and 1970, which repudiated the rights/privilege distinction and established procedural and substantial due process for the poor.

82. Memorandum titled "The Politics of Administrative Leadership," Box 38, Switzer Papers.

83. *Dandridge v. Williams,* 397 U.S. 471 (1970). The Court upheld a state ruling that limiting AFDC benefits to a maximum of $250 regardless of family size was acceptable.

84. Rand E. Rosenblatt, "Social Duties and the Problem of Rights in the American Welfare State," 90–114 in *The Politics of Law: A Progressive Critique,* edited by David Kairys (New York: Pantheon Books, 1982), 94–95.

85. Richard A. Grant to Switzer, regarding "Analysis of Comments by Social and Rehabilitation Service Regional Commissioners concerning National Citizens Conference on Rehabilitation of the Disabled and Disadvantaged," July 30, 1969, Box 42, Switzer Papers. On June 24, 1969, the National Citizens Conference on Rehabilitation of the Disabled and the Disadvantaged took place.

86. Walker, *Beyond Bureaucracy,* 246.

87. Switzer's address before the Florence Heller Graduate School at Brandeis University, April 1, 1969.

88. Walker, *Beyond Bureaucracy,* 247.

89. Switzer's address before the Florence Heller Graduate School at Brandeis University, April 1, 1969.

90. Herbert Rusalem, "A Personalized Recent History of Vocational Rehabili-

tation in America," 29–45 in *Contemporary Vocational Rehabilitation,* edited by Herbert Rusalem and David Malikin (New York: New York University Press, 1976), 39.

Chapter Four

1. Shortly before Switzer retired, Rusk, or "Mr. Rehabilitation" as she called him, penned his last column on December 7, 1969, *New York Times.*

2. Russell Jacoby, *Social Amnesia: A Critique of Conformist Psychology from Adler to Laing* (Boston: Beacon Press, 1975), 89.

3. Switzer presented her address titled "Rehabilitation" at the United Nations Conference of Ministers Responsible for Social Welfare, September 3–13, 1968, Mary Elizabeth Switzer Papers, Radcliffe College, Cambridge, Mass.

4. Gerben De Jong, "Independent Living: From Social Movement to Analytic Paradigm," in unpublished report by Disability Rights Education and Defense Fund, 1981, G-1.

5. Other factors include development of medical technology; popularizing ideology of deinstitutionalization and normalization, which encouraged growth of noninstitutional support and greater community life; changing age; Vietnam War. See Richard K. Scotch, *From Good Will to Civil Rights: Transforming Federal Disability Policy* (Philadelphia: Temple University Press, 1984), 6–7. Scotch argues that no cohesive disability movement or group is responsible for passage of the Rehabilitation Act.

6. Robert L. Burgdorf Jr., *Disability Discrimination in Employment Law* (Washington, D.C.: Bureau of National Affairs, Inc., 1995), 14–15.

7. Ibid., 26.

8. Two other projects were the National Center for Law and the Handicapped in South Bend, Ind., and the Children's Defense Fund Institute for Public Interest Representation in Georgetown University. See Scotch, *From Good Will to Civil Rights,* 37.

9. Marcia Pearce Burgdorf and Robert L. Burgdorf Jr., "A History of Unequal Treatment: The Qualifications of Handicapped Persons as a 'Suspect Class' under the Equal Protection Clause," *Santa Clara Lawyer* 15 (1975): 891.

10. *Rouse v. Cameron,* 373 F. 2d 451 (D.C. Cir. 1966), about involuntary admittance to mental institution.

11. See Burgdorf and Burgdorf Jr., "A History of Unequal Treatment," 887–89.

12. *Wyatt v. Stickey,* 325 F. Supp. 781 (M.D. Ala. 1971). Wyatt and least restrictive guidelines still did not settle the existence of segregated facilities.

13. Burgdorf and Burgdorf Jr., "A History of Unequal Treatment," 892.

14. Perry A. Zirkel, "Building an Appropriate Education from *Board of Education v. Rowley:* Razing the Door and Raising the Floor," *Maryland Law Review* 42 (1983): 466.

15. *Wolf v. Legislature of the State of Utah,* Civ. No. 182646 (3d Jud. Dist. Ct. Utah Jan. 8, 1969).

16. Burgdorf and Burgdorf Jr., "A History of Unequal Treatment," 876.

17. *Mills v. Board of Education,* 348 F. Supp. 866 (D.D.C. 1972). Peter Mills, who was twelve years old, was excluded because he was a discipline problem. Of 22,000 children with disabilities, up to 18,000 were not being furnished with programs of specialized education.

18. Burgdorf and Burgdorf Jr., "A History of Unequal Treatment," 876–77.

19. Ibid., 877.

20. Scotch, *From Good Will to Civil Rights,* 38–39.

21. James R. Baugh, "The Federal Legislation on Equal Educational Opportunity for the Handicapped," *Idaho Law Review* 15 (1978): 68–69.

22. *San Antonio Independent School District v. Rodriguez* 411 U.S. 1 (1973).

23. Baugh, "The Federal Legislation on Equal Educational Opportunity for the Handicapped," 69.

24. Burgdorf and Burgdorf Jr., "A History of Unequal Treatment," 881–83.

25. Judy Heumann, president of Disabled in Action, Ltd., to President Nixon, November 22, 1972, WHCF, Box 42, WE 8; and David N. Parker to Judy Heumann, December 12, 1972, WHCF, Box 42, WE 8; President Richard M. Nixon Papers, National Archives, College Park, Md. Heumann sent this letter asking Nixon to meet with her organization to the following members of Congress: Senators James L. Buckley (R-N.Y.), Robert Dole (R-Kans.), J. W. Fulbright (D-Ark.), Hubert Humphrey (D-Minn.), Jacob Javits (R-N.Y.), Ted Kennedy (D-Mass.), George McGovern (D-S.D.), Joseph M. Montoya (D-N. Mex.), Edmund Muskie (D-Maine), Charles H. Percy (R-Ill.), Harrison Williams (D-N.J.); and Representatives Bella Abzug (D-N.Y.), Herman Badillo (D-N.Y.), Mario Biaggi (D-N.Y.), Hugh Carey (D-N.Y.), Elizabeth Holtzman (D-N.Y.), Ogden Reid (R-N.Y.), John J. Rooney (D-N.Y.), Charles Vanik (D-Ohio), and Lester L. Wolf (D-N.Y.).

26. Memorandum entitled "The Rehabilitation Act of 1973," WHCF, Box 43, WE 8, Nixon Papers.

27. Edward D. Berkowitz, *Disabled Policy: America's Programs for the Handicapped* (New York: Cambridge, 1985), 175, 178.

28. Herbert Rusalem, "A Personalized Recent History of Vocational Rehabilitation in America," 29–45 in *Contemporary Vocational Rehabilitation,* edited by Herbert Rusalem and David Malikin (New York: New York University Press, 1976), 38.

29. David A. Rochefort, "Responding to the New Dependency: The Family Assistance Plan of 1969," 291–303 in *Poverty and Public Policy in Modern America,* edited by Donald T. Critchlow and Ellis W. Hawley (Chicago: Dorsey Press, 1989), 293.

30. Ibid.

31. Burgdorf Jr., *Disability Discrimination in Employment Law,* 40–41. Charles Vanik (D-Ohio) and Hubert Humphrey (D-Minn.) introduced bills in the 1970s.

32. *Congressional Record,* 92d Cong., 2d sess., 1971, 135, pt. 17:45945. H.R. 12154 was the bill introduced on December 9, 1971.

33. According to Drimmer, Humphrey spoke the language of civil rights, yet he justified his measure on "grounds reminiscent of the medical and social pathology models." Jonathon Drimmer, "Cripples, Overcomers, and Civil Rights: Tracing the Evolution of Federal Legislation and Social Policy for People with Disabilities," *UCLA Law Review* 40 (1993): 1380–81.

34. Burgdorf Jr. suggests that the reason the bill died is unknown. He speculates that the liberal members of Congress fought against it because they thought adding disability would dilute the Civil Rights Act. Burgdorf Jr., *Disability Discrimination in Employment Law,* 27. On January 20, 1972, "to prevent discrimi-

nation" of the disabled by amending the Civil Rights Act of 1964, Sen. Humphrey introduced S. 3044, *Congressional Record, 92d* Cong., 1st sess., 1971, 118, pt. 1:525–26.

35. Quoted from Burgdorf Jr., *Disability Discrimination in Employment Law,* 26–27.

36. *Congressional Record,* 92d Cong., 2d sess., 1972, 118, pt. 7:8965–75. The Brademas bill, H.R. 8395, was reported on October 13, 1972.

37. See Senate Report, no. 318, 93d Cong., 1st sess., 1973, 8–11, for the legislative history.

38. *Congressional Record,* 92d Cong., 2d sess., 1972, 118, pt. 7:8978.

39. Scotch, *From Good Will to Civil Rights,* 46.

40. Drimmer, "Cripples, Overcomers, and Civil Rights," 1382–83.

41. *Congressional Record,* 92d Cong., 2d sess., 1972, 118, pt. 7:8981.

42. The welfare rolls had increased. Aid to Families with Dependent Children had 90,000 people enrolled in 1967. See Frances Fox Piven and Richard A. Cloward, *Regulating the Poor: The Functions of Public Welfare* (New York: Pantheon Books, 1971), 303.

43. The first antidiscrimination provisions were included in the 1948 law against discrimination based on handicap in U.S. Civil Service. This law, however, was never enforced. The Architectural Barriers Act of 1968 was the first public accommodations measure. The impetus for this originated with the 1965 Vocational Rehabilitation Act Amendments. See Carolyn Gooding, *Disabling Laws, Enabling Acts* (London: Pluto Press, 1994), 22.

44. John D. Twiname, Social and Rehabilitation Service (SRS) administrator, February 9, 1971, Evaluation Plan of SRS presented at the commissioner's staff meeting. Richard Longmire, associate administrator for Planning, Research and Training, SRS, to James Callison, assistant administrator, Office of Program Planning and Evaluation, January 28, 1971, Record Group 363. Records of Social and Rehabilitation Service, HEW, National Archives, College Park, Md.; and memorandum to Jonathon Moore about the SRS Research and Development Strategy, February 19, 1971, Box 2, General Subject File, Rehabilitation Services Administration, Record Group 363; and Rochefort, "Responding to the New Dependency: The Family Assistance Plan of 1969," 292.

45. Memorandum to Jonathon Moore about the SRS Research and Development Strategy, February 19, 1971, Box 2, General Subject File, Record Group 363.

46. Twiname to Richard Verville, deputy assistant secretary, April 27, 1972, Box 4, General Service File, Record Group 363; Robert G. Bruce, assistant administrator, Program Planning and Evaluation, to Twiname, April 19, 1972; Report titled "Client Participation in Payment of Costs for Vocational Rehabilitation Services" by James H. McElroy, Office of Program Planning and Evaluation, Box 4, Congressional Correspondence, Record Group 363.

47. Twiname to Senator Alan Cranston, October 27, 1971, Box 6, General Subject File, Record Group 363.

48. Rusalem, "A Personalized Recent History of Vocational Rehabilitation in America," 30–34. Garrett, assistant administrator of Research and Demonstrations, was still in the Department of Health, Education and Welfare (HEW) in April of 1973.

49. See Rusalem, "A Personalized Recent History of Vocational Rehabilitation in America," 34–35.

50. Doyle R. Dobbins, president of the Delaware Chapter of the National Rehabilitation Association, to John D. Ehrlichman, March 20, 1973, WHCF, Box 43, WE, Nixon Papers.

51. See Rochefort, "Responding to the New Dependency: The Family Assistance Plan of 1969," 294. When Nixon gave his welfare speech about the Federal Assistance Plan, which was a negative income tax, 95 percent of the editorial comments around the country were favorable.

52. Rusalem, "A Personalized Recent History of Vocational Rehabilitation in America," 39, 43.

53. *Congressional Record,* 93d Cong., 1st sess., 1973, 119, pt. 2:1431, 1875.

54. Timothy M. Cook, "Nondiscrimination in Employment under the Rehabilitation Act of 1973," *American University Law Review* 27 (1977): 38.

55. Memorandum titled "The Rehabilitation Act of 1973, Summary of Major Provisions," WHCF, Box 43, WE 8, Nixon Papers.

56. Berkowitz, *Disabled Policy,* 182.

57. Chrisann Shiro-Geist and William A. Calzaretta, *Placement Handbook for Counseling Disabled Persons* (Springfield, Ill.: Charles C. Thomas, 1982), 8–39.

58. Timothy M. Cook and Daniel P. Butler, "Coverage of Employment Discrimination Pursuant to Section 504 of the Rehabilitation Act of 1973," *Wake Forest Law Review* 19 (1983): 582.

59. Quoted from *Congressional Record,* 93d Cong., 1st sess., 1973, 119, pt. 6:5882; *Congressional Record,* 93d Cong., 1st sess., 1973, 119, pt. 4:3893, for Senator Stafford's comment. Also see Senate Report, no. 318, 93d Cong., 1st sess., 1973, 8011.

60. Cook and Butler, "Coverage of Employment Discrimination Pursuant to Section 504 of the Rehabilitation Act of 1973," 582, 587.

61. Burdorf Jr., *Disability Discrimination in Employment Law,* 37–38. Before 1978, only a private right of action existed for enforcement. With the Rehabilitation Amendments of 1978, Section 505 was added. It provided, inter alia, that aggrieved employees or applicants would have available to them remedies, procedures, and rights.

62. See Colin Barnes, *Disabled People in Britain and Discrimination: A Case for Anti-Discrimination Legislation* (London: Hurst & Co., 1991), 85–88, for a good description of the quota system in Britain.

63. Stephen L. Percy, *Disability, Civil Rights, and Public Policy: The Politics of Implementation* (Tuscaloosa: University of Alabama Press, 1989), 196, 203.

64. Burgdorf Jr., *Disability Discrimination in Employment Law,* 38.

65. Section 504 reaches anywhere from 28 to 50 million people with disabilities. Senate Report, no. 1297, 93d Cong., 2d sess., 1974, 34.

66. Cook, "Nondiscrimination in Employment under the Rehabilitation Act of 1973," 33.

67. See *Congressional Record,* 93d Cong., 1st sess., 1973, 119, pt. 5:5861. Randolph Jennings was the chair of the Subcommittee of the Handicapped. Also see Scotch, *From Good Will to Civil Rights,* 47–49.

68. Scotch, *From Good Will to Civil Rights,* 3. Also see Cook, "Nondiscrimination in Employment under the Rehabilitation Act of 1973," 43.

69. Scotch, *From Good Will to Civil Rights,* 52.

70. Ibid., 54; and Percy, *Disability, Civil Rights, and Public Policy,* 67.

71. House Report, no. 93-500, 93d Cong., 1st sess., 1973, 41.

72. Mary Lenz Walker, *Beyond Bureaucracy: Mary Elizabeth Switzer and Rehabilitation* (Lanham, Md.: University Press of America, 1985), 218.

73. Cook, "Nondiscrimination in Employment under the Rehabilitation Act of 1973," 46.

74. See *Congressional Record*, 93d Cong., 1st sess., 1973, 119, pt.5:5861.

75. Caspar Weinberger, secretary of HEW, ND, Box 1, AASF, Record Group, 363; and Twiname to Weinberger, June 23, 1972, AASF, Record Group 363.

76. William E. Timmons to Ken Cole, January 16, 1973, WHCF, Box 5, FG 23, Nixon Papers.

77. Kathleen C. Arneson to Norm Silver, administrator Vocational Rehabilitation Division, Oregon, February 14, 1973, WHCF, WE8, Nixon Papers.

78. *Congressional Record*, 93d Cong., 1st sess., 1973, 119, pt. 9:10822–23. For passage see *Congressional Record*, 93d Cong., 1st sess., 1973, 119, pt. 7:7994.

79. Memorandum from W. Richard Howard via David N. Parker about Nixon's veto address, March 28, 1973, Box 43, WE 8, Nixon Papers.

80. William E. Timmons to Ken Cole, January 16, 1973, Box 5, WHCF, FG23, Nixon Papers.

81. Meanwhile, Timmons warned Kenneth Cole, deputy director to the president for domestic affairs: "We have little bargaining power without working with the subcommittees and privately assuring them that the President will sign these bills once modified." William E. Timmons to Ken Cole, January 16, 1973, Box 5, WHCF, FG23; and press conference of Roy Ash, director Office of Management and Budget (OMB), Box 33, WHCF, SMOF, Cauvenaugh, Nixon Papers.

82. Nixon's address to the Senate of the United States, March 27, 1973, WHCF, Box 43, WE8, Nixon Papers. Also see memorandum titled "Vocational Rehabilitation," March 12, 1973, Box 43, WE 8, Nixon Papers.

83. Nixon thanked Hugh Scott (R-Pa.) for his "successful efforts in the Senate to sustain my veto." Nixon to Hugh Scott, WHCF, Box 43, WE 8, Nixon Papers.

84. Rochefort, "Responding to the New Dependency," 293.

85. *Congressional Record*, 93d Cong., 1st sess., 1973, 119, pt. 14:18129.

86. Rusalem, "A Personalized Recent History of Vocational Rehabilitation in America," 38–39.

87. H.R. 8070 was sponsored by Brademas and other members of the Committee on Education and Labor. See *Congressional Record*, 93d Cong., 1st sess., 1973, 119, pt. 4:18129.

88. Berkowitz, *Disabled Policy*, 179.

89. Public Law 93-112. Nixon had a signing ceremony to "counter the assertions of those who claim that your vetoes of two earlier rehabilitation bills meant that the Administration was rejecting the handicapped." Casper Weinburger to Nixon, September 25, 1973, Box 43, WE 8, Nixon Papers.

90. Brademas had staged the hearings, moreover, so that Dwight and Reedy would "hear some criticisms being voiced in the field." Oversight Hearings before Select Subcommittee on Education of the Committee on Education and Labor, "On Future Directions of the Rehabilitation Service Administration," House of Representatives, 93d Cong., 1st sess., 1973, 85, 87, and 125.

91. Ibid., 125.

92. Ibid.

93. Ibid., 55.

94. Melvin R. Laird, counselor to the president for domestic affairs, to Senator Jennings Randolph, November 21, 1973, WHCF, Box 43, WE 8, Nixon Papers.

95. Janet A. Flaccus, "Discrimination Legislation for the Handicapped: Much Ferment and the Erosion of Coverage," *Cincinnati Law Review* 55 (1986): 84.

96. Cook, "Nondiscrimination in Employment under the Rehabilitation Act of 1973," 46.

97. *Cherry v. Matthews,* 419 F. Supp. 922 (D.C. 1976).

98. Cook, "Nondiscrimination in Employment under the Rehabilitation Act of 1973," 44.

99. Percy, *Disability, Civil Rights, and Public Policy,* 68.

100. Percy, *Disability, Civil Rights, and Public Policy,* 69; Scotch, *From Good Will to Civil Rights,* 102.

101. Memorandum titled "Rehabilitation for Independent Living," Chief of State, Box 5, Jimmy Carter Papers. President Jimmy Carter Library, Carter Center, Atlanta, Georgia.

102. The Carter transition team was well aware of all the implications of the battle over Section 504. In a very long and detailed memorandum, it listed the "pros" and "cons" for the following scenarios: possible congressional options, namely amending the Rehabilitation Act, which was due to expire in 1977; non-legislative action, which meant issuing federal regulations to implement Section 504; introducing new legislation; having administration officials present at congressional hearings when the new Rehabilitation Act was drafted; or finally extending any variation of the above "coupled" with a strong revised executive order to implement and enforce Section 504. Memorandum titled "Legislation and Non-Legislation Issues Affecting Handicapped Individuals"(n.d.), chief of state, Hamilton Jordan, Box 5, Carter Papers.

103. Dr. Frank Bowe to Stuart Eizenstat, April 21, 1977, Staff Offices, DPS, Eizenstat, Box 213, Carter Papers.

104. Joyce R. Starr to Jane Frank, David Rubinstein, Steve Selig, Mark Siegel, April 1, 1977, Staff Offices, DPS, Box 213, Carter Papers.

105. Children's Defense Fund, memorandum titled "To Substandard Changes in the January 21 Draft of the Section 504 Regulations Proposed by Secretary Califano."

106. Bowe to Eizenstat, April 21, 1977.

107. Children's Defense Fund, memorandum titled "To Substandard Changes in the January 21 Draft of the Section 504 Regulations Proposed by Secretary Califano."

108. Harrison A. Williams Jr. to Joseph A. Califano Jr., April 22, 1977, Staff Offices, DPS, Box 213, Carter Papers.

109. "Simple Rights" (n.d.), chief of state, Box 5, Carter Papers.

110. Starr to Frank, Rubinstein, Selig, Siegel, April 1, 1977.

111. Memorandum Dr. Frank Bowe to Eizenstat, April 21, 1977, Staff Offices, Domestic Policy Staff, Eizenstat, Box 213, Carter Center.

112. Knowing that the secretary's position would incite such a reaction from the disability rights movement, Carter still let Califano "continue to lead" the battle over Section 504. This is not to say, however, that the Carter administration

was unfazed by the demonstrations. Frank Raines, a member of White House DPS, wrote that Califano "is facing a very difficult problem, but it is being made worse by the delays." Frank Raines to Stuart Eizenstat, April 6, 1977, Staff Offices, DPS, Box 213, Carter Papers.

113. Sharon Bonney, "History of 504 Passage," 9–12 in *20th Anniversary: Victorious 504 Sit-In for Disability Rights* (Berkeley: Celebration and Commemoration Committee, 1997), 12.

114. Charles Raisch, "Our Demands—1977," *San Francisco Chronicle,* April 12, 1977, reprinted in *20th Anniversary: Victorious 504 Sit-In for Disability Rights* (Berkeley: Celebration and Commemoration Committee, 1997), 8.

115. Burgdorf Jr., *Disability Discrimination in Employment Law,* 41.

116. Mary Lou Breslin,"From Section 504 to the Americans with Disabilities Act," 20–25 in *20th Anniversary: Victorious 504 Sit-In for Disability Rights* (Berkeley: Celebration and Commemoration Committee, 1997), 22.

117. Percy, *Disability, Civil Rights, and Public Policy,* 197–98, 201. Carter gave the Civil Service Commission the authority to enforce these regulations.

118. Cook and Butler, "Coverage of Employment Discrimination Pursuant to Section 504 of the Rehabilitation Act of 1973," 582. When the Rehabilitation Act was amended in 1978, Congress stated this verbatim.

119. Percy, *Disability, Civil Rights, and Public Policy,* 213.

120. Drimmer, "Cripples, Overcomers, and Civil Rights," 1388–89.

121. Flaccus, "Discrimination Legislation for the Handicapped," 85.

122. Albert T. Hamlin, assistant general counsel, Civil Rights Division to Richard I. Beattie, September 19, 1979, DPS, Box 10, Carter Papers.

123. Ibid.

124. May 15, 1978, Senate Committee on Human Recourse, reported S. 2600 May 16,1978; whereas the House passed H.R 12467 under a suspension of the rules.

125. James T. McIntyre, director of OMB, to Carter, November 1, 1978, DPS, Box 213, Carter Papers.

126. Joseph A. Califano to Harrison A. Williams Jr., July 1978, Staff Offices, DPS, Box 213, Carter Papers.

127. These two memorandums provided a very comprehensive list of the policy issues as well as the political ramifications of a veto. Stuart Eizenstat to Jimmy Carter, November 4, 1978, DPS, Box 213, Carter Papers; and Eizenstat and Goldstein to Carter, November 6, 1978, DPS, Box 213, Carter Papers.

128. Dick Pettigrew to Jimmy Carter, November 3, 1978, DPS, Box 213, Carter Papers.

129. Ellen L. Goldstein and Christopher F. Edley Jr. to Stuart Eizenstat, July 19, 1978, DPS, Eizenstat, Staff, Box 213, Carter Papers.

130. Eizenstat and Goldstein to Jimmy Carter, November 6, 1978, DPS, Box 213, Carter Papers.

131. Goldstein and Edley to Eizenstat, July 19, 1978; and Eizenstat and Goldstein to Carter, November 6,1978. Although neither transportation nor treasury recommends veto, both have concerns with portions of the bill.

132. "Note for the Honorable Stuart Eizenstat," Fred Bohen, executive secretary, Department of HEW, Califano's Office, August 31, 1978, Staff Offices, DPS, Box 213, Carter Papers.

133. Frank Moore and Bill Cable to Jimmy Carter, November 1, 1978, DPS, Box 213, Carter Papers.

134. Eizenstat and Goldstein to Jimmy Carter, November 6, 1978, DPS, Box 213, Carter Papers.

135. McIntyre to Carter, November 1, 1978; and Eizenstat and Goldstein to Carter, November 6, 1978, DPS, Box 213, Carter Papers.

136. Ellen L. Goldstein and Diana Elmes to Stuart Eizenstat, August 7, 1979, Staff Offices, DPS, Box 213, Carter Papers. Moore and Cable to Jimmy Carter, November 1, 1978, DPS, Box 213, Carter Papers. Frank Moore, Bill Cable, and Bob Thomson to Jimmy Carter, November 4, 1978, DPS, Box 213, Carter Papers.

137. Frank White and Jeff Miller to Stuart Eizenstat, n.d., DPS, Box 10, Carter Papers.

138. See Cook and Butler, "Coverage of Employment Discrimination Pursuant to Section 504 of the Rehabilitation Act of 1973," 582–84.

139. S. 446, Equal Employment Opportunity for the Handicapped Act of 1979, testimony of Harold Russell, chairman, President's Committee on Employment of the Handicapped.

140. Drew S. Days III, assistant attorney general, Civil Rights Division, to Senator Harrison A. Williams Jr., chairman, Committee on Labor and Human Resources (received September 24, 1979), DPS, Box 10, Carter Papers.

141. "Memorandum for that Staff—Senate Labor and Human Resources Committee," Staff Offices, DPS, Box 10, Carter Papers.

142. White and Miller to Eizenstat, n.d., DPS, Box 10, Carter Papers; and "Memorandum for that Staff—Senate Labor and Human Resources Committee."

143. Darrell J. Anderson, counsel, Committee on Labor and Human Resources to Frank White, associate director, domestic policy staff, July 26, 1979, DPS, Box 10, Carter Papers.

144. Days to Williams (received September 24, 1979). Days made reference to *Trans World Airlines v. Hardison,* 432 U.S. 63 (1977): 83–85, in which the Supreme Court offered a weak interpretation of how an employer should accommodate an employee because of his or her religion.

145. White and Miller to Eizenstat, n.d.

146. Ibid.

147. See Berkowitz, *Disabled Policy,* 222.

148. Memorandum titled "Simple Rights," n.d.

Chapter Five

1. Ellen L. Goldstein and Diana Elmes to Stuart Eizenstat, August 7, 1979, staff offices, domestic policy staff, Box 213, Jimmy Carter Papers, President Jimmy Carter Library, Carter Center, Atlanta, Georgia.

2. See Judith A. Baer, *Equality Under the Constitution: Reclaiming the Fourteenth Amendment* (Ithaca: Cornell University Press, 1983), chap. 8, for an insightful overview of the Fourteenth Amendment and disability rights.

3. See *Levy v. Louisiana,* 391 U.S. 68 (1968); *Kramer v. Union Free School District,* 395 U.S. 621 (1961); and *Avery v. Midland County,* 390 U.S. 474 (1968).

4. Eric T. Sharpe, "A House Is Not a Home: *City of Cleburne v. Cleburne Living Center,*" *Pace Law Review* 6 (1986): 274–77.

5. *Reed v. Reed,* 404 U.S. 71 (1971). The Supreme Court ruled that a classification based on sex was subject to scrutiny. See *Frontiero v. Richardson,* 411 U.S.

677 (1973). Justice William J. Brennan joined William O. Douglas, Byron R. White, and Thurgood Marshall and found support in *Reed* to designate sex as inherently suspect. Brennan thought sex was like race and national origin in that it was immutable. It was not followed in *Stanton v. Stanton*, 421 U.S. 7 (1975), since there the Court found nothing rational requiring child support for males until the age of twenty-one and for females until only eighteen.

6. Sharpe, "A House Is Not a Home," 273.

7. *Craig v. Boren*, 429 U.S. 190 (1976).

8. Sharpe," A House Is Not a Home," 283.

9. *In re G.H.*, 218 N.W.2d 441 (N.D. 1974). The rationale was based on the federal district court in *Fialkowski v. Shapp*, 405 F. Supp. 946 (E.D. Pa. 1975). See James R. Baugh, "The Federal Legislation on Equal Educational Opportunity for the Handicapped," *Idaho Law Review* 15 (1978): 71.

10. Three federal courts followed this case. *Frederick L. v. Thomas*, 408 F. Supp. 832 (E.D. Pa. 1976); *Halderman v. Pennhurst*, 446 F. Supp. 1295 (E.D. Pa. 1977) at 1321–22; and *Medora v. Colautti*, 602 F.2d 1149 (3rd Cir. 1979) at 1152.

11. *Pennhurst State School and Hospital v. Haldeman*, 451 U.S. 1 (1981). In November 1976, the district court certified the case as a class action. It held that mentally retarded residents have both a constitutional and statutory right to minimally adequate and nondiscriminatory habilitation in "least restrictive environment" pursuant to the Eighth and Fourteenth Amendments and Section 504. The U.S. Court of Appeals for the Third Circuit affirmed the decision through a construction of the act. On appeal, the Supreme Court reversed. Section 6010 of the act does not create substantive rights for the mentally retarded to "appropriate treatment" in the "least restrictive environment." In the U.S. District Court for the District of Rhode Island, in *Naughton v. Bevilacqua*, 458 F. Supp. 610 (1978), it held that Section 6010 of the act gave the right to appropriate treatment. A moderately retarded schizophrenic minor suffered a severe reaction to a drug administered to control his behavior. The lower federal court found substantive statutory rights. The Supreme Court found that it did not in *Pennhurst*.

12. Anita L. Zimmer, "Statutes—Mental Health—Section 6010 of the Developmentally Disabled Assistance and Bill of Rights for the Mentally Retarded—*Pennhurst State School and Hospital v. Haldeman*, 451 U.S. 1 (1981)," *Cincinnati Law Review* 50 (1981): 901.

13. Rehnquist relied on the history in the House Report and the Senate Conference Committee Report in his ruling. The Senate bill had contained a detailed bill of rights and the House and the committee produced a compromise.

14. Judith Welch Wagner, "The Antidiscrimination Model Reconsidered: Ensuring Equal Opportunity without Respect to Handicap under Section 504 of the Rehabilitation Act of 1973," *Cornell Law Review* 69 (1984): 424.

15. Zimmer, "Statutes—Mental Health—Section 6010 of the Developmentally Disabled Assistance and Bill of Rights Act," 904.

16. Ibid. Also see Wagner, "The Antidiscrimiantion Model Reconsidered," 422–23.

17. Zimmer, "Statutes—Mental Health—Section 6010 of the Developmentally Disabled Assistance and Bill of Rights Act," 905.

18. *City of Cleburne, Texas v. Cleburne Living Center, Inc.*, 473 U.S. 432 (1985). Justice White delivered the opinion that Chief Justice Warren Burger,

Lewis F. Powell Jr., William H. Rehnquist, John Paul Stevens, and Sandra Day O'Connor joined. Thurgood Marshall concurred and dissented in part with William J. Brennan Jr. and Harry A. Blackmun joining him.

19. The federal court upheld the permit, arguing the zoning law was rationally related to the city's legitimate interests. The Court of Appeals for the Fifth Circuit, however, overturned its decision and recognized the mentally retarded as a "quasi-suspect category." See *City of Cleburne, Texas v. Cleburne Living Center, Inc.,* 726 F.2d 191 (5th Cir. 1984). Also see Sharpe, "A House Is Not a Home," 309; and Martha Minow, *Making All the Difference: Inclusion, Exclusion, and American Law* (Ithaca: Cornell University Press, 1990), 102.

20. *Cleburne v. Cleburne Living Center,* 443.

21. Ibid., 445. Also see Sharpe, "A House Is Not a Home," 294; and Minow, *Making All the Difference,* 103.

22. *Cleburne v. Cleburne Living Center,* 442, 446.

23. Sharpe, "A House Is Not a Home," 293.

24. *Cleburne v. Cleburne Living Center,* 450.

25. Minow, *Making All the Difference,* 104.

26. *Cleburne v. Cleburne Living Center,* 458.

27. Sharpe, "A House Is Not a Home," 301.

28. *Cleburne v. Cleburne Living Center,* 461–62.

29. Ibid., 455.

30. Sharpe, "A House Is Not a Home," 306–07.

31. *Cleburne v. Cleburne Living Center,* 468.

32. Judith A. Ravel, "*Board of Education v. Rowley:* Rather Roadblock or Another Signpost on the Road to State Courts," *Connecticut Law Review* 16 (1983): 165.

33. *Youngberg v. Romeo,* 457 U.S. 307 (1982); and Sharpe, "A House Is Not a Home," 284.

34. *Youngberg v. Romeo,* 310–11.

35. Ibid., 313.

36. Ibid., 313, 320. Justice Powell wrote for the majority. Blackmun wrote a dissenting opinion with Brennan and O'Connor concurring. Also, Burger wrote a separate dissenting opinion.

37. *Youngberg v. Romeo,* according to Bruce A. Arrigo, "The Logic of Identity and the Politics of Justice: Establishing a Right to Community-based Treatment for the Institutionalized Mentally Disabled," *Criminal and Civil Confinement* 18 (1992): 11–12.

38. Ibid., 319, 322–24.

39. *Youngberg v. Romeo,* 319.

40. *Cleburne v. Cleburne Living Center,* 323. Sharpe, "A House Is Not a Home," 286.

41. *Youngberg v. Romeo,* 320.

42. *Southeastern Community College v. Davis,* 442 U.S. 397 (1979).

43. Ibid., 400–02. Also see Wagner, "The Antidiscrimination Model Reconsidered," 453.

44. Wagner, "The Antidiscrimination Model Reconsidered," 455.

45. *Southeastern Community College v. Davis,* 410.

46. Other cases dealing with this were *Copeland v. Philadelphia Police Department,* 840 F.2d 1139, 1149 (3d Cir. 1988), about a policeman who was fired as a

drug user. Police should have allowed him to enter a rehabilitation program. Also in *Brennan v. Stewart,* 834 F.2d 1248 (5th Cir. 1988), in which a blind applicant sought Texas state board to modify licensing requirements for persons seeking to fit and dispense hearing aids.

47. *Southeastern Community College v. Davis,* 407, 410, and 414.

48. Ibid., 413.

49. Sally B. Schreiber, "Rights of the Handicap—to Be Otherwise Qualified: When Does Section 504 of the Rehabilitation Act Protect the Handicapped? *Nelson v. Thornburgh,* 567 F. Supp. 369 (E.D. Pa. 1983), *aff'd mem.,* No. 83-1626 (3d Cir. Mar. 6, 1984)," *Temple Law Quarterly* 57 (1984): 185–87.

50. Ibid., 409. *Edge v. Pierce,* 540 F. Supp. 1300 (D. N.J. 1982). In the Edge case, a New Jersey district court rejected the plaintiff's assertion that excluding persons who are, or are perceived to be, chronically mentally ill from certain federally subsidized housing opportunities violated Section 504.

51. Pamela Hussey Simon, "Employment Discrimination—Analyzing Handicap Discrimination Claims: The Right Tools for the Job," *North Carolina Law Review* 62 (1984): 561.

52. *Southeastern Community College v. Davis,* 409. Also see Bonnie P. Tucker, "Section 504 of the Rehabilitation Act after Ten Years of Enforcement: The Past and the Future," *University of Texas Law Review* 1989 (1989): 896–97.

53. Simon, "Employment Discrimination—Analyzing Handicap Discrimination Claims," 556.

54. *Southeastern Community College v. Davis,* 401–02.

55. *Alexander v. Choate,* 469 U.S. 287 (1985).

56. Carolyn Gooding, *Disabling Laws, Enabling Acts* (London: Pluto Press, 1994), 66.

57. *Alexander v. Choate,* 289, 306.

58. *Hendrick Hudson District Board of Education v. Rowley,* 458 U.S. 176 (1981), 200. Rehnquist wrote the opinion with Burger, Powell, Stevens, and O'Connor in agreement. Blackmun gave a concurring opinion. White wrote a dissenting opinion that Brennan and Marshall joined.

59. Lori A. Wenderoff, "*Board of Education v. Rowley:* Are Handicapped Children Entitled to Equal Educational Opportunities?" *California Western Law Review* 20 (1983): 133.

60. *Board of Education v. Rowley,* 198. The author added the italics for emphasis in the quote.

61. Ibid., 199.

62. Wenderoff, *Board of Education v. Rowley,* 137.

63. *Board of Education v. Rowley,* 200.

64. Wagner, "The Antidiscrimination Model Reconsidered," 423.

65. *Board of Education v. Rowley,* 185.

66. Paul F. James, "The Education for All Handicapped Children Act of 1975: What's Left after Rowley?" *Willamette Law Review* 19 (1983): 721; and Wenderoff, *Board of Education v. Rowley,*" 140–41.

67. *Board of Education v. Rowley,* 195, 198.

68. Wenderoff, *Board of Education v. Rowley,* 143.

69. *Board of Education v. Rowley,* 210.

70. James, "The Education for all Handicapped Children Act of 1975," 725.

71. John S. Harrison, "Comment, Self-Sufficiency under the Education for All

Handicapped Children Act: A Suggested Judicial Approach," *Duke Law Journal* 1981 (1981): 518–25.

72. *Board of Education v. Rowley,* 213, 215.

73. Perry A. Zirkel, "Building an Appropriate Education from *Board of Education v. Rowley:* Razing the Door and Raising the Floor," *Maryland Law Review* 42 (1983): 495.

74. Jeffrey O. Cooper, "Overcoming Barriers to Employment: The Meaning of Reasonable Accommodation and Undue Hardship in the Americans with Disabilities Act," *University of Pennsylvania Law Review* 139 (1993): 1462–66.

75. *Southeastern Community College v. Davis,* 405.

76. Wagner, "The Antidiscrimiantion Model Reconsidered," 460–61.

77. *Southeastern Community College v. Davis,* 405–06.

78. Note, "Employment Discrimination against the Handicapped and Section 504 of the Rehabilitation Act: An Essay on Legal Evasiveness," *Harvard Law Review* 97 (1984): 1007.

79. Schreiber, "Rights of the Handicap—to Be Otherwise Qualified," 181–82.

80. Ibid., 185–87.

81. Note, "Employment Discrimination against the Handicapped and Section 504 of the Rehabilitation Act," 1007.

82. An expansive interpretation of Section 504 was rendered in *Nelson v. Thornburgh,* 567 F. Supp. 369 (E.D. Pa. 1983); and *Strathie v. Department of Transportation,* 716 F.2d 227 (3rd Cir. 1983) A narrow interpretation of the section was given in *Walker v. Attorney Gen. of the United States,* 572 F. Supp. 100 (U.S. D.C. 1983); and *Upshur v. Love,* 474 F. Supp. 332 (N.D. Ca. 1979).

83. Simon, "Employment Discrimination—Analyzing Handicap Discrimination Claims," 555.

84. Wagner, "The Antidiscrimination Model Reconsidered," 4.

85. *School Board of Nassau County, Florida v. Arline,* 480, U.S. 273 (1987). Brennan delivered the opinion of the Court. Rehnquist wrote a dissenting opinion that Scalia joined.

86. Ibid., 274.

87. Ibid., 283.

88. Cooper, "Overcoming Barriers to Employment," 1435–37.

89. Elizabeth Clark Morin, "ADA of 1990: Social Integration through Employment," *Catholic University Law Review* 40 (1990): 203–05.

90. *School Board of Nassau County, Florida v. Arline,* 289, 292.

Chapter Six

1. Elaine S. Povich, "Senate Oks Bill Fixing Rights of the Disabled," *Chicago Tribune,* July 14, 1990.

2. Herman Wong, "Warrior for the Disabled: Brenda Premo Fought for the Front Line to Help Win Landmark Rights Bill," *Los Angeles Times,* July 25, 1990.

3. Robert J. Burgdorf Jr., "The Americans with Disabilities Act: Analysis and Implications of a Second Generation Civil Rights Statute," *Harvard Civil Rights–Civil Liberties Review* 26 (1991): 493.

4. John J. Sarno, "The Americans with Disabilities Act: Federal Mandate to Create an Integrated Society," *Seton Hall Legislative Journal* 17 (1993): 409.

5. Interview with Arlene B. Mayerson, Disability Rights Education and Fund, Berkeley, Calif., December 1997.

6. See Marta Russell, *Beyond Ramps: Disability at the End of the Social Contract* (Monroe, Maine: Common Courage Press, 1998), 123–24.

7. See Ruth Colker, "The ADA: A Windfall for Defendants," *Harvard Civil Rights–Civil Liberties Law Review* 34 (1999): 99–163.

8. Quoted from Bill Bolte, "Disabled Act: More Loophole than Law," *Los Angeles Times,* September 20, 1989.

9. Leslie J. Allen, "Varied Reaction to Disabilities Act . . . Business Gauges the Cost of Changes," editorial in *St. Louis Post-Dispatch,* May 24, 1990.

10. Senate Report, no.116, to accompany S. 933, Americans with Disabilities Act (ADA), Committee on Labor and Human Resources, 101st Cong., 1st sess., 9.

11. Harlan Hahn, "Antidiscrimination Laws and Social Research on Disability: The Minority Group Perspective," *Behavioral Sciences and the Law,*" 14 (1996): 41.

12. Senate Report, no. 116, to accompany S. 933, 101st Cong., 1st sess., "The Americans with Disabilities Act," 9–10.

13. Hahn, "Antidiscrimination Laws and Social Research on Disability," 53–54.

14. Hearings before the Subcommittee on Select Education of the Committee on Education and Labor in Boston, on October 24, 1988, 36.

15. Ibid., 9.

16. Hahn, "Antidiscrimination Laws and Social Research on Disability," 54.

17. Senate Report, no. 116 to accompany S. 933, 101st Cong., 1st sess., 1989, "The Americans with Disabilities Act," 9–10.

18. Hahn, "Antidiscrimination Laws and Social Research on Disability," 45.

19. Jeffrey O. Cooper, "Overcoming Barriers to Employment: The Meaning of Reasonable Accommodation and Undue Hardship in the Americans with Disabilities Act," *University of Pennsylvania Law Review* 139 (1993): 1424–25.

20. Bonnie P. Tucker, "The Americans with Disabilities Act: An Overview," *University of Illinois Law Review* (1989), 926.

21. See *Garrity v. Gallen,* 522 F. Supp. 171, 206 (D.N.H. 1981).

22. See Robert L. Burgdorf Jr., *Disability Discrimination in Employment Law* (Washington, D.C.: Bureau of Public Affairs, Inc., 1995), 44.

23. *Congressional Record,* 100th Cong., 2d sess., 1988, 134, pt. 7:9379–82, S. 2345, text on pages.

24. For H.R. 4498 see *Congressional Record,* 100th Cong., 2d sess., 1988, 134, pt. 2:1307. The list of fifty-seven in Tucker, "Section 504 of the Rehabilitation Act after Ten Years of Enforcement: The Past and the Future," *University of Illinois Law Review* (1989), 909–10. Steven B. Epstein, "In Search of a Bright Line: Determining When an Employer's Financial Hardship Becomes 'Undue' under the Americans with Disabilities Act," *Vanderbilt Law Review* 48 (1995): 422. Senator Lowell Weicker (R-Conn.) and Representative Tony Coelho (D-Calif.) introduced the legislation. Also see Burgdorf Jr., *Disability Discrimination in Employment Law,* 46.

25. Burgdorf Jr., "The American with Disabilities Act," 444.

26. *Congressional Record,* 100th Cong., 2d sess., 1988, 134, pt. 7:9381.

27. *Brown v. Board of Education of Topeka,* 347 U.S. 483 (1954).

28. Ibid. Senator Tom Harkin, a liberal Democrat from Iowa, also explained that people drafting the Weicker bill had been greatly influenced by two important

reports written by this council. These reports were "Towards Independence" and "On the Threshold of Independence."

29. Weicker's bill borrowed this rationale from the Supreme Court's ruling in *Davis*. See *Southeastern Community College v. Davis*, 442 U.S. 397 (1979).

30. *Congressional Record*, 100th Cong., 2d sess., 1988, 134, pt. 7:9386.

31. The Weicker bill developed the term "reasonable accommodations" from "Accommodating the Spectrum of Individual Abilities" (Washington, D.C.: U.S. Commission on Civil Rights, 1983).

32. *Congressional Record*, 100th Cong., 2d sess., 1988, 134, pt. 7:9377.

33. *Congressional Record*, 101st Cong., 1st sess., 1989, 135, H. 693.

34. For specific information on S. 933 see *Congressional Record*, 101st Cong. 1st sess., 1989, 135, S4978. For information on H.R. 2273 see *Congressional Record*, 101st Cong., 1st sess., 1989, 135, H1690. For the text of the final Americans with Disabilities bill see *Congressional Record*, 101st Cong., 1st sess., 1989, 135, S. 7422–36. Also see Burgdorf Jr., *Disability Discrimination in Employment Law*, 46.

35. Senate Report, no. 116, the changes in the substitute bill are discussed in the *Congressional Record*, 100st Cong., 2d sess., 1988, 135, S. 10732–63. See Senator Harkin. The Senate Committee on Labor and Human Resources reported a substitute bill on August 2, 1989.

36. See Senate Report, no. 116; "Oversight Hearing on H.R. 4498, American with Disabilities Act of 1988"; Hearing before the Subcommittee on Select Education of the Committee on Education and Labor, 100th Cong., 2d sess., 1989. Three other House Committees—Committee on Public Works and Transportation, Committee on Energy and Commerce, Committee on the Judiciary—also reported the substitute bill without amendment.

37. *Congressional Record*, 101st Cong., 1st sess., 1989, 136, E1840.

38. Ibid., 19841.

39. Ibid., 19840.

40. Ibid., 9840, 19481, 12889, 19903. It passed on September 7, 1989 The eight senators in opposition were John Glen (D-Ohio), Christopher S. Bond (R-Mo.), Jake Garn (R-Utah), Jesse Helms (R-S.C.), Gordon J. Humphrey (R-N.H.), Steve Symms (R-Idaho), James A. McClure (R-Idaho), and Malcolm Wallop (R-Wyo.).

41. Ibid., 19847.

42. Tucker, "The Americans with Disabilities Act," 924.

43. *Congressional Record*, 101st Cong., 2d sess., 1990, 136, H2638.

44. H.R. Conference Report, no. 558, 101st Cong., 2d sess., 1990; H.R. Conference Report, no. 569, 101st Cong., 2d sess., 1990.

45. The major differences were that the Senate bill made the ADA applicable to the Congress in the same way, with the same rights and remedies, as it applied to other entities covered by the act, while the House bill authorized the House and the instrumentalities of Congress to choose their own internal mechanisms for enforcement. The two bills also had different provisions about food handlers and the HIV, which was a politically sensitive issue.

46. *Congressional Record*, 101st Cong., 2d sess., 1990, 136, H. 4629 and S. 9695.

47. Burgdorf Jr., "The American with Disabilities Act," 413.

48. See Richard K. Scotch, *From Good Will to Civil Rights* (Philadelphia: Temple University Press, 1984), 15–40.

49. Senate Report, no. 116, 21–24.

50. Elizabeth Clark Morin, "ADA of 1990: Social Integration through Employment," *Catholic University Law Review* 40 (1990): 202.

51. These regulations were to be developed by July 26, 1991. See Burgdorf Jr., "The Americans with Disabilities Act," 463.

52. Cooper, "Overcoming Barriers to Employment," 1442–43.

53. Senate Report, no. 116, 38, refers to *Stutts v. Freeman*, 694 F.2d 666 (11th Cir. 1983).

54. Senate Report, no. 116, 31–32.

55. Epstein, "In Search of a Bright Line," 413.

56. Ibid., 425.

57. Ibid., 427.

58. Ibid., 441.

59. Ibid., 442; and Burgdorf Jr., "The Americans with Disabilities Act," 513.

60. Michael B. Laudor, "Disability and Community: Modes of Exclusion, Norms of Inclusion, and the Americans with Disabilities Act of 1990," *Syracuse Law Review* 43 (1992): 940, 942.

61. Epstein, "In Search of a Bright Line," 397–99, 433, 435. Between 1977 and 1990, only 265 lawsuits had been filed.

62. President's Committee on Employment of People with Disabilities, "Dispelling Myths about the Americans with Disabilities Act," July 1996, 1 (http://www.sopcepd.gov/pcepd/archivists/pubs/ek96/lawmyth.htm).

63. Tom D'Agostino, "Casey Martin Golf Cart Case about Fairness: ADA Not Con Artist's Tool," *Arizona Republic,* March 9, 1998.

64. Interview with Arlene Mayerson, Disability Rights Education and Defense Fund (DREDF), Berkeley, Calif., December 1997.

65. The ADA proved a broad definition that includes a person has a "physical or mental impairment that substantially limits one or more of the major life activities . . . ; second, a record of such an impairment; or third, as being regarded as having such an impairment." The major life activities are "functions such as caring for one's self, performing manual tasks, walking, seeing, hearing, speaking, breathing, learning, and working." That a major life activity is limited is not self-evident. Proof of a limitation is necessary. This is a broad definition. A physical impairment is a "physiological disorder or condition, cosmetic disfigurement, or anatomical loss affecting any of a list of body systems." A mental impairment is "any mental or psychological disorder, such as mental retardation, organic brain syndrome, emotional or mental illness, and specific learning disabilities." Analysis of the definition by the Department of Health, Education and Welfare regulations indicated that it was not feasible to list all the specific conditions. See Burgdorf Jr., "The Americans with Disabilities Act," 445–51. Also see Steven S. Locke, "The Incredible Shrinking Protected Class: Redefining the Scope of Disability under the Americans with Disabilities Act," *University of Colorado Law Review* 68 (1997): 107–46.

66. Locke, "The Incredible Shrinking Protected Class," 114.

67. Senate Report, no. 116, 21–24.

68. Mark Johnson, "What an Act Americans with Disabilities Act Lawsuits Are; Clogging the Courts, But 'Non-Traditional' Claims Range from: Backaches

to Infertility," *Buffalo News,* August 31, 1997; and Deborah Kaplan, "Employment Rights: History and Trends," an unpublished report by Disability Rights Education and Defense Fund, 1981, E-3.

69. Kaplan, "Employment Rights," E-3-4.

70. The federal courts have not been alone in voicing their queries about disabilities. There has been a great deal of public resistence to protecting people with nontraditional disabilities. See Johnson, "What an Act Americans with Disabilities Act Lawsuits Are."

71. John C. O'Connor, "ADA Maligned," *Chicago Tribune,* March 9, 1998. Also see Mona Charen, "EEOC Rules Have Touch of Madness," *Rocky Mountain News,* July 31, 1997.

72. Locke, "The Incredible Shrinking Protected Class," 114.

73. See *Deghand v. Wal-Mart Stores,* 926 F. Supp. 1002 (D. Kan. 1996); *Mathews v. TCI. Of Illinois,* 95.C4096, LEXIS 8274, at 12 (N.D. Ill. 1996); and *Roth v. Lutheran General Hospital,* 57 F.3d 1446 (7th Cir. 1995).

74. *Krocka v. Riegler,* 958 F. Supp. 1333 (N.D. Ill. 1997).

75. *Dertz v. City of Chicago,* 912 F. Supp. 319 (N.D. Ill. 1995). The police department had fired this officer on the grounds that this depression made him unfit to perform the duties of a police officer. At the same time, the department said this depression was not a disability, so that the officer would not collect disability benefits.

76. *Wood v. County of Alameda,* WL 705139 (N.D. Cal. 1995). (Not reported in F. Supp.)

77. *Schwartz v. Comex,* WL 187353 (S.D. N.Y. 1997). This is not a federal court decision.

78. *E.E.O.C. v. Chrysler Corp.,* 917 F. Supp. 1164 (E.D. Mich 1996). Also see *Pater v. Deringer Manufacturing Co.,* WL 530655 (N.D. Ill. 1995); and *Sarsycki v. United Parcel Service,* 862 F. Supp. 336 (W.D. Okla. 1994) for decisions that recognized insulin-dependent diabetes as a disability.

79. *Schluter v. Industrial Coils, Inc.,* 298 F. Supp. 1437 (W.D. Wis. 1996), 1444.

80. Ibid., 1445. Also see *Rodriguez v. Loctite Puerto Rico, Inc.,* 967 F. Supp. 653, WL 359020 (D. Puerto Rico 1997), for a decision in which lupus was not considered a disability because the symptoms did not affect a major life activity. Another federal court adopted a similar position with someone who had Graves's disease. *MacDonald v. Presbyterian Hospital,* WL 14436 (S.D. N.Y. 1996).

81. Skoler, Abbott, and Presser, "Epileptic Employee Deemed 'Unqualified' for Law's Protection," *Massachusetts Employment Law Letter* 8 (February 1998).

82. *Laurin v. The Providence Hospital, Inc., and Massachusetts Nurses Assn.,* Civ. No. 96-30012 (D. Mass. 1997).

83. L. M. Sixel, "Seeking to Define Worker Disabilities," *Houston Chronicle,* December 5, 1997.

84. *Mobley v. Bd. of Regents,* 924 F. Supp. 1179 (S.D. Ga. 1996).

85. *Chandler v. City of Dallas,* 2 F.3d 1385 (5th Cir. 1993).

86. *Erickson v. Bd. of Governors of State Colleges,* 911 F. Supp. 316–323 (N.D. Ill. 1995). She had been terminated from her job for taking sick leave to get treatments.

87. *Doe v. Kohn Nast & Graff, P.C.,* 862 F. Supp. 1310 (E.D. Pa. 1994).

88. *Sutton v. N.M. Dept. of Children, Youth & Families,* 922 F. Supp. 516 (D.N.M. 1996).

89. See *Murphy v. United Parcel Service, Inc.*, 946 F. Supp. 872 (D. Kan. 1996). Also see *Welsh v. City of Tulsa, Okla.*, 977 F.2d 1415 (10th Cir. 1992); *Otis v. Canadian Valley-Reeves Meat Co.*, 884 F. Supp. 446 (W.D. Okla. 1994); and *Wooten v. Farmland Foods*, 58 F.3d 382 (8th Cir. 1995).

90. *Gomez v. American Building Maintenance*, 940 F. Supp. 255 (N.D. Cal. 1996).

91. See Locke, "The Incredible Shrinking Protected Class," 117–18.

92. The EEOC's task-oriented definition of a disability working was created to settle a controversy between a federal court and the Department of Labor about a case involving Section 503. George Crosby entered a carpentry apprentice program in 1973. After performing 3,600 of the 8,000 hours of work in this program, Crosby failed a preemployment physical because of a congenital back problem. As a result of this impairment, Crosby's union would no longer send his services to any employers. Lodging a complaint at the Department of Labor, which oversaw Section 503, the assistant secretary of labor decided that Crosby did not have a disability, though he agreed with the union that his impairment prevented him from serving as an apprentice. See *E.E. Black, Ltd. v. Marshall*, 497 F. Supp. 1088 (D. Haw. 1980).

93. See *Dutcher v. Ingalls Shipbuilding*, 53 F3.d 723 (5th Cir. 1995); *Barfield v. Bell S. Telecommunications*, 886 F. Supp. 1321 (D. Miss. 1995); and *Coghlan v. H.J. Heinz Co.*, 851 F. Supp. 808 (N.D. Tex. 1994).

94. See *Kohnke v. Delta Air Lines, Inc.*, no. 93-C7096, LEXIS 12188 (E.D. Ill. 1995); *Soileau v. Guilford of Maine, Inc.*, 928 F. Supp. 37 (D. Me. 1996); and *Marschand v. Norfolk & W. Ry. Co.*, 876 F. Supp. 1529 (N.D. Ind. 1995).

95. *DePaoli v. Abbott Labs*, no. 95-C3069, LEXIS 5284 (E.D. Ill. 1996).

96. *Mobley v. Bd. of Regents.*

97. *Dutcher v. Ingalls Shipbuilding.*

98. *Venclauskas v. Conn. Dept. of Public Safety*, 921 F. Supp. 78 (D. Conn. 1995).

99. *McKay v. Toyota Motor Mfg. U.S.A., Inc.*, 878 F. Supp. 1012 (6th Cir. 1997). A patrol officer faced the same type of dilemma when he applied for training as a state trooper trainee. This officer failed the eye exam required for state trooper training and claims disability of visual acuity. The court ruled that it was enough of a disability to reject his application, but not enough of one that would enable him to receive accommodations.

100. *Bolton v. Scrivner, Inc.*, 36 F.3d 939 (10th Cir. 1994). A doctor determined that this worker could no longer perform his job, and as a result he was not rehired.

101. *Milton v. Scrivner, Inc.*, 901 F. Supp. 1541 (W.D. Okla. 1994).

102. *Ouzts v. U.S. Air*, no. 94-625, LEXIS 11610 (U.S. Dist. 1996); *Byrne v. Board of Education*, 979 F.2d 560 (7th Cir. 1992); and *Mathews v. TCI of Ill.*; and *DePaoli v. Abbott Labs.*

103. *Leslie v. St. Vincent New Hope, Inc.*, 916 F. Supp. 879 (S.D. Ind. 1996).

104. Ibid.

105. *Gray v. Ameritech Corp.*, 937 F. Supp. 762 (N.D. Ill. 1996).

106. *Howard v. Navistar Intern*, 904 F. Supp. 922 (E.D. Wis. 1995). In this case, the federal court held that if some people have an impairment they cannot be regarded as having one.

107. Arlene B. Mayerson, "Restoring Regard for the "Regarded As" Prong: Giving Effect to Congressional Intent," *Villanova Law Review* 42 (1997): 587.

108. *Pedigo v. P.A.M. Transport, Inc.*, 891 F. Supp. 482 (W.D. Ark. 1994).

109. *Mengine v. Runyon*, 114 F.3d 415 (3d Cir. 1997).

110. Also see *Borkowski v. Valley Cent. School Dist.*, 62 F.3d 131 (2d Cir. 1995). A teacher's case was not thrown out on summary judgment because there was some question about whether she would be otherwise qualified if she had the help of a teacher's aide.

111. *E.E.O.C. v. Chrysler Corp.*

112. *Norris v. Allied-Sysco Food Services, Inc.*, 948 F. Supp. 1418 (N.D. Cal. 1996).

113. *Mannell v. American Tobacco Company*, 871 F. Supp. 854 (E.D. Va. 1994).

114. *Turco v. Hoechst Celanese Chemical Group, Inc.*, 906 F. Supp. 1120 (S.D. Tex. 1995). Someone with epilepsy was also appropriately fired after having a number of seizures. This person excelled at selling shoes and wanted his employer to tolerate his seizures.

115. *U.S. E.E.O.C. v. AIC Security Investigations, Ltd.*, 820 F. Supp. 1060 (N.D. Ill. 1993). Also see *Bombrys v. City of Toledo*, 849 F. Supp. 1210 (N.D. Ohio 1993). A candidate for the position of police officer, who had insulin-dependent diabetes, was rejected on this basis. The court decided that a blanket policy, which was, therefore, based on stereotypes or suspicions, could not be used to disqualify an applicant.

116. *Erickson v. Bd. of Governors of State Colleges.* A woman using sick leave to attend infertility treatments was also required to have this reasonable accommodation entertained.

117. *Zamudio v. Patla*, 956 F. Supp. 803 (N.D. Ill. 1997).

118. *U.S. v. City and County of Denver*, 943 F. Supp. 1304 (D. Colo. 1996).

119. *Lyons v. Legal Aid Soc.*, 68 F.3d 1512 (2d Cir. 1995).

120. *Gile v. United Air Lines, Inc.*, 95 F.3d 492 (7th Cir. 1996).

121. *Heather K. by Anita K. v. City of Mallard, Iowa*, 887 F. Supp. 1249 (N.D. Iowa 1995). A mother of a thirty-two-month child, who had a respiratory and cardiac condition that resulted from the child's extremely premature birth, was sued by a neighbor who wanted an exception to her ban that prohibited open burning in backyards, which threatened her child's life. The court found that the neighbors had other reasonably convenient means of disposing of their waste than burning.

122. *Wood v. County of Alameda*, 1995 WL 705139 (N.D. Cal. 1995) (Not reported in F. Supp.) This case cites the following cases in support of this argument: *Emirck v. Libbey-Owens-Ford*, 875 F. Supp. 393, 398 (E.D. Tex. 1995); *Howell v. Michelin Tire Corp.*, 860 F. Supp. 1488, 1492 (M.D. Ala. 1994); and *Reigel v. Kaiser Foundation Health Plan*, 859 F. Supp. 963 (E.D. N.C. 1994).

123. *Pedigo v. P.A.M. Transport, Inc.*

124. *Shiring v. Runyon*, 9 F. Supp. 827 (3d Cir. 1996).

125. *Eckles v. Consolidated Rail Corp.*, 890 F. Supp. 1391 (S.D. Ind. 1995).

126. *Holbrook v. City of Alpharetta, GA*, 112 F.3d 1522 (11th Cir. 1997). A police detective who suffered from retinal detachment in both eyes, a disability that his department accommodated for a number of years, had his position modified and the accommodation taken away. The court found that the detective was

not legally required to accommodate plaintiff's disability with regard to the essential function of collecting evidence. Their previous accommodation may have exceeded the law's requirements.

127. *Harmer v. Virginia Electric and Power Co.,* 831 F. Supp. 1300 (E.D. Va. 1993).

128. *Valentine v. American Home Shield Corp.,* 939 F. Supp. 1378 (N.D. Iowa 1996).

129. *Pattison v. Meijer, Inc.,* 897 F. Supp. 1002 (W.D. Mich. 1995).

130. Quoted from Michael Doyle, "Disability Law Keeping Courts Busy," *Sacramento Bee,* November 26, 1998.

131. *Bragdon v. Abbott,* 524 U.S. 624(1998). (U.S. *cert. granted* Nov. 26, 1997). The First Circuit Court of Appeals of Boston ruled that people with HIV, but showing no symptoms, do have a disability. See Patricia Nealon, "Court Sets Ruling on AIDS Bias," *Boston Globe,* November 27, 1997. The Supreme Court might take it on because it will resolve two competing appeals court decisions. The Fourth Circuit ruled that it was not in *Ennis v. National Association of Business and Educational Radio, Inc.,* 53 F.3d 55 (4th Cir. 1995); and *Runnebaum v. Nations Bank of Maryland,* 123 F.3d 156 (4th Cir. 1997). Meanwhile, the First and Ninth Circuit Courts ruled that it did. See *Gates v. Rowland,* 39 F.3d 1439 (9th Cir. 1994); *United States v. Morvant,* LEXIS 13074 (E.D. La. 1994); and *Howe v. Hull,* 873 F. Supp. 72 (N.D. Ohio 1994).

132. Sidney Abbott, represented by Bennett H. Klein, director of AIDS Law Project for the Boston-based Gay and Lesbian Advocates & Defenders. One million people are currently living with AIDS. This information is included in the federal court decision. *Abbott v. Bragdon,* 912 F. Supp. 580 (D. Me. 1995).

133. The American Dental Association submitted a brief urging a decision for Bragdon. Peter M. Sfikas, Mark S. Rubin, and Jill A. Wolowitz, "Supreme Court Will Decide If Asymptomatic HIV Infection Is a Handicap," *AIDS Litigation Reporter* 11 (December 12, 1997): 3.

134. Linda Greenhouse, "Court to Weigh Whether HIV Is a Disability," *New York Times,* March 23, 1998.

135. Quoted from ibid.

136. *Bragdon v. Abbott,* 524 U.S. 624 (1998), 631.

137. Ibid., 641.

138. Ibid., 645.

139. Ibid., 659.

140. Ibid., 657.

141. Ibid., 659–60.

142. Ibid., 661.

143. Ibid., 664–65.

144. Quoted from Louis Freedberg, "HIV Ruled a Disability, Discrimination Barred," *San Francisco Chronicle,* June 26, 1998.

145. Robin Toner and Leslie Kaufman, "Ruling Upsets Advocates for the Disabled," *New York Times,* June 24, 1999.

146. David G. Savage, "High Court will Tackle Definition of Disability," *Los Angeles Times,* April 19, 1999.

147. The author highlighted the term in the text. *Sutton n v. United Air Lines,* 527 U.S.471 (1999), 482.

148. Quoted from ibid., 483–84.

149. Ibid.,486, 484–85. Writing a separate concurring opinion, Ruth Bader Ginsburg also had emphasized that the ADA was not as broad as 160 million people who wear glasses. Ginsburg concurred that the definition of a disability did not apply to this many people who could no longer be considered "a discrete and insular minority," if that was the case. The ADA, she said, did not reach "the legions of people with correctable disabilities." Recognizing that the legislative authors had included this language in an attempt to equate their protection with that under the Fourteenth Amendment, she dismissed the idea that they should be treated as a constitutional issue, and she underscored the term "minority" as evidence that the ADA did not include this many people.

150. Ibid., 489–90.

151. Ibid., 493.

152. Ibid., 492.

153. Ibid., 490–91.

154. Ibid., 479, 482.

155. Ibid., 482.

156. Ibid., 499.

157. Ibid., 495.

158. Ibid., 497.

159. *Hendrick Hudson District Board of Education v. Rowley,* 458 U.S. 176 (1981), 200. The Supreme Court overruled the lower court, which had held that she should receive an interpreter. Rehnquist wrote the opinion with Burger, Powell, Stevens, and O'Connor in agreement. Blackmun gave a concurring opinion. White wrote a dissenting opinion that Brennan and Marshall joined.

160. *Sutton v. United Air Lines,* 497–98.

161. Ibid., 507.

162. Ibid., 504, 511.

163. Ibid., 510.

164. Ibid., 511, 505, 506.

165. Ibid., 61. Breyer, who wrote his own dissenting opinion, concurred with Stevens on this point.

166. Ibid., 509.

167. Ibid., 504, 511.

168. *Albertsons Inc. v. Hallie Kirkingburg,* 527 U.S. 555 (1999).

169. Ibid.

170. Ibid., 577.

171. Ibid., 562.

172. Ibid., 565–66.

173. *Vaughn L. Murphy v United Parcel Service, Inc.,* 527 U.S. 516 (1999).

174. Ibid.

175. Ibid., 525.

176. The business community anxiously awaited these decisions since, as Ted Gies put it, "[T]he biggest human resource and legal challenge is the ADA." Quoted from Joan Biskupic, "Supreme Court Limits Meaning of Disability," *Washington Post,* June 23, 1999.

177. Toner and Kaufman, "Ruling Upsets Advocates for the Disabled."

178. Robyn Blumner, editorial titled "Hijacking the Disabilities Act: Incompe-

tent Students are Suing to Skirt Academic Requirements," *Denver Rocky Mountain News,* May 3, 1998.

179. "Job Laws," *Financial Times,* June 25, 1999; Leslie Kaufman, "From Eyeglasses to Wheelchairs; Adjusting the Legal Bar for Disability," *New York Times,* April 18, 1999.

180. David G. Savage, "High Court Reins in Disability Law's Scope," *Los Angeles Times,* June 23, 1999.

181. Blumner, "Hijacking the Disabilities Act."

182. Ibid.

183. Toner and Kaufman, "Ruling Upsets Advocates for the Disabled."

184. Joan Treadway, "Disabled People Can Gain Jobs, Dignity; But Legislation has a Way to Go," *Times-Picayune,* May 10, 1998.

185. Kevin Livingston, "Court Puts Harness on ADA Claims," *Recorder,* June 23, 1999.

186. Shannon P. Duffy, "U.S. Supreme Court's ADA Rulings Shake Plaintiffs' Employment Bar," *Legal Intelligencer,* June 24, 1999.

187. Toner and Kaufman, "Ruling Upsets Advocates for the Disabled."

188. Stacie E. Barhorst, "Note: What Does Disability Mean: The Americans with Disabilities Act of 1990 in the Aftermath of Sutton, Murphy, & Albertsons": *Drake Law Review* 48 (1999): 147.

189. Quoted from Biskupic, "Supreme Court Limits Meaning of Disability."

190. Toner and Kaufman, "Ruling Upsets Advocates for the Disabled."

191. Michael Remez, "Disabilities Act Could Be Broadened: Top Court to Tackle Issues of Correctable Conditions," *Hartford Courant,* April 27, 1999.

192. Interview with Judith E. Heuman, assistant secretary, U.S. Department of Education, Office of Special Education, Rehabilitative Services, July 1999, Washington, D.C.

193. Duffy, "U.S. Supreme Court's ADA Rulings Shake Plaintiffs' Employment Bar."

194. Acting as medical experts, however, is different from the doctrine of substituted judgment that Justice Powell used in *Youngberg v. Romeo,* 457 U.S. 307 (1982). Also see Bruce A. Arrigo, "The Logic of Identity and the Politics of Justice: Establishing a Right to Community-based Treatment for the Institutionalized Mentally Disabled," *Criminal and Civil Confinement* 18 (1992): 3.

Afterword

1. *Mondzelewski v. Pathmark Stores, Inc.,* WL 654137 (D. Del. 2000).

2. *Sharkey v. Federal Exp. Corp.,* WL 230330 (E.D. Pa. 2000), 13–14.

3. *Thalos v. Dillon Companies, Inc.,* 86 F. Supp. 2d 1079 (D. Colo. 2000).

4. Ibid., 1083.

5. Ibid., 1084.

6. *Gutwaks v. American Airlines, Inc.,* WL 1611328 (N.D. Tex. 1999), 13–14.

7. *Finical v. Collections Unlimited, Inc.,* 65 F. Supp. 2d 1032 (D. Ariz. 1999), 1039.

8. Ibid., 1041.

9. *Popko v. Pennsylvania State University,* 84 F. Supp. 2d 589 WL 232288 (M.D. Pa. 2000); and *Todd v. Academy Corp.,* 57 F. Supp. 2d 448 (S.D. Tex. 1999).

10. *Rowles v. Automated Production Systems, Inc.,* 92 F. Supp. 2d 424 (M.D. Pa. 2000).

11. *Schumacher v. Souderton Area School Dist.*, WL 72047 (E.D. Pa. 2000), 26.

12. *E.E.O.C. v. R.J. Gallagher Co.*, 181 F.3d 645 (5th Cir. 1999), 654–55.

13. *Taylor v. Phoenixville School Dist.*, 184 F.3d 296 (3d Cir. 1999), 308–9.

14. *Finical v. Collections Unlimited, Inc.*, 1038–39.

15. Ibid., 1038.

16. *Tangires v. Johns Hopkins Hosp.*, 79 F. Supp. 2d 587 (D. Md. 2000), 595–96.

17. *Mattice v. Memorial Hosp. of South Bend*, 87 F. Supp. 2d 859 (N.D. Ind. 2000).

18. Quoted at 861.

19. Colker came up with this figure after conducting a survey of cases from 1992 to 1998. See Ruth Colker, "The ADA: A Windfall for Defendants," *Harvard Civil Rights–Civil Liberties Law Review* 34 (1999): 99–163. The American Bar Association conducted a study of 700 Title I cases between 1992 and 1997 in which employers won 92 percent. The second figure is derived from the 168 cases the author found in the federal courts that were issued from June 1999 until May 2000.

20. Karen Orren, "Officers' Rights: Toward a Unified Field Theory of American Constitutional Development" (unpublished paper, 2000), 11–12.

21. Ibid.

22. *Franklin v. Consolidated Edison Co. of New York, Inc.*, WL 796170 (S.D.N.Y. 1999).

23. *Geneva M. Smith v. Midland Brake, Inc.*, 180 F.3d 1154 LEXIS 13185 (10th Cir. 1999).

24. *Taylor v. Phoenixville School Dist.*

25. See Stacie E. Barhorst, "Note: What Does Disability Mean: The Americans with Disabilities Act of 1990 in the Aftermath of Sutton, Murphy, & Albertsons," *Drake Law Review* 48 (1999): 142–43.

INDEX